P9-ASC-202

HIGH DEFINITION

An **A** to **Z** Guide to
Personal Technology

TECHNICAL COLLEGE OF THE LOWCOUNTRY
LEARNING RESOURCES CENTER
POST OFFICE BOX 1288
BEAUFORT, SOUTH CAROLINA 29901-1288

HOUGHTON MIFFLIN COMPANY
Boston • New York

Words are included in this Dictionary on the basis of their usage. No investigation has been made of common-law trademark rights in any word, because such investigation is impracticable. The inclusion of any word in this Dictionary is not, however, an expression of the Publisher's opinion as to whether or not it is subject to any proprietary rights. Indeed, no definition is this Dictionary is to be regarded as affecting the validity of any trademark.

Copyright © 2006 by Houghton Mifflin Company. All rights reserved.

No part of this work may be reproduced or transmitted in any form or by any means, electronic or mechanical, including photocopying and recording, or by any information storage or retrieval system without the prior written permission of Houghton Mifflin Company unless such copying is expressly permitted by federal copyright law. Address inquiries to Reference Permissions, Houghton Mifflin Company, 222 Berkeley Street, Boston, Massachusetts 02116.

Visit our website at www.houghtonmifflinbooks.com.

Library of Congress Cataloging-in-Publication Data

High definition : an A to Z guide to personal technology.
    p. cm.
 ISBN-13: 978-0-618-71489-6
 ISBN-10: 0-618-71489-8
 1. Household electronics--Dictionaries. 2. Electronic apparatus and appliances--Dictionaries.
 TK7804.H54 2006
 004.03--dc22

                                  2006019549

Illustration Credits

antialiasing Tech-Graphics; **Bézier curve** Tech-Graphics; **chip** Tech-Graphics; **connector** Elizabeth Morales; **dialog box** Elizabeth Morales; **DIP switch** Tech-Graphics; **DVORAK keyboard** Tech-Graphics and Christopher Granniss; **FITALY keyboard** Courtesy of Textware Solutions; **frame** Netscape Communications and Peter Dubuque; **hard drive** Tech-Graphics; **kerning** Katherine M. Getz; **landscape** Elizabeth Morales; **network** Tech-Graphics; **pixel** Library of Congress and Tech-Graphics; **printed circuit board** © 2001 PhotoDisc, Inc.; **QWERTY keyboard** Tech-Graphics; **sector** Tech-Graphics

Manufactured in the United States of America

MP 10 9 8 7 6 5 4 3 2 1

Table of Contents

Editorial and Production Staff

Vice President, Publisher of Dictionaries
Margery S. Berube

Vice President, Executive Editor
Joseph P. Pickett

Vice President, Managing Editor
Christopher Leonesio

Senior Editor
Steven R. Kleinedler

Project Editor
Erich M. Groat

Editor
Catherine Pratt

Associate Editors
Nicholas A. Durlacher
Uchenna Ikonné
Robert Knippen

Database Production Supervisor
Christopher Granniss

Art and Production Supervisor
Margaret Anne Miles

Production Associate
Katherine M. Getz

Text Design
Catherine Hawkes, Cat & Mouse

Preface

Historians tell us that we are living in the "Information Age." This period is often said to have begun with the widespread use of the telegraph in the 19th century, when information could be transmitted from place to place faster than people could carry it. Within decades, telegraph systems were largely replaced by telephones, and in a similar span of time the telephone had a new and formidable companion—radio—a mass medium for sound that allowed news, entertainment, and other forms of information to be broadcast over huge distances to vast numbers of people without the use of wires. With the advent of television, information in the form of moving images could be distributed using radio technology, supplementing the powerful impact of mass-produced still photographs in the press.

But there was more to the Information Age than the mere transmission of data. New ways of storing information were also developed. "Records" made of vinyl discs stored sound information in jagged spiral grooves. Later, tapes stored sound and ultimately video information on magnetized surfaces. Mass-produced and widely distributed, these storage devices gave people permanent access to music and images that in the past had been lost at the moment of production.

Revolutionary as these advances were, the Information Age has since undergone a further revolution with the introduction of digital technology. The computer was originally conceived as a calculating device, but has become yet another means of communication, and computer technology has spread far more extensively into the lives of ordinary people than previous generations of technology. Digital computing power is now found in everything from telephones and televisions to microwave ovens and wristwatches. The computer is thus part of a whole gamut of technologies geared toward both work and pleasure: the world of personal technology. This technology enables users to be more than passive recipients of broadcast information. It has turned ordinary people into active manipulators and even dispensers of information by connecting them to vast networks of information systems.

New technology brings with it new terminology. The information technology that now pervades our lives demands a new kind of dictionary—one that covers this new array of electronic devices not simply because they are technically forbidding, but because they are a primary means by which we interact with each other. It is to meet this demand that we present *High Definition: An A to Z Guide to Personal Technology*.

This book contains technical vocabulary from the worlds of telecommunications, computers, home entertainment systems, home electronics, and the World Wide Web. Each entry is defined with a simple question in mind: what kind of information might a user of this technology need to know? Both avid and occasional users of personal technology will find the definitions and explanations in this book clear, informative, and enlightening.

To keep the dictionary easy to read and use, we've provided simple explanations that are comprehensible to both the nontechnically minded and the techno-savvy. Where necessary, we've included additional explanations, as in presenting the exact specifications of a device. Cross-references to related terms help readers broaden their knowledge. Numerous tables and illustrations, as at **connector** and **Unicode**, provide technical detail, and five additional tables that are associated with a variety of entries, including truth tables for logic gates and a table of common audio-visual interfaces, appear in the Appendix for easy look-up.

High Definition provides the knowledge you need in this Information Age, and we hope you'll enjoy using this book to become more familiar with your own world of technology.

—Erich M. Groat, *Project Editor*

A/52 The ATSC standard corresponding to AC-3. *See* **AC-3.**

AAC *Abbreviation of* **Advanced Audio Coding.** A file format for compressing and transmitting audio data over the Internet with a higher sound quality than the MP3. The AAC codec was developed as a part of the MPEG-4 standard, so AAC files usually carry the *.m4a* file extension. *Also called* **MPEG-4 AAC.** *See also* **M4P.** *See* Table 3 at **codec.**

aacPlus The Coding Technologies trade name for an enhanced AAC format used for transmitting high quality digital audio, especially in satellite radio systems. AacPlus combines AAC with spectral band replication to compress the data twice as efficiently as standard AAC; thus they require much less bandwidth to transmit and can be efficiently streamed through lower-speed connections. Files of this type use the *.mp4* extension and are backward compatible with standard MP4 players. *Also called* **HE-AAC.**

abort To cancel a computer program while it is in progress. A program can usually be aborted on request; however, unsaved data may be lost or damaged when a program is aborted. Programs may also abort under certain conditions without user intervention. *See also* **crash.**

absolute address An address that references a location in memory directly by byte number, rather than by using an offset. *Also called* **direct address, machine address, real address.**

absolute pathname A pathname that identifies the location of a file or directory with respect to the root directory of the file system. An absolute pathname includes the names of all the directories above the file or directory, in order, starting with the root directory. In Windows, an absolute pathname begins with a backslash (\); in Linux and Unix, an absolute pathname begins with a forward slash (/). *Compare* **relative pathname.**

AC-3 *Abbreviation of* **adaptive transform coder 3.** An audio codec developed by Dolby Laboratories that can compress an audio signal with up to five full-range channels and one low-frequency channel into a serial bit stream between 32 Kbps and 640 Kbps. AC-3 is widely used in cable, satellite, and terrestrial broadcasting. *Also called* **Dolby Digital.** *See also* **surround sound.** *See* Table 3 at **codec.**

Accelerated Graphics Port *See* **AGP.**

accelerator board A printed circuit board that can be added to a computer to enhance its performance. Accelerator boards substitute a faster

CPU without replacing the entire motherboard and associated components. *Also called* **accelerator card.** *See also* **expansion card, graphics accelerator.**

Acceptable Use Policy *Abbreviated* **AUP.** A set of rules that determine what type of transactions are allowed on a given network. For example, at one time commercial activity was not allowed on the Internet. Also, some online service providers do not allow the posting of pornographic material.

access *n.* The ability to locate, gain entry to, and use a directory, file, or device on a computer system or over a network.

v. To locate and be able to use a directory, file, or device on a computer system or over a network.

access code A sequence of letters, numbers, or other symbols that must be entered on a keyboard or keypad in order to operate or gain access to something, such as a car, cell phone, or restricted location.

access control list A list of users or clients authorized to access resources of a computer system, generally accompanied by information describing how much access is allowed. Access control lists may govern who has access to which directories, files, or programs on a computer that has multiple users; an access control list for an individual file may designate who may read the file and who may alter the file.

access number A telephone number that allows a user to connect via modem to an ISP (Internet Service Provider) or another network provider, such as an online service.

access point *See* **wireless access point.**

access time The time required for a program or device to locate and retrieve, or to write and store, a piece of data. When used in reference to disk drives, for example, access time is the amount of time needed for the drive to respond to a request to read or write data. When such a request is made by the operating system, the disk drive must move the read/write heads over the proper location on the disk, settle the heads into position, and wait for the desired location on the disk to rotate under them. Hard drives for personal computers have average access times under six milliseconds. The quoted access time for hard disks is an average, so a given instance of accessing may take significantly longer than the average.

account An arrangement with the provider of a computer service, such as an Internet email account, a newspaper whose content is available online, or an Internet retail service, that allows a user access to the service, and may in some cases keep track of information particular to the user, such as payment information or user preferences for the service. Accounts often require the use of a username and password to prevent unauthorized parties from accessing them.

account ID   *See* **username.**

account name   *See* **username.**

ACM   *Abbreviation of* **Association for Computing Machinery.**

acoustic coupler   A part of a modem that attaches to the earpiece and mouthpiece of a telephone so that a computer can make a connection over the telephone. The coupler allows digital signals to be changed to sound and back again. This device is now rarely used due to the widespread availability of modular phone jacks, which allow modems to connect directly with a telephone using a telephone connector.

ACPI   *Abbreviation of* **Advanced Configuation and Power Interface.**   A power-saving system that allows control of the amount of electricity each peripheral attached to the computer uses, so that power to items such as a CD-ROM can be shut off when not in use. This feature is included in Microsoft Windows 98 and subsequent versions.

Acrobat   A suite of programs developed by Adobe Systems that allows documents formatted by desktop publishing software to be viewed on a wide variety of computer platforms. Acrobat allows printable documents to be placed online without being reformatted in HTML, which would cause them to lose their original format and design.

active   **1.** Relating to a file, device, or portion of the screen that is currently operational and ready to receive input. **2.** Capable of amplifying an electrical or audio signal. *Compare* **passive.**

Active Desktop   The collective set of desktop features available in Microsoft Windows that are integrated into Microsoft Internet Explorer, giving the desktop the look and feel of a webpage interface.

active-matrix display   A type of LCD that uses one individual transistor for each cell in the liquid-crystal layer to control the electrical power delivered to that cell. Most large color LCDs are active-matrix displays.

ActiveServer Pages   *See* **ASP.**

ActiveX   An OLE technology developed by Microsoft for running programs through web browsers and email clients. Programmers can write ActiveX components called   *controls*   that can be embedded in any webpage or email. When a user clicks on the control, a program is downloaded and run on the user's computer. ActiveX controls are designed to be used with Microsoft software and operating systems, though some other programs and systems can use them. They usually have the file extension *.ocx.*

3

Not all web browsers support ActiveX components. Furthermore, ActiveX allows a wide variety of software to be downloaded and executed on a user's computer without the user's full knowledge. *Compare* **applet.** *See also* **client-side script.**

Ada   A high-level programming language, based on Pascal and developed for the US Department of Defense in the late 1970s. Ada was designed to be a standard, general-purpose language for saving the military the expense and trouble of maintaining many incompatible computer systems.

adapter   **1.** *See* **expansion card. 2.** A device used to connect two pieces of apparatus or to effect compatibility between different parts of one or more pieces of apparatus; for example, an adapter can be used to allow a device that requires a 1/4-inch plug to accept a 1/8-inch plug, or allow a USB device to transmit signals to and from a FireWire device.

adaptive differential pulse code modulation   *See* **ADPCM.**

adaptive transform coder 3   *See* **AC-3.**

ADB   *Abbreviation of* **Apple Desktop Bus.**

ADC   *Abbreviation of* **analog-to-digital converter.**

A/D converter   *Abbreviation of* **analog-to-digital converter.**

add-in   *See* **plug-in.**

additive color   Color produced by emitting light, as pixels on a display, rather than by absorbing and reflecting light, as inks on a sheet of paper. Additive colors are usually combinations of red, green, and blue. *Compare* **subtractive color.** *See also* **color model.**

add-on   **1.** A hardware device that is added to a computer to increase its capabilities. Common add-ons include additional hard drives, DVD-ROM drives, graphics cards, sound cards, and modems. *See also* **expansion card, peripheral. 2.** *See* **plug-in.**

address   **1.** The name, usually in the form of a number, assigned to a location in memory or a peripheral storage device. *See also* **physical address, virtual address. 2.** Any name that identifies a file on a computer, a computer on a network, or a user or service on a computer or network, such as an email or IP address.

address bus   A bus that carries the addresses of data storage locations back and forth between the CPU (central processing unit) and RAM. The address bus enables the CPU to select a specific location in memory for the transfer of data that the CPU needs in order to execute a specific instruction.

Address Resolution Protocol   *See* **ARP.**

Adobe Reader   A program for viewing and printing PDF documents that can be downloaded without charge from Adobe Systems, Inc. While Adobe Reader cannot be used to create PDF files, it can be used to fill in and save PDF forms. Plug-ins allow Adobe Reader to display PDFs from within many web browsers.

ADPCM   *Abbreviation of* **adaptive differential pulse code modulation.**   A form of pulse-code modulation (PCM) that produces a lower bit rate than standard PCM. Applications use ADPCM to digitize voice signals to allow them to be sent with data on lines designed for digital signals. When used on CD-ROMS, ADPCM allows for up to 16 hours of audio recording.

ADSL   *Abbreviation of* **Asymmetric Digital Subscriber Line.**   A type of DSL technology that provides higher bandwidth for receiving data than for sending data. ADSL connections allow users to receive data at speeds up to 9 Mbps and send data at speeds up to 640 Kbps. An ADSL modem is needed to use this service.

Advanced Audio Coding   *See* **AAC.**

Advanced Encryption Standard   *See* **AES.**

Advanced IBM Unix   *See* **AIX.**

Advanced Interactive Executive   *See* **AIX.**

advanced mobile phone service   *See* **AMPS.**

Advanced Research Projects Agency   *Abbreviated* **ARPA.**   *See* **DARPA.**

Advanced Research Projects Agency Network   *See* **ARPANET.**

Advanced Streaming Format   *See* **ASF.**

Advanced Systems Format   *See* **ASF.**

Advanced Technology   *See* **AT.**

Advanced Technology Attachment   *Abbreviated* **ATA.**   *See* **IDE.**

Advanced Technology Extended   *See* **ATX.**

Advanced Television Systems Committee   *See* **ATSC.**

adware   Software that displays advertisements on personal computers. Malicious adware can be surreptitiously installed when users view certain webpages on the World Wide Web, causing unwanted advertisements to appear on the user's screen. However, some legitimate software is distributed as adware; users agree to view ads that appear when using the software, but they do not have to pay a licensing fee. Adware is often accompanied by spyware.

AES   *Abbreviation of* **Advanced Encryption Standard.**   A standard encryption algorithm defined by the US government. AES is a block cipher that may use a variety of key sizes and block sizes, depending on the level of security and efficiency of encryption and decryption desired. AES supersedes DES as the form of encryption used by the US government for the transmission of both unclassified and classified information.

AES/EBU *Abbreviation of* **Audio Engineering Society/European Broadcasting Union.** A digital audio transmission standard developed jointly by the Audio Engineering Society and the European Broadcasting Union and used in professional grade equipment. The AES/EBU cables are balanced STP cables terminating in an XLR connector. An unbalanced, consumer-grade version of AES/EBU called S/PDIF also exists. *Also called* **AES3.**

AF *Abbreviation of* **audio frequency.**

AGC *Abbreviation of* **automatic gain control.**

agent A program that performs a task such as data transfer on behalf of a particular machine or human.

aggregate To collect several web feeds into one webpage or newsreader. By aggregating web feeds from webpages, blogs, and news services, users can create a custom view of web content. *See also* **syndicate.**

aggregator A program or website that allows users to subscribe to and collect web feeds so they can view content from different sources in one place. Some email clients can also be used as aggregators. *Also called* **feed reader, news aggregator, newsreader, RSS reader.**

AGP *Abbreviation of* **Accelerated Graphics Port.** A computer bus developed by Intel Corporation that enables a device, typically a graphics card, to access a computer's main memory directly, rather than requiring the CPU to handle the reading and writing of data. AGPs thus free the processor for other tasks. AGPs have a bus width of 32 bits.

AI *Abbreviation of* **artificial intelligence.**

AIFF *Abbreviation of* **Audio Interchange File Format.** An audio format for storing and transmitting sound developed by Apple and commonly used on its Macintosh computers. This format is also often utilized on the Internet and on Silicon Graphics machines. AIFF does not compress the data, so AIFF files are comparatively large. AIFF files commonly have the *.aiff* file extension. *See* Table 4 at **container format.**

airtime **1.** The amount of time that a cell phone is connected to a network, for incoming and outgoing calls. In North America, most cell phone service plans bill based on airtime. **2.** A period of time used or reserved for the broadcast of radio, television, or other media programming.

AIX *Abbreviation of* **Advanced Interactive Executive** or **Advanced IBM Unix.** A proprietary operating system developed by IBM based on an early version of Unix and compliant with the Single Unix Standard. AIX runs on computers using IBM microprocessors such as the PowerPC.

alert box   A window or box that appears on the screen to alert the user to something requiring attention. An alert box may warn a user, for example, that a requested file cannot be found. Unlike a dialog box, an alert box does not request user input. *Also called* **message box.**

algorithm   A finite set of unambiguous instructions that, given some set of initial conditions, can be performed in a prescribed sequence to achieve a certain goal and that has a recognizable set of end conditions. To follow a recipe or the instructions for building a model plane is to follow an algorithm. Computers are constantly executing algorithms, and the goal of much computer programming is to implement algorithms in terms of a set of instructions. The creation of efficient algorithms is vital to applications in which difficult computational tasks must be performed quickly, as for example in the cryptography used to conceal private information such as credit card numbers during Internet transactions. In many countries, newly devised algorithms can be patented.

alias   **1.** An email address that does not store incoming email, but instead sends it on to another email address. Aliases are used for a variety of purposes, for example to act as an alternative name for an email address that is difficult to remember. **2.** An alternative filename for a file or application in Apple Macintosh operating systems, allowing the file to appear in more than one location in the file structure, allowing it for example to be seen both within a directory and on the desktop. Aliases are equivalent to shortcuts in Windows and symbolic links in Linux and Unix operating systems. **3.** An alternate name associated with an object, such as a computer, computer user, or variable. **4.** Aliasing in telecommunication links resulting from interactions between signal frequency and sampling frequency, resulting in the transmission of false signals. *See also* **artifact.**

aliasing   An artifact introduced into digital information, such as audio signals or images, caused when a continuous line or transition cannot be smoothly captured or represented given the resolution of a digital medium. In computer graphics, aliasing is most often seen in the form of jagged distortions called jaggies in curves and diagonal lines. In this case, aliasing occurs because of limited display screen resolution: pixels are arranged in rows and columns, but if the pixel grid is too coarse, the pixels cannot be turned on in a pattern that will be perceived as a smooth curve or diagonal.

Aliasing can occur in other contexts as well, especially in the digitization of audio signals, in which a smoothly rising or falling waveform is rendered digitally as a sequence of discrete steps. Such distortions of the waveform can have audible effects.

The problems associated with aliasing can be reduced by introducing a larger sample size in the digital representation of the signal, for example, by using more pixels to represent an image or a higher sample rate for an audio signal. Aliasing that has already been introduced into digital information can sometimes be effectively reduced by antialiasing techniques. *See also* **artifact.**

alignment   **1.** The placement of objects in fixed rows or columns, such as icons in a folder or on the desktop. **2.** The placement of the read/write heads of disk drives over the tracks so that they are in the correct position to read and write. **3.** *See* **justification.**

alkaline battery   A common disposable battery made of zinc and manganese dioxide. Alkaline cells last longer than zinc-carbon cells but not as long as lithium, silver-oxide, or zinc-air cells. Most have a maximum voltage of 1.5 volts per cell.

alphanumeric   Consisting of any combination of alphabetic characters and the decimal numerals 0 through 9. In some contexts certain punctuation characters and other symbols are also included. *See also* **ASCII, Unicode.**

alpha testing   The initial stage in the testing of a new software or hardware product conducted by testers within the company that developed the product, before it is released to independent testers outside the company.

alpha version   The first version of a software or hardware product, used during alpha testing.

Alt key   A key that is pressed in combination with another key to execute an alternate function. In some Microsoft Windows applications, for example, Alt-F4 exits and closes a running program. *See also* **Control key, Shift key.**

ALU   *Abbreviation of* **arithmetic-logic unit.**

AM   *Abbreviation of* **amplitude modulation.**   A method of transmitting signals, such as sound or digital information, in which the value of the signal is given by the amplitude of a high-frequency carrier wave. In AM radio transmission, for example, the signal to be carried is a sound wave, and its increasing and decreasing value is reflected in the increasing and decreasing amplitude of the radio frequency carrier wave. In AM fiber-optic transmission, the carrier wave is a beam of light. *See also* **FM, PCM.**

Amaya   A free, open-source web browser developed by the W3C. Amaya has an integrated editor for HTML, CSS, and XML. It supports a wide range of standard XML markup languages, such as XHTML, SVG, and MathML.

AMD64   *See* **x86-64.**

American National Standards Institute   *See* **ANSI.**

American Standard Code for Information Interchange   *See* **ASCII.**

America Online or **AOL**   A commercial online service that provides access to services such as chatrooms, instant messaging, and the Internet.

amp   **1.** *Abbreviation of* **ampere. 2.** *Abbreviation of* **amplifier.**

ampere   *Abbreviated* **amp.**   A measure of electrical current flow through a conductor. One ampere is equal to the current flowing through a conductor with an impedance (or resistance) of one ohm when a voltage of one volt is applied across the conductor.

Amphenol Precision Connector   *See* **APC-7.**

amplifier   *Abbreviated* **amp.**   An electronic device that is used to increase the magnitude of an electrical signal.

amplitude   The maximum absolute value of a periodically varying quantity, especially an electrical or sound signal. *Compare* **loudness, volume.**

amplitude modulation   *See* **AM.**

AMPS   *Abbreviation of* **advanced mobile phone service.**   A standard for analog cellular communications in which each base station transmits at a different frequency. Most AMPS service worldwide has been replaced with the GSM and CDMA digital cellular standards.

analog   **1.** Measuring or representing data by means of one or more physical properties that can express any value along a continuous scale. Analog modes are contrasted with digital modes, in which a variable must assume one of a number of discrete values and can only approximate values that lie between these points. A mercury thermometer and a clock with hands, for example, are analog devices. Analog signals are common in electrical and radio transmission, especially of sound signals, where the changing amplitude of the sound wave is represented by a corresponding change in the amplitude of a voltage in an electrical circuit, or the intensity or frequency of a radio wave.

   Most computers are strictly digital devices; they can accept input and produce output in analog form, but only with the help of digital-to-analog and analog-to-digital converters. Analog computers, which operate on continuously varying input data, are primarily used in specialized industrial and scientific contexts.

2. Designating a type of display, as on a watch or radio, that makes use of a pointer or other indicator moving against a fixed scale rather than a series of changing numerical digits. *Compare* **digital.**

analog stick   A small vertical stick on a game controller that can be tilted to indicate direction. Analog sticks are typically capped with a disk and operated with the thumb. *Also called* **thumbstick.**

analog-to-digital converter   *Abbreviated* **A/D converter** or **ADC.**   A device that converts an analog signal, such as a varying electrical voltage, into digital form that can be stored or manipulated by a computer or other digital sound-processing device. Analog-to-digital converters are often used to convert voice signals picked up by a microphone into digital signals, for example for transmission by a cell phone, and in voice-recognition products that allow computers to accept spoken input. They are also used in joysticks and computer mice to convert physical motion into a digital signal interpreted by a computer. *Compare* **digital-to-analog converter.**

anamorphic DVD   A DVD with a widescreen image that is recorded so as to use the full vertical resolution of a widescreen television. For display on a screen with a 4 : 3 aspect ratio, the anamorphic image must be converted to letterbox format by the DVD player or the television. *See also* **widescreen.**

anamorphic lens   A lens that produces optical imaging effects, especially shrinking along one axis, by refracting light differently along one axis than along another. Anamorphic lenses are used on projectors to show widescreen images on a display with a 4 : 3 aspect ratio using the display's entire vertical resolution. Such projectors have a digital processor that compresses the widescreen image along the horizontal axis until it fits onto the 4 : 3 display. The distorted 4 : 3 image is projected through an anamorphic lens that compresses it along the vertical axis to restore its original widescreen aspect ratio.

anchor   **1.** An HTML tag that sets off an item of text or graphics as a hyperlink to another item in the same or another HTML document. **2.** A formatting code that is used to fix an object, such as a graphical item, to a place that is permanent or relative to another object, so that it remains in that position when the document is repaginated. For example, in dictionary publishing, marginal artwork may be anchored to the entry word with which it corresponds, so that if text shifts cause an entry associated with a piece of art to flow to the following page, the art will follow along with it.

AND   A logical operator that returns the value TRUE as its output if both of its inputs (or *operands*) are TRUE. If either input is FALSE, AND returns the value FALSE. *See* Table E on page 361.

animated GIF   A series of GIF files saved as one large file. Animated GIFs, when viewed by the appropriate software (such as a web browser displaying the GIF on a webpage), provide short animations that typically repeat as long as the GIF is being displayed. This technology has largely been replaced by dedicated animation programs.

animation   The creation of the illusion of motion through the display of a series of static pictures that change slightly from one to the next. Computer software is often used to facilitate the production of cartoons or animated multimedia presentations by eliminating the need for a human to redraw each image; instead, the computer can modify each step.

anonymous FTP   A method of downloading publicly available files or other data from an FTP server. If a file is available by anonymous FTP, a user does not need a username or password in order to download the file; the username *anonymous* can be used with an email address as a password. Because of the widespread use of web browsers, most publicly available files are now available via HTTP on the World Wide Web and so anonymous FTP is not commonly used. *See also* **file transfer protocol.**

ANSI   *Abbreviation of* **American National Standards Institute.**   A private organization that maintains US standards in many areas, including computers and communication. ANSI represents the United States in the ISO and the IEC.

answering machine   A device for answering telephone calls and recording callers' messages. Most answering machines record messages digitally and store them on a chip.   *See also* **voice mail.**

answer mode   A mode of operating in which a modem is ready to answer incoming calls and establish a connection with calling modems or fax machines in order to receive data. *Also called* **auto-answer mode.**

antenna   A device used to capture energy from a radio signal in order to convert it into an electrical signal, or to convert electrical energy into a radio signal for broadcast.

   Antennas that pick up broadcast radio or television signals are generally made of metallic extensions that project out from the device (such as a tuner or amplifier) that processes the signals, while antennas used in cell phones and wireless devices are generally internal. Both types of antenna usually have specialized shapes that maximize their receptiveness to a specific range of frequencies. Antennas do not themselves amplify the electrical or radio signals they capture or transmit.

antialiasing   A software process for removing the effects of aliasing. Jaggies, for example, are a kind of aliasing that result in jagged distortions of an image on a graphic display with limited resolution; antialiasing can diminish the conspicuousness of jaggies by surrounding them with shades of gray (for gray-scale images) or color (for color images). *See also* **aliasing.**

bitmap (with jaggies)   antialiasing   smoothing

antialiasing

antiblooming gate   A gap between the sensor pixels of a CCD imaging device that prevents an overexposed pixel from triggering neighboring pixels and causing blooming. Antiblooming gates reduce overall resolution of the pixel, since the size of the pixel is effectively reduced, and the pixel can absorb less light before being saturated than a pixel without antiblooming gates.

antistatic   Relating to devices or techniques for reducing the risk of electrostatic discharge (static shock) while working on a computer or other device. Static electricity can harm microprocessors, RAM chips, hard disks, and other computer components. Antistatic devices, such as bracelets and mats, generally work by reducing the buildup of static electricity.

antivirus program   A program that checks memory, disks, or files being downloaded from a network for computer viruses or other suspicious programs or information, typically removing those that it finds. Since new viruses are often being developed, such software needs to be updated regularly. *See also* **firewall.**

AOL   *Abbreviation of* **America Online.**

Apache server   Free, open-source web server software, based on code originally developed by the National Center for Supercomputing Applications and supplemented by a number of patches (hence, *a patchy server*). Originally written for Unix, versions of Apache now exist for other operating systems, including Linux and Microsoft Windows.

APC-7   *Abbreviation of* **Amphenol Precision Connector.**   A 7mm, sexless coaxial connector often used for high-frequency transmissions up to 18 GHz. APC-7 is a registered trademark of the Amphenol Corporation, but other companies also produce this cable, using the first letter of their names to replace the *A* in the acronym.

aperture grill   A series of fine vertical wires on the inside of a CRT screen that separate the three colors of phosphors into columns. Aperture grills have two horizontal stabilizing wires running across the screen that are sometimes visible. *Compare* **shadow mask.**

API *Abbreviation of* **application program interface.** A set of routines and protocols through which one program can communicate with another. APIs make it easier for programmers to write an application that uses the functionality of another application.

app An application. Used informally in phrases such as *a killer app.*

append To add data to the end of a file or string. Commands that write data to a file can often be configured to append the data to the file, rather than overwriting the file. *See also* **concatenate.**

Apple Desktop Bus *Abbreviated* **ADB.** An interface developed by Apple and used in older Macintosh computers. The Apple Desktop Bus allows up to 16 serial input devices (mouse, keyboard, trackball, etc.) to be connected to the computer through two 4-pin ports on the back. The Apple Desktop Bus is no longer in use in current Macintosh computers.

Apple key *See* **Command key.**

Apple Mail *See* **Mail.**

applet A small program designed to be downloaded from the Internet to run on a webpage that a user is accessing. Applets are usually written in the Java programming language, have limited features, and require limited memory resources. Some browsers require a plug-in to run Java applications. *Compare* **ActiveX.**

application A computer program that serves as a tool to help the user accomplish some specific task or range of related tasks. Popular applications includes word processors and text editors, spreadsheet and accounting packages, database management programs, communications software, and programs for entertainment and education. *See also* **system software, utility.**

application and power interface *See* **ACPI.**

application program interface *See* **API.**

applications software Software that executes the variety of tasks that users want their computers to perform. Examples are word processing programs, database management systems, spreadsheets, Internet browsers, and games. *Compare* **system software.** *See also* **software.**

application window The main window of an application, typically consisting of a title bar, which lists the name of the application; the menu bar, which hierarchically lists the names of the available commands or options; and a work area, which itself may consist of multiple windows.

architecture   The overall design or structure of a computer system. In general, architecture applies to the entire system including all the hardware components and systems software needed to make it run. More specifically, it often refers to the internal structure of a microprocessor, either in terms of the size of its registers (8 bits, 16 bits, 32 bits, or 64 bits) or the type of instruction set it uses. The instruction set consists of all instructions or commands in the computer's machine language that the microprocessor can recognize and execute.

archival backup   *See* **full backup.**

archive   *n.* **1.** A long-term storage area, often on magnetic tape or a hard disk, for backup copies of files or for files that are no longer in active use. **2.** A file containing other files, often in compressed format. Archives allow efficient storage and file transfer. They are created by archiving programs, such as tar, or compression programs, such as WINZIP, and must be unarchived by such a program in order to be used. *See also* **data compression, packed file. 3.** An attribute in DOS and Microsoft Windows 95 that indicates files that have been changed since the last backup.
   v. To create a long-term storage area archive or an archive file.

ARCnet   *Abbreviation of* **Attached Resource Computer network.**   A popular, inexpensive local access network (LAN) first produced in 1968 by Datapoint Corporation. ARCnet employs a star topology and allows a mixture of different kinds of cables on the same network. ARCnet is capable of transmitting data at rates of up to 2.5 Mbps.

areal density   The amount of data that can be fit on a storage medium, expressed in megabits or gigabits per square inch. *See also* **TPI.**

arg   *Abbreviation of* **argument.**

argument   *Abbreviated* **arg.**   In spreadsheet programs and in programming languages, a value that is passed to a function so it can be operated on to produce a result. For example, if a function called LOG computes the common logarithm of a number, then the statement LOG(100), where the argument is 100, would return the value 2. The term is often used as a synonym for both *option* and *parameter,* as in the phrase *command line argument,* which refers to an option to a command.

arithmetic expression   An expression that can be calculated to yield a numerical value. Arithmetic expressions can contain constants and variables. Examples are $6 \times (5 + 4)$ and PRICE $\times$ QUANTITY $\times$ 0.05.

arithmetic-logic unit   *Abbreviated* **ALU.**   A component of the CPU (central processing unit) that performs arithmetic and logical operations. Arithmetic-logic units can only perform calculations on whole numbers and thus floating-point units are used for many numerical calculations. One CPU may have several arithmetic-logic units. *See also* **control unit.**

arithmetic operator   A symbol that stands for a numerical operation, such as addition or multiplication. *See also* **logical operator, relational operator.**

ARM   A microprocessor architecture developed by ARM Ltd. ARM is a 32-bit RISC architecture designed to consume small amounts of power and to be inexpensive to produce. ARM microprocessors are commonly used in cell phones, PDAs, and other wireless devices, as well as handheld games, calculators, and digital music players.

ARP   *Abbreviation of* **Address Resolution Protocol.**   A protocol often used in conjunction with TCP/IP to determine the MAC address of a given IP address. The requester broadcasts a message giving the IP address and requesting the MAC address. The machine with that IP address responds with its own MAC address. *See also* **MAC address.**

ARPA   *Abbreviation of* **Advanced Research Projects Agency.**   *See* **DARPA.**

ARPANET   *Abbreviation of* **Advanced Research Projects Agency Network.** A network developed by ARPA in the 1960s and 1970s as a means of communication between research laboratories and universities. Used by researchers for testing networking technologies, it is the predecessor of the Internet.

array   **1.** In mathematics and computer programming, a structure consisting of a collection of single elements or pieces of data, all having the same data type, any of which can be located and retrieved by specifying the name of the array and the element's location within the array. A one-dimensional data structure, with values arranged in a single row or column, is known as a vector. An array of more than one dimension, such as a two-dimensional array of rows and columns, is known as a matrix. **2.** A group of many single elements, all of the same kind, arranged in a regular pattern and connected together to perform a single task.

arrow key   Any of a set of keys labeled with arrows pointing left, right, up, and down, that control the movement of the cursor or insertion point on the display screen. Depending on which program is running, the arrow keys may have additional functions when combined with other keys, such as the Shift key. For example, Shift + Up-arrow may send the cursor to the beginning of a document.

artifact   A phenomenon or feature that is not originally present or intended in a system and is a by-product of some aspect of processing. For example, the intended smooth gradation of color generally appears on a computer monitor as an artifact consisting of very narrow bands of even color, with each band slightly different from the adjacent bands. Lossy compression of data is especially likely to create artifacts.

artificial intelligence *Abbreviated* **AI.** A branch of computer science whose goal is to develop electronic devices that can operate with some of the characteristics of human intelligence. Among these properties are logical deduction and inference, creativity, the ability to make decisions based on past experience or insufficient or conflicting information, and the ability to understand natural language. *See also* **expert system.**

ascending sort A sort in which the items are listed from first to last or smallest to largest, as from A to Z or from 0 to 9. *See also* **descending sort.**

ASCII *Abbreviation of* **American Standard Code for Information Interchange.** **1.** A character encoding that assigns a 7-bit digital sequence to each of 128 characters so they can be stored and transmitted by computers. ASCII (pronounced AS-kee) encodes letters of the Roman alphabet, as well as control characters such as carriage returns and tabs. Because computers generally store data in 8-bit bytes, various extensions of ASCII were developed that use 8 bits, and thus encode 256 characters. The most common extension in use today is ISO Latin-1. More recently, the Unicode standard was developed in order to represent the letters of all the world's languages. *See also* **extended ASCII.** *See* Table 1. **2.** The set of characters encoded by the ASCII standard.

ASCII file A text file that contains only characters in the standard ASCII character set.

ASCII sort A sort in which items are listed in order according to their numerical position in the ASCII character set. Numbers precede uppercase letters, which precede lowercase letters. *See also* **dictionary sort.**

ASF *Abbreviation of* **Advanced Systems Format** or **Advanced Streaming Format.** A container format used in the Windows Media platform for streaming audio and video. Files of this type usually have the *.asf* extension.

ASP *Abbreviation of* **ActiveServer Pages.** A scripting language developed by Microsoft for using server-side scripts to generate webpages, often from data in databases. For example, a webpage written using ActiveServer Pages can be used to generate HTML that reflects changing information, such as dynamic numerical information, or information that is specific to a particular user or session. This new HTML is generated for the page every time it is accessed. ASP is used primarily with web servers running a Windows operating system.

aspect ratio The ratio of width to height of a display screen, or of an image on a given display device. Digital cameras generally produce images with an aspect ratio of 4 : 3 (1.33 : 1), which is the aspect ratio

TABLE 1   **Standard ASCII Character Encoding**

Decimal Value	Hexadecimal Value	Character	
0	0	NUL	(null character)
1	1	SOH	(start of heading)
2	2	STX	(start of text)
3	3	ETX	(end of text)
4	4	EOT	(end of transmission)
5	5	ENQ	(enquiry)
6	6	ACK	(acknowledge)
7	7	BEL	(terminal bell)
8	8	BS	(backspace)
9	9	HT	(horizontal tab; normal tab character)
10	A	LF	(line feed)
11	B	VT	(vertical tab; soft return)
12	C	FF	(form feed)
13	D	CR	(carriage return)
14	E	SO	(shift out; changes meaning of following characters)
15	F	SI	(shift in; reinstates normal meaning of following characters)
16	10	DLE	(data link escape)
17	11	DC1	(device control 1)
18	12	DC2	(device control 2)
19	13	DC3	(device control 3)
20	14	DC4	(device control 4)
21	15	NAK	(negative acknowledge)
22	16	SYN	(synchronous idle)
23	17	ETB	(end transmission block)
24	18	CAN	(cancel)
25	19	EM	(end of medium)
26	1A	SUB	(substitute)

TABLE 1 Standard ASCII Character Encoding *(continued)*

Decimal Value	Hexadecimal Value	Character	
27	1B	ESC	(escape)
28	1C	FS	(file separator)
29	1D	GS	(group separator)
30	1E	RS	(record separator)
31	1F	US	(unit separator)
32	20	SP	(space)
33	21	!	(exclamation point)
34	22	"	(double quote)
35	23	#	(pound sign)
36	24	$	(dollar sign)
37	25	%	(percent sign)
38	26	&	(ampersand)
39	27	'	(single quote)
40	28	(	(left parenthesis)
41	29	)	(right parenthesis)
42	2A	*	(asterisk)
43	2B	+	(plus sign)
44	2C	,	(comma)
45	2D	-	(hyphen)
46	2E	.	(dot; period)
47	2F	/	(slash; forward slash)
48	30	0	
49	31	1	
50	32	2	
51	33	3	
52	34	4	
53	35	5	
54	36	6	
55	37	7	
56	38	8	

TABLE 1 **Standard ASCII Character Encoding** *(continued)*

Decimal Value	Hexadecimal Value	Character	
57	39	9	
58	3A	:	(colon)
59	3B	;	(semicolon)
60	3C	<	(left angle bracket)
61	3D	=	(equals sign)
62	3E	>	(right angle bracket)
63	3F	?	(question mark)
64	40	@	(at sign)
65	41	A	
66	42	B	
67	43	C	
68	44	D	
69	45	E	
70	46	F	
71	47	G	
72	48	H	
73	49	I	
74	4A	J	
75	4B	K	
76	4C	L	
77	4D	M	
78	4E	N	
79	4F	O	
80	50	P	
81	51	Q	
82	52	R	
83	53	S	
84	54	T	
85	55	U	
86	56	V	

TABLE 1   Standard ASCII Character Encoding *(continued)*

Decimal Value	Hexadecimal Value	Character	
87	57	W	
88	58	X	
89	59	Y	
90	5A	Z	
91	5B	[	(left square bracket)
92	5C	\	(backslash)
93	5D	]	(right square bracket)
94	5E	^	(caret)
95	5F	_	(underscore)
96	60	`	(backtick)
97	61	a	
98	62	b	
99	63	c	
100	64	d	
101	65	e	
102	66	f	
103	67	g	
104	68	h	
105	69	i	
106	6A	j	
107	6B	k	
108	6C	l	
109	6D	m	
110	6E	n	
111	6F	o	
112	70	p	
113	71	q	
114	72	r	
115	73	s	

TABLE 1   **Standard ASCII Character Encoding** *(continued)*

Decimal Value	Hexadecimal Value	Character	
116	74	t	
117	75	u	
118	76	v	
119	77	w	
120	78	x	
121	79	y	
122	7A	z	
123	7B	{	(left curly bracket)
124	7C	|	(vertical bar; pipe symbol)
125	7D	}	(right curly bracket)
126	7E	~	(tilde)
127	7F	DEL	(delete)

of typical computer monitors and televisions. High-definition television displays have an aspect ratio of 16 : 9 (1.78 : 1). *See also* **widescreen.** *See* Table B on page 357.

ASR   *Abbreviation of* **automatic speech recognition.**   *See* **speech recognition.**

assembler   A program that converts a set of instructions written in assembly language into machine language.

assembly language   A low-level programming language that very closely reflects a machine language, in which each instruction generally corresponds to a single machine language instruction. Assembly languages have the same structure as machine language, the difference being that commands and functions are expressed using text rather than the binary numbers of machine code. Assembly language programs are converted into machine language by an assembler. Assembly language programming is useful when detailed control of the operation of the computer is required; for everyday programming, however, assembly language is difficult and tedious to work with, since each procedure must be spelled out in extreme detail. Assembly programs also must be rewritten if they are transferred from one type of microprocessor to another.

Association for Computing Machinery *Abbreviated* **ACM.** The first professional society for computer technology experts, founded in 1947. The ACM publishes journals and books, maintains a web portal for computing literature, sponsors conferences, promotes computing standards, and has formulated a code of ethics and professional conduct.

asterisk A character (*) found in most standard character sets, often used to indicate multiplication (as in 4 * 2 = 8). It is also used when referring to character strings, such as filenames, as a wild card; in this use, it stands for any arbitrary set of characters. For example, *dog** would match any filename beginning with the letters *dog* (*dog1, dog5, dogsandcats, dog.exe,* and so on).

ASV *Abbreviation of* **audio still video.** A still image on a DVD-Audio disk that is displayed onscreen when the disk is played.

Asymmetric Digital Subscriber Line *See* **ADSL.**

asynchronous Relating to or being a telecommunications mode that does not rely on an independent timing signal to identify the beginning and end of each byte of data that is transmitted. In asynchronous mode, the communicating devices are free to send data in a continuous stream whenever both devices are ready. The beginning of each byte is identified by a start bit, and the end by a stop bit. Most communication between personal computers is asynchronous, because the relatively lower transmission speeds permit the use of standard telephone lines. *See also* **modem, parity, synchronous.**

asynchronous transfer mode *See* **ATM.**

AT *Abbreviation of* **Advanced Technology.** An obsolete standard for desktop computer components that is based on the design of the IBM AT computer, introduced in 1984. *See also* **ATX.**

ATA *Abbreviation of* **Advanced Technology Attachment.** *See* **IDE.**

AT Attachment Packet Interface *Abbreviated* **ATAPI.** The IDE protocols pertaining to drives other than hard drives, such as CD-ROM drives. *See also* **IDE.**

AT command set *Abbreviation of* **Attention command set.** A standardized set of instructions developed by Hayes Microcomputer Products and used to control and configure modems. Practically all modern modems made today are compatible with this standard. *Also called* **Hayes command set.**

ATM *Abbreviation of* **asynchronous transfer mode.** A high-speed communications standard for voice, data, and video traffic. The standard achieves its speed because it does not require the clock signals of the communicating devices to be coordinated. Instead, each device sends signals to the other(s) indicating whether it is ready to receive or send. ATM combines the efficiency of packet switching with the path and bandwidth reliability of circuit switching.

Atom   An XML language for representing headlines and summary information about web content. Atom is used for distributing news briefs, as well as alerting people about new content available on websites. An API governs the functioning of programs that create, edit, and display web feeds written in Atom. *See also* **web feed, web syndication.**

ATSC   *Abbreviation of* **Advanced Television Systems Committee.**   A digital television transmission standard based on the MPEG-2 video standard and the AC-3 audio standard. ATSC supports all major display formats including SDTV, EDTV, and HDTV. ATSC is used alongside NTSC for terrestrial broadcasting in the United States. *Compare* **DVB.**

at sign   The character @. At signs are used in email addresses to separate the name of a mailbox and the computer name at which it resides, as in *trade@hmco.com.*

Attached Resource Computer Network   *See* **ARCnet.**

attachment   A file that is attached to an email using the MIME standard. The contents of an attachment usually do not appear within the body of the email, and non-ASCII data is encoded as ASCII text. Most email programs automatically encode documents that are sent as attachments and automatically decode received attachments. While email viewers can usually display text, HTML, and image attachments, some attachments, such as word processing documents, have to be saved as a separate file in order to be viewed. *Also called* **MIME attachment.** *See also* **MIME type.**

Attention command set   *See* **AT command set.**

attribute   **1.** A named characteristic of a data object such as a block of text or an HTML element. Attributes generally take one of a defined set of values. For example, the style attribute of a block of text can have values such as *italic* or *bold.* **2.** *See* **file attribute.**

ATX   *Abbreviation of* **Advanced Technology Extended.**   A standard for computer motherboards and other basic components, such as power supplies, that evolved from the AT standard. Most desktop computers have ATX motherboards.

audio   Audible or recorded sound.

audio card   *See* **sound card.**

audiocassette   A cassette containing blank or prerecorded audiotape. *Also called* **audiotape.**

audio CD   A compact disk that contains digital audio data in the format used by special-purpose CD players, as opposed to other digital audio formats. *See also* **compact disk.**

Audio Engineering Society/European Broadcasting Union   *See* **AES/EBU.**

audio frequency   *Abbreviated* **AF.**   A frequency that is within the range of human hearing, typically between 20 Hz and 20 kHz.

Audio Interchange File Format   *See* **AIFF.**

audio still video   *See* **ASV.**

audiotape   **1.** A relatively narrow magnetic tape for recording and playing back sound. *Also called* **tape. 2.** *See* **audiocassette.**

AUDIO_TS   A folder in the directory of a DVD where files in the DVD-Audio format are stored.

Audio Video Interleave   *See* **AVI.**

audio-visual or **audiovisual**   *Abbreviated* **A/V.**   Relating to materials and devices that present information in audible and pictorial form. *Compare* **text.**

audit trail   **1.** In accounting and database management software, a complete record of all transactions and changes made to a document. An audit trail allows the document's history to be reconstructed in case of data loss or error. **2.** In systems management, a record of all activity on a network, used primarily for security purposes.

AUP   *Abbreviation of* **Acceptable Use Policy.**

authentication   The process of verifying the identity of a computer user or of a device with which a computer communicates. Authentication is used to prevent unauthorized access to computer resources, as when a user is required to provide a login name and a password; it is also used in networks to guarantee that messages are being received by the intended recipients.

authoring   The process of creating or writing a hypertext document using a markup language. Examples of authoring include combining text, graphics, and sound objects to create content for webpages, multimedia presentations, slide shows, DVDs, and other applications.

authoring language   A computer language designed to make it easier to create graphics, multimedia presentations, webpages, or programs. Authoring languages provide ways to link together text, graphics, and sounds without using a complex programming language. HTML is often considered an authoring language, though the term is sometimes restricted to proprietary languages used by special-purpose authoring software.

authoring software   Programs used to create graphics, multimedia presentations, webpages, and programs. Authoring programs usually provide an easy-to-use graphical interface rather than working directly with an authoring language.

auto-answer mode   *See* **answer mode.**

auto exposure   A system that automatically sets the exposure time or the aperture value (or both) used in making an image taken by a camera or video device.

automatic gain control   *Abbreviated* **AGC.**   An electronic circuit in an amplifier that compensates for variations in the input level of an audio or video signal by boosting or lowering the gain sufficiently to maintain a constant level.

automatic speech recognition   *Abbreviated* **ASR.**   *See* **speech recognition.**

autoplay   The ability of some optical disk drives to launch disks automatically upon insertion to the drive. *Also called* **autorun.**

auto-redial   A feature that allows a modem to dial a number repeatedly when it receives a busy signal.

autorepeat   A feature that allows a key on a keyboard to repeat its assigned keystroke continuously as long as the key is held down.

autorun   *See* **autoplay.**

autosave   To save automatically files that are open in an application to a disk at periodic intervals to reduce the chances of losing data. Many applications autosave documents, creating temporary backups of each file that are used to restore the file in case of a crash or a power loss while the file is open. *Also called* **timed backup.** *See also* **save.**

AUX   In DOS, the name of a serial port for connecting an auxiliary device. This port is usually the same as COM1, the first serial port.

A/V or **AV**   *Abbreviations of* **audio-visual.**

avatar   **1.** A graphical representation of a person in an IRC chatroom, interactive game, instant-messaging system, or other interactive web environment. An avatar can be a cartoon drawing, photograph, or other item that the user chooses to represent his or her virtual identity. **2.** The character a user controls in a multiplayer computer or video game, especially a role-playing game. **3.** The name of the superuser account on some Unix systems.

AVI   *Abbreviation of* **Audio Video Interleave.**   A container format for the Microsoft Windows environment used for storing, transmitting, and playing audio and video data. AVI files are named with an *.avi* extension.

awk   A programming language designed for processing text. Awk is part of the standard set of tools available on almost all Linux and Unix operating systems. It has powerful pattern matching capabilities because it uses regular expressions.

backbone   A high-speed communications line that connects smaller, local networks to each other, especially in a wide area network.

backdoor   A property of a computer system that allows users to gain access without going through normal authentication procedures. For example, a backdoor program can be surreptitiously installed on a computer, allowing another user to access the computer. Some part of the source code of a program or operating system, included when the software is created, might also function as a backdoor, allowing users who know about it to gain access.

back end   The parts of an application that run on a server instead of on a user's machine. For example, making purchases online usually involves processing on the back end. *See also* **client/server, front end, server-side script.**

background printing   Printing a document by means of a spooler so the program used to create the document can work on something else during printing. When background printing is used, print jobs are sent first to the spooler, which stores the job on disk until the printer can process it. If background printing is not used, programs send data to the printer directly, and so remain busy until all the data has been accepted by the printer. Some operating systems allow background printing to be turned on or off.

background process   A program that is running without user interaction. Background processes take up space in RAM and may use the CPU to make calculations. A program may be a background process because its window is inactive, because it is not currently in control of a terminal, or because it is a daemon. *Compare* **foreground process.** *See also* **process.**

backlighting   A technique used to increase the legibility of a liquid crystal display screen by illuminating it from behind. The display screens of laptops, digital camera viewscreens, and personal digital assistants typically use backlighting, which heightens the contrast of the text or images on the screen, but requires considerable electrical power; most portable devices therefore turn backlighting off if they have not been in use for some period to prevent battery power from draining needlessly.

back-side bus   A bus that allows data transfer between a CPU and an external cache. *Compare* **front-side bus.**

backslash   A character (\) used in Windows pathnames to separate directory names.

A character (\) used as an escape character, as when including special characters in regular expressions so that they are interpreted as literal characters. For example, the asterisk is a wildcard, so when using a regular expression to search for text containing asterisks, many systems require the asterisk to be preceded by a backslash—otherwise the regular expression interpreter will treat it as a wildcard.

Backspace key   A key that moves the cursor one space to the left, typically deleting the character that is there. *See also* **Delete key.**

backup   **1.** An instance or the process of backing up a set of files, such as the files on a drive or in a directory. **2.** A copy of a file or set of files produced during a backup. **3.** A disk, tape, or other storage device that contains files copied for use as a backup.

back up   To copy a file or files from one storage area, such as a hard disk, to another to prevent their loss in case of disk or power failure. It is generally considered crucial to maintain one or more backup files for information of any importance. When backing up large files, or large numbers of files, as when backing up an entire hard disk, data compression is sometimes used to reduce the storage needed.

backward compatible   Relating to new versions of technology, especially computer hardware or software, that do not make earlier versions obsolete. For example, a backward-compatible word processing program still retains the features of earlier versions, and is capable of reading word processing files saved by earlier versions; a backward-compatible microprocessor can still run the software run by its predecessors. Backward-incompatible technology may render earlier technology obsolete, being difficult or impossible to use along with the older technology. *Also called* **downward compatible.** *See also* **compatible, upward compatible.**

backward incompatible   Not backward compatible. Used of new versions of technology that are incompatible with earlier versions.

bad sector   A sector of a hard disk or floppy disk that cannot be used for reading and writing information because of a manufacturing defect or a flaw in the surface. It is normal for a new hard disk to have a small number of bad sectors; the operating system or a disk utility program can locate and mark these areas so they will not be used. As a hard disk gets older, more sectors may occasionally fail, but if this happens frequently it is a sign of a malfunctioning disk drive or impending disk failure. If bad sectors appear on a floppy disk, some data will usually be lost and the entire disk may become unusable; the safest policy generally is to copy the remaining files to a fresh disk, if possible, and discard the one that has failed. *See also* **disk, format, head crash, sector.**

baffle   A partition that prevents interference between sound waves in a speaker.

.bak   A file extension commonly used for backups of individual files. Many programs can be configured so that when a document named, for example, *foo.doc* is saved, a backup called *foo.bak* is created, which contains the previous version of the file.

balanced audio   Audio equipment that uses balanced cables for the transmission of audio signals.

balanced cable   A cable that transmits electrical signals using three separate conductors. One conductor carries the signal with positive phase, another carries the signal with negative phase, and the third serves as the ground. The difference between the signal-carrying conductors is used to retrieve the signal at the receiving end, meaning that any stray signals (such as hum) that enter both signal-carrying conductors are cancelled out at the receiving end. Balanced cables are used in many audio applications because they allow for high sound quality with low outside noise when long cables are used. *Compare* **unbalanced cable.**

Balanced Technology Extended   *See* **BTX.**

band   A range of frequencies in the electromagnetic spectrum between two defined limits. Government agencies generally regulate how various bands of frequencies can be used. Some bands, such as those used for broadcast television, are reserved by law for licensed users of particular services. Protocols such as Wi-Fi usually define a band to be used for communication. Bands are usually divided into a number of smaller bands, called *channels.*

banding   An artifact of color gradation in computer imaging in which a gradual change in the color or brightness of an image appears as a set of distinct bands, each of a single color or brightness. Banding can be reduced by the application of dithering.

bandwidth **1.** A measure of the amount of data that can be transmitted in a given amount of time. In general, the bandwidth of a channel directly affects the speed of data transfer—the higher the bandwidth, the faster data can be sent. For analog devices, or digital devices that use carrier waves to transmit signals, bandwidth is the range of frequencies that can be transmitted and is expressed in hertz. The bandwidth of digital devices is usually measured in bps (bits per second). A standard telephone line, for example, has a bandwidth of about 3,000 Hz while a USB 2.0 cable has a bandwidth of 480 Mbps.

The bandwidth of a video signal is a function of the resolution of the image and the number of frames displayed per second. A 720p60 HDTV signal requires a video system—including the cables, set-top box, and television—with a bandwidth of around 90 MHz. A lower bandwidth will reduce the quality of the image. *See also* **data transfer rate.**

2. The difference between the highest and lowest effective frequencies of a signal, such as a radio, electrical, or sound signal, or between the highest and lowest frequencies that are processed by a device. For example, the bandwidth of a typical AM radio signal is about 10 kHz, meaning that most of the energy of the signal is found within a 10 kHz range around its base carrier frequency. Thus, a station broadcasting at 1260 kHz would be best received by a radio tuned to receive frequencies between 1255 kHz and 1265 kHz.

banner A rectangular box for advertisements on webpages. Clicking on a banner links you to the advertiser's website and often supplies the advertiser with data about you or your computer that is used to track the effectiveness of the advertisement and to generate leads.

barrel distortion Distortion of an image in which the horizontal and vertical lines curve outward away from the center of the image. Barrel distortion often arises from imperfections in an optical system, such as a lens. *See also* **pincushion distortion.**

base64 A format used in the MIME protocol for encoding binary data as ASCII text. Base64 is commonly used to encode graphics and other binary files so they can be sent as email attachments. *See also* **MIME.**

baseband transmission A digital signal transmission technique that allows only a single channel for communication at any given time. The transmission may be either simplex or duplex. Baseband transmission is typically used in radio and infrared transmission; most Ethernet networks use broadband transmission as well.

base font In word processing, the default font that is used in a document wherever a different font is not specifically selected.

base station **1.** In a cell phone network, a set of transceivers and antennas at one location, providing service for one or more cells. When a user of a cell phone makes or receives a call, data is transmitted by antenna between the phone and one of the transceivers at a base station. **2.** A device containing a transceiver and antenna, used with cordless phones or other cordless mobile devices such as headphones or speakers. The base station is connected by wire to a telephone network or to a fixed device, and data is transmitted by antenna between the base station and the mobile devices. **3.** *See* **wireless access point.**

bash *Abbreviation of* **Bourne-again shell.** A shell that interprets commands for Linux and Unix operating systems. Bash is an extension of the Bourne shell and uses similar shell script commands. It is a very popular shell because of features such as allowing users to define their own functions. Bash is free software and part of the Gnu project.

BASIC *Abbreviation of* **Beginners' All-purpose Symbolic Instruction Code.** A simple, high-level programming language. It was first developed in the mid-1960s by John Kemeny and Thomas Kurtz of Dartmouth College, and many other versions with proprietary extensions have also been developed over the years. Despite being criticized by professional programmers for its unwieldiness, BASIC is still often taught to students as a first programming language. Visual Basic is based on BASIC.

basic input/output system *See* **BIOS.**

bass reflex A speaker enclosure with a vent that augments low frequency sounds.

.bat An extension typically used for batch files on a Windows operating system.

batch file A text file that consists of a set of commands. Batch files are often used to execute sequences of commands that are commonly done in the same order. On Windows operating systems, batch files often have the extension *.bat;* hence they are often called *bat* files. *See also* **shell script.**

batch processing Processing in which a complete program or set of instructions is carried out from start to finish without any intervention from a user. Batch processing does not allow for any input while the batch is running, or any corrections in the event of a flaw in the program or a system failure. For these reasons it is primarily used for CPU-intensive tasks that can run reliably without supervision. *See also* **transaction processing.**

battery A device containing an electric cell or a series of electric cells storing energy that can be converted into electrical power. Most consumer batteries are made of dry cells (the chemicals producing the current are made into a paste), although some, such as car batteries, contain chemicals in a liquid form.

Common household batteries, such as those used in a flashlight, consist of a single dry cell. These batteries come in a variety of standard sizes and voltages, ranging from large sizes, such as AAA, AA, A, C, and D, to tiny button cells for which each manufacturer uses a different notation. A positive and negative sign on the cell indicates how the cell should be oriented when it is inside an electrical device. Other batteries, such as laptop and cell phone batteries, consist of multiple dry cells housed within a single case and are designed for use with a specific device. Individual cells are typically capable of producing between 1.2 and 3 volts of electricity, depending on the technology they use.

The least expensive disposable batteries are made of zinc and carbon, but in many applications these have been replaced by longer-lasting types such as alkaline (made of zinc and manganese dioxide), lithium, silver-oxide, and zinc-air batteries. Rechargeable battery types include lithium ion (Li-ion), nickel-metal-hydride (NiMH), and nickel-cadmium (NiCad) batteries.

baud   A unit of data transfer speed equal to one change in a carrier signal per second. Since most data transmission schemes transfer more than one bit of data with each change in the carrier signal, one baud is usually equal to several bits per second. For example, a modem which transfers data at 14,400 bps is operating at 2400 baud and transferring 6 bits of data with every signal change. The term *baud* is outdated and often confused with *bps,* which is now more commonly used to describe data transfer rates.

bay   A space in the cabinet of a personal computer where a storage device such as a disk drive, CD-ROM drive, or removable storage drive can be installed. A bay is *internal* or *hidden* when it cannot be used for removable media, such as floppy disk drives; otherwise it is called *exposed* or *accessible. Also called* **drive bay.**

Bayer interpolation   The use of any of a variety of algorithms for converting digital images in which each pixel represents information about a single color (typically blue, green, and red) into a new image in which each pixel represents a combination of those colors. Bayer interpolation is often used in the processing of images produced by digital cameras and camcorders. Different Bayer interpolation algorithms produce images of different quality and file size.

BBS   *Abbreviation of* **bulletin board system.**

31

beam   To transfer data from one computer or handheld device to another by transmitting infrared energy. If two users have devices equipped with infrared ports, they can establish a connection between the devices and beam files or other data to each other. *See also* **IrDA.**

Because It's There Network or **Because It's Time Network**   *See* **BITNET.**

beeper   *See* **pager.**

Beginners' All-purpose Symbolic Instruction Code   *See* **BASIC.**

benchmark   A set of calculations performed by an application, used as a standard for measuring the performance of a device or system. Benchmarks make it possible to compare hardware or software across different platforms, especially with regard to processing speed.

beta   Relating to the final stage of testing of new software or hardware. Beta versions of products are often released to the public or to independent testers outside the company. Beta testing determines how software or hardware performs in actual work environments.

bezel   The plastic frame around the screen of a television or monitor.

Bézier curve   A smooth, free-form curve used to describe the shapes of characters and images in nearly all draw programs. The shape of the curve is determined mathematically by the location of two midpoints called *control handles*, or simply *handles*. Usually the handles are book-ended by two small boxes called *control points*. By clicking on the control points or the handles themselves and dragging them with the mouse, the user can change the shape of the curve to create image outlines. Bézier is pronounced BEZ-ee-ay.

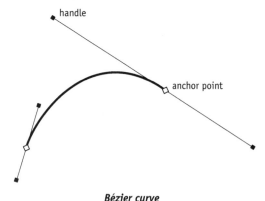

Bézier curve

bidi   *Abbreviation of* **bidirectional text.**   Computer text that contains both scripts that are read left to right and scripts that are read right to left.

TABLE 2 Decimal, Binary, Octal, and Hexadecimal Equivalents

Decimal	Binary	Octal	Hexadecimal
0	0	0	0
1	1	1	1
2	10	2	2
3	11	3	3
4	100	4	4
5	101	5	5
6	110	6	6
7	111	7	7
8	1000	10	8
9	1001	11	9
10	1010	12	A
11	1011	13	B
12	1100	14	C
13	1101	15	D
14	1110	16	E
15	1111	17	F
16	10000	20	10
17	10001	21	11
18	10010	22	12
19	10011	23	13
20	10100	24	14
21	10101	25	15
22	10110	26	16
23	10111	27	17
24	11000	30	18
25	11001	31	19
26	11010	32	1A
27	11011	33	1B
28	11100	34	1C

Special-purpose software is required to display or print such texts properly.

Big Blue   A nickname for IBM Corporation.

binaries   Binary files that contain the executable version of a program.

binary   Relating to the base 2 numeral system. The binary system uses only two symbols: 0 and 1. Each place in a binary number represents a power of 2, in contrast with the commonly used decimal system, in which each place in a number represents a successive power of 10. Thus the decimal number 165, which stands for

$$(1 \times 10^2) + (6 \times 10^1) + (5 \times 10^0)$$

is written in binary notation as 10100101, which stands for

$$(1 \times 2^7) + (0 \times 2^6) + (1 \times 2^5) + (0 \times 2^4) + (0 \times 2^3) + (1 \times 2^2)$$
$$+ (0 \times 2^1) + (1 \times 2^0).$$

This kind of notation is unfamiliar and difficult for people to read, but it is ideal for computers because they are built from binary circuits, which have two possible states. *See also* **hexadecimal, octal.** *See* Table 2 on page 33.

binary coded decimal notation   A notation for representing numbers in which each decimal digit from 0 to 9 is represented by a string of four binary digits. For example, since the binary equivalent of 3 is 0011 and the binary equivalent of 6 is 0110, 36 is represented as 0011 0110. Binary coded decimal notation allows a greater degree of precision in storing numbers and making calculations, but generally requires more storage space. It is often used in computing, especially in applications such as accounting and financial transactions, for which accuracy is important. Most calculators use binary coded decimal notation. *Compare* **fixed-point notation, floating-point notation.**

binary digit   *See* **bit.**

binary file   Any nontext file, especially a data file or program file. *Compare* **text file.** *See also* **executable file.**

Binary Runtime Environment for Wireless   *See* **BREW.**

binaural   Relating to a stereo audio recording created specifically for playback on headphones.

BinHex   A file format formerly used on Macintosh operating systems for encoding binary data as text, as for transmission. Files in BinHex format typically have the extension *.hqx.*

BIOS *Abbreviation of* **basic input/output system.** A set of instructions and routines that controls communication between the various components of a computer system, such as memory, disk drives, keyboard, monitor, printer, and communications ports. Just as the operating system lets applications interact with the computer without having to tell it exactly how to carry out every operation, the BIOS mediates between the operating system and the hardware, taking care of the intricate details of timing and communication required for the devices to work together. The BIOS is often contained in read-only memory (ROM), making it available when the system boots up. Much of the work of the BIOS in older computers has been taken over by the operating system working with device drivers, and the BIOS is mostly responsible for the startup of the computer before the operating system has been loaded.

B-ISDN *Abbreviation of* **Broadband ISDN.**

bit The smallest unit of information or memory within a computer. A bit can hold only one of two values, 0 or 1. In the binary number system, the digits 0 and 1 are also called bits. The term comes from the phrase *binary digit. See also* **byte.**

bit depth The range of color or brightness that can be represented by an individual pixel, measured in terms of how many binary bits are used to represent the information. The greater the bit depth, the more information can be represented concerning the pixel's color and brightness. A pixel using 8 bits of information for the red, green, and blue color channels has a total bit depth of 24 bits; these 24 bits provide enough information to represent around 16.8 million (2^{24}) distinct colors. *Compare* **color depth.**

bitmap or **bit map** *n.* **1.** A set of bits that represents a graphic image. Each bit corresponds to a dot in a pattern. For a monochromatic image, the bitmap consists of rows and columns of 0's and 1's. Each value determines whether its dot is to be filled in (1) or not (0). For a color image or one with shades of gray, each dot requires more than one bit of data. Images and text are almost always translated into bitmaps in order to be printed or displayed. To print an image, the printer creates a bitmap and translates the bitmap into ink dots. To display an image on a screen, the computer's graphics card translates the image into a bitmap, and the monitor translates the bitmap into pixels. Optical scanners and fax machines convert text or pictures into bitmaps. *See also* **bit depth, outline font, resolution.** *See figure at* **antialiasing. 2.** A bitmapped format for color graphics files that represents images to a color depth of 24 bits. The bitmap format does not include compression, so bitmap files are generally larger than GIF or JPEG files. The Windows operating system uses the bitmap format internally, and the format is also widely used for storing and exchanging images. Bitmap files often have an extension ending in *.bmp. Also called* **BMP.**

v. To convert an image into a bitmap.

bitmapped font   A font in which each character is represented by a pattern of dots, where each dot corresponds to the value of a pixel or set of pixels. Bitmapped fonts cannot be easily scaled up, as from Times Roman 12 point to Times Roman 16 point; such scaling generally results in jaggies. Typically, a bitmapped font is used for displaying text on the screen, while an associated outline font is used for printing. *Also called* **screen font.** *See also* **antialiasing, bitmapped graphics, outline font.**

bitmapped graphics   Graphics in which objects are stored in memory as arrays of bits that specify the appearance of individual pixels. Examples of bitmapped graphics include icons used for files in window-based systems, the representations of letters in bitmapped fonts, and the output of paint programs. Because an image made with bitmapped graphics is not mapped in memory as a set of objects but only as an undifferentiated set of dots, it is difficult to pick out one element of a bitmapped drawing for editing. Scaling bitmapped graphics up in size produces pronounced jaggies. *Also called* **raster graphics.** *Compare* **vector graphics.** *See figure at* **pixel.**

BITNET   *Abbreviation of* **Because It's There Network** or **Because It's Time Network.**   A former wide area network (WAN) founded in 1981 and run by the Corporation for Research and Educational Networking in Washington, DC. BITNET linked North American, European, and Japanese universities and research institutions, using a different set of protocols than those currently used on the Internet. It featured email, chat, newsgroups, and file sharing, but did not allow hypertext browsing like the World Wide Web.

bit rate or **bitrate**   **1.** *See* **data transfer rate. 2.** The average number of bits used to store one second of audio or video data. Most codecs for storing audio and video data allow the data to be represented with different bit rates. Higher bit rate versions of the same recording produce higher quality sound or video, but take up more space.

bits per pixel   *Abbreviated* **bpp.**   The number of bits of information used to represent the color or brightness of an individual pixel. Bits per pixel is a measure of bit depth.

bits per second   *See* **bps.**

bit stream or **bitstream**   A serial transmission of bits. Bit streams are common in telecommunications, as when binary data is transmitted over optical cables. *Compare* **byte stream.**

BitTorrent   A protocol that is used for the peer-to-peer distribution of large files over the Internet. BitTorrent users connect directly to each other to send and receive files while a central server, or *tracker*, manages and coordinates the connections. Because the network users are connected to each other rather than to the central server, less bandwidth is required than with client-server modes of file transmission.

.biz   A top level domain operated by Neulevel, intended to be used for commercial enterprises. The registration policy for the .biz domain only allows businesses to register domain names for commercial purposes.

black-and-white   **1.** A visual medium employing only black and white or black, white, and values of gray. **2.** In computer graphics, a binary range of color values used to represent images, where the color of any location on the image, such as a single pixel, may be only black or white. *See also* **gray scale.**

Blackberry device   A PDA made by Research In Motion, Ltd. Unlike other PDAs, Blackberry devices have small keyboards rather than numerical keypads. They use a proprietary operating system and software that allows them to send and receive email and instant messages by connecting to Wi-Fi networks. Blackberry devices are popular with large corporations, which use them to provide email and other messaging services to traveling employees.

black level   *See* **brightness** (sense 2).

blank character   Any character that causes blank space to appear on the screen or in print. Tabs and spaces, for example, are blank characters. *Also called* **whitespace.**

blast email   Email that is sent to a large number of recipients simultaneously, especially to a targeted group.

bleed   Text or graphics that extend to the edge of the page or that are printed so as to go off the edge after trimming.

bloatware   Software requiring large amounts of system resources, such as disk space and working memory, especially as compared with previous versions. Bloatware often contains additional unused features.

block   **1.** A section of text in a word processing document. Word processing programs allow users to select and manipulate blocks of text. For example, text blocks can be moved, deleted, copied, reformatted, printed, or saved as a new file. **2.** A unit of storage or transmission for digital data. The bytes of data that make up computer files are usually grouped into blocks by systems and protocols used for storage or transmission. For example, data is grouped into blocks for storage on a hard disk and file transfer protocols group data into blocks for transmission. *See also* **fragmentation.**

block cipher A cipher which divides the plaintext being encrypted into pieces of definite size, called blocks, and encrypts each block separately, normally using a single key for all blocks, or keys derived from a single key for each block. Given large plaintexts, block ciphers are more efficient than ciphers that encrypt the entire plaintext at once, since the calculations involved can be executed much more easily on smaller chunks of data.

blocking The freezing of rectangular sections of a digital video image that occurs when the video is transmitted too slowly. *See also* **artifact.**

blog *n. A shortened form of* weblog. A website that displays the posts of one or more individuals and usually has links to comments on specific posts. Blogs list posts in reverse chronological order, with the most recent post appearing first.

v. To write in, add materials to, or maintain a blog.

blogosphere The set of blogs, blog-related websites, the information contained on them, and the writers who maintain and update them, considered as a whole or as a general phenomenon.

blook A book whose contents are derived primarily from a blog.

blooming The effect of overexposure of a CCD, in which pixels neighboring an overexposed, saturated sensor pixel register a light signal, even though no light is actually striking them, causing streaks or fuzziness of resolution or color. Blooming is prevented in some cameras by use of antiblooming gates; blooming can also be prevented by taking multiple exposures, none of which are exposed long enough to be subject to blooming, and overlaying them to get a fully exposed image.

Bluetooth A technology for short-range wireless data transmission between computers or other devices such as printers, PDAs, speakers, headsets, etc. Bluetooth networks transmit data over the 2.4 GHz frequency band at rates up to 720 Kbps for distances up to 30 feet. Bluetooth technology standards are developed and maintained by Bluetooth SIG, Inc. *Compare* **Wi-Fi.** *See* Table D on page 360.

Blu-ray Disc *Abbreviated* **BD.** An optical disk designed for storing digital video and capable of storing much more data than a DVD. Blu-Ray Discs, developed by the Blu-Ray Disc Association, have the same physical dimensions as DVDs and compact disks but use a different type of laser and a different physical format. Single-layer Blu-Ray Discs can store 25 GB of data. They are similar in function to HD-DVD disks, with the main difference being that a single-layer HD-DVD disk can store 15 GB of data.

Blu-Ray Discs are available in read-only form, called *BD-ROM,* as well as a form that can be written once, called *BD-R,* and a form that can be rewritten many times, called *BD-RW.*

BMP   *See* **bitmap** (sense 2).

BNC connector   A small, twist-and-lock RF connector used for terminating thin coaxial cables in professional video and audio equipment, and as an alternative to the RCA connector in composite video.

board   *See* **printed circuit board.**

boilerplate   Text or graphical elements that need to be used frequently in numerous documents, such as standard language required in mortgage documents, or a company logo and letterhead. By saving boilerplate to a memory device, you can copy it into any documents or programs that require its use.

boldface   A typeface in which the letters are heavier and darker than normal. The entry words in this dictionary are printed in boldface. *Also called* **bold.**

bookmark   A record of a selected webpage or URL kept by a program such as a web browser or help utility. Bookmarks allow the user to quickly find and return to the selected site by clicking an easily recognizable link.

Boolean   **1.** Having only two possible values, TRUE and FALSE. For example, a Boolean variable can hold only one bit of information, taking the value 1 for TRUE, or 0 for FALSE. **2.** Relating to the logical operators, also known as Boolean operators. For example, many search engines have a Boolean search feature that allows users to combine search terms with logical operators.

Boolean algebra   A form of algebra that employs only two values, TRUE and FALSE. Boolean algebra, developed by the 19th-century English mathematician George Boole, is particularly well suited for use with computers because it provides a formal way to work with logical relations and because it works so well with the binary number system. A bit with value 1 corresponds to TRUE; a bit with value 0 corresponds to FALSE. *Also called* **Boolean logic.**

Boolean operator   *See* **logical operator.**

boot   *v.* To load and run a computer's operating system. A special program, usually stored in ROM, loads the operating system and transfers control of the computer to it.

   n. The process of booting a computer. *Also called* **startup.** *See also* **cold boot, warm boot.**

boot disk   *See* **startup disk.**

boot sector   A sector on a hard drive, optical disk, or other storage device that contains the instructions that the computer needs in order to start up. The boot sector is usually the first sector of a partition. *See also* **master boot record.**

bot   **1.** A software program that imitates the behavior of a human, as by querying search engines or participating in chatrooms or IRC discussions. *Also called* **robot. 2.** *See* **spider. 3.** *See* **robot** (sense 1).

bounced mail   An email message that cannot be delivered to its destination and is returned to its sender. Bounced mail usually includes some indication of why it could not be delivered.

Bourne-again shell   *See* **bash.**

Bourne shell   *Abbreviated* **sh.**   A shell that interprets commands for Linux and Unix operating systems. The Bourne shell was developed by Stephen Bourne at AT&T Bell Laboratories and is the oldest of the shells that are still in use. Popular for a time because of its support for shell scripts, and still used for that purpose, it is no longer commonly used as an interactive shell. *See also* **bash.**

box   **1.** An enclosed display area in a GUI (graphical user interface). Boxes are similar to windows in appearance, but generally cannot be resized. Alert boxes and dialog boxes are two kinds of boxes. **2.** A particular kind of computer. Used informally in phrases such as *a Unix box.*

BPL   *Abbreviation of* **broadband over power line.**   Any of various methods for providing high-bandwidth telecommunications services by transmitting data over existing power lines rather than special-purpose cables. Services such as Internet access, telephone, and television can be provided using BPL technologies. *See also* **power line communications.**

bpp   *Abbreviation of* **bits per pixel.**

bps   *Abbreviation of* **bits per second.**   The basic unit of measure of the data transfer rate. Data transfer rates are usually reported in kilobits, megabits, or gigabits per second.

Break key   *See* **Pause key.**

BREW   *Abbreviation of* **Binary Runtime Environment for Wireless.**   A set of programs and standards that allows cell phone users to download and run software. Cell phones that contain an application called the *BREW Application Execution Environment* can run any software that is developed using BREW technology and standards. BREW is licensed by Qualcomm, Inc., but others use BREW technology to create programs for cell phones.

bridge   A device that connects two local area networks and allows them to exchange data, even though they may have different topologies or communications protocols. Bridges are used to connect local area networks of computers and peripherals to wireless devices and to connect older telephone circuits to more modern ones. *See also* **router.**

brightness **1.** The light output of a display. The brightness of a projector is measured in ANSI lumens. Projectors generally range from 1,000 to 4,000 ANSI lumens. The brightness of other displays is measured in candelas per square meter (cd/m^2), or nits. A large plasma television has a brightness of around 1,000 cd/m^2, and an LCD monitor is usually around 250 cd/m^2. The symbol for brightness is Y. *Also called* **luminance. 2.** A display setting that adjusts the darkness of the darker portions of the image. *Also called* **black level.**

broadband **1.** Relating to high bandwidth digital data transmission, as with cable modems. Broadband connections transmit high-quality audio and video data, allowing a variety of services such as fast Internet connections, transmission of phone calls using VoIP and other technologies, and video on demand. **2.** Relating to digital data transmission that uses multiple channels so that multiple pieces of data can be transmitted simultaneously.

Broadband ISDN *Abbreviated* **B-ISDN.** A standard for data transmission over fiber-optic cable at rates of up to 1.5 Mbps. *See also* **ISDN.**

broadband over power line *See* **BPL.**

broadcast **1.** To simultaneously send one message to a number of receivers, as in an email system or over a network. **2.** To transmit a radio or television program for public or general use.

brouter A networking device that combines the functions of bridges and routers.

brownout A reduction in electric power, usually as a result of a shortage, a mechanical failure, or overuse. A computer subject to a power interruption caused by a brownout can crash and possibly lose data. *See also* **surge protector, UPS.**

browse To view information on a website or in another kind of document without searching. Browsing involves following hyperlinks or scrolling through pages rather than issuing queries. *See also* **surf.**

browser *See* **web browser.**

BTX *Abbreviation of* **Balanced Technology Extended.** A standard for computer motherboards and other basic components that modifies the ATX standard to improve airflow within the computer case.

Bubble-Jet Printer A trademark for a thermal inkjet printer developed by Cannon. *See also* **thermal inkjet printer.**

buddy icon   An avatar as used in an instant-messaging service.

buffer   A temporary storage area for data, typically in RAM. Buffers are used to hold data that is being transferred from one location to another at a faster rate than can be processed by the recipient device. For example, the operating system of a computer can send information to a printer much faster than the printer can print it, so the printer stores information in a buffer until it can be printed. Writing data to disk is another relatively slow task, so many word and image processors save text changes in a buffer. Then, either at set intervals or at the end of an editing session, they transfer the updated text from the buffer to the document's disk file. *See also* **print buffer, spooler.**

buffer overflow   An overflow error that results when a unit of data is too large to be stored in the buffer that it is written to. *Also called* **buffer overrun.**

bug   A defect in software or hardware that causes it to perform inconsistently, crash, or otherwise malfunction.

built-in font   *See* **resident font.**

bullet   A graphical element used to highlight a particular passage, as an item in a list or outline. Bullets are typically heavy, filled-in dots (●), but can also have other shapes (■, ◆, ○) serving a similar function.

bulletin board system   *Abbreviated* **BBS.**   An electronic communication system that allows users to write and read email, chat, play games, and upload and download files, including software. Computers are connected to a BBS by modem. Thousands of BBSs are active in the United States, although due to the proliferation of the Internet, most of the services they provide are now more commonly provided by newsgroups and websites. *See also* **message board.**

bundled software   **1.** Programs that are included with a computer at the time of purchase. **2.** Several programs packaged and sold together. *See also* **suite.**

bunzip2   A program that decompresses files compressed with bunzip2. Bunzip2 is available for most operating systems.

burn   To write data onto a blank optical disk, most commonly a CD or DVD.

burn-in   *v.* To run a newly manufactured device continuously for an extended period in order to test for defective parts, such as memory chips, microprocessors, and other computer components.
  n. See **ghosting** (sense 1).

burst mode   **1.** Any of several methods for high-speed data transfer in which a device or system sends data without waiting for acknowledgment from another device or without waiting for an internal process to finish. **2.** A mode of operation in which a memory controller reads a sequence of nearby addresses from working memory when data from one address is requested by the CPU. Burst mode can speed processing, because the CPU often needs data from addresses near previously requested data; if the CPU needs data that the controller has already read, it can access that data very quickly.

bus **1.** A system that connects digital components or devices, allowing the transfer of electric signals from one connected component to another. The electric signals that travel across a bus can provide power to each connected component, as well as encoding information according to a specific protocol. There are many buses in use in any computer, each acting as a pathway for transferring information, for example, between chips on the motherboard, or between the motherboard and external devices.

Synchronous buses, such as the bus by which the CPU is connected to main memory, use a clock which controls the transmission of electrical signals by sending out regular pulses. Asynchronous buses, such as the buses typically used to communicate with peripheral devices such as keyboards and mice, use other control mechanisms. *See also* **external bus, parallel bus, serial bus.**

2. A standard governing the functioning and physical design of a bus. Bus standards specify the wiring, electrical signals, and protocol used on a bus. Standard buses make it easier for different companies to create components and devices that will work together. *See* Table C on page 358.

3. The central cable used in a bus network. *See also* **network topology.**

bus network   A network in which all devices (network nodes) are connected to a single cable along which information is passed. Ethernet is configured as a bus network. Many local area networks (LANs) are configured as star networks. *See also* **network topology, ring network, star network.** *See figure at* **network.**

bus width   The amount of data, measured in bits, that a parallel bus can carry at once. A parallel bus is composed of a certain number of single-bit channels which together determine its bus width. Common bus widths include 16 bits, 32 bits, and 64 bits.

button **1.** A small outlined area within a dialog box that is clicked to select a command. *Also called* **pushbutton. 2.** In a hypertext database, an icon that when selected allows a user to view a particular associated object. Text, pictures, recorded music, and other forms of information are called objects; associated objects are linked together.

button cell   A tiny disk-shaped battery used in watches, hearing aids, calculators, and other small devices. Like most battery cells, button cells provide a voltage in the range of 1.2 to 3.6 volts, 1.55 volts being typical. Some button cells are actually composed of multiple cells and supply higher voltages.

byte   **1.** A unit of data equal to eight bits. Each bit has a value of either 0 or 1, and the various eight-bit combinations represent all of the data in a computer. Amounts of computer memory are often expressed in terms of megabytes (1,048,576 bytes). *See also* **megabyte. 2.** A basic unit of information for a computer system or transmission protocol. Computers process and store binary data in units of a specific number of bits. For storage and processing in modern computers, eight-bit bytes are common, but other byte sizes are also used, particularly in systems for transmitting data.

bytecode   A computer language used to represent programs that are executed by interpreters. For some interpreted languages, a program written in a high-level programming language is first translated into a bytecode file by a compiler. An interpreter executes the program by processing the bytecode file. Java is an example of an interpreted language that is compiled into bytecode. Unlike machine language, bytecode can be used on any machine with the appropriate interpreter.

byte stream   A bit stream in which the bits being transmitted are processed in discrete units that are the length of a byte. *Compare* **bit stream.**

.bz   An extension used for files compressed with bzip2.

bzip2   An open-source data compression program. Bzip2 only compresses individual files and is therefore not an archiving program. It is typically used with tar to create compressed archives. Bzip2 compresses files to a smaller size than similar programs such as gzip, but is slower. It is available for most operating systems. Files compressed with bzip2 typically have the file extension *.bz2. See also* **bunzip2.**

C   **1.** A popular high-level programming language. Known as an efficient and flexible language, C was developed at AT&T Bell Laboratories in the 1970s. Before the advent of object-oriented languages like C++ and Java, it was the most popular language for both writing systems and application software. It is widely used for both purposes. **2.** *Symbol for* **chrominance.**

C++ An object-oriented programming language based on C. C++ was developed in the early 1980s at AT&T Bell Laboratories. C++ is one of the most commonly used languages for the development of new commercial software.

.cab A filename extension for cabinet format files.

cabinet A format used for archiving and compressing files on Windows operating systems. Cabinet files typically have the extension *.cab,* and are used to distribute software.

cable **1.** A bundle of wires designed to carry electric power or electric signals, or a bundle of optical fibers designed to carry light signals. Cables usually include insulators or shielding materials that prevent interference, both from the outside and from adjacent wires or fibers on the inside. Cables are also made with strengthening materials to prevent damage caused by stress. Certain cables are used with specific kinds of plugs or connectors that attach to the devices that are sending or receiving the electricity or light signals. *See* Table A on page 356. **2.** A subscription television or broadband Internet service that uses cables to carry signals between local distribution antennas and the subscriber's location. Only cable systems that have been upgraded to two-way data transmission can support broadband Internet, video on demand, or interactive television menus. *Also called* **CATV.**

cable modem A broadband modem that allows computers to transmit data over the coaxial lines used for cable TV. Because of the high bandwidth of the coaxial cables, cable modems are much faster than modems that make dial-up connections over telephone lines.

cache **1.** An area of storage devoted to the high-speed retrieval of frequently used or requested data. Data can be retrieved much more quickly from a cache than it can from another storage area, such as a disk or RAM. A cache typically mimics a larger, slower area of storage. **2.** A part of RAM set aside to facilitate access to the data that is needed most often. The cache uses faster, more expensive static RAM chips. Every time a request for data is sent to RAM, the cache intercepts the request. If the data is already in the cache, it can be sent immediately. Otherwise, the cache accesses the data from the slower chips in RAM and sends it to the microprocessor, but also keeps a copy in case it is needed again soon. When no requests are made, the cache copies and stores data from RAM addresses near the data most recently needed on the theory that they may be needed next. When the cache is full, it erases the data that has waited the longest without being needed. *Also called* **RAM cache.**

CAD *Abbreviation of* **computer-aided design.** The use of computer programs and systems to create detailed two- or three-dimensional models of physical objects, such as mechanical parts, buildings, and molecules. CAD software is used in engineering, architecture, and other design professions.

CAD/CAM *Abbreviation of* **computer-aided design/computer-aided manufacturing.** A computer system that designs and manufactures products. An object is designed with the CAD component of the system, and the design is then translated into manufacturing or assembly instructions for specialized machinery.

CAI *Abbreviation of* **computer-aided instruction.** The use of computer programs as teaching tools. CAI software usually offers tutorials, drills, and tests and allows the student to proceed at his or her own pace. CAI may also make use of the Internet to provide access to source materials.

calculated field A field in a database or spreadsheet that contains results of calculations performed on other fields of a record. In a database showing an employee's earnings from hourly wages and bonuses, a calculated field could give total earnings.

calculator A program that enables the user to perform arithmetic calculations, usually with an onscreen representation of a handheld calculator. The calculator is operated with the keyboard or with a mouse.

calendar An application that works as an electronic datebook. Besides allowing the user to set appointments, many calendar programs can automatically set entries for weekly or monthly events. Some calendar programs can issue a signal as a reminder for an important engagement or a significant day.

calibrate To adjust the display settings on a television, monitor, or projector for the accurate reproduction of recorded images. Common display settings include brightness, contrast, color, tint, sharpness, and color temperature. There are various calibration tools, such as sensors that are mounted on the screen or DVDs with special graphics, that can assist in calibrating a display. Some retailers offer professional display calibration.

caller ID A feature available on most telephone networks that displays the phone number of incoming calls. If used with a phone that does not have a display, a display device can be connected to the phone line.

call forwarding A feature available on most telephone networks that allows users to redirect phone calls to another number. When call forwarding is enabled, a user of a phone line specifies the phone number that calls will be forwarded to and calls to the phone line ring at the new number until forwarding is disabled.

call waiting   A feature available on most telephone networks that alerts the user of a phone line to an incoming call when a call is already in progress, allowing the user to suspend the current call and switch to the incoming call. On a North American land line, users are often alerted to a new call by a short beep and switch to the new call by quickly depressing and releasing the button that normally hangs up the phone.

CAM   *Abbreviation of* **computer-aided manufacturing.**   The use of computer systems to control manufacturing tools. CAM software translates designs created with CAD software into manufacturing and assembly instructions for specialized machinery.

camcorder   A handheld video camera and recorder. Modern camcorders use CCD or CMOS light sensors to convert light into a signal which is then recorded in a digital video format, such as DV, and stored on a tape, DVD, or hard disk. Most have a small LCD screen that can function as a viewfinder and display video as it is being recorded.

camera   1. *See* **digital camera.** 2. *See* **camcorder.**

canalphone   A headphone that fits inside the ear canal. Canalphones are designed to block ambient noise. *Also called* **earbud.**

candela   A unit of luminous intensity equal to 1/60 of the luminous intensity per square centimeter of a blackbody (a theoretically perfect absorber of all incident radiation) radiating at the temperature of solidification of platinum (2,046 degrees Kelvin).

candela per square meter   *Abbreviated* **cd/m^2.**   A unit of illuminative brightness equal to one candle per square meter, measured perpendicular to the rays of the source. The brightness of monitors and televisions is measured in candelas per square meter. A large plasma television has a brightness of around 1,000 cd/m^2, and the brightness of an LCD monitor is usually around 250 cd/m^2. *Also called* **nit.**

candy bar phone   A cell phone that is rectangular and has no hinge, slider, swivel, or other major moving part. *Compare* **flip phone, slider phone.**

cap code   A numeric code assigned to a pager that identifies messages intended for that pager. A pager's cap code is usually printed somewhere on the device. Since paging systems transmit all messages on the same frequency, each pager detects messages sent with its cap code.

Caps Lock key   A toggle key on a computer keyboard that when activated locks the keyboard so that the user can enter uppercase letters without pressing the Shift key. The key has no effect on number and punctuation keys. Most keyboards have a light that goes on when the Caps Lock key is pressed.

caption   A transcription of film or video dialogue that is displayed in synchronization with the soundtrack, especially for the deaf and hard of hearing. *Compare* **subtitle.**

capture   To save data, especially audio or video data, to a digital file so it can be stored or manipulated on a computer. For example, a television show or movie on a videotape can be captured to digital form. When analog data is captured, it must be digitized. When digital data is captured, it is often converted to a different format. *See also* **video capture card.**

capture card   An expansion card that plugs into a computer, enabling it to import video or audio data from external sources. Some capture cards can convert analog signals to digital form before capturing it on the computer's hard drive. *Also called* **video capture card.**

card   A printed circuit board with an edge connector. Different cards serve different functions; for example, they may contain a modem, flash memory, or a radio or television tuner. Expansion cards plug into slots on the motherboard inside a computer. Other cards, such as memory cards and PC Cards, plug into a port on the outside of a device. *See also* **expansion card, memory card, PC Card.**

caret   A symbol (^) usually found above the 6 on the keyboard. This symbol sometimes indicates the Control key, especially in manuals or documentation; that is, ^A would indicate to press the Control key and the A together. The caret is also used to indicate that the number following it is an exponent; that is, 2^4 is the same as 2^4.

carpal tunnel syndrome   *Abbreviated* **CTS.**   A condition characterized by pain and numbing or tingling sensations in the hand and resulting from compression of a nerve in the carpal tunnel, a passageway in the wrist through which nerves and the flexor muscles of the hands and fingers pass. Carpal tunnel syndrome is often a repetitive stress disorder caused by overuse or misuse of hands and arms when using a computer keyboard or mouse.

carriage return   *Abbreviated* **CR.**   A control character often used in indicating the end of a line in a text file. Carriage return is coded with a bit sequence corresponding to the number 13 in ASCII and most other character encodings. It was originally designed to signal that the cursor in a text display or the print head of a printer should be returned to the beginning of the line. *See also* **end of line, hard return, linefeed, soft return.**

carrier   **1.** A telecommunications company. **2.** *See* **carrier signal.**

carrier sense multiple access   *See* **CSMA.**

carrier signal   The basic signal used to transmit information in a communications system. In order to transmit information, the carrier signal is changed or modulated, as in frequency, amplitude, or phase. Carrier signals are used in most common transmission systems, including those that transmit data through the air, as with radio and television broadcasts, and those that transmit data through cables, as through telephone lines and coaxial and fiber-optic cables. Modems use a carrier signal for transmission.

carrier wave   A carrier signal in the form of an electromagnetic wave.

cascade   To arrange all active windows on a computer display so they overlap each other, with only the topmost window displayed in full, and usually with the title bar of every window left visible. Applications often have a single command or menu option for cascading windows. *Compare* **tile.**

cascading menu   A submenu that appears on the screen when a choice from another menu is selected. Menu items that trigger cascading menus are usually identified by a triangular arrow.

cascading style sheets   *Abbreviated* **CSS.**   A computer language for specifying the visual format of HTML webpages. While HTML provides means for specifying many aspects of visual formatting, CSS allows formatting information, such as fonts, colors, or spacing, to be separated from the content of a webpage. This makes formatting much more flexible and helps webpages load faster.

case-sensitive   Distinguishing between uppercase (capital) and lowercase (small) letters. A case-sensitive search function can get different results for *APPLE*, *apple*, and *Apple*, for example. Linux and Unix file systems are case-sensitive, so they allow filenames to be distinguished by capitalization. Most passwords are case-sensitive, but most email addresses and URLs are not.

CAS latency   *Abbreviation of* **column address strobe latency** or **column address select latency.**   On an SDRAM chip, the number of bus cycles required to transfer a piece of data from an address in memory to the output buffer, after the address has been selected. Smaller values indicate faster SDRAM. CAS latency is one important part of the latency of an SDRAM chip, though its contribution to the overall processing speed of a computer is usually relatively small. Values of 2 and 3 are common, and are sometimes indicated with the terms *CL2* and *CL3,* respectively.

cassette   A small, flat case containing two reels and a length of magnetic tape that winds between them, used in audio and video recorders and players and as a medium for storing data in digital form.

cathode-ray tube   *Abbreviated* **CRT.**   The display used in traditional computer monitors, televisions, and projectors, consisting of a special vacuum tube that beams electrons onto a phosphorescent screen. An electron gun at the rear of the glass vacuum tube shoots streams of electrons against a phosphorescent screen; when the electrons hit the screen, the phosphor on the screen glows. Magnets or electrical plates guide the beam, making it trace out horizontal lines called *scan lines* starting at the top of the screen. These scan lines constitute the display's vertical resolution. The phosphorescent screen, which fades rapidly, must be reilluminated, or refreshed, many times each second to maintain the image. The refresh rate is adjustable on computers with CRT monitors and generally set above 75 hertz to prevent the image from flickering noticeably.

The screen size of a CRT television or monitor is measured as the diagonal of the entire glass screen, even though some of the screen is usually covered by the plastic frame. CRT displays produce a very high-quality image, especially when displaying pictures and video, but are becoming less popular because of their weight (large CRT televisions can weigh hundreds of pounds).

CATV   *Abbreviation of* **community antenna television.**   *See* **cable.**

CAV   *Abbreviation of* **constant angular velocity.**

CB   *Abbreviation of* **citizens band.**   A system for wireless communication over short distances in which one or more unlicensed base stations, mobile radios, or walkie-talkies transmit and receive analog voice signals. CB systems use half-duplex communication and have a range of about nine kilometers (five miles). They are commonly used in vehicles, especially trucks.

C band   A band of microwave frequencies from 3.7 to 6.4 gigahertz, used for satellite television broadcasting.

CBR   *Abbreviation of* **constant bit rate.**

CBT   *Abbreviation of* **computer-based training.**

CC   *Abbreviation of* **closed captioning.**

CCD   *Abbreviation of* **charge-coupled device.**   A photosensitive chip used as a light sensor to capture images in digital cameras, scanners, and similar devices. Each pixel in a CCD sensor generates a voltage signal based on the amount of light striking it. The signal from each pixel is passed to adjacent pixels and eventually out of the chip, where it is converted to a digital signal by an A/D converter. CCD sensors are more light-sensitive than CMOS sensors, but require considerably more power.

CCITT *Abbreviation of* **Comité Consultatif International Téléphonique et Télégraphique.** A former organization based in Geneva, Switzerland, that developed many important standards for telecommunications, particularly protocols used by modems and fax machines to transmit data over telephone lines. Its standards work was subsumed in 1993 by its parent organization, the International Telecommunications Union (ITU).

CD *Abbreviation of* **compact disk.**

CD burner A device used to write data onto compact disks. The CD burner encodes data onto the disk by using a laser to etch patterns of lands and pits which can be read by the optical sensor of a CD or DVD player. Drives also exist which allow CDs to be both read and written in the same device; current machines write at a speed of 1x (150 KBps) to 8x (1.2 MBps).

CD drive A disk drive that reads data stored on compact disks. Many CD drives can also write data to compact disks, and many can also read and write DVDs. CD drives read data from a compact disk by shining one or more lasers on the surface of the disk and detecting patterns of light reflecting off the surface of the disk. To write data to CD-Rs and CD-RWs, disk drives use a laser to create patterns of light and dark on the disk by causing tiny sections of the surface of the disk to become opaque.

The speed that a CD drive spins a disk determines how fast data can be read from the disk, and maximum speeds are reported as multiples of 500 rpm—the speed used to play audio CDs. For example, speeds of 56x (56 × 500 rpm, or 2800 rpm) are common. Drives that can write data to compact disks have different maximum speeds depending on whether they are reading, writing, or rewriting. *See also* **CD burner, head.**

CD-I *Abbreviation of* **compact disk-interactive.** An obsolete standard for storing audio, video, and text on high-capacity compact disks.

cd/m *Abbreviation of* **candela per square meter.**

CDMA *Abbreviation of* **Code Division Multiple Access.** A method of transmission for wireless communications, such as voice, text messaging, and wireless networking. On CDMA networks, multiple users simultaneously access the same spectrum of frequencies. Each transmission is split into segments and all segments are sent simultaneously on different frequencies. Each segment is coded so the intended recipient can identify and reassemble the transmission, thereby preventing interference between simultaneous transmissions on the same frequency band. *Compare* **TDMA.** *See also* **multiplex, spread spectrum.**

cdma2000   A CDMA standard for digital mobile communication, allowing for data transmission speeds up to 2Mbps. Considered a 3G standard, it is an incompatible competitor with UMTS, and is licensed by a US consortium called the Telecommunications Industry Association.

CDPD   *Abbreviation of* **Cellular Digital Packet Data.**   A packet-switching protocol for transmitting and receiving digital data on analog cellular networks. CDPD allows users to communicate with the Internet and send and receive text and multimedia. *Compare* **GPRS, HSCSD.**

CD-R   *Abbreviation of* **compact disk-recordable.**   A compact disk that can have data written onto it once by a CD burner. CD-Rs are typically less expensive than CD-RWs and are commonly used for recording music and distributing software.

CD-ROM   *Abbreviation of* **compact disk read-only memory.**   A compact disk that functions as ROM (read-only memory), having been encoded with data when it is produced. CD-ROMs can contain many different kinds of digital data, including audio and video, but are distinguished from audio CDs, which use a specific format to store digital audio data, and DVDs, which have a different physical format than compact disks.

CD-ROM XA   *Abbreviation of* **CD-ROM extended architecture.**   A specification standard developed by several companies that allows the interleaving of audio and data sectors on CD-ROM tracks. CD-ROM XAs contain special sectors that allow data, graphics, video, and audio to be read and displayed simultaneously, but they can be played only on drives that support this technology.

CD-RW   *Abbreviation of* **CD-rewritable.**   A compact disk that data can be written to more than once.

Celeron   A series of microprocessors designed by Intel as an alternative to the Pentium series.

cell   **1.** A hexagonal geographic zone served by one or more base stations in a cell phone network. Each cell is commonly served by three base stations, located at alternating corners of the hexagon. **2.** A cell phone.

cell phone   A mobile phone that transmits and receives data using radio frequency energy. Cell phones communicate by means of a network of short-range transmitters with overlapping ranges with a central station making connections to regular telephone lines. *Also called* **cellular phone.** *See also* **cell, landline, satellite phone.**

cellular Relating to wireless communications, typically by cell phones, that take place over a network of short-range transmitters located in overlapping cells.

Cellular Digital Packet Data *See* **CDPD.**

cellular phone *See* **cell phone.**

central processing unit *See* **CPU.**

Centrino One of several combinations of a chipset, a CPU, and a wireless card sold by Intel and integrated into laptops.

Centronics port A 36-pin D-subminiature connector found on some peripheral devices, such as printers and scanners. Centronics ports are used to create a parallel bus as defined in IEEE 1284, and can be connected to the 25-pin parallel ports typically found on computers by using an IEEE 1284 cable.

CERN *Abbreviation of* **Conseil Européen pour la Recherche Nucléaire (European Council for Nuclear Research).** A laboratory in Geneva, Switzerland for research in physics. The basic protocols that make the World Wide Web possible—HTML, URL, and HTTP—were developed at CERN in the late 1980s to facilitate the transmission of information among scientists.

CF *Abbreviation of* **CompactFlash.**

CGA *Abbreviation of* **Color Graphics Adapter.** The first color graphics card and video standard used with PC-compatible computers, introduced in 1981. The CGA system has been superseded by VGA and Super VGA systems.

CGI *Abbreviation of* **Common Gateway Interface.** A standard that specifies how server-side scripts or programming languages interact with web browsers. CGI allows a web server program to invoke an interpreter to process a script and specifies how the results of the script are returned to the web browser as part of a webpage. The language most commonly used with CGI is Perl. Some languages, such as ASP and PHP, are interpreted by web server programs and do not require CGI.

CGM *Abbreviation of* **Computer Graphics Metafile.**

CGMS *Abbreviation of* **Copy Generation Management System.**

channel **1.** A course or pathway through which information is transmitted. **2.** A specified frequency band for the transmission and reception of electromagnetic signals, as for television signals. **3.** In television and radio, a link to a specific content provider or a specific set of content. **4.** *See* **chatroom.**

character   A letter, digit, punctuation mark, symbol, whitespace or control character that can be encoded as a series of binary bits by using a character encoding. Unicode, for example, contains characters for representing the scripts of most languages, as well as many technical symbols, such as those used in mathematics and linguistics. *See also* **ASCII.**

character encoding   A standard way of translating characters into bits of digital data so computers can store and transmit them. Some character encodings, such as ASCII, are simple matchings of characters and binary numbers. For example, in ASCII, uppercase D is coded as 68 (binary 0100 0100). In contrast, the Unicode standard translates characters to code numbers, and then gives several different ways of translating code numbers to sequences of binary bits. *Also called* **character map, character set.** *See also* **ASCII, code page, extended ASCII, unicode.**

character map   *See* **character encoding.**

character recognition   *See* **optical character recognition.**

character set   *Abbreviated* **charset.   1.** A group of characters made available together in a character encoding, a font, or for some other purpose. **2.** *See* **character encoding.**

characters per inch   *Abbreviated* **cpi.**   The number of characters that fit into a one-inch-long line of type of a particular font. In monospace fonts, all characters have a constant width. In proportional fonts, characters have varying widths, so measurements of the number of characters must be averaged to compute characters per inch.

character string   *See* **string.**

charge-coupled device   *See* **CCD.**

charset   *Abbreviation of* **character set.**

chat   To communicate in real-time on a computer network using typed messages. A person chatting with another person or group of people on the network types in a message and waits for the other party to type in a response. *See also* **instant messaging, IRC.**

chatroom   A site on a network, as on IRC, where online conversations are held in real time by a number of computer users. *Also called* **channel.**

cheat code   A sequence of keystrokes, a password, or any other normally disallowed technique used to advance to a higher level in a computer or video game.

check box   An element of a GUI (graphical user interface) that allows a user to make a yes/no choice. Check boxes are typically square. When a check box is clicked on, an X or a checkmark appears in it. If a list of items with check boxes appear, more than one item on the list may be selected.

checksum **1.** A technique for detecting errors or changes in digital data by recording the sum of all the bytes in a data file. A computer creating a file or transmitting information calculates the sum of all the bytes in the file and includes it when the data file is transmitted or stored. Any computer receiving the file or taking the file from storage makes the same calculation on the file and compares the result to the stored number. If they match, the data in the file is presumed to have remained the same. **2.** Any technique for detecting errors or other changes in digital data that involves storing a value, including those for creating message digests or hashes. *See also* **CRC, MD5.**

child directory A subdirectory in a parent dictionary. *See also* **parent directory.**

chip A device containing circuits that have been built from layers of various semiconductors and other materials deposited on a thin silicon substrate. The circuits are called integrated circuits because they are located on a single substrate. A chip smaller than a fingernail can hold millions of circuits. Most of a computer's circuitry, including that of its CPU, RAM, and ROM, is built on chips that are mounted on circuit boards or inserted into sockets mounted on circuit boards. *See also* **DIMM, DIP switch, PGA, SIMM, SIP.**

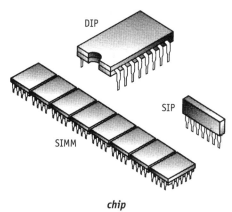

chip

chipset A set of chips that are designed to function together as a unit to perform a specific task and are mounted together on one circuit board. For example, one kind of chipset is found on a computer's motherboard and functions to control the flow of data between the CPU and other components, such as main memory.

chrominance   The portion of a video signal that carries the signal's color information but not the brightness. The chrominance is composed of two components, hue and saturation. The symbol for chrominance is C. *Also called* **chroma.**

cipher   A cryptographic method in which letters or numbers used to represent text or other information are transformed into other letters or numbers by means of algorithm. Most electronic ciphers also involve the use of one or more keys to encrypt and decrypt the information.

ciphertext   The data that results from encrypting a text. *Compare* **plaintext.** *See also* **cryptography, decrypt.**

circuit   **1.** A system of electrically connected parts or devices.   **2.** A closed path through which an electric current flows or may flow.

circuit board   *See* **printed circuit board.**

circuit breaker   An electrical switch that interrupts the flow of electric current in a circuit if the voltage, current, or power running through the circuit goes above a set threshold, or if the circuit is otherwise stressed, for example by excessive heat. Circuit breakers are found in many electrical and electronic devices, especially in power supplies, as a protection against damage to components or from fire that can be caused by excessive levels of electricity.

circuit switching   A technique for establishing connections between nodes in a network, especially common in telephone networks and smaller computer networks, in which a path for the communication is chosen before communication begins, and that path remains fixed for the duration of the communication. The fastest route linking the two communicating nodes is established at the beginning of the communication and remains fixed even if other faster routes become available. The bandwidth of the connection is reserved for communication between those two parties only; thus, even if there are gaps in data transmission, no other two parties can use the connection. *See also* **packet switching.**

circumaural headphone   A headphone with a cup that surrounds the ear. *See also* **headphone.**

CISC   *Abbreviation of* **complex instruction set computer.**   A complex microprocessor design that allows the CPU to recognize and carry out more complex instructions than the RISC design. Many instructions understood by a CISC microprocessor have to be translated into sets of simpler instructions. The idea behind CISC is to create a more powerful assembly language and thus make it easier to design programs. The microprocessors in most personal computers have CISC architecture. CISC is pronounced as one syllable, as though it were spelled SISK. *See also* **RISC.**

citizens band   *See* **CB.**

CL1.5, CL2, CL2.5, CL3   *See* **CAS latency.**

clamping area   The region near the inner hole of an optical disk where the disk drive grips the disk in order to spin it.

Class A   A standard, set by the FCC (Federal Communications Commission), for how much radiation a personal computer can emit. Computers with Class A certification are suitable for office and industrial use.

Class B   A standard, set by the FCC (Federal Communications Commission), for how much radiation a personal computer can emit. Class B is a tougher emissions standard than Class A. Computers with Class B certification are unlikely to interfere with radio and television reception in residential areas and are suitable for use in the home.

clean boot   A boot in which a computer loads only the files necessary to run the operating system. A clean boot is often run to track down problems caused by device drivers and other software that is loaded during a normal boot. Most operating systems have software that allows users to configure the computer to perform a clean boot. *See also* **safe mode.**

clear   To erase data from a display screen or document. The *clear* command in most operating systems deletes the selected data from memory, in contrast to the *cut* command, which copies the selected data to the clipboard. *See also* **undo.**

cleartext   *See* **plaintext.**

click   To press down and immediately release a button on a mouse. Clicking the mouse when its pointer is touching an object or text on the screen will select the object or text. *See also* **double-click, drag, shift clicking.**

clickwrap license   A software license whose terms of use the user accepts by clicking on buttons in dialog boxes or pop-up windows that appear when the software is installed. *See also* **shrinkwrap license.**

client   **1.** A computer that relies on other computers for services such as file storage or printing. *See also* **client/server network. 2.** A program that requests a service from another program, called a *server*. Often the server program is on a different machine on a network. Web browsers, programs used to read email, and programs used to perform instant messaging are examples of clients.

client/server   Relating to a computer system in which a client program running on a user's machine requests services from a program running on the server. In client/server systems, the server typically controls a central repository of data that is manipulated in some way by the client.

client/server network   A network of personal computers in which a relatively small number of server computers provide services such as communications, file storage, and database access to the other computers (the clients) on the network. Most networks of personal computers are client/server networks. *Compare* **peer-to-peer network.**

client-side script   A script embedded in a webpage. Client-side scripts run on the machine from which the webpage is viewed and can provide functions that require some computer processing, such as responding to user input. Common languages used for client-side scripts are JavaScript, JScript, and ECMAScript. *Compare* **server-side script.**

clip art   Ready-made pieces of printed or computerized graphic art, such as illustrations, borders, and backgrounds, that can be electronically copied and used to decorate a document.

clipboard   An area of memory where cut or copied text and graphics are temporarily stored so they can be pasted into another location within the same document or into a new document. Some clipboards hold only one item at a time and are overwritten when new information is copied or cut. Others hold several items, allowing the user to choose among previously cut or copied items.

clock   1. *See* **real-time clock. 2.** *See* **system clock.**

clock cycle   The interval of time between two pulses of a system clock.

clock-doubled   Running at two times the clock speed of an attached bus or motherboard. Used of a CPU.

clock radio   A radio having a built-in alarm clock that can be set to turn the radio on automatically.

clock speed   The number of electrical pulses per second generated by a system clock on a computer, usually reported in megahertz (MHz). Because each unit of processing in a device or bus occurs on a pulse, the clock speed determines the smallest amount of time that one unit of processing can take.

  The central clock in a computer is the one that controls the system bus, determining the rate at which data can be transferred between the CPU and main memory. Other devices and buses may have clocks that run faster or slower than the system bus clock, but in order to synchronize different parts of the system, the speed of every device or bus is determined by multiplying or dividing the system bus speed by a factor. For example, the clock speed of the CPU (central processing unit) is determined by multiplying the speed of the system bus by a constant factor. *Also called* **clock rate.** *See also* **overclock, processor speed, underclock.**

clock-tripled   Running at three times the clock speed of an attached bus or motherboard. Used of a CPU.

clone   *n.* A computer, program, or component that resembles an original model in appearance and function. Personal computer clones often have the same components, run the same software, and use the same peripherals as the computers that they imitate.

   v. To illegally encode a cell phone, SIM card, or other cellular device with data that identifies another subscriber and device. When a legitimate subscriber's phone is cloned, that subscriber is billed for calls made on the illegally encoded phone.

close   **1.** To exit a data file and save it. *Compare* **open. 2.** In graphical user interfaces, to exit a file and remove its window from the screen. *Compare* **open.**

closed architecture   A computer system design whose specifications are proprietary—that is, not available to outside software developers or manufacturers. Closed architecture prevents outside companies from developing products for such a system. *Compare* **open architecture.**

closed captioning   *Abbreviated* **CC.**   A system for providing film or video captions in which viewing the captions is optional.

cloud   *See* **wireless cloud.**

cluster   **1.** A unit of storage on a disk, consisting of a set of adjacent sectors of a track (known as track sectors). The number of adjacent sectors that constitutes a cluster depends on the kind of formatting used for the disk. *See also* **block, fragmentation. 2.** A group of computers that work together, usually on a high-speed LAN, to provide a service that is more reliable or faster than could be provided by a single computer. Some clusters provide more reliable service by having each computer perform the same operations; if one computer fails, another is very likely to be able to complete the operation. Others provide faster and more reliable service by distributing requests for service to whichever computer is free. Still other clusters provide faster service by distributing the calculations required to multiple computers, which complete the calculations in parallel. Many of the most powerful supercomputers are examples of this last type of cluster. *See also* **grid computing.**

CLV   *Abbreviation of* **constant linear velocity.**

CMOS   *Abbreviation of* **complementary metal oxide semiconductor.   1.** A static RAM chip that draws very little power and is therefore typically connected to a battery and used as nonvolatile memory. Most computers use a CMOS chip (pronounced SEE-moss) and a battery to keep the time, date, and system setup data. **2.** A photosensitive chip used as a light sensor to capture images in digital cameras, scanners, and similar devices. Each pixel on a CMOS chip consists of a light-sensitive part and several digitizing transistors, which convert the pixel's response to light into digital information. CMOS sensors use considerably less power than CCD sensors, but are slightly less sensitive to light, since the transistors on the chip reduce the amount of area of each pixel that responds to light.

CMY *Abbreviation of* **cyan-magenta-yellow.** A color model from which all colors can be made using subtractive primary colors that absorb light instead of additive primary colors that emit light. When the spectrum contains the full amount of cyan, magenta, and yellow, the result is white. When these three colors are removed from the spectrum completely, the result is black. By varying the amount of each pigment that is removed, all the colors of the spectrum can be achieved. *Compare* **CMYK.**

CMYK *Abbreviation of* **cyan-magenta-yellow-black.** A color model that uses the same subtractive primary colors as the CMY color model (cyan, magenta, and yellow), but which adds an additional black component. CMYK allows for a deeper, richer black than the basic CMY color model. *Compare* **CMY.** *See also* **color model.**

coaxial cable A cable consisting of a conducting outer metal tube enclosing and insulated from a central conducting core, used for high-frequency transmission. Coaxial cables are commonly used by cable television and computer networks. They are typically used in conjunction with RF connectors. *Also called* **RF cable.** *See* Table A on page 356.

coax plug *See* **RF connector.**

COBOL *Abbreviation of* **common business-oriented language.** A high-level programming language developed in the late 1950s and early 1960s as a common language for business programming. It is still widely used, especially in financial and business applications. COBOL was designed to mimic English as closely as possible.

code *n.* **1.** The information that constitutes computer programs. Code written by programmers in programming languages is often called *source code,* while code in the form of machine language, normally generated by compiling source code, is called *machine code. Compare* **data. 2.** Information, or a discrete piece of information, sent to a computer in a specified form in order to give it a command or make a request. For example, in handshaking between two programs, codes may be exchanged that provide information about how the programs should interact. **3.** A set of symbols for representing characters in binary form for storage in a computer. For example, most computers recognize characters in ASCII code.

v. To write instructions in a programming language.

codec *Abbreviation of* **compression/decompression.** Any of various technologies that compress and decompress data. Codec technologies allow information such as video or audio data to be compressed to make it easier to store or transmit, and to be decompressed when needed. Examples of codec technologies include MPEG and GIF compression. *See* Table 3.

Table 3 Common Audio and Video Codecs

Standard	Standard Owner	Data Type	Lossy/Lossless
AAC	MPEG	audio	lossy
AC-3	Dolby	audio	lossy
ADPCM	public domain	audio	lossy
Apple Lossless	Apple	audio	lossless
ATRAC	Sony	audio	lossy
Cinepak	Compression Technologies, Inc.	video	lossy
DivX	DivX	video	lossy
DTS	Digital Theater Systems	audio	lossy
FLAC	public domain	audio	lossless
GIF	Compuserve	graphics	lossless
H.264	ITU/MPEG	video	lossy
JPEG	JPEG	still images	lossy
MP3	MPEG	audio	lossy
MPEG-1	MPEG	video/audio	lossy
MPEG-2 Video	MPEG	video	lossy
MPEG-4 Audio Lossless	MPEG	audio	lossless
Musepack	public domain	audio	lossy
Sorenson	Sorenson Media	video	lossy
3ivx	3ivx	video	lossy
TwinVQ	NTT	audio	lossy
Vorbis	public domain	audio	lossy
WMA	Microsoft	audio	lossy
WMA Lossless	Microsoft	audio	lossless
XviD	public domain	video	lossy

Code Division Multiple Access   *See* **CDMA.**

code page   One of the ANSI-standard character encodings developed by IBM or Microsoft and used, for example, in the Windows operating system. Windows-1252, for example, is a code page that encodes the Latin alphabet as used in many Western European languages. Code pages are not fully compatible with existing international standards, such as ISO 8859. *See also* **ASCII, extended ASCII.**

cold boot   The processing of booting a computer that has been turned off. When the computer is turned on, it automatically loads its operating system. *Compare* **warm boot.**

collaborative software   *See* **groupware.**

collapse   To compress the view of an object so that its internal parts are not visible or are only partly visible. For example, collapsing a node on a hierarchical tree display of a file structure (often done by clicking on the node) leaves only that node visible.

color   A display setting that adjusts the color saturation of the image. The minimum color setting displays the image in black and white.

color depth   **1.** The number of discrete colors that can be represented by an individual pixel. If a pixel has only two color values (for example, black and white), it has a color depth of 2 and can be encoded by one bit of information. Color depth can be increased by increasing the number of bits used to represent each pixel. A 24-bit image, for instance, uses 24 bits for each pixel, making it possible to display 2^{24} (nearly 16.8 million) different colors or shades of gray. **2.** *See* **bit depth.**

Color Graphics Adapter   *See* **CGA.**

color model   A way of representing a range of colors by using a small set of variables (usually three of four) that can each take on a different value. Common variables used are hue, saturation, and value (HSV), red, green, and blue (RGB), and cyan, magenta and yellow (CMY). For example, using an RGB color model, the color white is represented by high and equal values of red, green, and blue, while the color yellow is represented with high values for green and blue, but a low value for red. *Compare* **color space.** *See also* **CMYK, HSV, YCbCr, YPbPr.**

color space   **1.** A color model, together with the map that links any given color to the numbers used by the model to describe the color. Devices or applications, such as a digital camera and a monitor, might use the same color model, but have differing color spaces, due to differences in the way the color signals are transmitted and converted. This can result in slight differences in color as they appear on different devices or with different applications. **2.** *See* **color model.**

color temperature **1.** A measure of the color of a sample of unfiltered light based on the temperature, in kelvins, at which a blackbody (a theoretically perfect absorber of all incident radiation) radiates light of that color. The color temperature spectrum ranges from red at 1800 K to yellow at 4000 K to white at 5500 K to blue at 16000 K. Light bulbs that reproduce the color of the midday sun have a color temperature of 5500 K. **2.** A display setting that adjusts the color balance of the image to simulate a certain color temperature. The NTSC standard for television is 6500 K, which typically corresponds to a low, or *warm,* setting. Higher color temperature settings, which cause the white portions of the image to appear blue, are sometimes labeled *cool.* The color temperature setting on a digital camera is called *white balance.*

column A vertical arrangement of data. On a display screen in character mode, a column is a vertical line that is one character wide and extends from the top of the screen to the bottom. In a spreadsheet, a column is a set of vertically aligned cells.

column address strobe latency or **column address select latency** *See* **CAS latency.**

.com **1.** A top-level domain operated by Verisign, Inc. and originally intended for commercial organizations. Currently, any individual or organization can register a name in the .com domain. **2.** A file extension used for executable files on some MS-DOS and Windows operating systems.

COM *See* **COM port.**

comb filter A device inside a television that separates the luminance and chrominance components of a composite video signal. The best comb filters are known as *3D* or *motion adaptive filters.* S-video and component video signals do not require a comb filter.

combo drive **1.** A DVD drive that is also capable of reading and writing to CDs. *See also* **CD-R. 2.** A removable external hard drive, often used to supplement the data storage space of a computer's main internal hard disk.

Comité Consultatif International Téléphonique et Télégraphique *See* **CCITT.**

comma-delimited Relating to data tables stored as text by representing each row as a line in the file and separating columns of data with commas. *See also* **CSV, tab-delimited.**

command   A signal that tells a program or operating system to do a specific task. Users issue commands by making selections from a menu displayed on the screen, typing a keyboard shortcut, or entering a command at a command prompt.

command button   A button on a GUI that a user clicks on to activate a command, such as confirming choices made in a dialog box or performing some action in a program.

command-driven   Relating to software that recognizes and accepts typed-in commands, rather than displaying menus from which users can make choices. *Compare* **menu-driven.**

command history   A record of commands previously typed into a command line interpreter. Most command line interpreters maintain a command history and provide ways that users can quickly edit and reissue commands.

Command key   A key on Apple Macintosh computer keyboards that is marked with a four-leaf clover and/or the Apple logo and functions is used for keyboard shortcuts. *Also called* **Apple key.**

command language   A programming language that consists of the commands understood by an operating system or program. For example, the MS-DOS command language includes the command DIR, which lists the names of the files in the current directory.

command line   **1.** A line in a text box that begins with a command prompt. When commands are typed, they appear on the command line; in most command line interfaces, typing "enter" at the end of the line then submits the command to the computer. **2.** A string of characters comprising a command and its arguments.

command line interpreter   A program that accepts and interprets commands for an operating system. A command line interpreter usually displays a text box with a command line at which commands can be typed. Most command line interpreters can interpret shell scripts or batch files as well as commands typed by users. *Also called* **command line interface, command processor, command shell.** *See also* **shell.**

command prompt   A character or set of characters in a text box or terminal window, next to which a cursor is set for the user to type in a command to a computer. The printing of a command prompt on the screen indicates that the computer is ready to accept a new command. The command line of a command line interface begins with the command prompt.

comma-separated values   *See* **CSV.**

common business-oriented language   *See* **COBOL.**

Common Gateway Interface   *See* **CGI.**

communications protocol   A set of standards that defines the manner in which data is transmitted between two or more pieces of computer equipment over a telephone line or other communications link. Two pieces of equipment must be using the same protocol in order to communicate, and even then may have to negotiate agreement over variable parts of the standard.

There are several different families of communications protocols, each governing a different aspect of the communications process. For example, modem protocols govern the way in which modems convert digital signals into analog signals for transmission over telephone lines, while other protocols govern the way in which computers attached to those modems convert data into a series of bits for transmission. Still more protocols control data compression, encryption, and error detection, for example. *See also* **handshaking.**

communications software   Software that transmits and receives data via a communications protocol. While the software required to connect to most networks is included in most computer operating systems, additional software is sometimes required for certain kinds of data transmission, such as VoIP or the use of webcams to transmit video data over the Internet.

community antenna television   *Abbreviated* **CATV.**   *See* **cable.**

compact disk or **compact disc**   *Abbreviated* **CD.**   An optical disk that stores digital data in one of several related formats. The first compact disks were read-only disks designed by Philips to store digital audio data. These disks, sometimes called *audio CDs* or *music CDs,* are still a popular storage medium for music, and can be played in standard CD players used with home and portable audio systems, as well as in computer CD drives. Later, formats were developed so other kinds of data, including text, computer programs, and even video, could be stored on read-only compact disks; these disks, usually called *CD-ROMs,* can contain many different kinds of digital data and are usually read by CD drives on computers. Finally, formats were developed to allow digital data, including audio CD data, to be recorded to compact disks with a CD burner; data can be written once to CD-R disks and CD-RW disks can be rewritten multiple times.

DVDs are the same size as compact disks, but use a different underlying physical format that provides a much greater storage capacity. *See also* **disk.**

compact disk-interactive   *See* **CD-I.**

compact disk-recordable   *See* **CD-R.**

CompactFlash *Abbreviated* **CF.** One of two open-source memory card formats developed by SanDisk and adopted by a consortium of electronics manufacturers called the CompactFlash Assocation. CompactFlash memory cards typically use flash memory to store data, but Microdrives also use the format and store data on small disk drives. CompactFlash cards are used as a storage medium in a range of devices manufactured by various companies, including digital cameras, PDAs, digital audio players, and computers. CompactFlash II cards are slightly thicker than CompactFlash I cards.

compatible Capable of being used with or substituted for another computer, component, file, or program. Software is often said to be compatible with the various operating systems and computer hardware it can run on, and replacement components such as ink cartridges are sometimes said to be compatible with a given component if they can replace that component.

compile To translate a program written in a high-level language into object code or bytecode. The result of compiling may be machine language that can be directly executed by the computer, it may be an intermediate assembly language that must be transformed into machine language by an assembler, or it may be a format such as bytecode that can be executed by an interpreter. *See also* **executable file.**

compiled language A programming language whose programs are translated into another language by a compiler before being executed. Typically, compiled languages are translated into machine languages, which can be executed by a CPU. The compiler outputs the machine language to a file for later execution. C, C++, and Fortran are examples of compiled languages. *Compare* **interpreted language.**

compiler A program that translates a program written in a high-level language into another language, usually machine language or bytecode. A compiler outputs the compiled version of the program to a file for later execution. Compilers take programs written in high-level languages, which are easy for people to read, and change them into a form that is easy for computers to read. *Compare* **interpreter.**

compile time The period of time during which a compiler translates a program's source code into a form that is executable by a computer. *Compare* **runtime.**

complementary metal oxide semiconductor *See* **CMOS.**

complex instruction set computer *See* **CISC.**

component **1.** A self-contained piece of software that can usually be integrated with other applications in order to add predefined functionality. For example, you can add a map that zooms in and out to your web application by adding a mapping ActiveX component. **2.** A completely functional device that is part of a larger system. For example, a sound card is a component of a computer, and a television is a component of a home-theater system.

component video   **1.** A video signal in which the luminance and chrominance components are transmitted through separate wires or channels rather than being encoded into a single composite signal. Component video allows richer and more detailed color than composite video because the use of two separate chrominance components, along with a luminance component, allows the transmission of more color information. Component video signals are divided according to a color model. For example, analog component video signals often use the YPbPr color model, which consists of one luminance component (Y) and two chrominance components (Pb and Pr). Each component is transmitted over a separate RCA cable. *Compare* **composite video. 2.** A video signal in which the information corresponding to each variable of the color model is transmitted through a separate wire or cable. For example, an RGB component video connection is composed of three wires: one for red, one for green, and one for blue. DVI cables separate signals in this way. *See* Table A on page 356.

COM port   *Abbreviation of* **communications port.**   On a computer running Windows, one of four possible serial ports, designated by MS-DOS as COM1, COM2, COM3, and COM4.

composite video   An analog signal in which the luminance and chrominance components are transmitted through the same cable. NTSC and PAL are the composite video standards most often used for terrestrial television transmission. Composite video cables typically have an RCA connector. *Compare* **component video.**

compound document   A file that contains data from two or more different applications, for example, a document that contains text from a word processing program and a spreadsheet from a spreadsheet program. Compound documents are often produced by office suite software.

compress   To encode data in a form that minimizes the space it requires for storage or transmittal. Users can compress data by using programs such as WinZIP or gzip. Many communication protocols compress transmitted data. Compression is also called *packing*. *See also* **data compression.**

compression   *See* **data compression.**

compression artifact   A data error resulting from the loss of information when data is compressed using lossy compression. Compression artifacts are common in file formats such as MPEG and JPEG. In sound files, compression artifacts take the form of reduced sound quality or unwanted sounds accompanying the desired signal; in graphics files, compression artifacts may take the form of overall blurriness, jaggedness of boundaries between colors, blotchiness, and so on.

computer   A programmable machine that performs high-speed processing of numbers, as well as of text, graphics, symbols, and sound. Modern computers are digital. The computer's physical components are called hardware; its programs and data are called software. Almost all computers include these components:

- a CPU that interprets and executes instructions
- input devices, such as a keyboard or a mouse, through which data and commands enter the computer
- memory, such as RAM and ROM, which enables a computer to store programs and data
- mass storage devices, such as disk drives, that store large amounts of data
- output devices, such as printers and display screens, that show the results after the computer has processed data

See also **mainframe, personal computer, supercomputer.**

computer-aided design   *See* **CAD.**

computer-aided instruction   *See* **CAI.**

computer-aided manufacturing   *See* **CAM.**

computer-based training   *Abbreviated* **CBT.**   The use of CAI teaching tools to provide workers with the necessary computer skills to perform their jobs effectively.

computer case   The hard shell and metal chassis that contain the components of a computer. The computer case supports the drives, motherboard, fans, and power supply unit. *See also* **desktop, tower.**

computer game   An electronic game that is played on a personal computer. Computer games are compatible with standard operating systems. *Compare* **video game.**

Computer Graphics Metafile   *Abbreviated* **CGM.**   A graphics file format that allows both vector and bitmapped graphics, used in engineering and other technical applications. Files in the computer graphics metafile format often have the extension *.cgm.*

computer language   *See* **programming language.**

computer literacy   The ability to operate a computer and to understand the terms used in working with computers and related technology.

computer science   The scientific study of computation, computer programming, and computing hardware.

computer virus   *See* **virus.**

concatenate   To join together. For example, two or more files can be concatenated into a single file by placing the data for one after the data for the other. Similarly, two or more character strings, such as *super* and *computer*, can be concatenated into one string, *supercomputer.*

condensed   Relating to type in which characters are placed closer together than in ordinary text and sometimes narrowed. Most word processing applications have a feature that allows users to modify character spacing and create condensed type.

conference call   A telephone call in which three or more persons in different locations participate. Conference calls can be initiated by using the three-way calling feature on some telephones or by using a special conference calling service.

CONFIG.SYS   A configuration file in DOS, OS/2, and Windows 95 or 98 operating systems. The file is not used in more recent Windows systems.

configuration   The way in which a computer is set up in terms of both hardware and software. For example, a PC-compatible computer's configuration may consist of 256MB of RAM, a 4GB hard drive, a 3.5-inch floppy drive, a 40x CD-drive, a mouse, a monitor, and the Microsoft Windows 2000 operating system. When configuring a computer, a user must attach all the physical components with the necessary cables and connectors, set various switches and jumpers, and select the software parameters that tell the computer what the configuration looks like and how its various components should interact with each other. For example, the operating system needs to know what type of monitor and printer the computer is hooked up to.

configuration file   An ASCII file containing information about the current parameters used to run a specific application. For a word processing program, for example, the parameters might include the current settings for line spacing, margin width, and font specifications. If these parameters are changed while using the application, the configuration file is rewritten to indicate these changes, so that the next time the application is run, the new parameters are preserved.

connectivity   The ability to make and maintain a communications link between two or more devices.

connector   **1.** A coupler used to join two cables or to plug a cable into a port or interface. Different types of connectors are closely associated with standards for the transmission of different signals. For example, DVI standards for transmission of digital and audio video use special connectors having 17 to 29 pins. *See* Table A on page 356. **2.** A cable using such connectors.

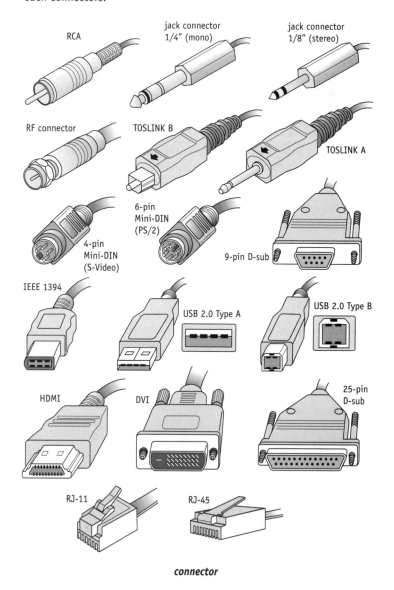

connector

70

connect time **1.** The period of time that a cell phone maintains a radio connection with a cell site. Connect time is longer than the time a conversation lasts, because a cell phone connects to the network as soon as a number is dialed. **2.** The elapsed time during which a user or computer is connected to a network. **3.** The time it takes a device or service to connect to a network.

console **1.** A terminal or device that controls a computer, providing input and receiving output. Mainframe computers are often operated by remote and local terminals; the console terminal is the one that has special administrative privileges to start and stop the machine and to which system administration messages are sent. Most computers are attached to a keyboard and display, which together serve as a console. Often, a single keyboard and display are attached to a number of server computers by a device that allows the user to choose which computer to control. **2.** *See* **video game console. 3.** *See* **terminal window.**

console application A program designed to be run from a command line in a text window.

console game *See* **video game** (sense 2).

constant angular velocity *Abbreviated* **CAV.** A technique for reading data from or writing data to a disk in which the disk rotates at a uniform rate, regardless of whether the read/write head is near the center of the disk or near its rim. Constant angular velocity is used in hard disks, floppy disks, and some optical disk drives. *Compare* **constant linear velocity.**

constant bit rate or **constant bitrate** *Abbreviated* **CBR.** A method of encoding data, especially audio or video, so that it is transmitted as a steady stream of bits that remains fixed regardless of variances in the levels of the signal. *Compare* **variable bit rate.**

constant linear velocity *Abbreviated* **CLV.** A technique for reading data from or writing data to a disk in which the read/write head traces a path over the spinning disk at a constant speed. The closer the head moves toward the center of the disk, the slower the motor rotates the disk in order to compensate for the decreased linear space the head must travel. Constant linear velocity is still used in most optical disk drives, but some newer and faster drives have replaced it with constant angular velocity, or with a combination of CLV and CAV. *Compare* **constant angular velocity.**

contact manager An application for storing and organizing lists of people and companies along with their addresses and other personal information. Contact managers are commonly used by businesses to keep track of customers. *See also* **PIM.**

container format A file structure that is capable of encapsulating various media components such as audio, video, tags, and menus in a single package. Common container formats include AVI, ASF, WAV, and AIFF. *See* Table 4.

Table 4 Common Audio and Video Container Formats

Standard	Standard Owner	Data Type	File Extensions
AIFF	Apple	audio	.aiff
ASF	Microsoft	audio/video	.asf
AVI	Microsoft	audio/video	.avi
DivX Media Format	DivX	audio/video	.divx
Flash	Macromedia	audio/video	.swf
Matroska	public domain	audio/video	.mka, .mkv
MP4	MPEG	audio/video	.mp4
MXF	SMPTE	audio/video	.mxf
Ogg/OGM	public domain	audio/video	.ogg
QuickTime	Apple	audio/video	.mov, .qt
RealMedia	RealNetworks	audio/video	.ra, .ram, .rm, .rv
3GP	3GPP	audio/video	.3gp
VOB	MPEG	audio/video	.mpg, .vob
WAV	Microsoft	audio	.wav

content Text, pictures, video, sound, or other kinds of information distinct from the hardware, software, and format used to provide them. Some content is available free, as over broadcast television channels, while other content is copyrighted or available only for a fee. *See also* **medium.**

content protection Any of various methods of preventing the unauthorized use or modification of copyrighted digital content. Copy protection, for example, prevents unauthorized copying of digital data (such as data stored on a DVD).

Content Scrambling System *Abbreviated* **CSS.** A method of content protection that encrypts the content of a DVD so that it can be decoded only by licensed DVD players. The Content Scrambling System continues to be used in most commercial DVDs despite the fact that its encryption algorithm has since been broken and distributed widely on the Internet.

context-sensitive help A mode of help in which the information first presented to the user varies according to the operation the user is performing so that the user sees the most useful information right away, without having to search for it.

continuous paper Paper that is produced in a single, long strip, having sheets that are separated by perforations, and often having holes down the margins to allow for use in the tractor feed mechanism of impact printers.

continuous tone A method of creating an image out of smoothly gradated colors or shades of gray, as in photography. Color printers and some color graphics programs use continuous tone, but some black-and-white printers and most black-and-white graphics software use patterns of black dots of variable size and density to simulate continuous tone. *See also* **halftone.**

contrast **1.** The difference in brightness between the lightest and darkest parts of an image. **2.** A display setting that adjusts the overall range of brightness of an image by establishing the brightness of the lighter portion of the image. Setting contrast too high can damage CRT and plasma displays. *Also called* **picture, white level.**

contrast ratio The ratio between the brightness of a white image and the brightness of a black image on a given display. Contrast ratios are commonly used as a specification for backlit displays, such as LCDs. Displays with low contrast ratios may produce a washed-out image; however, published contrast ratios are often unreliable.

control character or **control code** A character that has no visual representation and does not take up any space in a display or printout. Control characters are used for indicating the end of a line of text or for transmitting a backspace or delete, for example. The first 32 characters of the ASCII character set contain control characters as well as whitespace characters.

Control key *Abbreviated* **Ctrl.** A key used in combination with other keys, typically in keyboard shortcuts. When pressed in combination with a letter key, the Control key produces a control character, which is then interpreted as a command by an application such as a word processor.

controller   **1.** A unit that controls the flow of data along the bus between a computer's CPU and devices such as a display, a disk drive, or a printer. Each device attached to the motherboard has its own controller. *See also* **bus. 2.** An input device used with a video game console. Controllers typically consist of a directional pad or analog stick and a set of buttons. *Also called* **gamepad.**

Control Panel   A part of the Microsoft Windows GUI (graphical user interface) containing configuration programs that set such system parameters as screen colors, speaker volume, the date and time in the computer's clock, the double-click speed for a mouse, or the keyboard repeat rate.

control unit   The component of the CPU that directs the operations of the other components. *See also* **arithmetic-logic unit, floating-point unit.**

conventional memory   In PC-compatible computers, the first 64 kilobytes of main memory addresses. DOS was designed to use only conventional memory, although DOS and DOS programs can access extended memory by using special software. *See also* **upper memory area.**

convergence   The process of rendering a color image using separate red, green, and blue pixels or images.

cookie   A piece of data sent by a website to a web browser and stored on the computer where the browser is running. A cookie records information, such as user preferences, registration information, or sites visited, that is later sent back to websites. Web browsers allow users to control how cookies are stored and retrieved. Many websites require cookies to be enabled in order to access all their features.

cooperative multitasking   Multitasking in which the operating system only interrupts the processing of the active program at points specified by the programmer. Cooperative multitasking requires a less complex operating system than preemptive multitasking, because the programmer who designs each program determines when it can and cannot be interrupted. It was used in Macintosh operating systems before OS X and in Windows operating systems before Windows NT. *Compare* **preemptive multitasking.**

coprocessor   A device for data processing that is distinct from the CPU and is designed to perform specified functions that the CPU cannot perform as well and as quickly. For example, although CPUs can perform the calculations necessary to do encryption and decryption, a cryptographic coprocessor is designed to perform them more quickly, leaving the CPU available for other kinds of processing.

copy   To duplicate data. Text can be copied from the document and pasted into another document or into a different location within the same document. Files can be copied from one directory or storage medium to another. The ability to copy can be found in nearly every electronic environment.

Copy Generation Management System *Abbreviated* **CGMS.** A method of controlling the unauthorized duplication of DVDs by limiting the number of sequential copies that can be made. CGMS allows only a first-generation copy of the disk, which is encoded with data that prevents the production of further copies. CGMS comes in two forms, CGMS-A (for encoding analog signals) and CGMS-D (for encoding digital signals).

copyleft A type of license for software and other creative works that allows free distribution and ensures that any works derived from the original are also free from copyright or other legal restrictions on distribution. *See also* **open source.**

copy protection Any of various methods used to prevent the unauthorized duplication of copyrighted material on electronic media such as DVDs, CDs, or Internet servers. Copy protection is achieved primarily by ensuring that any copies made of the content of the media will be unusable, using a wide variety of methods, including watermarking and encryption. *See also* **content protection.**

cordless phone A portable telephone that uses radio waves, rather than a wire, to connect to a standard landline. Cordless phones typically have a range of about 100 yards. *Compare* **mobile phone.**

corrupt To change or destroy the data in a file accidentally, often due to software problems, damage to the disk or disk drive, or a fluctuation in power.

courseware Software that is used for educational or training purposes, including distance learning and CAI (computer-aided instruction).

coverage area The geographical area in which a cell phone network offers service to subscribers.

cpi *Abbreviation of* **characters per inch.**

CPU *Abbreviation of* **central processing unit.** The part of a computer that interprets and executes instructions. A mainframe has a CPU consisting of one or more printed circuit boards, but the CPU of a personal computer is contained on a small chip called a microprocessor.

The CPU fetches, decodes, and executes instructions, and transfers information to and from other components—such as disk drives, expansion boards, and the keyboard—over the computer's bus, its main data highway. The part of the CPU known as the arithmetic-logic unit (ALU) performs all arithmetic and logic operations on data. The CPU's control unit coordinates the steps necessary to execute each instruction. It tells the other parts of the CPU what to do and when. The data registers of the CPU function as a scratch pad for the ALU and as working memory for the CPU. *See also* **processor speed.**

CR   *Abbreviation of* **carriage return.**

cracker   *See* **hacker** (sense 1).

crash   To stop functioning suddenly and become unusable, used, for example, of an application, operating system, or disk. When software crashes, it may freeze and stop functioning, or it may suddenly terminate. Crashes often result in the loss of data.

crawler   *See* **spider.**

CRC   *Abbreviation of* **cyclical redundancy check.**   A technique for detecting errors in the transmission of digital data by means of a particular type of hash function. CRC is more complex and more likely to detect errors than a simple checksum. It is used in many communications and file transfer protocols. *See also* **checksum.**

crop   In a graphics or desktop publishing program, to cut away parts of an image in order to resize or reshape it, or to remove unwanted material.

cross-luma   *See* **dot crawl.**

crossover   A filter that separates audio signals according to frequency. Audio signals separated by crossover can be used to drive different kinds of speakers, for example, sending high frequencies to tweeters, low frequencies to woofers, and midrange frequencies to standard speakers. This provides more efficient and more accurate conversion of electrical energy into sound from the speakers.

crossover frequency   A frequency at which a crossover filter divides a single audio signal into separate signals of different frequency ranges. For example, two-way crossovers have a single crossover frequency; all the frequencies above it go into one signal path, while all the frequencies below it go into another signal path.

cross-platform   Relating to the capability of hardware or software to function in the same way on different platforms. Cross-platform applications generally can be run on Apple Macintosh, Unix, or Microsoft Windows operating systems, for example.

cross-posting   The act of posting a single message simultaneously to multiple newsgroups or in multiple discussion threads of an online forum. Cross-posting is generally considered bad netiquette.

crosstalk   Interference caused by the unintended transmission of signals from one communications circuit or channel to another, especially voice signals transmitted over a telephone circuit that can be heard on another circuit.

CRT   **1.** *Abbreviation of* **cathode-ray tube. 2.** A computer monitor, television, or projector that displays an image using a cathode-ray tube. *See also* **direct-view television.**

cryptanalysis   **1.** The analysis of encrypted data in the attempt to recover the original, unencrypted data. **2.** The study and development of techniques for deciphering encrypted data.

cryptography   Any of various techniques, especially those involving the mathematical manipulation of data, for converting information into and out of unreadable forms, especially in order to keep the information private when stored in an accessible place or when transmitted over a public medium such as the Internet. *Compare* **steganography.** *See also* **private-key cryptography, public-key cryptography.**

C shell   *Abbreviated* **csh.**   A shell that interprets commands for Linux and Unix operating systems and uses a command structure that is similar to the C programming language. The C shell was initially popular because of interactive features such as allowing earlier commands to be recalled and edited. Bash and tcsh are now more popular.

CSMA   *Abbreviation of* **carrier sense multiple access.**   A method of data transmission for networks in which multiple transmissions are sent on the same channel by requiring senders to detect the presence of other transmissions before they transmit. CSMA allows a form of half-duplex communication on networks and is used on some Ethernet and wireless networks.

CSS   **1.** *Abbreviation of* **cascading style sheets. 2.** *Abbreviation of* **Content Scrambling System.**

CSV   *Abbreviation of* **comma-separated values.**   A file format for storing tables in which each line of the file represents a row of a table and columns of data are separated by commas. CSV files contain only character data. They often have the file extension *.csv.*

Ctrl   *Abbreviation of* **Control key.**

Ctrl-Alt-Del   A command available in Windows operating systems issued by pressing the Delete key while holding down the Control and Alt keys. The command gives the user several options, such as locking the computer, restarting it, changing a user password, or forcing an application that is not responding to quit. The command interrupts all applications currently running to provide these options.

CTS   *Abbreviation of* **carpal tunnel syndrome.**

current directory   The directory that an operating system or program is using at a given point in time. New directories and files are usually created in the current directory unless a different directory is specified, and files in the current directory are displayed in response to a request for a list of files. *Also called* **working directory.**

current drive   In DOS, the drive on which the current directory is located and that the operating system uses for commands that involve the entire drive.

cursor   A moveable indicator that marks the place at which a command from a particular input device, such as a keyboard or mouse, will be executed. Text cursors, which are associated with text input devices, such as keyboards, are used in text boxes and text editors, and typically appear as a small blinking vertical line or rectangle. Other cursors, such as those associated with mice, touch pads, and directional pads, can usually be moved across the entire display screen. These typically appear as an arrow but may change shape depending on what functions are available to the user at a particular position on the screen. For example, when such a cursor is positioned over a hyperlink in a web browser it may change into the shape of a hand to indicate that clicking a button on the input device will command the browser to follow the hyperlink to a new webpage.

cursor movement key or **cursor control key**   Any of various keys that change the position of the cursor on a display screen, usually comprising the arrow keys and the Home, Page Up, Page Down, and End keys.

cut   To remove text or graphics from a document or file. Such removed data can usually be pasted into other locations within the same document or file or into other documents or files. *Compare* **delete.**

cut-sheet feeder   *See* **sheet feeder.**

cyan-magenta-yellow   *See* **CMY.**

cyan-magenta-yellow-black   *See* **CMYK.**

cyber-   A prefix used to refer to computers and computing. Many new words have been coined by adding *cyber-* to already existing words. For example, *cyberculture* refers to the culture arising from the use of computer networks. *Cyberpunk* is a subgenre of science fiction often involving futuristic computer-based societies. The prefix was taken from the word *cybernetics*.

cybernetics   The theoretical study of communication and control processes in biological, mechanical, and electronic systems, especially the comparison of these processes in biological and artificial systems.

cyberspace   The electronic medium of computer networks, in which online communication takes place.

cyclical redundancy check *See* **CRC.**

cylinder The set of all tracks located in the same corresponding position on every recording surface of a disk or on both sides of a platter in a hard disk drive. Each circular track in a cylinder lies on the edge of an imaginary column running through the disk drive, and the columns of the inner tracks are embedded inside the columns of the outer tracks, just as the inner tracks form concentric circles inside the outer tracks. Thus, on a double-sided disk drive with a single platter, each cylinder consists of two tracks, one track on each side. If a hard disk drive made of four platters has 600 tracks on each platter, it will have 300 cylinders, each consisting of 8 tracks.

DAB A standard for the transmission of digital radio over terrestrial radio networks. Unlike Digital Radio Mondiale, DAB signals are transmitted separately from analog signals. The DAB standard is used outside of the United States. *See also* **digital radio.**

DAC or **D/A converter** *Abbreviations of* **digital-to-analog converter.**

DAE *Abbreviation of* **digital audio extraction.**

daemon A program that operates in the background without human input and waits for requests to perform a specific task. For example, a mail delivery program is usually a daemon that waits for a request to send email.

daisy chain A set of hardware devices that are linked in a series, with each device linked to another device or a terminator rather than all being linked to a hub.

DARPA *Abbreviation of* **Defense Advance Research Projects Agency.** A research agency (formerly called ARPA) at the US Department of Defense that funds and researches technology for the military. DARPA funded development of ARPANET, which was the precursor to the Internet.

DASD *Abbreviation of* **direct access storage device.** A storage device, such as a hard drive, that is connected to an IBM-compatible computer and allows any of its data to be accessed directly. In contrast, tape drives require data to be accessed sequentially. DASD is pronounced either dee-ay-ess-DEE or DAZZ-dee.

dashboard software   Software that monitors information that is subject to change and displays the information dynamically, typically on a window or windows on a computer monitor. Dashboard software is used to keep track of changing stock prices, inventory, meteorological conditions, and other data for which constant monitoring is useful.

DAT   *Abbreviation of* **digital audio tape.**   A storage medium that uses a magnetic tape with a width of four millimeters to store digital data. Originally designed to store high-quality audio data, DAT can store general data on DAT cartridges by means of the DDS format. A DAT cartridge is approximately two by three inches in size and can hold up to 180 minutes of audio recordings or 72 GB of data. Because DATs allow only sequential access, their use with non-audio data is primarily restricted to backups.

data   Numerical, textual, audio, visual, or other information, especially in a machine-readable form that can be processed and stored by a computer. Words or numbers entered into a database, for example, are stored as data in binary form, as is the information determining the shapes, brightness, and color of a video image. The word *data* is the plural form of *datum,* which means a single fact, but *data* is often considered a singular entity and used with a singular verb. *Compare* **code.**

data area   *See* **program area.**

database   An organized collection of information that can be searched, retrieved, and changed using a collection of programs known as a database management system. Most current databases are relational databases, although XML databases are becoming more common. *See also* **flat-file database.**

database administrator   *Abbreviated* **DBA.**   A person who is responsible for the design and management of an organization's databases. A database administrator is usually responsible for implementing and maintaining database management software, as well as designing the structure of databases and the queries used to access them.

database management system   *Abbreviated* **DBMS.**   The program or combination of programs that stores, retrieves, updates, and protects the data in a database. Database management systems create and manage the files that data is stored in, and provide sophisticated ways for users or applications to query and change the data. Database management systems usually allow different users or applications to access the data simultaneously, and include tools to control which users can access specific parts of the database. Most database management systems also protect against data loss by backing up data and checking data integrity.

Database management systems generally allow users to perform all the most common database management functions by using the SQL language. However, those systems designed primarily to be used on personal computers, such as Microsoft Access, also have a GUI (graphical user interface) that makes it easier to perform certain tasks, as in creating tables and generating reports. Two very widely-used database management systems for larger-scale projects are DB2 and Oracle.

database server A computer system on a network that stores a shared database and enables network users to retrieve the data they request. *See also* **client/server network, server.**

data compression The encoding of data in a form that reduces the amount of space required to store it or the time required to transmit it. For example, the popular data compression programs PKZIP and WinZip assign special codes to frequently used words in a text file so that they take up fewer bits than they would if each letter were coded separately. Lossy compression techniques result in the loss of some information and are used for data such as images and audio. Lossless compression techniques are more appropriate for textual data and software.

data dictionary In database management systems, a file that contains the file specifications needed to operate the database.

data-encoding scheme A format in which data is encoded for storage or transmission.

Data Encryption Standard *See* **DES.**

data entry The process of putting data into a computer, especially the typing of text and figures into a database or spreadsheet from the keyboard.

data entry form In database or related applications, a single record appearing onscreen in a form that is easy for the user to fill in or update. Most database applications let the user create a custom data entry form in addition to displaying a default form.

data file A file containing data created by an application, such as a document, a graphics design, or database records. *Compare* **program file.**

datagram *See* **packet.**

data integrity **1.** The condition of data that has not been lost or modified in unintended or malicious ways. **2.** In databases, the consistency and accuracy of the data.

data mining The process of extracting useful information from large bodies of data. Data mining is usually performed using automated processes that search for meaningful patterns in the data without much prior knowledge of the data content or relationships.

data processing The storing or processing of data by a computer, especially the processing of large amounts of data by a company or government institution. *Also called* **electronic data processing.**

data rate **1.** *See* **bit rate** (sense 2). **2.** *See* **data transfer rate.**

data transfer rate The rate at which digital data is transmitted between devices, measured in bits or bytes per second. For example, a typical broadband Internet connection allows data to be downloaded at 1.5 Mbps. *Also called* **bit rate, data rate, transfer rate.** *See also* **bandwidth.**

data type or **datatype** A named category of data used by a computer language or computer program to indicate how much memory to allocate for a given piece of data, what operations can be performed on it, or how to display it. Data types are primarily defined by computer languages such as C, SQL, and XML. However, programs like spreadsheets and database management systems sometimes define their own data types.

data warehouse A collection of databases for one organization or on one topic, usually accessible through one database management system or related software system.

daughter board A printed circuit board that attaches either to a computer's main circuit board or to an expansion card. Daughter boards are added to improve a computer's performance or enhance its capabilities and are often used with sound or graphics cards. *Compare* **expansion card, motherboard.**

dB *Abbreviation of* **decibel.**

DB2 A database management system designed by IBM that is popular for use on mainframe computers. DB2 is available for many different operating systems.

DBA *Abbreviation of* **database administrator.**

DB connector *Abbreviation of* **D-subminiature connector.**

DBMS *Abbreviation of* **database management system.**

DBS *Abbreviation of* **direct broadcast satellite.** A subscription television service in which television content is transmitted by satellite to a small fixed satellite dish and a proprietary receiver connected to the subscriber's television. *Compare* **TVRO.**

DCII *Abbreviation of* **DigicipherII.**

D connector *See* **D-subminiature connector.**

DCR *Abbreviation of* **digital-cable ready.**

DDE *Abbreviation of* **Dynamic Data Exchange.** A system that allows two applications programs to be linked together so that a change made in one application, called the *server*, is immediately reflected in the other, called the *client*. A common example of this linking process is the use of a communications program to monitor an online service for stock prices and trading information, together with a spreadsheet program that receives the new data as it comes in, makes changes in its tables, and recalculates its formulas automatically. Applications must be specifically designed as DDE servers or clients for this technique to work. DDE was developed by Microsoft Corporation and IBM.

DDR *Abbreviation of* **double data rate.** Relating to SDRAM that transfers data twice during each bus cycle. DDR SDRAM effectively doubles the bus rate, so the clock speeds used to categorize it are generally doubled; 400 MHz DDR SDRAM operates with a 200 MHz clock. *See also* **SDR.**

DDR2 *Abbreviation of* **double data rate 2.** Relating to DDR SDRAM that can be run at higher clock speeds than standard DDR chips because of an improved electrical interface. *See also* **SDR.**

DDS *Abbreviation of* **digital data storage.** A format for storing digital data on magnetic tapes. DDS allows digital data, as from hard disks, to be backed up onto DAT cartridges. Drives that read and write DAT cartridges usually use either the DAT audio format or the DDS data format, but not both.

dead pixel An LCD pixel that has stopped responding, especially one that no longer transmits light. *Compare* **stuck pixel.**

debug To search for and eliminate errors or malfunctions in a program or device.

decibel *Abbreviated* **dB.** Any of various measures of the relative voltage, power, sound level, or other property of two signals. As a measure of sound level, the sound pressure of the quietest sound audible to human ears is commonly used as a reference level, and volume reported relative to this level typically has a positive value. On voltage meters showing signal levels in audio equipment, a reference level is usually set by the maximum level that the equipment can process without serious distortion, and decibel levels tend to have negative values. Decibel measures are logarithmic; using the definition of *decibel* assumed in nearly all commercial applications, a measurement of 0 decibels indicates equal signal level, 3 decibels indicates roughly a doubling of the signal level, -3 decibels indicates roughly a halving of the signal level, 20 decibels indicates a 100-fold increase, and so on. The abbreviation *dBSPL* is sometimes used for measurements of sound pressure.

decimal   Relating to the base 10 numeral system. Numbers are usually written in the decimal system, which uses the 10 different symbols 0—9. Each place in a decimal number represents a successive power of 10, with places to the right of the decimal point representing negative powers. Computers use the binary numeral system internally, and still other numeral systems are often used in computing. *See also* **binary, hexadecimal, octal.** *See* Table 2 at **binary.**

decode   To convert data from a format used for transmission or storage back into its original form. *Compare* **encode.**

decoder   **1.** Any of various devices used to convert proprietary signal formats, such as a pay-TV transmission, for display on standard devices such as televisions or monitors. *See also* **set-top box. 2.** Any of various devices or programs that convert digitized data back into its original form. Decoder cards are used in DVD players to convert MPEG-2 data into analog video signals.

decompress   *See* **uncompress.**

decrypt   To decode data that has been encrypted, usually by using a password or key. Encrypted data must be decrypted before it can be used. *See also* **ciphertext, cryptography, plaintext.**

dedicated circuit   A telecommunications line that connects two specific locations together, often providing a private network between a LAN and an ISP. Dedicated circuits frequently use leased lines that carry no other traffic, but they can also be paths defined across a circuit-switched network serving multiple users. *See also* **WAN.**

dedicated short-range communications   *See* **DSRC.**

default   **1.** A setting used by a program, device, or system until the first time a user chooses a different setting. Defaults are set when a program is written or a device is manufactured. *Also called* **factory setting. 2.** A setting that determines what a program, device, or system will do in the absence of further information about what to do in a given situation. For example, most operating systems allow users to select a default printer, to which documents will be sent for printing unless the user specifically chooses another printer when starting a new print job.

Defense Advanced Research Projects Agency   *See* **DARPA.**

defrag   To defragment.

defragment   To reorganize the way files are stored on a disk or in memory to eliminate fragmentation. Most operating systems include utility programs for defragmenting disks.

degauss   **1.** To erase data from a magnetic storage device. **2.** To rebalance the magnetic field of a CRT to correct image distortion. Some CRTs can be degaussed by pressing a button or by selecting the degauss option on a display menu.

deinterlace   To convert interlaced video into progressive video, as by combining pairs of fields into single frames. Complex algorithms are required to deinterlace video without creating noticeable artifacts. Displays other than CRTs, such as an LCD or plasma television, must deinterlace all interlaced signals in order to display them. Most progressive-scan DVD players are capable of deinterlacing interlaced DVDs.

Del   *Abbreviation of* **Delete key.**

delete   **1.** To erase content internal to a file. For example, a user can delete characters in a document by using the Delete or Backspace keys and can delete a document in a file system by using the Delete key, a menu option, a text command, or by dragging the document into the trash. *Compare* **cut. 2.** To remove a file from a directory. Deleting a file, unlike erasing it, does not necessarily cause the data to disappear from the memory (such as RAM or a hard disk) on which it is stored, but simply redefines the parts of memory in which the data was stored as free space. Files whose content has been completely erased are sometimes said to be *permanently deleted*.

Delete key   *Abbreviated* **Del.**   On a computer keyboard, a key that is pressed to erase characters, files, or other information. Pressing the Delete key erases a character to the right of the cursor, or a group of characters that have been highlighted. *See also* **Backspace key.**

delimiter   A character marking the start or end of a unit of data. For example, the backslash (\) is used as a delimiter in Windows pathnames, such as C:\WP\MEMOS\CURPROJ.ABC.

Delphi   An object-oriented programming language based on Pascal, developed and licensed by Borland Software Corporation.

demand paging   A technique for virtual memory in which a page of data is transferred to working memory from swap space only after data in that page has been requested by the CPU. *Compare* **prepaging.** *See also* **page fault.**

demodulation   The conversion of a modulated carrier signal into a copy of the data encoded in the signal. For example, when digital data is transferred from one computer to another computer over a phone line by modulating—or making changes to—a carrier signal, the carrier signal must be demodulated in order to recover the bits that make up the data. *Compare* **modulation.**

denial-of-service attack *Abbreviated* **DoS attack.** A malicious attack on a server in a network, or on an entire network, in which the server or network is bombarded with large numbers of unnecessary data requests. As a result, the server or network is unable to provide regular services to legitimate requests.

density A measure of how many bits can be stored in a given amount of physical space on some storage medium. Higher density means more bits can be stored in the same amount of space. Different storage formats for the same type of device often differ in density. For example, DVDs can store much more data than CDs even though they use the same size disk, because DVDs have higher density.

DES *Abbreviation of* **Data Encryption Standard.** A standard encryption algorithm defined by the US government and first developed by IBM. DES is a block cipher, encrypting data by breaking it into 64-bit blocks and using a 56-bit key for each block. Due to the short length of its key, DES is no longer secure in itself, but a technique called triple DES, in which data is encrypted multiple times, is considered secure and is commonly used in Internet data transmission. DES has been superceded by AES as the standard used for the transmission of unclassified data by the US government.

descending sort A sort in which the items are listed from last to first or largest to smallest, as from Z to A or from 9 to 0.

desktop **1.** The background of a GUI (graphical user interface) for an operating system, on which windows, icons, and dialog boxes appear. **2.** A desktop computer. **3.** A rectangular computer case that is designed to lie horizontally on top of a desk. *Compare* **tower.**

desktop computer A personal computer that is generally larger and less portable than a laptop or notebook computer. Desktop computers usually have keyboards that are separate from the computer case that houses the CPU. *Compare* **laptop, notebook.** *See also* **slimline computer, small form factor.**

desktop environment A GUI (graphical user interface) used to operate a computer. The desktop environment allows users to choose commands, start programs, and manage files using drag-and-drop and mouse clicking, rather than by typing text commands. It provides standard windows, icons, and menus for the operating system, as well as toolbars and applications such as calendars, calculators, and clocks.

Some operating systems, such as Microsoft Windows and the Macintosh operating systems, come with an integrated desktop environment. Others, such as Linux and Unix, work with several different environments. Most desktop environments provide some control over the look and feel of the interface, including the choice of different themes. The Linux and Unix desktop environments typically consist of distinct, interchangeable modules, so they are highly customizable. *See also* **environment, window manager.**

desktop publishing   The design and production of publications, such as newsletters, trade journals, books, or brochures, using ordinary personal computers running specialized computer software. Desktop publishing software typically includes a combination of word processing and graphics software.

detail   *See* **sharpness.**

device driver   A piece of software that enables the operating system of a computer to communicate with a device such as a printer, sound card, or scanner. Device drivers convert generic commands from an operating system or applications program into the specific commands needed to perform a requested action on a particular piece of hardware.

   Device drivers may be provided along with the operating system, an applications program, or the piece of hardware. It is sometimes necessary to install the device driver from a disk in order to make it available to the programs that use it.

DHTML   *Abbreviation of* **Dynamic HTML.**

dialog box   A window that presents information to the user or requests input from the user. Dialog boxes often explain why a program cannot complete a command or request input, such as a choice among options, that a program needs in order to complete a command.

   In some operating systems, a menu option followed by an ellipsis (. . .) will bring up a dialog box if selected. *See also* **alert box.**

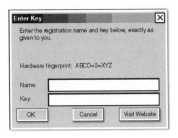

dialog box

dial-up   Relating to temporary network connections made over the public telephone network using a modem. Dial-up Internet accounts allow users with a modem to connect to the Internet by having the modem dial an access number. DSL also uses modems to make network connections over telephone lines, but DSL connections are permanent connections with much faster data transfer rates.

dictionary sort   A sort that puts items in alphabetical order but disregards capitalization and styling features such as hyphens and apostrophes. *See also* **ASCII sort.**

differential backup   A backup which copies only those files that have been changed or added since the last full backup. When using differential backups, data can be completely restored by copying the last full backup and the last differential backup. *Compare* **incremental backup.**

digicam   *See* **digital camera.**

DigicipherII   *Abbreviated* **DCII.** A digital television broadcasting standard developed by Motorola based on the MPEG-2 video standard and the AC-3 audio standard. DigicipherII is used for digital TVRO systems and by many cable television operators to distribute signals to local antennas. DigicipherII supports all major display formats including SDTV, EDTV, and HDTV.

digital   **1.** Representing information by means of a set of discrete values, usually the digits 1 and 0. Digital technology is distinguished from analog technology, which represents data using continuously varying quantities. A digital clock uses a series of changing digits to represent time at discrete intervals, for example, every second. In contrast, a clock with hands is an analog device, because the hands move continuously around the face of the clock. All modern computers are digital because they use the digits 0 and 1 to represent and manipulate all information. **2.** Designating a type of display, as on a watch or radio, that makes use of a series of changing numerical digits, rather than a pointer or other indicator moving against a fixed scale. *Compare* **analog.**

digital audio extraction   *Abbreviated* **DAE.** The process of extracting the digital data stream from an audio CD and storing it on a hard disk. *See also* **rip.**

digital audio player   A device that stores and plays digital sound files. Most digital audio players are able to play audio files stored in a wide variety of formats, including AAC, MP3, Ogg Vorbis, and WMA. Some digital audio players incorporate digital rights management technology, allowing them to be used to play music that is purchased from websites that use such technology to restrict access to music files. They are typically portable devices that play music through headphones, though there are models designed for use in the home, as well as some designed for use in cars.

A variety of storage media are used for digital audio players, including small hard disks, internal flash memory, and removable memory cards.

Most popular digital audio players can be connected to a computer's USB port in order to share files with a computer or other device, and some use the power available in a USB connection to recharge their batteries. Other common features are the ability to play FM radio and the ability to record audio. *Also called* **MP3 player.**

digital audio tape   *See* **DAT.**

digital-cable ready   *Abbreviated* **DCR.**   Capable of receiving digital cable without being connected to a separate tuner or set-top box. Digital-cable ready televisions require a subscription to a cable service but do not require the purchase or rental of additional equipment.

digital camera or **digicam**   A camera that uses CCD or CMOS light sensors to take photographs. Digital cameras store the images in digital form on memory chips or small disks rather than on film. Pictures taken with digital cameras can be downloaded to a computer for storage, display, or manipulation. Some cameras additionally allow direct hookup to a television or printer for display or printout of images without the use of a computer. Most have a small LCD screen that can function as a viewfinder. Digital cameras are often classified by the number of megapixels they can capture and by whether or not they use single-lens reflex technology.

The most common file formats used by digital cameras for storing the digital image (and transferring it to a computer or other device) are JPEG, TIFF, and RAW file formats. Some cameras allow the user to select which format to use. *See also* **camcorder, memory card, resolution.**

digital cash   *See* **e-cash.**

digital certificate   A digital signature issued by a trusted third party and used as part of security protocol such as SSL to verify the authenticity of a public key. Digital certificates are typically issued by specially designated certificate authorities to websites such as those operated by online merchants or financial institutions. They are used by web browsers and other software to confirm that a given public key that will be used to encrypt information actually belongs to the appropriate organization. Digital certificates are protection against unwittingly encrypting information with a public key held by a malicious third party, as the third party could then decrypt the information using the corresponding private key. *Also called* **SSL certificate.** *See also* **public-key cryptography.**

digital data storage   *See* **DDS.**

digital light processing   *See* **DLP.**

digital microphone   A microphone that converts incoming sound signals directly into digital signals, rather than providing an analog output. Some digital microphones also provide additional digital signal processing, such as reducing background noise, or simulating the response characteristics of traditional microphones.

digital object identifier *Abbreviated* **DOI.** An identification code for intellectual property on the Internet. Unlike a URL, which uses a location to identify a webpage or article published on the Internet, the digital object identifier is designed to identify digital content wherever it is located. *See also* **URN.**

digital radio Radio content that is encoded in a digital format. Within the United States, digital radio is broadcast by satellite radio providers using proprietary standards and by traditional radio stations using HD Radio or Digital Radio Mondiale (DRM), a worldwide standard. In other parts of the world the dominant standard is DAB. Satellite radio, HD Radio, DRM, and DAB all require special receivers. Radio programming is also available in standard digital audio formats over the Internet.

Digital Radio Mondiale *Abbreviated* **DRM.** A standard for the transmission of digital radio over terrestrial radio networks. Using DRM, traditional AM and FM radio stations can broadcast digital signals alongside analog signals. *See also* **digital radio.**

digital rights management *Abbreviated* **DRM.** The use of special software and other technology to allow the owners of music, video, text, or other content in digital form to control the conditions under which the content can be accessed. For example, digital rights management technology allows only the purchaser to play back or copy songs purchased at certain music websites. DRM systems usually involve a way of marking or encoding the content so it can only be viewed or played by special software.

digital signal processing *See* **DSP** (sense 1).

digital signal processor *See* **DSP** (sense 2).

digital signature An authentication that is unique to an individual or individual computer, used for signing digital information, such as documents or messages. Attaching a digital signature to an email message allows the recipient to verify that the sender is who he or she claims to be.

For security, signatures are often encrypted. For this, public-key cryptography is most often used. The originator of the information includes along with it a signature that is made by encrypting that information (or more often a hash of the information) using his or her private key. Others who wish to verify the authenticity of the information then decrypt the signature using the originator's public key: if the messages match, then authenticity is assured, since only the someone with the corresponding private key could have created the signature. *Also called* **e-signature.**

digital subscriber line   *See* **DSL.**

digital television   *Abbreviated* **DTV.**   Television content that is encoded in a digital format. Compressed digital formats, such as MPEG-2, require less bandwidth than traditional analog television. Consequently, digital television broadcasters can provide high-resolution picture formats such as HDTV, a large number of channels, data such as program titles, or interactive services. In the United States, digital terrestrial television is broadcast using the ATSC standard. Cable and satellite operators use the DVB or Digicipher II standards. Digital television transmitted over IP-based networks is called IPTV.

digital terrestrial television   *Abbreviated* **DTT** or **DTTV.**   The public distribution of digital television using ground-based antennas. Digital terrestrial television can be received using a standard digital tuner and antenna.

Digital Theater Systems   *See* **DTS.**

digital-to-analog converter   *Abbreviated* **D/A converter** or **DAC.**   A device that converts digital data into an analog signal, especially into an electrical signal whose voltage reflects the value of digitally represented values. Digital-to-analog converters are used in CD players and related devices to convert digitally stored sound into electrical signals for amplification and playback through headphones or speakers. *Compare* **analog-to-digital converter.**

Digital Versatile Disk   *See* **DVD.**

Digital VHS   *See* **D-VHS.**

digital video   *Abbreviated* **DV.**   **1.** Video encoded in a digital format. Digital video can be created with a digital camcorder or by digitizing analog video. Common digital video formats include MPEG-2, M-JPEG, and DV. *See also* **digital television. 2.** *See* **DV** (sense 2).

Digital Video Broadcasting   *See* **DVB.**

Digital Video Disk   *See* **DVD.**

Digital Video Interface connector   *See* **DVI connector.**

digital video recorder   *See* **DVR.**

digital watermarking   A method of copy protection that encodes within digital video, image, and music files information that authenticates the file's content and identifies the copyright holder. In video and image files, this code may be either visible or invisible.

digital zoom   In digital cameras, the use of computer graphics, often built into the software and hardware of the camera, to magnify or zoom in on an image being photographed. With digital zoom, an image already captured by the camera is used; the desired part of the image is then modified using special algorithms. Digital zoom typically provides an image of lower resolution than the comparable optical zoom.

digitize To convert analog data or signals to digital form. For example, optical scanners detect the color and brightness of different locations of a printed image, and store these values digitally as a bitmapped image. Audio signals are typically digitized by sampling the amplitude of a sound wave at different points and storing the measured amplitudes as a sequence of digital values, effectively providing a digital model of the shape of the audio signal. *See also* **analog-to-digital converter.**

digitizer **1.** A device that digitizes data. Optical scanners and A/D converters are examples of digitizers. **2.** *See* **digitizing tablet.**

digitizing tablet An input device consisting of an electronically sensitive tablet and a light pen or puck used to input drawings directly into the computer. A puck, also called a cursor, is a mouselike device with an attached plastic window with cross hairs to aid in precise placement and movement. The tablet records the movement of the puck or light pen and digitizes each point through which the puck or light pen passes. *Also called* **digitizer, graphics tablet.**

DIMM *Abbreviation of* **dual inline memory module.** A memory module used to provide RAM for personal computers, having 168 or 184 pins and providing up to 1 GB of memory. Unlike SIMMs, DIMMs do not have to be installed in pairs. *See also* **SIMM.**

DIN connector A connector that conforms to the standards of Deutsches Institut für Normung (DIN), the organization that sets standards for German hardware. The DIN connector that was once used to connect the keyboard to the computer has since been replaced by smaller Mini-DIN connectors, USB connectors, and IEEE 1394 connectors. *See also* **Mini-DIN connector.**

dingbat A typographical ornament or symbol, such as a bullet (●), check mark (✓), or arrow (↔), that can be inserted into a document. Many clip-art packages contain dingbats. One of the most popular sets of dingbats is the Zapf dingbats, available as a PostScript font.

DIP *Abbreviation of* **dual inline package.** An electronic component housing commonly used for chips, having rows of connecting pins sticking out downward from the two long sides. *Compare* **SIP.** *See figure at* **chip.**

dipole speaker A type of surround speaker designed with two or more drivers pointing in opposite directions for maximum diffusion of sound.

DIP switch   A series of tiny rocker or slider switches contained in the housing of a DIP. The housing has downward-facing pins so that it can be inserted into a socket on a printed circuit board or soldered directly to the board. Some devices have settings that are controlled by DIP switches.

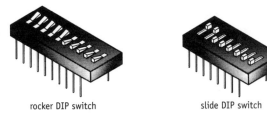

rocker DIP switch   slide DIP switch

two types of DIP switch

Direct Access Storage Device   *See* **DASD.**

direct address   *See* **absolute address.**

direct broadcast satellite   *See* **DBS.**

directional pad   *Abbreviated* **D-pad.**   A small pad located on a game controller that can be pressed at points around its center to indicate direction. Users usually manipulate directional pads with the thumb.

direct memory access   *See* **DMA.**

directory   An object maintained by a computer's operating system for organizing files of data, applications, and other information used by the computer. Directories are generally given names that describe their contents. They may contain files and other directories; these other directories are considered lower in the directory structure and are called subdirectories. On Macintosh computers, directories are known as folders and may contain both subfolders and files.

directory tree   A tree structure used to organize the files on a storage device.

Direct Stream Digital   *See* **DSD.**

direct-view television   A television that uses a cathode-ray tube to display an image. Direct-view televisions can display both progressive and interlaced video, and many are HDTV-compatible. Most standard TV sets are direct-view televisions. *Compare* **rear-projection television.**

DirectX   A collection of APIs for Microsoft Windows that allows programmers to write multimedia programs such as games without regard to the specific graphics and sound hardware used to run them. Programs written using DirectX technology often perform faster and look and sound better when run on systems that have DirectX installed.

disc An alternate spelling of disk used mostly in reference to optical disks. *See* **disk.**

discussion group A public forum on the Internet where multiple users can share and discuss ideas about a topic.

dish antenna A transmitter or receiver of electromagnetic energy, especially microwaves or radiowaves, consisting of a concave parabolic reflector.

disk or **disc** The most common medium for permanent data storage. The two types of disks are magnetic disks and optical disks. A magnetic disk is a round plate, as of plastic or metal, covered with a magnetic coating. Data is encoded on the disk by magnetizing microscopically small iron particles that are scattered throughout the coating. Magnetic disks include floppy disks, hard disks, and removable cartridges.

Optical disks are composed of a layer of reflective material encased in a protective plastic coating. Data is encoded by a pattern of tiny pits or of aligned metal alloy crystals on the reflective layer. The data is read by means of a laser. The laser light is scattered by the pits or crystals, but when it strikes the flat reflective surfaces between them, it is reflected directly into a detector. Optical disks include CDs and DVDs.

The word *disk* was originally spelled with a *k,* while the *c* spelling arose later as a learned spelling derived from the word's Latin source, *discus*. With the advent of electronic technology, the spellings began to be sorted out by function; the spelling *disc* was used to refer to the new method of making phonograph recordings on a flat plate (as opposed to Edison's cylindrical drum), and the *c* spelling became conventional for this sense. With the advent of flat magnetic storage devices, the spelling *disk* was pervasive among computer scientists, becoming conventionalized in such compounds as *hard disk*. Computer specialists preferred the familiar *k* spelling, while people in the music industry, who saw the shiny circular plates as another form of phonograph record, referred to them as *compact discs*. *See also* **magneto-optical disk.**

disk cache RAM that is set aside to speed access to data on a disk. When data is read from a disk, a copy is stored in the disk cache. When the CPU requests data from the disk, the disk cache is first checked to see if it contains the necessary data. If it does, the data can be sent back to the CPU much more quickly than if it has to be read from the disk. Typically, data in the disk cache that has not been used recently is overwritten with new data, under the assumption that the most recently used data is most likely to be used again soon. Most hard disks come with a dedicated cache, although portions of a computer's main memory can sometimes be used as a disk cache. *Also called* **disk buffer.**

disk cloning   *See* **ghosting** (sense 2).

disk crash   A major problem with a hard disk, especially a problem with the physical mechanism, such as a head crash. Disk crashes often result in a loss of data.

disk drive   A hardware device that reads data stored on a disk and writes data to the disk for storage. Disk drives include hard drives, floppy drives, and optical drives. A hard drive reads hard disks, a floppy drive reads floppy disks, and an optical drive reads optical disks.

Disk drives are distinguished by their data storage capacity and access times (the amount of time it takes the drive to access a single piece of data). Optical drives can store much more data than floppy or hard drives, but are slower, and they generally cannot read and write data in quick succession, as magnetic drives can. Hard drives are faster and have larger storage capacities than floppy drives. Techniques such as disk caching and interleaving are used to improve the performance of disk drives. *See also* **cache.**

diskette   *See* **floppy disk.**

disk fragmentation   The fragmentation of files on a disk.

diskless workstation   A personal computer that has a CPU and RAM, but does not have its own disk drive. Diskless workstations store data and program files on a network file server, and usually serve as thin clients, which means that a lot of the processing required by applications is done by a server. *See also* **thin client.**

disk operating system   *See* **DOS.**

disk optimizer   A program that defragments the files on a disk.

disk pack   A removable device used in early disk drives consisting of a stack of several magnetic disks encased as a unit.

disk sector   A set of sectors on a formatted disk that lie on separate tracks but within a single wedge-shaped section of the disk.

display   **1.** The part of a monitor, television, computer, handheld, or other device that displays visible content. Common display types include CRT, LCD, LCoS, DLP, OLED, and plasma. **2.** A device, such as a monitor or television, for displaying visible content.

display adapter   *See* **graphics card.**

display rate   In video transmission, the number of frames displayed per second. Higher display rates can produce clearer and more accurate depictions of moving images than lower display rates. Low display rates may also produce an unwanted flickering effect.

distance learning   Education in which students take academic courses by accessing instructional materials and communicating with the instructor over the Internet.

distortion   The alteration of the original form of a signal representing an image, a sound, a waveform, or other information. Distortion is generally an unwanted alteration; deliberate alterations of a signal into a form from which the original signal can be restored are not thought of as distortion.

Distortion has a wide variety of causes. Nearly every point at which a signal is processed or transmitted is susceptible to it. One very common cause of audio distortion is a signal level that is so high that a device using the signal, such as a speaker, an amplifier, or an analog-to-digital converter, cannot accommodate it. A change in the shape of an image resulting from or as if from the image passing through a lens, as in pincushion distortion, is common in video distortion.

Distortion is sometimes deliberately introduced in audio signals, especially electric guitar signals, in order to alter or add to the richness and tone of the sound. *See also* **artifact.**

distributed processing   The use of multiple computers, communicating over a network, to perform a single task or a set of related tasks. Distributed processing can take place in parallel, with multiple computers running a single application and jointly accomplishing a single task. However, distributed processing can also involve distributing parts of a workload to different computers running different applications. *See also* **cluster, grid computing, parallel processing.**

distribution   A collection of related programs that are packaged together. Different distributions of the same product may include different programs, or different versions of the same programs. For example, distributions of Linux all include a version of the Linux kernel and Gnu system tools, but different desktop environments and other software.

dithering   Any of various signal processing techniques in which a small amount of noise is introduced into a signal in order to mitigate unwanted distortion or artifacts that result from digitizing the signal.

In digital audio, for example, digital signals often undergo mathematical manipulation to adjust for volume or tone. This manipulation can result in round-off errors, since most digital audio equipment uses a limited number of bits to represent the signal, and these repeated errors result in tonal distortion of the signal. Adding a small amount of randomness, or *dither,* to the signal makes the round-off errors less consistent; the signal thus may sound noisier or hissier, but will not sound as distorted. Dithering also may help reduce the bandwidth needed to transmit signals, since the degradation of signal quality that results from sending fewer bits of information can be partly overcome.

In computer graphics, the values of adjacent dots or pixels can be alternated to create the illusion of intermediate values. Thus, in printing color or displaying color on a computer screen, making adjacent dots or pixels different colors gives the effect of a third color. For example, a printed field of alternating cyan blue and yellow dots appears green. On a monochrome display or printer, altering the ratio of black to white dots can create the illusion of a particular shade of gray. Thus dithering can give the effect of more colors or shades of gray on a small display, such as that found on many cell phones, than that display is capable of displaying. As in the case of audio dithering, dithering images also allows the transmission of much smaller image files than would otherwise be required for images of acceptable quality. *See also* **antialiasing, banding, halftone.**

DivX A codec developed by DivX, Inc. for the storage and transmission of digital video over the Internet. DivX uses MPEG-4 technology to compress high quality video up to seven times more efficiently than MPEG-2. DivX files usually have the *.avi* extension. *See also* **XviD.**

DL *Abbreviation of* **dual-layer.**

.dll The file extension for DLLs.

DLL *Abbreviation of* **dynamic link library.** A library file used on Windows operating systems containing executable routines that can be used by any program. Programs that use routines from a DLL can only run if that DLL is installed. DLL files have the *.dll* extension. *See also* **shared library.**

DLP **1.** *Abbreviation of* **digital light processing.** A display type used in projectors and rear-projection televisions. A DLP display reflects light onto the screen with an array of tiny mirrors (each corresponding to a pixel) arranged on a semiconductor chip. The mirrors tilt toward and away from the light source thousands of times per second. The brightness of a pixel is controlled by the proportion of time that its mirror reflects the light source.

Most DLPs color the light using a red, green, and blue filter mounted on each of the mirrors. High-end DLPs, however, use a separate chip for each color, producing three monochrome images, which are then combined into the multicolored image that is projected on the screen. Some people notice an artifact caused by the color filters on single-chip DLPs called the *rainbow effect*. DLPs are known for their high contrast ratio.

2. A projector or rear-projection television that uses such a display.

DMA **1.** *Abbreviation of* **direct memory access.** The ability to transfer data between main memory and a peripheral device, such as a disk drive, without involving the CPU. Most modern computers contain a simple processor, called a *DMA controller,* that allows data to be transferred to and from a peripheral without slowing down the CPU. **2.** *See* **Ultra DMA.**

DNS *Abbreviation of* **Domain Name System.** The system for using textual domain names, rather than numerical IP addresses, to identify computers and services on the Internet. The DNS consists primarily of a system for assigning and registering domain names, a database that stores the IP addresses associated with each domain name, and a protocol that programs use to communicate when translating domain names into IP addresses. When the name of a web server is typed into a web browser, for example, it must first be translated into an IP address so the web browser can contact the web server. The operating system translates the name by using the DNS protocol to get information from the DNS database. Different parts of the DNS database are stored on different name servers throughout the Internet. *See also* **domain name, name server.**

DNS server *See* **name server.**

.doc The file extension typically used for files created by Microsoft Word, Microsoft's word processing program.

docking station A device to which a laptop, digital audio player, PDA, or other portable device is connected for stationary use. Docking stations make it easy to connect a small portable device to stationary devices, such as speakers, desktop computers, monitors, or keyboards. They usually provide a power supply that can recharge the batteries of the portable device. Docking stations for laptops typically allow the laptop to be used as a desktop computer by connecting it to a keyboard, monitor, or network, as well as peripherals such as printers. *Also called* **dock.**

document A piece of work that is created with an application such as a word processor and is given its own name.

documentation The set of instructions, tutorials, and technical information that comes with a program or a piece of hardware. Documentation may be in the form of printed manuals, but often it is provided in electronic form. Software often also has an online help system that can be summoned from the application with a help command or by pressing a designated help key.

document type definition   *See* **DTD.**

DOI   *Abbreviation of* **digital object identifier.**

Dolby Digital   *See* **AC-3.**

domain   **1.** On the Internet, a set of IP addresses associated with the same domain name. *See also* **domain name. 2.** On a LAN, a group of computers that are administered together, usually sharing a common group of users and a common security policy.

domain name   A unique alphanumeric string that identifies a computer, service, organization, or domain on the Internet. Fully qualified domain names, such as *www.hmco.com,* can be translated into IP addresses, and thus serve as easy-to-remember identifiers for individual computers or services such as websites. Each fully qualified domain name is made up of at least two character strings connected by dots. The rightmost character string is a top-level domain name. Examples are *com,* designed to be used for commercial enterprises, *edu,* used for educational organizations, and *uk,* used for individuals and organizations in the United Kingdom. Since each top-level domain is controlled by a different registry that makes its own rules as to how names are assigned within its domain, not all top-level domains are reliable indicators of the nature or location of the individual or organization to whom a name is assigned. A domain name such as *hmco.com* is a second-level domain name. Second-level domain names must be registered by an organization or individual with the registry that controls the top-level domain. The organization or individual can then either associate a computer or service with the second-level name or create and register further names by adding character strings to the left, separated by periods. *See also* **DNS, hostname, IP address.**

Domain Name System   *See* **DNS.**

dongle   **1.** *See* **flash drive. 2.** A hardware device used to discourage the copying of certain software. A dongle must be physically attached to the computer (usually by being plugged into an I/O port) in order for the software to run on that computer, so that even if the software is copied onto many machines, only those machines with a dongle can run the software. Dongles are usually provided along with the software or bought for a fee.

doorway page   *See* **portal.**

DOS   *Abbreviation of* **disk operating system.**   An operating system developed by IBM for PC-compatible computers in which users may type written commands in a text box. Microsoft Windows was originally a graphical user interface (GUI) for DOS, but later developed into a full-fledged operating system based around DOS.

DoS attack   *See* **denial-of-service attack.**

dot   **1.** The basic unit of composition for an image produced by a device that prints text or graphics on paper. *See also* **dots per inch. 2.** A period, as used in URLs and email addresses to separate strings of words, as in *www.hmco.com.*

dot-com   *adj.* **1.** Relating to business conducted on the Internet, as in *dot-com* advertising. **2.** Relating to a company whose products or services deal with or are sold on the Internet, as in *dot-com brokerage firm.*

   n. A company whose products and services are a part of the Internet industry.

dot crawl   A type of artifact that occurs mainly in composite video signals in both PAL and NTSC systems, but is also present in some digital sources. Dot crawl appears as blocks of irregularly colored animated dots around the transitions between colors. Dot crawl cannot be completely eliminated once it has been introduced into a video signal. *Also called* **cross-luma.**

dot-matrix printer   An impact printer that prints text and graphic images by hammering the ends of pins against an ink ribbon, producing characters and images made up of a patterns of dots. Dot-matrix printers are relatively cheap, relatively fast, and able to print graphics. They are noisier, slower, and have poorer print quality than inkjet and laser printers, and are no longer in common use. *See also* **printer.**

dot pitch   A measure of the distance between the pixels of a display or digital camera. Traditionally dot pitch is measured diagonally between like-colored subpixels, but some manufacturers measure it horizontally. A typical high-resolution CRT display has a diagonal dot pitch of 0.25 mm and a horizontal dot pitch of 0.21 mm. *Also called* **pixel pitch.**

dots per inch   *Abbreviated* **dpi. 1.** A measure of the resolution of a printer or printed image; the more dots per inch, the higher the resolution. A laser printer with a resolution of 1200 dpi can print 1200 dots per linear inch, or 1.44 million (1200 $\times$ 1200) dots per square inch. Note that printer resolutions are not comparable to the resolutions of other devices. For instance, an image printed at a resolution of 1200 dots per inch will not be as finely detailed as an image displayed on a computer monitor at 1200 pixels per inch. *See also* **resolution. 2.** *See* **samples per inch. 3.** *See* **pixels per inch.**

double-click   To click a mouse button twice in quick succession without moving the mouse. Double-clicking is usually a way of initiating a specific action such as opening a file. Most operating systems let users set the double-click speed, which indicates the longest interval between clicks that the computer will interpret as a double-click rather than as two separate clicks.

double data rate   *See* **DDR.**

double-density disk   A floppy disk that can hold twice the data of the now obsolete single-density disk. Double-density 3.5-inch disks hold 720,000 bytes of data; double-density 5.25-inch disks hold 360,000 bytes of data. Double-density disks have less data storage capacity than high-density disks.

double-sided disk   A disk, such as a CD, hard disk, or floppy disk, that can hold data on both its top and bottom surfaces.

down   Malfunctioning or not operating, especially temporarily. Used especially of computers, servers, networks, or connections. *Compare* **up.**

Down-arrow key   A key used to move the cursor down one line of text, or to scroll up the contents of a window so that the lower portions of its contents come into view. *Compare* **Up-arrow key.**

download   To transfer a copy of a file from a central source to a local computer or other device. For example, files can be downloaded from websites or a network file server to a computer, or from a desktop computer to a handheld device.

downmix   To mix a multichannel audio recording, such as one with five channels, in order to create a compatible version with fewer channels. Downmixing a recording optimizes it for playback on devices that play fewer channels.

downsampling   The process of resampling a digital signal at a lower sampling rate. Downsampling is used in graphics, video, and audio applications to reduce the size of files or accommodate the signal to the rate required by some application or device. *Compare* **upsampling.** *See also* **interpolation.**

downward compatible   *See* **backward compatible.**

D-pad   *Abbreviation of* **directional pad.**

dpi   *Abbreviation of* **dots per inch.**

draft-quality   Relating to or producing low-quality printed output suitable for drafts of documents.

drag   To hold down the mouse button while moving the mouse. In many word processing programs, for instance, dragging the mouse selects a block of text. On a computer desktop, an icon or graphics object can be moved from one part of the screen to another by dragging it.

drag-and-drop Relating to an operation that is executed by dragging an item (such as an icon representing a document) and placing it elsewhere in the GUI (such as on a program icon or in the Trash Can or Recycle Bin). Most operating systems allow users to manage files using drag-and-drop, as well as open files in a specified program or perform other functions.

DRAM *Abbreviation of* **dynamic RAM.** A type of RAM chip that stores information as electrical charges in very small capacitors. Because such capacitors hold a charge for only a very short time, DRAM must be periodically refreshed and is thus slower than SRAM (static RAM). However, DRAM requires fewer components and is thus cheaper to make. Most RAM in personal computers is DRAM. DRAM is pronounced DEE-ram. *See also* **SDRAM.**

draw program A graphics application that allows the user to create line art using objects such as lines, circles, squares, and Bézier curves. Because draw programs use vector graphics, objects created in draw programs can be sized and scaled without distortions and moved without affecting surrounding objects. Some draw programs allow the creation of objects modeled in three dimensions. *See also* **paint program.**

drive Any mass storage device for a computer. The term *drive* originally referred to a device, such as a disk drive or tape drive, containing a motor that moved a removable magnetic storage medium such as a tape or a disk. Now the term is applied to hard disks, optical disks such as CDs and DVDs, and flash drives.

drive bay *See* **bay.**

driver **1.** *See* **device driver. 2.** The component of a speaker that vibrates to produce audible sound waves. *See also* **speaker.**

DRM **1.** *Abbreviation of* **digital rights management. 2.** *Abbreviation of* **Digital Radio Mondiale.**

drop-down menu *See* **pull-down menu.**

dropout **1.** A segment of magnetic tape on which expected information is absent. **2.** A loss of data due to an interruption in a transmission.

DSD *Abbreviation of* **Direct Stream Digital.** A method developed by Sony and Philips for digitizing analog signals, used for encoding audio data on Super Audio CDs.

DSL *Abbreviation of* **digital subscriber line.** Any of various technologies for creating high-bandwidth network connections over standard telephone lines. DSL systems use a special-purpose modem to create a permanent network connection, typically between a subscriber and an Internet service provider. DSL technologies transmit data over phone lines without interfering with voice service. *See also* **ADSL.**

DSP   **1.** *Abbreviation of* **digital signal processing.**   The manipulation of digital signals, typically audio and image data, while they are in digital form. Digital signal processing is often used to reduce noise in a signal and can also be used to encrypt or decrypt a signal and perform other kinds of modifications, such as adding audio effects. **2.** *Abbreviation of* **digital signal processor.**   A coprocessor that is designed to perform efficient digital signal processing. DSPs are typically embedded in devices that rely on processing signals quickly, such as sound cards, cell phones, and digital TVs, and are dedicated to performing only those operations that require digital signal processing.

DSRC   *Abbreviation of* **dedicated short-range communications.**   A protocol for wireless communication between vehicles and stationary devices located on or near the roadside. DSRC allows for the transmission of data over ranges up to 1 kilometer (0.6 miles) and is primarily used for electronic toll collection and in systems that monitor commercial vehicles. *See also* **telematics.**

D-subminiature connector   *Abbreviated* **D-sub connector** or **DB connector.** A standard plug and socket used by a computer's parallel ports, serial ports, and VGA connectors. D-subminiature plugs consist of a number of pins arranged in two, three, or four rows and circumscribed by a D-shaped band, which fits over a protruding socket. The body of the plug and socket come in five different sizes, designated *DE, DA, DB, DC,* and *DD,* with DE connectors being the smallest and DDs the largest. The number of pins are usually indicated following the size, as in *DE-9* and *DB-25.* Note that sometimes the number is listed after the abbreviation *DB* standing for *D-subminiature,* as in *DB-9. Also called* **D connector.** *See figure at* **connector.**

DTD   *Abbreviation of* **document type definition.**   A formal definition of the structure of a given type of SGML or XML document. The DTD states the constraints on the structure of the document and the kind of data each of its components may contain.

DTS   *Abbreviation of* **Digital Theater Systems.**   The trade name for an audio codec originally developed by the company of the same name, for use in the soundtracks of theatrical films, but used increasingly in DVD-Video and DVD-Audio disks. Like Dolby Digital, DTS contains up to six channels but compresses audio signals at a lower rate, losing less data. *See also* **AC-3.** *See* Table 3 at **codec.**

DTT or **DTTV**   *Abbreviations of* **digital terrestrial television.**

DTV   *Abbreviation of* **digital television.**

dual-band phone   A cell phone that transmits at two different frequency bands. Dual-band phones usually transmit at 800 MHz and 1900 MHz, frequencies that are primarily used in North and South America. While networks at both frequencies are fairly widespread in North America, there are still areas in which only one of the two bands are available, so dual-band phones allow users access to cell phone service in a wider geographic area.

dual-channel   Relating to memory controllers that allow two communication paths between a computer's CPU and working memory. Computers with dual-channel memory controllers speed memory access and thus make better use of faster processors.

dual-core   Relating to chips that contain two CPUs or GPUs. *See also* **multicore, multiprocessing.**

dual-display   Relating to a computer or graphics card that can simultaneously display images on two monitors.

dual-head   Dual-display.

dual inline memory module   *See* **DIMM.**

dual inline package   *See* **DIP.**

dual-layer   *Abbreviated* **DL.** Relating to a technique for optical disk recording that makes it possible to write two layers of data on a single side. The second layer is accessed by refocusing the read laser through the top layer. With this dual-layer recording, the storage capacity of a single DVD can be almost doubled to 8.5 GB, in contrast to 4.7 GB of capacity on a single-layer DVD.

dual-mode phone   A cell phone that can transmit and receive using Wi-Fi as well as GSM standards. Dual-mode phones can use VoIP technology to route calls over the Internet when the phone is near a wireless access point.

dual-monitor   Dual-display.

dual-ported RAM   RAM that can be accessed simultaneously by two independent buses. Dual-ported RAM is commonly used on video cards, where it is connected to both a microprocessor and to video display circuitry. In such an application, using dual-ported RAM increases processing speed because the microprocessor can write data to one part of memory while the display circuitry can read data from another part. *See also* **VRAM.**

dumb   Having little or no capability for processing data. *Compare* **smart.**

104

dumb terminal A terminal that has no internal microprocessor and thus no processing power independent of the computer it is used to interact with. *Compare* **smart terminal.**

dump To transfer data from one location to another often without reformatting it, usually for the purposes of debugging. For example, the contents of main memory or the screen can sometimes be dumped to a file. *See also* **screen shot.**

duplex Any mode of two-way transmission, especially over the same channel of communication. *Compare* **simplex.** *See also* **full duplex, half duplex.**

duplex printing A printing process in which the printer prints on both sides of a piece of paper. Many printers are capable of duplex printing. *Compare* **simplex printing.**

DV **1.** *See* **digital video** (sense 1). **2.** A digital videotape format that stores up to 720 lines of horizontal resolution. DV tapes have a 1/4-inch magnetic tape that is typically housed in a small *miniDV,* or *S,* cassette (approximately 2.56 × 1.89 inches). Video can be recorded on DV tapes using either the NTSC or PAL television standards. NTSC, which is the predominant standard in North America, allows approximately 480 lines of vertical resolution. DV uses a YCbCr color model and samples video data at a rate of 13.5 MHz for the luminance component (Y) and 3.375 MHz for the chrominance component (Cb and Cr), which results in a ratio between sampling rates of 4 : 1 : 1. Compressed DV video (including audio and video data) requires approximately 3.6 MB of storage space per second, or 12.9 GB per hour.

DVB *Abbreviation of* **Digital Video Broadcasting.** A digital television transmission standard based on the MPEG-2 standard. DVB supports all major display formats including SDTV, EDTV, and HDTV. DVB is used worldwide for satellite and cable broadcasting and outside the United States for terrestrial television. *Compare* **ATSC.**

DVD *Abbreviation of* **Digital Versatile Disk** or **Digital Video Disk.** An optical disk that can store seven times as much data as a compact disk. Using the MPEG-2 compression format, DVDs are capable of storing a full-length movie up to 133 minutes long in high-quality video and audio. DVD drives are also able to read conventional CD-ROMs and music CDs. DVDs have a capacity of 4.7 GB, 8.5 GB, or 17 GB. Write-once DVD-R (recordable) drives can record a 3.9 GB DVD-R disk that can be read on any DVD drive.

DVDs can be recorded in all the major television formats including NTSC (used in North America), PAL, and SECAM, but must be played on a compatible DVD player and television (most televisions sold in the United States can only display NTSC signals). In addition, DVD publishers typically encrypt DVDs in such a way that they can only be displayed on DVD players sold in one of six regions of the world. The United States and Canada are in region 1, most of Europe is in region 2, and Central and South America are in region 4. Only DVD players labeled *region-free* or *multiregion* are capable of playing DVDs from multiple regions. *See also* **compact disk, data compression, regional management.**

DVD-Audio   A format that delivers high-fidelity audio content on DVD. Because of its higher storage capacity, a DVD can store more music than a CD, as well as provide additional channels for spatial sound reproduction, optional text, images, videos, and menus.

DVD player   A device for recording and playing back video images and sound on a DVD. DVD players are designed to correct for small errors which are often present on DVDs. DVD players are often programmed to play only DVDs that have been sold in a specific region of the world. Many progressive-scan DVD players can deinterlace signals and reverse the process of 3 : 2 pulldown to restore the video to its original frame rate of 24 frames per second. *See also* **regional management.**

DVD-R   *Abbreviation of* **DVD-Recordable.**   A DVD onto which data can be written only once. DVD-Rs are typically less expensive than DVD-RW disks and are commonly used for recording movies and making permanent backup disks.

DVD-ROM   A DVD containing data that cannot be erased or overwritten. DVD-ROM drives lack the ability to burn DVDs.

DVD-RW   *Abbreviation of* **DVD-Rewritable.**   A DVD that allows data to be written onto it more than once. DVD-RWs are typically more expensive than DVD-Rs and less compatible with conventional set-top DVD players.

DVD+RW   *Abbreviation of* **DVD+Rewritable.**   A rewritable DVD format that combines the capabilities of the DVD-R and DVD-RAM while being compatible with set-top players.

D-VHS   *Abbreviation of* **Digital VHS.**   A digital videotape format based on VHS that is capable of storing high-definition video.

.dvi   A file extension for DVI files.

DVI connector   **1.** *Abbreviation of* **Digital Video Interface connector.**   A video connector used especially to connect flat-panel displays to a digital video source. The DVI standard comprises an analog, digital, and hybrid version, called *DVI-A, DVI-D,* and *DVI-I,* respectively. A DVI plug and socket has between 17 and 29 pins depending on the version. The DVI cable contains a set of four wires: one wire for each component of the red, green, and blue color signals and one for a clock signal. DVI-D and

DVI-I often come with two sets of wires, in which case they are some-times labeled *Dual Link* or *DVI-DL.* Each set of wires has a maximum clock frequency of 165 MHz, meaning that a single-link connector can transmit a 2.6-megapixel image with a refresh rate of 60 Hz. *See figure at* **connector.** *See* Table A on page 356. **2.** *Abbreviation of* **device independent.** A file format used with the TeX word processing system. Files written in the TeX page description language are converted into DVI format for viewing. DVI files are usually converted to PostScript format for printing. They typically have the file extension *.dvi.*

Dvorak keyboard **1.** An alternative keyboard designed for faster typing rates. Unlike the QWERTY keyboard, the Dvorak keyboard is designed so that the letters of most English words fall in the middle row of keys. Common letter positions are placed together for quicker typing. The Dvorak keyboard was designed in the 1930s by August Dvorak and his brother-in-law William Dealy. **2.** A keyboard layout that uses the Dvorak key arrangement.

Dvorak keyboard

DVR *Abbreviation of* **digital video recorder.** A device that records and plays back television broadcasts, storing the video on a hard drive. *Also called* **personal video recorder.**

dye-sublimation printer A photo printer with a heated print head that transfers dye from a sheet of film to paper or other material by vaporizing the dye. The dyes—usually cyan, magenta, yellow, and a clear coating—are applied in separate layers which overlap and blend on the page, thereby producing a continuous image in which the pixels are not discernible.

Dynamic Data Exchange *See* **DDE.**

Dynamic HTML *Abbreviated* **DHTML.** A combination of technologies by which web servers generate webpages on demand. Dynamic HTML is usually interactive, meaning that user input changes the webpage. Client-side scripting and CSS are the most common methods used for Dynamic HTML.

dynamic link library *See* **DLL.**

dynamic RAM *See* **DRAM.**

dynamic range   **1.** A measure of the range between the highest level and lowest discernible or detectable level of an audio or video signal, usually expressed in decibels. For audio signals, the value of the lowest level is given either by a reference voltage or current or by the minimal audible signal level. **2.** The capacity of a piece of signal processing equipment, such as audio or visual equipment, to process a range of signal levels, expressed as the range of the signal levels it can handle without loss or significant distortion. High dynamic ranges indicate the capacity to handle very high signal levels or a wide range of levels.

dynamic range compression   The process of limiting the range between the highest and lowest discernible levels of an audio or video signal. For example, dynamic range compression is used in the night listening mode of stereo systems, so that when the volume is turned to its highest setting, the audio signal does not exceed a preset threshold.

E911   *Abbreviation of* **enhanced 911.**   A service provided to cell phone and VoIP customers ensuring that calls to 911 from cell phones and VoIP phones are forwarded to public safety agencies and that the agencies are given accurate information about the phone number, identity, and especially the location of the caller. Telecommunications companies are required by law to provide E911 service.

earbud   **1.** A headphone that fits in the auricle of the ear. Earbuds are lightweight and easily portable. **2.** *See* **canalphone.**

earphone   A small speaker worn inside or near the ear, such as a headphone, earbud, or canalphone.

Easter egg   A hidden feature that is embedded within a computer application, video game, DVD, or CD. Examples of Easter eggs include bonus scenes or audio tracks on DVDs. Easter eggs are usually accessed by following a sequence of keystrokes or other actions. Sometimes they appear spontaneously or at a date and time predetermined by the engineer or software developer.

EB   *Abbreviation of* **exabyte.**

EBCDIC *Abbreviation of* **Extended Binary-Coded Decimal Interchange Code.** A character encoding developed by IBM and used primarily in mainframe computers. EBCDIC is pronounced EBB-see-dik.

e-cash Any of various privately issued currencies used to conduct electronic transactions. *Also called* **digital cash.**

ECC *Abbreviation of* **error correction code** or **error checking and correction.** Relating to memory modules that contain extra circuitry for detecting errors in stored data. ECC memory stores parity information along with the data in such a way that external hardware or software can not only detect small errors in the stored data, but correct them. Not all computer systems are capable of using ECC memory.

ECD *Abbreviation of* **enhanced compact disk.**

Ecma International A computer industry association that develops and maintains standards for computing and household technology. Ecma was responsible for the first standard for the physical structure of a CD-ROM and recently developed the ECMAScript standard, which incorporates JavaScript and JScript. Until 1994, Ecma was known as the European Computer Manufacturer's Association.

ECMAScript A scripting language based on JavaScript and JScript which has been made into a standard by Ecma International. ECMAScript contains the major features of both JavaScript and JScript, so both are considered compliant with the standard.

e-commerce Commerce that is transacted or conducted electronically, as over the Internet.

EDGE *Abbreviation of* **Enhanced Data rates for GSM Evolution.** A standard for transmitting and receiving digital data on GSM cellular networks. EDGE allows users of cell phones, PDAs, and other mobile devices to communicate with the Internet and send and receive text and multimedia. It is an enhancement to the HSCSD and GPRS protocols which allows transmission rates up to 384 Kbps.

edge connector A set of metal contacts on the edge of an expansion card that fits into an expansion slot on a motherboard.

EDI *Abbreviation of* **electronic data interchange.** The set of standards for the transmission of business documents and data over the Internet. These protocols specify the formats companies use for invoices, orders, and other exchanges of information, thereby reducing paperwork and miscommunication.

EDP *Abbreviation of* **electronic data processing.** *See* **data processing.**

EDTV *Abbreviation of* **enhanced-definition television.** A class of television display formats with the same resolution and aspect ratio as SDTV formats but with double the number of frames displayed each second. Common EDTV formats include 480p60 and 576p50. The first number refers to the vertical resolution in visible lines per frame, the *p* to progressive scanning, and the second number to the fields or frames per second. *See* Table B on page 357.

.edu A top-level domain operated by Educause and used by educational institutions, primarily those in the United States. Only accredited post-secondary institutions are allowed to register domain names in the .edu domain.

EEPROM *Abbreviation of* **electrically erasable programmable read-only memory.** Nonvolatile memory that is similar to EPROM, but can be erased by applying an electrical charge. EEPROM differs from flash memory in that it takes much longer to write data to it. It is often used to store the BIOS in a personal computer.

EFF *Abbreviation of* **Electronic Frontier Foundation.**

EFT *Abbreviation of* **electronic funds transfer.**

EGA *Abbreviation of* **Enhanced Graphics Adapter.** A graphics card and video standard developed by IBM and introduced in 1984. EGA is capable of displaying 16 colors from a palette of 64 and has a resolution of 640 horizontal pixels by 350 vertical pixels. EGA, which represented an advance over CGA technology, is now also obsolete, having been replaced by VGA and SVGA.

EIDE *Abbreviation of* **Enhanced IDE.**

802.11 *See* **IEEE 802.**

EISA *Abbreviation of* **Extended Industry Standard Architecture.** A bus architecture used in older PC-compatible computers that has a 32-bit data path. The EISA architecture is downward compatible with the earlier 16-bit ISA cards. EISA is pronounced EE-suh.

electrically erasable programmable read-only memory *See* **EEPROM.**

electronic bulletin board *See* **message board.**

electronic data interchange *See* **EDI.**

electronic data processing *See* **data processing.**

electronic document *See* **document.**

Electronic Frontier Foundation An advocacy organization working on issues relating to civil liberties and copyright law as they apply to digital communication technologies.

electronic funds transfer   *Abbreviated* **EFT.** The transfer of money using an electronic system that automatically subtracts money from one account and deposits it in another. Examples of such transfers include ATM withdrawals, purchases made with a debit card or check card, and preauthorized payments.

electronic mail   *See* **email.**

electronic program guide   *Abbreviated* **EPG.** A television menu that lists movies or television shows that are scheduled for broadcast or are available for ordering. Electronic program guides can be manipulated using a remote control. *Also called* **interactive program guide.**

electronic serial number   *See* **ESN.**

electrostatic discharge   *Abbreviated* **ESD.** The movement of static electrical charge that has built up on one object to another object. Electrostatic charge commonly builds up on certain materials that rub against other materials, as in the contact of clothing or shoes with rugs or other materials. Electrostatic discharge is usually sudden, and the electric current flow that results can permanently damage delicate electronic circuitry such as computer memory and microprocessors. Antistatic devices are often used to reduce this risk when contact with computer circuitry is necessary.

electrostatic speaker   A speaker that produces sound by vibrating a large flexible panel sandwiched between two conductive plates. Electrostatic speakers are most commonly employed as tweeters. *See also* **speaker.**

element   A piece of data in an XML or SGML document. An element consists of a tag combined with the data it is tagging.

EM64T   A 64-bit microprocessor architecture developed by Intel and based on the x86 architecture. *See also* **x86-64.**

emacs   An open-source text editor commonly used in Linux and Unix environments, and available for most operating systems. While emacs has a GUI that includes menus and command buttons, it is primarily used as a command-based editor. Many add-ons for emacs are available free of charge on the Web, making it a popular tool for programmers and for editing files in computer languages such as HTML and LaTeX.

email or **e-mail** **1.** An electronic message in a special form for transmission over a computer network, especially the Internet. Each email message specifies the network address of each intended recipient of the message, and includes optional information about the subject of the mail as well as other information about the message. Email clients may sort incoming email according to sender, subject, size, and other criteria.

111

Email typically consists of text, but can contain any kind of digital data, such as pictures, audio, or video. Often, information other than the basic text message of the email, such as an image or audio file, is included in the form of an attachment. *See also* **chatroom, instant messaging, text message. 2.** A system, or any part of a system such as special software, for sending, receiving, or viewing email. *See also* **webmail.**

email address   An address to which email can be sent. An email address usually consists of a username and a domain name, joined by an at sign (@); for example, president@whitehouse.gov.

email client   A program used to read and download email from a server computer where it is received and stored, or to transfer email to a server for sending. Some popular email clients are Microsoft Outlook, Pine, and Mozilla Thunderbird. *See also* **IMAP, POP, webmail.**

email spoofing   The disguising of identification data in email, especially the sender's name and email address, so that the email's true source is concealed and difficult to trace. Email spoofing is often used by people who pose as well-established financial institutions in order to trick email recipients into revealing confidential information. *See also* **phish, spam.**

embedded object   A part of a document that is created by a different application than the document and remains in its original format. For example, a multimedia file can be an embedded object in a word processor document or a webpage. *Compare* **linked object.** *See also* **OLE.**

embedded system   A special-purpose computer system that is part of another system or device. Embedded systems are typically made up of a single printed circuit board that contains a microprocessor, main memory, and some form of NVRAM to store programs. They often include special-purpose hardware. Most digital devices, from controls in appliances and automobiles to digital audio players, contain embedded systems. There are many different kinds of embedded systems performing a wide range of different functions, from controlling mechanical components to digital signal processing. *See also* **firmware.**

EMF   *Abbreviation of* **Enhanced Metafile.**   A vector graphics file format developed by Microsoft and commonly used on its Windows operating systems as the format in which documents are sent to a printer. EMF is based on the earlier WMF format.

emoticon   A combination of characters used to represent a human emotion or attitude. Emoticons usually suggest a facial expression and are typically oriented sideways. For example, the characters :-) suggest a happy face or humor (and are often called *smileys*), while the characters :-(suggest an unhappy face or displeasure.

emulate   To behave in the same way as another device or program. For example, a newer computer can be made to emulate an older model in order to run software that is designed for the older computer.

Encapsulated PostScript   *Abbreviated* **EPS.**   A file format for using the PostScript page description language to represent graphic images. Encapsulated PostScript files contain additional information about the size and shape of the image, allowing programs that cannot display standard PostScript images to include Encapsulated PostScript images in documents; even if they do not display, they can be printed on any PostScript-compatible printer. The extension usually used for Encapsulated PostScript files is *.eps.*

encode   To convert data into an alternate format, especially to facilitate transmission or storage. *Compare* **decode.**

encrypt   To encode data in a form that makes it inaccessible to unauthorized users but allows users with a key or password to convert it back to its original state. *See also* **cryptography, decrypt.**

End key   A key that moves the cursor to the end of a line, page, or document, depending on the application that is running. *Compare* **Home key.**

end of line   *Abbreviated* **EOL.**   One or more characters in a text file used to mark the end of a line of text. End of line in Windows and DOS operating systems consists of the carriage-return character followed by the line-feed character. Linux and Unix systems use the line feed by itself, and Macintosh systems prior to OS X use the carriage return by itself. *See also* **control character.**

Energy Star   A set of guidelines for power consumption recommended by the Environmental Protection Agency. For electronic devices, such as computers, televisions, or printers, Energy Star recommends maximum amounts of wattage that each device should use. Products that are compliant with the guidelines are allowed to display the Energy Star logo.

engine   A program, or part of a program, that performs a common, essential task, especially in a video or computer game.

enhanced 911   *See* **E911.**

enhanced compact disk   *Abbreviated* **ECD.**   A compact disk format that stores audio data and multimedia content on the same disk and is playable either in a standard CD player or a CD-ROM drive. Enhanced compact disks use multisession capability to store up to 98 audio tracks in the first session and one CD-ROM XA data track in the second session. A CD player will play the first session and ignore the second, while a CD-ROM drive will play the second session first.

Enhanced Data rates for GSM Evolution   *See* **EDGE.**

enhanced-definition television   *See* **EDTV.**

Enhanced Graphics Adapter   *See* **EGA.**

Enhanced IDE   *Abbreviated* **EIDE.**   An early version of the IDE standard with a higher data-transfer speed than previous versions. The Enhanced IDE standard includes a specification permitting two drives to be attached to each IDE connector on the motherboard. *Also called* **Fast ATA.** *See also* **IDE.**

enhanced keyboard   A 101-key keyboard having a row of function keys at the top rather than on the left side and an extra set of cursor control keys between the main typing keys and the numeric keypad. The enhanced keyboard and the Windows keyboard are the most popular keyboards for PC-compatible computers.

Enhanced Metafile   *See* **EMF.**

Enhanced Small Device Interface   *See* **ESDI.**

enhanced specialized mobile radio   *See* **ESMR.**

Enter key   The key used to enter or confirm a command or other textual input to a computer. Computer programs generally receive and respond to typed commands only after the Enter key is pressed. *Also called* **Return key.**

environment   The set of conditions under which a user operates a computer. The term can refer to a number of different aspects of computer operation. With reference to operating systems, a user can be in the DOS, Windows, Unix, Macintosh, multitasking, or other environment. The term also refers to different types of user interface, such as window or command-line environments.

environment variable   One of various configuration settings for an operating system, determining such parameters as the path to use to find executable files and the location of temporary files.

EOL   *Abbreviation of* **end of line.**

EPG   *Abbreviation of* **electronic program guide.**

EPROM   *Abbreviation of* **erasable programmable read-only memory.**   A type of nonvolatile memory that can hold data for 10 to 20 years and is erased by exposure to ultraviolet light. A special device is required to program EPROM chips. EPROM is commonly used to store the BIOS in personal computers. *See also* **EEPROM.**

.eps   *Abbreviation of* **Encapsulated PostScript.**   A file extension commonly used for Encapsulated PostScript files.

erasable programmable read-only memory   *See* **EPROM.**

erase   To remove information from a storage medium, especially a magnetic tape or disk. *See also* **delete.**

ergonomics   The applied science of equipment design and arrangement, intended to reduce user fatigue and discomfort, especially in the workplace. People who work at computers benefit from the proper ergonomic design and arrangement of monitors, keyboards, input devices, and chairs, to prevent muscular discomfort or physical impairment, such as carpal tunnel syndrome.

error message   A message displayed on the screen to inform the user that the system is unable to carry out an operation or that something is not operating as expected.

ESC   *Abbreviation of* **Escape key.**

escape character   A character that changes the meaning of characters that follow, often used in escape sequences. The character generated by pressing the Escape key is used as the escape character in many escape sequences. However, characters such as the ampersand (&) are used in other contexts, as when including special characters in HTML documents—for example, the character   is coded as an opening ampersand followed by *aelig* and a closing semicolon.

Escape key   *Abbreviated* **ESC.**   A key that, when pressed, generates an escape character.

escape sequence   A string of characters beginning with an escape character, used as a code for a special character or symbol, or to give commands to a device such as a printer.

ESD   *Abbreviation of* **electrostatic discharge.**

ESDI   *Abbreviation of* **Enhanced Small Device Interface.**   An interface standard used in older computers for connecting hard disks, floppy disks, and tape drives.

e-signature   *See* **digital signature.**

ESMR   *Abbreviation of* **enhanced specialized mobile radio.**   A newer, digital version of SMR that allows full-duplex communication so multiple users can speak and hear at the same time. ESMR systems also include paging, fax, and data transmission capabilities.

ESN   *Abbreviation of* **electronic serial number.**   A unique number that identifies some wireless communications devices that do not use GSM technology. Until early 2006, 32-bit ESNs were encoded in the chips of non-GSM cell phones in order to prevent fraudulent users from making calls and billing them to the accounts of legitimate subscribers. New non-GSM phones have a 56-bit MEID. GSM devices use an IMEI for

115

identification. Fraudulent users can clone a phone by illegally duplicating its ESN and MIN. *Compare* **MIN.**

Ethernet   A widely used local area network developed by Xerox, DEC, and Intel. It is used primarily to connect computers, printers, storage media, servers, and other devices, generally within a small area such as a building or building complex, typically using coaxial cable or twisted-pair wiring. Ethernet (pronounced EE-ther-net) uses a bus topology and provides raw data transfer rates of 10 megabits per second. *Compare* **Fast Ethernet, Gigabit Ethernet.** *See* Table C on page 358 and Table D on page 360.

Ethernet card   A network interface card that allows a computer to be con-nected to an Ethernet network. Some Ethernet cards have two jacks so the computer can be connected to Ethernet networks using either twisted-pair or coaxial cables. *Also called* **Ethernet adapter, Ethernet interface card.**

Ethernet interface card   *See* **Ethernet card.**

ETLA   *Abbreviation of* **extended three-letter acronym.**   An acronym con-sisting of four or more characters. *See also* **TLA.**

Eudora   An email client available as freeware or by subscription from Qual-comm, Inc., for both Apple Macintosh and Microsoft Windows platforms. Eudora was formerly quite popular, especially on Macintosh platforms.

European Computer Manufacturer's Association   *Abbreviated* **ECMA.**   *See* **Ecma International.**

even footer   In word processing, a footer that appears on even-numbered pages.

even header   In word processing, a header that appears on even-numbered pages.

evil twin attack   An attempt to collect secure information such as pass-words and credit card numbers from unsuspecting users by setting up a fraudulent "evil twin" wireless access point in the vicinity of an authentic one. If wireless users connect to the fraudulent access point, their com-munications, such as passwords, email, and information they send to websites, is intercepted. *See also* **man-in-the-middle attack, phish.**

exabyte   *Abbreviated* **EB.**   A unit of measurement of computer memory or data storage capacity equal to 1,152,921,504,606,846,976 (2^{60}) bytes. One exabyte equals 1,024 petabytes. Informally, *exabyte* is sometimes used to refer to 1,000,000,000,000,000,000 (one quintillion) bytes.

exception   A problem that occurs during the execution of a computer pro-gram. Some exceptions can cause a program to abort or crash, but others can be handled by the program and may not be noticeable to the user, or they may simply result in an error message.

exclusive OR   *See* **XOR.**

executable file   A file containing a program, or part of a program, that has been compiled for fast execution by a computer. Such files are typically binary files written in the computer's machine language, and can include program files, DLL files, and device drivers.

execute   To run a program, carry out a command, or perform a function.

.exe   An extension commonly used for executable files.

expanded   Relating to type in which characters are spaced farther apart than in ordinary type. Most word-processing programs have a feature that allows users to modify character spacing and create expanded type.

expansion board   *See* **expansion card.**

expansion card   A printed circuit board that plugs into a slot in the computer's motherboard. Common expansion cards include graphics cards, disk drive controllers, sound cards, network interface cards, and modems. Some expansion cards have cable connectors that are exposed to the outside of the case. *Also called* **adapter, expansion board.**

expansion slot   A long, narrow socket on a computer's motherboard, designed to accept the edge connector on an expansion card. Motherboards typically have one expansion slot for a graphics card and several other expansion slots for other devices, such as disk drive controllers, a sound card, or a network interface card.

expert system   A program designed to help solve problems or make decisions in a particular field by modeling some of the knowledge that would be used by an expert. Expert systems typically have a knowledge base consisting of rules of inference; given a set of data defining a particular situation, the expert system derives a range of possible conclusions. For example, expert systems in the field of medicine have been used to derive sets of possible diseases or dysfunctions that are consistent with a patient's symptoms presented to the system as data. Expert systems are sometimes used in financial analysis, engineering, and other fields as well. *See also* **artificial intelligence.**

exploit   A computer program or system designed to take advantage of a particular error or security vulnerability in computers or networks. Exploits may cause damage to software, collect personal information, or make use of computer resources without authorization. *See also* **malware.**

exponent   A number or symbol that indicates the amount of times a number is to be multiplied by itself. Exponents are used to render memory capacity, quantities of pixels, bit rates, and many other quantities. The exponent is usually placed above and to the right of the number being multiplied. In $1,000 = 10^3$, 3 is the exponent of 10, meaning that $1,000 = 10 \times 10 \times 10$. In environments where superscripts cannot be used, such as text format files, exponents are often expressed using the caret symbol; thus $1,000 = 10^3$.

A number with an exponent is said to be *raised to the power* of that exponent; thus in both examples using the exponent 3 above, we read "one thousand equals ten to the power of three," "ten to the third power," or simply "ten to the third."

exponential notation   *See* **scientific notation.**

export   To send data created in one program or system to another one. The first program performs whatever format conversion is necessary so that the second program can read the data. Many word processing programs can export files created in them to other applications in ASCII or other formats. *See also* **import.**

ExpressCard   A PC Card with a 16-pin edge connector and a higher data transfer rate than CardBus PC Cards. ExpressCards come in two sizes, 75×34 mm and 75×54 mm, and have a USB 2.0 or PCI Express interface. *See also* **PC Card.** *See* Table C on page 358.

expression   A combination of symbols that represents a value. An expression can consist of a single value, such as a number or variable. More commonly it consists of one or more values, or operands, and one or more operators, which specify what calculations are to be performed with the operands. Some examples of expressions are 3.1415, $x < 5$, and 2*pi*radius.

Expressions are used in programming, database management systems, and spreadsheets. *See also* **arithmetic expression, formula.**

ext2   *Abbreviation of* **second extended file system.**   A file system commonly used with Linux operating systems. Ext2 is part of the Linux kernel.

ext3   *Abbreviation of* **third extended file system.**   A file system commonly used with Linux operating systems. Ext3 is an extension of ext2 that has security features for keeping track of changes to files, allowing older versions of files to be recovered.

extended ASCII   Any of various character encodings that extend the ASCII character set by assigning codes to 128 more characters. Extended ASCII encodings use eight bits for each character, yielding a total of 2^8, or 256, codes. The additional codes represent non-English characters, mathematical symbols, and symbols for drawing pictures. ISO Latin-1 and Windows-1252 are the most common extended ASCII encodings. *See* Table 5.

118

Table 5   Extended ASCII Character Encodings

Decimal Value	Hexadecimal Value	Windows-1252		ISO Latin-1
128	80	€	(euro sign)	Unused
129	81	Unused		Unused
130	82	‚	(low single quote)	Unused
131	83	ƒ	(guilder sign)	Unused
132	84	„	(low double quote)	Unused
133	85	…	(ellipsis)	Unused
134	86	†	(dagger)	Unused
135	87	‡	(double dagger)	Unused
136	88	^	(circumflex)	Unused
137	89	‰	(permille sign)	Unused
138	8A	Š		Unused
139	8B	‹	(small left angle bracket, used for quotations in some languages)	Unused
140	8C	Œ		Unused
141	8D	Unused		Unused
142	8E	Ž		Unused
143	8F	Unused		Unused
144	90	Unused		Unused
145	91	'	(left single curly quote)	Unused
146	92	'	(right single curly quote)	Unused
147	93	"	(left double curly quote)	Unused
148	94	"	(right double curly quote)	Unused
149	95	•	(bullet)	Unused
150	96	–	(en dash)	Unused
151	97	—	(em dash)	Unused
152	98	~	(small tilde)	Unused
153	99	™	(trademark sign)	Unused
154	9A	š		Unused
155	9B	›	(small right angle bracket, sometimes used for quotations)	Unused

Table 5   Extended ASCII Character Encodings *(continued)*

Decimal Value	Hexadecimal Value	Windows-1252		ISO Latin-1
156	9C	œ		Unused
157	9D	Unused		Unused
158	9E	ž		Unused
159	9F	Ÿ		Unused
160	A0	NBSP	(nonbreaking space; a space that separates two words that must stay on the same line)	Same
161	A1	¡	(inverted exclamation point, used in Spanish)	Same
162	A2	¢	(cent sign)	Same
163	A3	£	(pound sign—currency)	Same
164	A4	¤	(currency sign)	Same
165	A5	¥	(yen sign—currency)	Same
166	A6	¦	(broken vertical bar)	Same
167	A7	§	(section sign)	Same
168	A8	¨	(dieresis)	Same
169	A9	©	(copyright sign)	Same
170	AA	ª		Same
171	AB	«	(left double angle bracket, used for quotations in some languages)	Same
172	AC	¬	(negation sign)	Same
173	AD	SHY	(soft hyphen, for hyphenation that occurs at the end of a line)	Same
174	AE	®	(registered trademark sign)	Same
175	AF	¯	(macron)	Same
176	B0	°	(degree sign)	Same
177	B1	±	(plus-or-minus sign)	Same
178	B2	²	(superscript 2)	Same
179	B3	³	(superscript 3)	Same
180	B4	´	(acute accent)	Same

Table 5 **Extended ASCII Character Encodings** *(continued)*

Decimal Value	Hexadecimal Value	Windows-1252		ISO Latin-1
181	B5	μ	(Greek mu, used as an abbreviation for micro)	Same
182	B6	¶	(paragraph sign, Pilcrow sign)	Same
183	B7	·	(middle dot)	Same
184	B8	¸	(cedilla)	Same
185	B9	¹	(superscript 1)	Same
186	BA	º	(superscript 0)	Same
187	BB	»	(right double angle bracket; used for quotations in some languages)	Same
188	BC	¼		Same
189	BD	½		Same
190	BE	¾		Same
191	BF	¿	(inverted question mark, used in Spanish)	Same
192	C0	À		Same
193	C1	Á		Same
194	C2	Â		Same
195	C3	Ã		Same
196	C4	Ä		Same
197	C5	Å		Same
198	C6	Æ		Same
199	C7	Ç		Same
200	C8	È		Same
201	C9	É		Same
202	CA	Ê		Same
203	CB	Ë		Same
204	CC	Ì		Same
205	CD	Í		Same
206	CE	Î		Same

Table 5 **Extended ASCII Character Encodings** *(continued)*

Decimal Value	Hexadecimal Value	Windows-1252		ISO Latin-1
207	CF	Ï		Same
208	D0	Ð	(capital eth)	Same
209	D1	Ñ		Same
210	D2	Ò		Same
211	D3	Ó		Same
212	D4	Ô		Same
213	D5	Õ		Same
214	D6	Ö		Same
215	D7	×	(multiplication sign)	Same
216	D8	Ø		Same
217	D9	Ù		Same
218	DA	Ú		Same
219	DB	Û		Same
220	DC	Ü		Same
221	DD	Ý		Same
222	DE	þ	(capital thorn)	Same
223	DF	ß		Same
224	E0	à		Same
225	E1	á		Same
226	E2	â		Same
227	E3	ã		Same
228	E4	ä		Same
229	E5	å		Same
230	E6	æ		Same
231	E7	ç		Same
232	E8	è		Same
233	E9	é		Same
234	EA	ê		Same
235	EB	ë		Same
236	EC	ì		Same
237	ED	í		Same

Table 5   Extended ASCII Character Encodings *(continued)*

Decimal Value	Hexadecimal Value	Windows-1252		ISO Latin-1
238	EE	î		Same
239	EF	ï		Same
240	F0	ð	(eth)	Same
241	F1	ñ		Same
242	F2	ò		Same
243	F3	ó		Same
244	F4	ô		Same
245	F5	õ		Same
246	F6	ö		Same
247	F7	÷	(division sign)	Same
248	F8	ø		Same
249	F9	ù		Same
250	FA	ú		Same
251	FB	û		Same
252	FC	ü		Same
253	FD	ý		Same
254	FE	þ	(thorn)	Same
255	FF	ÿ		Same

Extended Binary-Coded Decimal Interchange Code   *See* **EBCDIC.**

Extended Graphics Array   *See* **XGA.**

Extended Industry Standard Architecture   *See* **EISA.**

extended memory   In PC-compatible computers, all main memory with addresses above the first megabyte. While most programs and operating systems can use extended memory directly, DOS and DOS programs can only access extended memory by using special software. *Also called* **XMS memory.** *See also* **conventional memory, upper memory area.**

extended TLA   *See* **ETLA.**

extended VGA   *See* **SVGA.**

extensible markup language   *See* **XML.**

extensible stylesheet language   *See* **XSL.**

123

extension An optional string of characters following the filename and separated from it by a period. Filename extensions can be assigned by programs; for example, *.exe* is a common extension for executable files, *.bat* is used for batch files, and so on. Users sometimes choose descriptive extensions for data files, such as *.ltr* for *letters* or *.jan* for *January*. *Also called* **file extension.**

external bus A bus that connects the CPU and motherboard to external devices. Some external buses connect the motherboard to devices inside the computer, such as expansion cards; some connect it to peripherals outside the computer, such as printers, keyboards, or handheld devices; some can be used with both kinds of devices.

external command In DOS, a command that is defined by an separate utility program rather than the core operating system program. *See also* **internal command.**

external modem A modem, especially one used to make a dial-up connection, that is housed in a case separate from the computer. External modems are usually connected to a computer by a cable attached to a serial port.

extranet An extension of an institution's intranet, especially over the World Wide Web, that provides customers and other outsiders with limited access.

F1, F2, F3 . . . *See* **function key.**

facsimile machine A fax machine.

factory setting *See* **default** (sense 1).

FALSE One of two values used in logic gates, equivalent to the binary value zero. *Compare* **TRUE.** *See* Table E on page 361.

family radio service *See* **FRS.**

FAQ *Abbreviation of* **frequently asked questions.** A list of questions that might be asked by newcomers to a website, Usenet newsgroup, or other source of information or by someone unfamiliar with a given subject, along with the answers to those questions.

Fast ATA *See* **Enhanced IDE.**

Fast Ethernet An Ethernet specification that allows for transmission speeds of up to 100 megabits per second, 10 times faster than the original Ethernet transmission rate. *Also called* **100Base-T.** *Compare* **Gigabit Ethernet.** *See* Table C on page 358 and Table D on page 360.

Fast Infrared *See* **FIR.**

FAT *Abbreviation of* **file allocation table. 1.** The file system developed for MS-DOS and used in most home versions of Windows prior to the release of Windows 2000. While no longer the preferred file system for personal computers, FAT is supported by most Linux and MacOS operating systems, as well as more recent versions of Windows, and is commonly used as the file system on floppy disks, digital cameras, and USB flash drives. It uses a file allocation table to keep track of the location of each file stored on a device. **2.** A file used by some operating systems to store information about the physical location of each piece of every file managed by the system. If the part of the disk containing the file allocation table is erased or corrupted, no files on the disk can be read, even though they may be physically intact.

fatal error An error in program execution that causes the program to terminate.

fat client The client in a client/server architecture in which most of the processing is run on the client. Such a system does not take advantage of the benefits of working on a network, because instead of having programs residing on the server, each computer in the network must have its own copy of every program needed.

fault tolerance A computer system's ability to operate normally, avoiding data loss or severe slowdowns, despite the occurrence of software or hardware errors.

favicon An icon associated with a particular web browser or website, generally appearing in the URL bar of the browser and in references to particular sites within the browser, such as a list of favorite links.

fax or **facsimile 1.** A technology for transmitting copies of documents over the public telephone network. Documents transferred by fax may be printed documents that are scanned, or electronic documents that are converted into a bitmapped image. They are usually printed by the machine that receives them, but they may be stored electronically. **2.** A document transmitted by fax. **3.** A fax machine or fax modem.

fax board A printed circuit board containing components for receiving and sending faxes. Most fax boards can also function as modems. *See also* **fax modem.**

fax machine A device that sends and receives printed pages over telephone lines. The basic components of a fax machine are an optical scanner for digitizing the page, a modem for transmitting the information over a telephone line, and a printer for printing received faxes. Some fax machines are a combination fax, printer, and copier, and some can store faxes electronically and forward them via email.

fax modem   A modem that communicates over a phone line and can also send and receive fax transmissions. Since fax modems don't have optical scanners, documents they transmit must first be stored as files in the computer, either by simply creating a file such as a word processor document, or by using a scanner. Likewise, received documents are written to files before they can be printed.

FCC   *Abbreviation of* **Federal Communications Commission.**

FCC certification   A statement that a given make and model of an electrical device conforms to guidelines set by the Federal Communications Commission. The FCC maintains regulations covering radio frequency interference, the legal use of radio frequency bands, transmission power, specific absorption rate, and other properties of communications devices.

   In personal technology, the limits concerned often regard radio frequency emissions, which can cause interference with other electrical devices. Class A certification signifies that a device is suitable for use in commercial and industrial environments. Class B certification requires lower levels of radio frequency radiation and is for devices to be used in the home. Class B certification does not guarantee that the device will not cause interference to nearby radios and television sets, but the levels should be low enough not to be disruptive under normal use.

F connector   An RF connector that is typically used for cable and satellite television, cable modems, and other high-frequency transmissions.

FDD   *Abbreviation of* **floppy disk drive.**   *See* **floppy drive.**

FDDI   *Abbreviation of* **Fiber Distributed Data Interface.**   A set of standards for LANs using fiber-optic cable, supporting data rates of up to 100 Mbps. FDDI has been largely supplanted by Fast Ethernet.

feathering   Streaking or blurring on the edges of objects in an image. Feathering sometimes occurs as an artifact of deinterlacing.

Federal Communications Commission   *Abbreviated* **FCC.**   The United States government agency that regulates interstate and international communications by wire, cable, radio, television, and satellite.

Federal Information Processing Standard   *See* **FIPS.**

feed   A transmission or locus of transmission of raw data, information, or television programming to one or more recipients for processing, analysis, or distribution. *See also* **web feed.**

126

feed reader   *See* **aggregator.**

female connector   A connector that has one or more receptacles into which pins from a male connector are inserted.

FEP   *Abbreviation of* **front-end processor.**

FHS   *Abbreviation of* **file system hierarchy standard.**   A standard for the location of operating system and other files on Linux and Unix file systems. FHS defines a set of standard directory names and a standard directory structure in which to put common files.

Fiber Distributed Data Interface   *See* **FDDI.**

fiber optics   The transmission of light over optical fibers, especially any of various methods of communicating data via pulses of light transmitted over cables made from such fibers. Data transmission using fiber optics is common in telecommunication—it typically offers greater transmission bandwidth than wire or radio waves, can transmit data for longer distances without degradation, and is much less susceptible to interference.

FidoNet   **1.** A protocol for sending email and newsgroup posts over telephone lines, begun in 1984 by Tom Jennings for use with his Fido BBS. The FidoNet protocol came to be used by thousands of BBSs. **2.** The network of BBSs and other organizations that use the Fidonet protocol. The size of the network is dwindling as BBSs are replaced by similar functions on the Internet.

field   **1.** In a database, a space for a single item of information contained in a record. For example, in a database containing records of names, addresses, and account histories for individual clients, one field might hold the Zip code, another the telephone number, and another the date of last contact. When arranged in a table with each record in a single horizontal row, the fields are displayed in vertical columns. In most database management systems, each field is assigned a specific data type such as text, date, or currency. **2.** A single frame of an interlaced video, composed of only the odd or the even lines of resolution.

field rate   The number of individual fields of an interlaced video that are displayed each second to create the illusion of a moving picture.

file   A sequence of bits treated as a unit in a computer under a single name, called the *filename*. Although a single file is often stored in pieces scattered across many places on a hard disk, a computer retrieves all the pieces and makes them available as a single entity. *See also* **file system.**

file allocation table   *See* **FAT.**

file attribute   A piece of data associated with a file that records information such as the file's creation date, the date it was last modified, and its size, as well as information about permissions, such as who can access or modify the file.

file compression *See* **data compression.**

file extension *See* **extension.**

file format The format that a program uses to encode data in digital form. Some formats are proprietary, and a file so encoded can only be read by a program distributed by the company that owns the format. Some standard formats, such as JPEG, can be read by many kinds of programs.

file fragmentation *See* **fragmentation.**

file management The organization and manipulation of computer files and directories in a file system. Operating systems typically provide programs called *file managers,* which provide file management services, allowing users to delete, copy, move, name, back up, search for, and view files. Independent file managers are also available. *See also* **directory, hierarchical.**

filename A text string used to identify files on a computer system. Different file systems have different rules for the length and composition of filenames. In NTFS, a file system commonly used with Windows, a filename can be up to 254 characters long and must not include any of the following characters:

$$" / \backslash : ? * < > |$$

The file systems used with Mac OS X allow filenames up to 255 characters long, and only exclude the colon (:). Linux and Unix filenames are case-sensitive, while those in Windows are not. HFS+, a file system commonly used with Mac OS X, is not case-sensitive. See also extension.

file server **1.** A computer connected to a network on which users of the network can store files. **2.** A program that provides file storage services to computers on a network. *See also* **client/server network.**

file sharing network A network designed to enable users to share digital files. File sharing networks are typically peer-to-peer networks that operate over an existing physical network such as the Internet, allowing participating computers to connect to each other so users can search for and transfer files, especially music and video files. Napster, one of the first and largest file sharing networks specializing in music, was shut down in 2001 because the music files being shared were protected under copyright law. Napster is now a commercial online music service.

file system **1.** The organizational structure, software, and data that a computer operating system uses to manage files. The file system is responsible for how files are named and how they are stored on and retrieved from different sorts of devices, such as hard disks or CDs. File systems generally represent a set of files to the user as a set of hierarchical directories, even though files are not physically organized this way. File systems include data other than the files themselves, such as file allocation tables. Common file systems include FAT, NTFS, HFS, and ext2. **2.** All the files available on a given computer or device, along with the directory structure used to organize them.

file system hierarchy standard   *See* **FHS.**

file transfer   The process of sending files from one computer to another. For example, when a file is downloaded from the Internet, a copy of the file is transferred to a local computer from a server.

file transfer protocol   *Abbreviated* **FTP. 1.** Any of various communications protocols that enable the transfer of files from one computer to another over a telephone line or network. Unlike more general communications protocols, file transfer protocols only allow sending and receiving the binary data that make up computer files. More advanced protocols allow data to be compressed or encrypted for transmission. FTP (see sense 2 below), SCP, and XMODEM are commonly used file transfer protocols. **2.** *usually* **FTP**   One of these protocols, designed to transfer files over the Internet. Applications, including web browsers, use the FTP protocol to transfer files between computers connected to the Internet. FTP is gradually being replaced by more secure protocols, such as SCP. **3.** *usually* **FTP**   A program found on most Unix and Linux operating systems that uses the FTP protocol to transfer files. The FTP program is a client that connects to a computer running server software.

file type   A designation for a class of files with the same general structure or function. In some operating systems, such as Microsoft Windows, the file type is usually indicated by the file's extension.

fill   *v.* In graphics programs, to fill in an enclosed area with a color or pattern.

   n. In spreadsheet programs, a command that automatically fills a range of cells with a series of values based on a starting value and an algorithm.

filter   **1.** Any of various electronic or optical devices that block some signals, or parts of signals, while allowing other signals or parts of signals to pass through. For example, a high-pass audio filter allows signals of high frequencies to pass, while attenuating or blocking lower frequencies. Filters have a wide variety of uses in audio and image processing, including noise reduction, special effects, tone control, mitigating processing artifacts, and signal splitting in the crossover circuits used in

129

speakers. **2.** A program or device used to block unwanted email or block access to certain websites, such as those that offer pornography.

finalization   The process of writing the lead-in and lead-out data when burning a compact disk. Finalization is necessary for a DVD or CD to be playable in standard players, although some disk burners can read unfinalized disks.

Finder   The core of the Apple Macintosh operating system. The Finder controls the file system, the desktop, and the clipboard, allowing users to manage files, launch applications, and copy and paste text.

finger   A program that provides information about users of a computer system. If a computer is running the appropriate server software, finger can be used to look up users' names, email addresses, phone numbers, and similar information. It can also be used to look up information about users of a remote computer attached to the Internet.

FIPS   *Abbreviation of* **Federal Information Processing Standard.**   Any of a series of standards created by the National Institute of Standards and Technology to be used for US government computing systems. Many FIPS standards are developed in private industry, but some have been developed by the US government, such as the DES and AES encryption algorithms and a set of codes for geographic areas.

FIR   *Abbreviation of* **Fast Infrared.**   An IrDA protocol for infrared data transmission at up to 4 Mbps.

firewall   Software or hardware that restricts communication between a local area network (LAN) or a single computer and outside networks, such as the Internet. Firewalls authenticate the identity of users or machines attempting to communicate with the LAN or computer from outside before granting permission, keeping out unauthorized parties. Firewalls may also regulate what kinds of communication are permitted, providing more fine-tuned access restrictions. Well-designed firewalls are crucial for maintaining the privacy and security of small networks and computers that are connected to the Internet. *See also* **antivirus program, authentication.**

FireWire   The Apple Computer trade name for IEEE 1394. *See* **IEEE 1394.**

firmware   Software that is stored in a computer system's read-only memory (ROM). Firmware is commonly used with embedded systems, such as those in cell phones, digital audio players, and DVD players.

first-person shooter   *Abbreviated* **FPS.**   A computer or video game in which the player controls a character that defends or attacks with a weapon. The player operates from the point of view of that character.

Fitaly Keyboard   A keyboard layout designed by Textware Solutions and used as a soft keyboard on handhelds. The Fitaly Keyboard groups commonly used letters in the center of the keyboard and keeps letters that are frequently typed together adjacent to each other. *Also called* **One-Finger Keyboard.**

→	z	v	c	h	w	k	⁻ ₁	! ₂	←
caps	f	i	t	a	l	y	, ₃	? ₄	↵
shift		n	e				' ₅	: ₆	☒	/
123	g	d	o	r	s	b	' ₇	(₈	←	⟸
ℹ	q	j	u	m	p	x	/ ₉	) ₀	::	^

Fitaly keyboard

5.1   A six-channel sound-reproduction system that has become the standard for movies, music, and video-game systems. In 5.1 configuration, an audio signal is split into five full-bandwidth channels—left, center, and right front channels, left and right rear channels—and one low-frequency effects (LFE) channel. *See also* **surround sound.**

fixed disk   *See* **hard disk.**

fixed pitch   *See* **fixed space.**

fixed-pixel display   A display that uses discrete pixels to display an image. All non-CRT displays are fixed-panel displays, including LCD, LCoS, plasma, and DLP displays.

fixed-point notation   A method of representing numbers in which a fixed number of digits represents the whole-number portion, and another fixed number of digits represents the remaining fractional portion. Fixed-point notation is useful in some computer applications because mathematical operations can be performed on them very quickly, but it lacks the flexibility of floating-point notation for working with wide ranges of very large or very small numbers. *See also* **binary coded decimal notation, floating-point notation.**

fixed space   An equal amount of space assigned to all characters in a font. Fixed space contrasts with proportional space, which gives each character its own particular width. In a fixed space font, a narrow letter such as *I* is given the same amount of horizontal space as a wider letter such as *w*, while in a proportional space font, *I* would be allocated a smaller amount of space. Many computer display screens show text in a fixed space font, while books, magazines, and newspapers are printed in proportional space. *Also called* **fixed pitch, fixed width.** *See also* **monospace font, pitch.**

fixed width   *See* **fixed space.**

FLAC *Abbreviation of* **Free Lossless Audio Codec.** An open source audio codec used for storing and transmitting digital audio over the Internet. Because FLAC encodes audio data using lossless compression, it maintains a higher sound quality than MP3 and other lossy formats. Files of this type usually have the *.flac* extension. *See* Table 3 at **codec.**

flame A hostile email or post on a public forum on the Internet, especially one containing abusive language or personal insults.

flash **1.** To blink or change color in order to get the user's attention. For example, Microsoft Windows will cause an icon or title bar to flash if the printer is out of paper. **2.** To momentarily hang up a telephone line, as when using a call waiting service. Most modems have a special command to do this.

Flash A file format developed by Macromedia for graphics, audio, and video data. Flash files are commonly used for transmitting animation over the Internet. They allow streaming, and are viewed with a web browser plug-in called *Flash Player.* Flash files usually have the file extension *.swf.*

flash drive A portable data storage device that is small enough to fit in a pocket and can be connected to the USB port of a computer or other device. Flash drives use flash memory chips for storage. *Also called* **flash disk, key drive, thumb drive, USB flash drive, USB key.**

flash memory Nonvolatile memory that uses transistors to store data, allows random access, and can be erased and rewritten many times. Because it allows random access, flash memory is much faster than most other forms of nonvolatile memory such as hard disks. Writing to flash memory is slower than writing to volatile memory such as DRAM or SRAM, and flash memory wears out after 10,000–100,000 write operations. It is commonly used in portable storage devices such as memory cards and flash drives, as well as other handheld devices that require storage, such as digital cameras and portable music players.

flat cable *See* **ribbon cable.**

flat-file database A simple database that typically stores data in a single table, similar to a spreadsheet. Flat-file databases can be inefficient when dealing with large, complex data sets.

flat-panel display *Abbreviated* **FPD.** A thin, lightweight display, such as an LCD, plasma, or OLED display. Flat-panel displays are components of many portable and handheld devices such as laptops, cell phones, and digital cameras. Flat-panel monitors and televisions, which can be hung on the wall, are popular alternatives to CRTs. *Also called* **flat-screen display.**

flicker *See* **screen flicker.**

flip phone   A cell phone that has a horizontal hinge, such that the upper part—which houses the display—folds down to cover the lower part—which contains the keypad.

floating graphic   A graphics file that is embedded in a document, such as a word processing document or a webpage, and remains in position on the page when other objects around it, such as text, are altered or moved, rather than moving along with the other objects. Text that is moved typically realigns itself around a floating graphic. *Compare* **inline graphic.**

floating-point   Relating to or using numbers in floating-point notation.

floating-point coprocessor   An FPU (floating-point unit) that is on a separate chip from the CPU (central processing unit). Before 1990, floating-point coprocessors were commonly used to help computers process numerical data more quickly. Since then, most CPUs have come with integrated FPUs. *See also* **superscalar architecture.**

floating-point notation   A method of representing numbers that uses a fixed number of digits before a decimal point and a fixed number after it. This combination of digits may then be multiplied by a power of some predetermined base, also represented by a fixed number of digits. In computer memory, a number in floating-point notation is represented as a binary number (the first digit of which is to the left of the decimal point, and the rest to the right of it) multiplied by a power of the base 2. The number 60 5/8 can be expressed in base 10 floating-point notation as 60.625 or 6.0625×10^1. In binary floating-point notation this same number is represented as 1.11100101 (base 2) $\times 2^5$.

Floating-point representations of numbers are useful in computing because each number occupies precisely the same amount of space in memory, simplifying the storage and manipulation of numerical data. Also, since the same number of digits is used to represent each number, each number is represented with the same degree of numerical accuracy. *See also* **binary coded decimal notation, fixed-point notation, scientific notation.**

floating-point operations per second   *See* **FLOPS.**

floating-point unit   *Abbreviated* **FPU.** A circuit or set of circuits that enables a computer to process mathematical operations very quickly. Floating-point units are very useful for applications that require heavy mathematical calculations, as with high-resolution animated graphics. They may be installed as independent coprocessors or built into a central processor. Special software may take the place of floating-point units by emulating them.

floppy disk   A round, flat piece of Mylar coated with magnetic material and covered by a square protective jacket, used as a storage medium for

133

personal computers. Originally, floppy disks were the principal storage medium for personal computers, but the development of inexpensive hard disks has diminished their role. Floppy disk drives are slower than hard disk drives, and floppy disks themselves have less storage capacity and are more easily damaged than hard disks. But floppy disks are more portable and considerably less expensive than hard disks, and they are useful for loading some programs into a computer and for backup. CDs are largely replacing floppy disks as a distribution and backup medium. *Also called* **floppy, diskette.**

FLOPS *Abbreviation of* **floating-point operations per second.** A measure of the speed of a computer in operations per second, especially arithmetic operations involving floating-point numbers. Although the final *s* is not properly a plural ending, the singular form *flop* is sometimes found, especially in compounds such as *gigaflop*.

floptical disk An optical disk developed by Insite Peripherals that is the size of a 3.5-inch floppy disk. Floptical disks can store over 20 megabytes of data magnetically. The read/write head of the disk drive is aligned by means of a laser. Floptical disks are no longer in common use.

flow control A system by which a receiving device in a communications link can signal a sending device to stop transmission until the receiving device can accept more data. When data comes in faster than a receiver can process it, it is normally stored in a buffer; flow control is used to prevent data from being lost if such a buffer becomes full.

flush Aligned evenly with a margin. *Flush left* means that the text is aligned with the left margin, and *flush right* means that it is aligned with the right margin. *See also* **justification.**

FM *Abbreviation of* **frequency modulation.** A method of transmitting signals, especially in radio broadcasting, in which the value of the signal is given by the frequency of a high-frequency carrier wave. In FM radio transmission, the signal to be carried is a sound wave, and its increasing and decreasing value is reflected in the increasing and decreasing frequency of a radio frequency carrier wave. *See also* **AM.**

FM synthesis *Abbreviation of* **frequency modulation synthesis.** A technique for mimicking the sound of a musical instrument, used by systems that utilize MIDI. FM synthesis creates multiple sine waves for audio transmission and modulates their frequencies according to a predetermined algorithm for a particular musical instrument. *Compare* **wavetable synthesis.**

folder An organizing structure that contains multiple files and is associated with a directory. A folder is usually represented on the screen by the image of a file folder. Like a directory, a folder may contain other folders. In Macintosh operating systems, the directories are usually referred to and represented as folders.

font **1.** A complete set of characters of one size and typeface. The height of a font is measured in points (72 points equal one inch). The most common weights are lightface and boldface. Popular styles include roman and italic. Another font specification is pitch, which refers to the number of characters printed per inch. A fixed pitch (also called a fixed space or monospace) font allocates the same amount of space for every character. A proportional pitch (or proportional) font gives each character its own particular amount of space. *See also* **bitmapped font, outline font. 2.** *See* **font family.**

font cartridge A ROM cartridge that is plugged into some printers to add to the number of resident fonts. Font cartridges are obsolete because increased memory in printers and increased processing speed make it possible for nonresident fonts to be downloaded quickly to the printer while a document is printing.

font family A set of fonts in various weights and sizes that share the same typeface. For example, Times Bold 10 point and Times Italic 12 point are in the same font family.

footer In word processing, printed information—such as a title, page number, or date—placed in the bottom margin of a page and repeated on every page or every other page of the document. A footer that repeats only on odd-numbered pages is an odd footer; one that repeats only on even-numbered pages is an even footer. *Compare* **header.**

footprint **1.** The amount of space a device occupies on a desk or on the floor. **2.** The geographic area covered by transmissions from a particular communications satellite.

foreground process A program that is both running and accepting input from the user. A foreground process either has an active window or is in control of a terminal. *Compare* **background process.** *See also* **process.**

format *n.* An arrangement of data for storage, display, transmission, or hard copy presentation. Database, spreadsheet, graphics, audio and video files, and word processing files come in a wide variety of formats. *See also* **file format.**

   v. **1.** To arrange the data in a document for display or hard copy presentation. In word processing, for example, setting such attributes in a document as the typeface, point size, margins, headers or footers, line spacing, and justification is referred to as formatting the document. **2.** To run an operating system or utility program that prepares a disk for use by organizing its storage space into addresses that can be recognized and accessed.

Reformatting a disk usually deletes or erases the data on a disk. *Also called* initialize, especially with reference to Apple Macintosh computers.

form factor **1.** The size of a device, measured by its physical dimensions as opposed to its storage capacity. The term is often used with respect to hard disks and hard drives. **2.** A specification for the dimensions and layout of a motherboard, power supply unit, computer case, or other basic components of a computer. *See also* **AT, ATX, BTX.**

form feed **1.** A button or command that tells the printer to advance to the top of a new page or form. **2.** A control character used to tell a printer to advance to the top of a new page. The form feed character is no longer commonly used for this purpose in text files.

formula An expression that instructs an application, such as a spreadsheet, to perform an operation on one or more values. For example, in a spreadsheet program, a formula can be used to perform a calculation with a column of cells containing numerical values. Formulas in spreadsheets and similar applications can perform operations on any kind of data, including modifying or counting strings.

Fortran *Abbreviation of* **formula translator** or **formula translation.** The first high-level language, developed in the 1950s by IBM and released in 1957. Fortran was designed to be used for scientific and numerical tasks and is still used in science and engineering, particularly for applications that model complex systems.

forward **1.** To route a message to a different address than that intended by the sender. Users with multiple email addresses, for example, sometimes have email sent to one address automatically forwarded to another address. Email messages received by a user can also be forwarded to other users. **2.** To route a telephone call to a different number than that dialed by the caller. *See also* **call forwarding.**

forward compatible *See* **upward compatible.**

FPD *Abbreviation of* **flat-panel display.**

fps *Abbreviation of* **frames per second.** *See* **frame rate.**

FPS *Abbreviation of* **first-person shooter.**

FPU *Abbreviation of* **floating-point unit.**

fragmentation **1.** The condition of having different parts of the same file scattered throughout a disk. Fragmentation occurs when the operating system breaks up a file and fits it into the spaces left vacant by previously deleted files. Fragmentation slows down the operating system by making the read/write head search for files over a larger area. *Also called* **file fragmentation.** *See also* **defragment. 2.** A similar scattering in a computer's random-access memory (RAM) that takes place when programs and data are repeatedly stored and released.

frame   **1.** A rectangular area in which text or graphics can be shown. In HTML, frames divide a browser's window into segments that are scrolled independently of each other; each frame is a separate HTML document. **2.** In animation and video, an individual image in a set of images that, when viewed rapidly in sequence, create the illusion of a moving picture. **3.** A pair of fields in an interlaced video. Fields are often combined into frames through a process called deinterlacing.

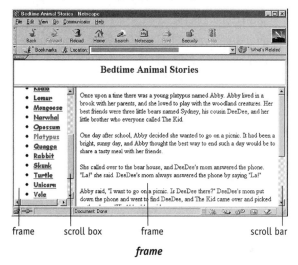

frame   scroll box   frame   scroll bar

frame

frame rate   In video and animation, the number of still frames that are displayed each second to create the illusion of a moving picture. Most movies shot on film have a frame rate of 24 frames per second (fps). In North America, television is usually displayed at 30 or 60 fps (the NTSC and ATSC standard) and in other parts of the world at 25 or 50 fps (the PAL and SECAM standard). A high-end graphics card and monitor can render and display 3D graphics at 60 fps.

Films shot at 24 fps must be converted to different frame rates in order for them to be displayed on most televisions. The speed of a 24 fps film can be increased to 25 fps without significantly distorting the image or sound, but higher rates require the creation of additional frames. A process called 3 : 2 pulldown is used to reach 30 fps. Frame rates of 50 or 60 fps are attained simply by duplicating each frame of a 25 or 30 fps film.

Most camcorders record video at the standard television frame rates, but some high-end camcorders are capable of recording at the film standard of 24 fps or slower.

137

frames per second   *See* **frame rate.**

Free Lossless Audio Codec   *See* **FLAC.**

free software   *See* **open source.**

freeware   Computer programs that are given away free of charge. Unlike public domain software, freeware remains copyrighted. The copyright owner of a freeware program may restrict its use or distribution, and its source code may be unavailable. *Compare* **open source, shareware.**

frequency   The number of cycles, expressed in hertz, that a wave completes within a specified period of time. *Compare* **wavelength.**

frequency modulation   *See* **FM.**

frequency modulation synthesis   *See* **FM synthesis.**

frequently asked questions   *See* **FAQ.**

friction feed   A mechanism that draws paper through a printer by pinching it between plastic or rubber rollers. Most printers are friction feed printers. *Compare* **tractor feed.**

front end   The part of an application that runs on a client computer, rather than a server. The front end typically displays a GUI (graphical user interface) and performs tasks that require access to information, such as user preferences, stored on the user's machine. *See also* **back end, client/server, client-side script.**

front-end processor   *Abbreviated* **FEP.** A small computer that handles network communication for a mainframe, using a network protocol to transmit and receive messages, and perform error correction.

front-projection television   A television that projects an image onto the side of the screen from which it is viewed. *See also* **projector.**

front-side bus   *Abbreviated* **FSB.** The high-speed data pathway between the CPU and main memory in a computer. *Compare* **back-side bus.** *See also* **bus.**

FRS   *Abbreviation of* **family radio service.** A system for wireless communication over short distances in which an unlicensed network of walkie-talkies and base stations transmit and receive analog voice signals. FRS systems use half-duplex communication and have a range of about three kilometers (two miles). Most walkie-talkies sold for consumer use are FRS walkie-talkies.

FSB   *Abbreviation of* **front-side bus.**

FTP   *Abbreviation of* **file transfer protocol.**

full backup   A backup that copies every file in a given set of files, for example, all the files on a disk or in a directory. Full backups are often used in conjunction with differential or incremental backups, so full backups, which take more time, can be performed infrequently, and faster incremental or differential backups can be performed more frequently. *Also called* **archival backup.**

full duplex   A mode of two-way transmission in which data can be sent in two directions simultaneously. Telephone communication involves full-duplex channels because both participants can speak and listen at the same time. Some modem communication also allows a full-duplex mode. *Compare* **half duplex, simplex.**

full-height drive   A 3.25-inch-tall disk drive used in the first generation of PC-compatible computers. The current disk drives on desktop computers are roughly half the height of full-height drives. *Compare* **half-height drive.**

full-range   Having or relating to frequencies between approximately 20 and 20,000 hertz. Used mostly of audio signals or devices that process audio signals.

full-tower   A tower computer case that is larger than a midtower. A full-tower is typically around 23 inches tall. *See also* **tower.**

fully qualified domain name   *See* **hostname** (sense 2).

function key   One of a set of computer keys usually located on the top or the left side of the keyboard that enters specific commands defined by the application in use. Keyboards are equipped with either 10 or 12 function keys that are labeled F1, F2, F3, and so on. Function keys execute different commands when they are pressed in combination with the Alt key, the Control key, and/or the Shift key.

fuse   A safety device that protects an electric circuit from becoming overloaded. Fuses contain a length of thin wire (usually of a metal alloy) that melts and breaks the circuit if too much current flows through it. *See also* **circuit breaker, surge protector.**

G   **1.** *Abbreviation of* **giga-. 2.** *Abbreviation of* **gigabyte.**

G3   **1.** A microprocessor developed by Apple Computer and used in the Power Macintosh G3 computer line. It runs at speeds of up to 400 megahertz per second, with low power consumption requirements. **2.** A computer that uses such a microprocessor.

G4   **1.** A microprocessor developed by Apple Computer and used in the Power Macintosh G4 computer line. It runs at speeds of up to 500 megahertz per second. **2.** A computer that uses such a microprocessor.

gain   **1.** The ratio between the output and input level of a signal going through a device, such as a volume knob or an amplifier. A gain of more than one means that the signal level is increased; a gain of less than one means the signal level is decreased. **2.** A control, such as a volume knob, that sets the gain of a device. **3.** A relative measure of a projection screen's reflectivity, defined as the ratio between its actual reflectivity and the reflectivity of a standard magnesium oxide surface. A light gray matte surface has a gain of around 0.8 while a highly reflective surface made of glass beads can have a gain of 2.5. The ideal gain for a given setup depends on the brightness of the projector that will be used, the projector's position in relation to the screen, and the required viewing angle. High-gain screens have narrower viewing angles than low-gain screens.

GameCube   A video game console developed by Nintendo. The GameCube belongs to the same generation of products as the Sony PlayStation 2 and the Microsoft Xbox.

gamepad   *See* **controller** (sense 2).

game port   A port into which joysticks and similar input devices for games can be connected.

gaming   The playing of computer or video games.

gateway   A software or hardware system that enables communication between different computer networks. Gateways are necessary when communicating networks use different communication protocols. *See also* **router.**

gateway page   *See* **portal.**

Gb   *Abbreviation of* **gigabit.**

GB   *Abbreviation of* **gigabyte.**

Gbps or **Gbit/s**   *Abbreviations of* **gigabits per second.**

GBps or **GB/s**   *Abbreviations of* **gigabytes per second.**

GDI   *Abbreviation of* **Graphical Device Interface.**

general mobile radio service   *See* **GMRS.**

general packet radio service   *See* **GPRS.**

general protection fault   *Abbreviated* **GPF.**   A severe failure of a program that usually causes its unexpected termination. General protection faults occur when a program tries to access invalid or inaccessible memory locations.

General Public License   *See* **GPL.**

generation   A stage or period of sequential technological development and innovation.

GFLOPS or **GFLOP**   *Abbreviations of* **gigaflops** or **gigaflop.**

ghosting   **1.** The permanent etching of an image into a display screen when the same image has been left on the screen for a long period of time. Ghosting is a problem only for displays, such as CRTs or plasmas, that use phosphor. Screen savers prevent ghosting either by dimming the screen brightness or by displaying moving images on a screen that has displayed a fixed image for a specified period of time. *Also called* **burn-in. 2.** The creation of a copy, or ghost image, of the programs and configuration settings on a computer's main hard drive, to be stored on another device such as an optical disk, a server, or another hard drive. Ghosting is done to make safety or backup copies of the hard drive, especially to preserve everything about the state of the computer as configured in its operating system, along with all of the files currently stored. Ghosting is therefore useful when upgrading a computer to a larger main hard disk, since the operating system is transferred to the new disk as is without the need to reinstall and reconfigure it. *Also called* **disk cloning, ghost imaging. 3.** A visual artifact caused by poor television reception that appears as a faint secondary image superimposed on the desired television picture. **4.** The smearing of an image on an LCD monitor or television resulting from a slow pixel response time.

GHz   *Abbreviation of* **gigahertz.**

Gibbs effect   *See* **mosquito.**

GIF   *Abbreviation of* **Graphics Interchange Format.**   A bitmapped color graphics file format that can reproduce up to 256 distinct colors in an image. GIF is used in many web applications to exchange graphics because it supports efficient, lossless data compression. Its restriction to only 256 gradations of color makes it unsuitable for high-quality photographs, but suitable for simple graphics such as icons, table, and graphs. GIF is pronounced JIFF or GIFF. *See also* **PNG.**

gig   A gigabyte. Used informally.

giga-   *Abbreviated* **G.   1.** A prefix indicating one billion (10^9), as in *gigahertz*. This is also the sense in which *giga-* is generally used in terms of data transmission rates, where a bit is a signal pulse and is counted in the decimal system, which is based on multiples of 10. **2.** A prefix indicating 1,073,741,824 (2^{30}), as in *gigabyte*. This is the sense in which *giga-* is generally used in terms of data storage capacity, which, due to the binary nature of bits, is based on powers of 2.

gigabit *Abbreviated* **Gb.** One billion (10^9) bits, used as a unit for expressing the rate of data transmission per unit of time (usually one second). In highly technical contexts involving data storage capacity, it can refer to 1,073,741,824 (2^{30}) bits.

Gigabit Ethernet An Ethernet specification that allows for transmission speeds of up to 1 gigabit per second. Gigabit Ethernet was formerly used only in network backbones, but network cards that support it are becoming more popular for personal computers. It uses both twisted-pair cables and fiber optic cables. *Compare* **Fast Ethernet.** *See* Table C on page 358 and Table D on page 360.

gigabyte *Abbreviated* **G** or **GB.** **1.** A unit of measurement of computer memory or data storage capacity, equal to 1,073,741,824 (2^{30}) bytes. One gigabyte equals 1,024 megabytes. **2.** One billion (10^9) bytes, especially when reporting the storage capacity of a hard disk or DVD.

gigaflops or **gigaflop** *Abbreviated* **GFLOPS** or **GFLOP.** A measure of computing speed equal to one billion (10^9) floating-point operations per second. *See also* **FLOPS.**

gigahertz *Abbreviated* **GHz.** A unit of frequency equal to one billion (10^9) hertz.

glitch **1.** A small programming error that generally goes unnoticed and does not have an impact on usability. **2.** A false or spurious electronic signal caused by a brief, unwanted surge or loss of electric power, especially one that causes a computer or other piece of hardware to malfunction.

global **1.** Relating to all the users in a computer network. **2.** Relating to an entire program, document, or file. A global format for a spreadsheet, for example, is a format that applies to every cell in that spreadsheet.

Global Positioning System *See* **GPS.**

Global System for Mobile communications *See* **GSM.**

GMRS *Abbreviation of* **general mobile radio service.** A system for wireless communication over short distances in which a network of walkie-talkies and base stations transmit and receive analog signals. GMRS systems include the ability to page other users. They use half-duplex communication and have a maximum range of around 20 kilometers (12 miles).

Repeaters can be used in GMRS systems to allow transmissions over longer distances. While GMRS systems are designed to be used by consumers, using them in the US requires a license.

GNOME *Abbreviation of* **GNU Network Object Model Environment.** A free, open-source desktop environment for Linux and Unix operating systems. GNOME is part of the Gnu project.

Gnu *Abbreviation of* **Gnu's not Unix.** A project to develop open-source, freely distributed, UNIX-compatible system software. The Gnu project was instrumental in developing the Linux operating system. It is sponsored by the Free Software Foundation.

Google A company that provides a variety of Internet servies, including a widely used search engine, email services, and online book search.

Gopher A protocol for distributing documents over networks such as the Internet. The gopher protocol and associated software tools provide capabilities similar to the World Wide Web, but with a text-based interface. Gopher has largely been supplanted by the World Wide Web; however, Gopher servers still exist and many web browsers support the Gopher protocol.

.gov A top-level domain operated by the US General Services Administration and used by US governmental organizations. Any government organization in the United States can register a domain name in the .gov domain, including cities and states.

GPE *Abbreviation of* **GPE Palmtop Environment.** A GUI for Linux operating systems running on handheld devices. GPE is open-source software, released by Gnu.

GPF *Abbreviation of* **General protection fault.**

GPL *Abbreviation of* **General Public License.** An open-source software license created and published by Gnu. Software developers can release a program under the GPL by including a copy of the license text with the program. The GPL ensures that the source code of programs released under it is available for inspection and modification, and that any programs derived from the source code are also covered by the agreement.

gppm *Abbreviation of* **graphics pages per minute.**

GPRS *Abbreviation of* **general packet radio service.** A packet-switching protocol for transmitting and receiving digital data on GSM cellular networks. Part of the GSM standard, GPRS allows users to communicate with the Internet and to send and receive text and multimedia at relatively high data transmission rates (up to 115 Kbps). The EDGE standard enhances this protocol to provide greater transmission rates. *Compare* **CDPD, HSCSD.**

GPS   *Abbreviation of* **Global Positioning System.**   A system of satellites, computers, and receivers that is able to determine the latitude and longitude of a receiver on Earth by calculating the time difference for signals from different satellites to reach the receiver. GPS receivers are commonly installed in cars and handheld devices.

GPU   *Abbreviation of* **graphics processing unit.**   A coprocessor designed for graphical applications such as rendering 3D images. GPUs speed up the processing of computer graphics by removing much of the processing load from a computer's main CPU and by being designed to perform the necessary computations very efficiently. GPUs are usually located on graphics cards.

grabber   **1.** A device that digitizes images from a video camera or other video source. **2.** An onscreen cursor, often represented by an icon of a hand, that allows the user to grab onscreen objects and move them around on the screen.

Graffiti   A handwriting recognition program for the Palm OS that requires users to write with an alphabet consisting of a modified version of standard block letters.

Graphical Device Interface   *Abbreviated* **GDI.**   A Microsoft Windows API for displaying or printing text and graphical images. Printers that use GDI rely on the operating system to process text and graphics files and create printable bitmaps, rather than creating bitmaps from page description languages like PostScript or PCL. *Also called* **Graphics Device Interface.**

graphical user interface   *See* **GUI.**

graphics   **1.** The display and manipulation of pictorial information by computers. The two basic forms of computer graphics are vector graphics and bitmapped graphics.

   Many graphics-based applications exist, including desktop publishing software, presentation graphics, and CAD (computer-aided design) software. *See also* **bitmapped graphics, vector graphics.**

   2. The images or pictorial information presented in such displays.

graphics accelerator   A computer graphics card containing a GPU. *Also called* **video accelerator.** *See also* **graphics card.**

graphics adapter   *See* **graphics card.**

graphics-based   Relating to applications that represent and allow manipulation of information using visual images. Graphics-based applications represent information using bit maps or with a set of geometrical objects.

Examples of graphics-based software include presentation graphics, desktop publishing programs, and most computer games. *Compare* **text-based.**

graphics card   A computer expansion card that processes and converts video signals for display on a monitor. Some video cards have powerful GPUs and VRAM that allow them to correct and embellish the image data that they receive. On some motherboards, the video card is integrated into the system. *Also called* **graphics adapter, video adapter, video card.**

graphics file format   The way in which a program reads and stores information so as to create and manipulate graphics images. There are numerous proprietary graphics file formats, with little standardization among them, although graphics software often includes the capacity to work with several different formats and convert a file in one format into another format.

Graphics Interchange Format   *See* **GIF.**

graphics pages per minute   *Abbreviated* **gppm.**   The speed at which a printer can print pages of graphics images. This measurement contrasts with pages per minute (ppm), the speed at which a printer prints pages of text. Given the relative complexity for many printers of printing graphics versus text, a printer's graphics-pages-per-minute rating may be slower than its pages-per-minute rating.

graphics processing unit   *See* **GPU.**

graphics tablet   *See* **digitizing tablet.**

gray scale   A series of shades ranging from pure white to pure black, used to represent or display black-and-white images. In computer graphics, the number of gradations within this scale varies depending on the number of bits used to store the shading information for each pixel. Gray-scale computer monitors allow higher quality representations of images than black-and-white monitors.

greeking   In desktop publishing, the use of gray bars or garbled text to simulate how text will appear on a page. Greeking is used when evaluating the layout and design of a document rather than its content. *See also* **preview, thumbnail.**

grep   *n.* A software tool, originally developed for the Unix platform, that allows the user to search text files for specific text patterns.
   v. To search for something in a text file using this command.

grid computing   The calculation and storage of data by using resources available on computers that are distributed across the Internet on different LANs. Many grid computing projects involve programs that run on participating computers when they are idle, using the computers' CPU and free disk space and transmitting information to other computers on the grid. *See also* **cluster.**

ground   *n.* A part of an electrical circuit that serves as a baseline voltage of zero volts. The entire chassis of an electrical device, or at least the metallic parts of the chassis, may serve as a ground. Grounds are often directly connected to part of a power supply, such as the negative terminal of a battery, and may also be connected to an external ground, such as the third terminal of a wall socket, or directly by wire to the earth itself. A ground shared by multiple devices serves as a safety feature, since it guarantees that all devices share a common baseline of zero volts, so that there is no risk of sudden current flow if the devices touch each other, or of shock if a person touches more than one device. Shared grounds may also reduce the influence of stray signals, such as electrical hum or radio wave interference, on audio or video signals.

   v. To connect an electrical device to a ground.

Group 3 Protocol   An international standard developed by the ITU for faxes over standard telephone lines.

Group 4 Protocol   An international standard developed by the ITU for the technology involved in transmitting faxes over ISDN lines.

groupware   Any of various software applications designed to support multiple users working on the same project at the same time, often in different locations. Examples of groupware include schedulers that help employees plan meetings, electronic newsletters, programs for file sharing, and electronic discussion groups. *Also called* **collaborative software.**

GSM   *Abbreviation of* **Global System for Mobile communications.**   A standard for digital mobile communication using TDMA technology, used for mobile telephony, text messaging, and data. First introduced in 1991 to replace a variety of incompatible analog systems, GSM quickly became the dominant mobile technology in Europe, the Middle East, Africa, and Asia. It is gradually replacing CDMA and iDEN networks in North America and South America. The standard allows networks at different frequency bands: 800 MHz, 900 MHz, 1800 MHz, and 1900 MHz. 800 MHz and 1900 MHz networks are restricted to North and South America. *See also* **PCS, SIM.**

GUI   *Abbreviation of* **graphical user interface.**   A set of images displayed on a computer screen that allow users to choose commands, see lists of files, and otherwise interact with a program or operating system. Commands can be entered by using the mouse or keyboard to select and move icons, menu items, and other parts of the GUI. An operating system's desktop environment includes standard elements, such as menus, buttons, and text boxes, that are used by the GUIs of different programs to make them look similar and function in similar ways. GUI is pronounced GOO-ee.

gunzip   A program for Linux and Unix systems that decompresses files compressed with gzip. On Windows systems, the WinZip program can be used to decompress such files. *See also* **gzip.**

.gz   An extension used for files compressed with gzip.

gzip   A data compression program commonly used on Linux and Unix systems. While gzip uses a similar compression method to that used with zip archives, it only compresses individual files and is thus not an archiving program. It is typically used with tar to create compressed archives. Files compressed with gzip typically have the extension *.gz. See also* **gunzip.**

H.264   An MPEG standard for transmitting digital video. Because H.264 compresses files at a lower bit rate and higher quality than MPEG-2, H.264 has been used in some HDTV and SDTV broadcast systems, as well as in HD DVD technology. *Also called* **MPEG-4 AVC, MPEG-4 Part 10.**

H.323   An international standard developed by the ITU for audio and video conferencing and telephony in real time over the Internet.

hacker   **1.** A person who breaks into a computer system to view, alter, or steal restricted software or data. *Also called* **cracker. 2.** A person who is proficient at using or programming a computer; a computer buff.

half duplex   Any mode or channel of two-way communication in which data can be sent in only one direction at a time, so that two senders must alternate their transmissions. Walkie-talkies are examples of half-duplex transmission, as are some modem transmission protocols. *Also called* **local echo.** *Compare* **full duplex, simplex.** *See also* **communications protocol.**

half-height drive   A disk drive for current PC-compatible computers that is roughly half as tall as the first generation of desktop computer drives, which were about 3.25 inches high. Half-height drives are now standard for PC-compatible computers. *Compare* **full-height drive.**

halftone   A photograph or other continuous-tone image in which the gradation of tones is simulated by the relative darkness and density of tiny dots. Dark shades are reproduced by dense patterns of large dots, and lighter shades by less dense patterns of smaller dots. *See also* **dithering.**

handheld A computer or other digital device small enough to be held in one hand and operated with the other. Common types of handhelds include cell phones, PDAs, and portable music players. Most handhelds have more than one function.

handheld scanner A compact, portable scanner whose scan head is moved manually over text or images. *See also* **sheet-fed scanner.**

handle *See* **screen name.**

handset **1.** The part of a telephone that contains the speaker and the microphone. **2.** A cell phone that consists of only a handset.

hands-free kit Equipment that permits drivers to use a cell phone without holding a handset to their ear. A hands-free kit usually includes a speaker, a microphone, power cables, and a cradle in which the phone rests.

handshaking An exchange that takes place between two devices so that communications can begin. Hardware handshaking occurs over a special communications line between a computer and a peripheral, such as a serial printer, before a transfer of data takes place. In software handshaking, codes are exchanged through modems to establish a file transfer protocol for the exchange of information.

handwriting recognition The conversion of handwritten characters into text by a device or software. Many handheld PDAs, for example, use handwriting recognition technology. The user writes onto the screen with a stylus, using a modified alphabet system that allows each letter to be written without lifting up the stylus. *See also* **speech recognition.**

hang To enter into or be in a state that is not responsive to any input, as from the keyboard or mouse of a computer. Computer applications can hang when their processing is greatly slowed down for some reason or when the programming or system has errors or incompatibilities. When the operating system of a computer hangs, the computer usually must be rebooted. *See also* **crash.**

hard card An expansion card containing a hard disk drive. A hard card fits into an expansion slot instead of a disk drive bay. Hard cards are easy to install and generally have less storage capacity than drives installed in drive bays.

hard copy A printed version of data stored on a disk or in memory, such as an image or document. *Compare* **soft copy.**

hard disk **1.** *See* **hard drive. 2.** One of the platters used in a hard drive.

hard drive   A rigid magnetic disk or disks fixed within a disk drive and used for storing computer data. Hard disks typically offer more storage and quicker access to data than optical disks do.

A single hard drive consists of one or more disk platters that rotate at between 5,000 and 15,000 rpm. Each platter has two read/write heads, one for each side of the platter, that float on a thin sheet of air just above a magnetized surface. All the read/write heads are attached to a single head arm so that they don't move independently. Each platter has the same number of tracks, and the group of tracks in corresponding locations on all the platters is called a cylinder.

There are several interface standards for connecting hard disks to computers. These include SCSI, SAS, IDE (also called ATA), and SATA. *Also called* **fixed disk, hard disk, hard disk drive.**

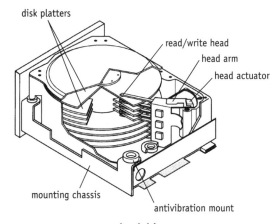

disk platters

read/write head

head arm

head actuator

mounting chassis

antivibration mount

hard drive

hard link   In Linux and Unix operating systems, a name for a file in the file system. Each file has at least one hard link, which makes it show up in a directory. Multiple hard links can be created for the same file, allowing the file to show up in multiple directories or under multiple names in the same directory. A file is deleted when all hard links to it are deleted. *Compare* **symbolic link.**

hard return   An instruction in a word processing program that ends a line, usually to begin a new paragraph. Unlike soft returns, which are typically inserted by a program's word wrap feature and can be moved automatically when the document changes, hard returns are typically inserted by the user, and are not moved by word wrap. *See also* **line break, soft return.**

hardware   The physical components that carry out the processing, display, or storage of information by a computer or CPU. Hardware includes chips, disk drives, display screens, cables, expansion boards, modems, speakers, printers, and any other physical object that is part of a computer system. *Compare* **software.** *See also* **firmware.**

hardware address   *See* **MAC address.**

hardwired   **1.** Implemented through logic circuitry that is permanently connected within a computer and therefore not subject to change by programming. **2.** Connected by electrical wires or cables.

hash   A value generated by performing a hash function on a string of data. The hash is generally much shorter than the original data, but it can be used to identify the original data because the chances that any other data would yield the same hash are quite small. The original data cannot normally be retrieved from the hash, but the hash can be used for verification of the data.

Computer passwords are usually stored as hashes to keep them secure. When a user types a password, the computer verifies that it is correct by creating a hash from the typed string and comparing it with the stored hash. Hashes are also often used in cryptography to verify that a message has not been altered, particularly as part of a digital signature protocol. *See also* **public-key cryptography.**

hash function   A mathematical function performed on a piece of data, such as the binary representation of a file, that produces a hash that can be used as a tag, shorthand, or identifier for that piece of data.

Hayes command set   *See* **AT command set.**

HDCP   *Abbreviation of* **High-bandwidth Digital Content Protection.** A digital rights management protocol developed by Intel. HDCP encryption is used to protect digital video and audio signals carried by DVI and HDMI cables. An HDCP-compatible display is required to decode HDCP signals.

HD DVD   An optical disk designed for storing digital video and capable of storing much more data than a DVD. HD DVD disks, developed by the DVD Forum, have the same physical dimensions as DVDs and compact disks, but use a different type of laser and a different physical format. Single-layer HD DVD-ROM disks can store 15 GB of data, compared to 4.78 GB for standard DVDs and 25 GB for Blu-Ray disks. Dual-layer disks have twice the capacity of single-layer disks.

HD DVD disks are available in read-only form, called *HD DVD-ROM,* as well as a form that can be written once, called *HD DVD-R,* and a form that can be rewritten many times, called *HD DVD-RW.* An HD DVD-R disk can store 15 GB of data per side and an HD DVD-RW disk can hold 20 GB per side. *Compare* **Blu-Ray Disc.** *See also* **DVD.**

HDMI connector *Abbreviation of* **High-Definition Multimedia Interface connector.** A connector used to transmit digital video and audio between a source, such as a DVD player, and a display. The standard 19-pin HDMI connector has a maximum clock frequency of 165 MHz, allowing it to transmit a 2.6-megapixel image with a refresh rate of 60 Hz. *See figure at* **connector.** *See* Table A on page 356.

HD Radio A technology developed by iBiquity Digital Corporation for transmitting digital radio over terrestrial radio networks. Using HD Radio, traditional AM and FM radio stations can broadcast digital signals alongside analog signals. *See also* **digital radio.**

HDTV **1.** *Abbreviation of* **high-definition television.** A class of television display formats that has over 576 visible lines per frame and a widescreen aspect ratio (image proportions) of 16 : 9. Common HDTV formats include 720p24, 720p25, 720p30, 720p50, 720p60, 1080i50, 1080i60, 1080p24, and 1080p25, where the first number refers to the vertical resolution in visible lines per frame, the letter *p* or *i* to progressive scanning or interlacing, and the second number to the fields or frames per second. *See also* **digital television.** *See* Table B on page 357. **2.** A television that is capable of displaying HDTV. HDTVs that are advertised as *HDTV-compatible* or *HDTV-ready* usually require an external tuner or set-top box to receive HDTV broadcasts. Those labeled *integrated HDTV* typically have a built-in tuner for receiving digital terrestrial television. *Digital-cable ready* means that the HDTV can receive digital cable without the purchase or rental of a separate set-top box, though a subscription to a cable service is still necessary.

HE-AAC *Abbreviation of* **High Efficiency Advanced Audio Coding.** *See* **aacPlus.**

head **1.** The device in a disk or tape drive or player that enables it to read data, and in some cases also to write data, to the disk or tape.

In magnetic media such as hard disks, there are one or two small coils in the head through which electric current can pass. When the head of a disk or tape drive writes data to the disk or tape, current passes through the coils toward the magnetic fields on the disk or tape and causes the magnetic particles directly beneath the head to align either north-south or south-north. When the head reads the data, the magnetic particles directly beneath the head send a current back through the coils that is to be translated into binary code. The direction in which the particles are aligned determines whether the bit will have a value of 0 or 1.

The heads of optical drives contain one or more lasers that shine light on the disk. To read data, sensors in the head detect the pattern of light reflecting off the disk as it spins, decoding this information into a stream of binary values (1's and 0's). To write data, stronger lasers in the head are focused on the disk and burn patterns of small pits on its surface, encoding the patterns of 1's and 0's corresponding to the data being written.

Tape drives often have separate heads for reading, recording, and sometimes erasing data. *See also* **magneto-optical disk, read/write head.** *See figure at* **hard disk.**

2. *See* **monitor.**

3. *See* **print head.**

head crash   The sudden dropping of the read/write head onto the surface or platter of a hard disk. When a head crash occurs, the oxide coating on the disk or platter is scratched off or burned, the data stored on that part of the disk is destroyed, and the disk usually must be replaced. A head crash can be caused by rough handling of the drive, by dirt particles in the drive, or by mechanical failure. *See also* **disk crash, park.**

header   **1.** Data stored at the beginning of a file or other unit of memory to provide information about a given file, program, or device. Headers usually contain information for use by the operating system or the program the information concerns. **2.** In word processing, printed information, such as a title or name, that is placed in the top margin of the page and usually repeated on every page or every other page of the document. A header that repeats only on odd-numbered pages is an odd header; one that repeats only on even-numbered pages is an even header. *Compare* **footer.**

headphone   A device that converts electric signals, as from an audio receiver or MP3 player, to audible sound and fits over or in the ear. Headphones are held in place either by a band worn around the head, by a clip attached to the ear, or simply by being set inside the ear. This last type includes those known as *canalphones,* which are inserted into the ear canal, and those called *earbuds,* which are held in the auricle. Of those worn outside the ear, some, called *circumaural headphones,* have cups that cover the entire ear to block ambient noise; others, called *supra-aural headphones,* lay flat against the ear but are more portable. *See also* **noise-canceling headphone.**

headset   **1.** A headphone or pair of headphones with a microphone attached. **2.** A pair of headphones.

heat sink   A device designed to prevent the overheating of computer components, such as integrated circuits or microprocessors, by absorbing and dissipating heat, often through metal fins. *Also called* **heat spreader.**

heat spreader   *See* **heat sink.**

help   Information about an application that can be accessed from within the application. This information usually includes instructions on using the application and what to do if errors or problems arise. Some applications require an Internet connection in order for the user to have full access to the help features of that application. *See also* **context-sensitive help.**

hertz *Abbreviated* **Hz.** A unit of frequency equal to one cycle per second. The rate of any kind of repeated event, such as the transmission of bits of information on the Internet (which proceeds one bit at a time), the vibration of a radio wave, or the refreshing of images on a display screen, can be measured in hertz.

heterogeneous network A network of computers running different operating systems, such as Windows, MacOS, and Linux.

Hewlett-Packard Graphics Language *See* **HPGL.**

hex *Abbreviation of* **hexadecimal.**

hexadecimal *Abbreviated* **hex.** Relating to the base 16 numeral system. The hexadecimal system uses the digits 0 through 9 and the letters A through F. Programmers often use the hexadecimal system instead of the binary system that computers use because the hexadecimal representation of a number uses fewer characters than its binary representation. It is also fairly easy to translate hexadecimal into binary because each hexadecimal digit can be translated directly into a group of four binary digits. For example, 12 in decimal is C in hexadecimal and 1100 in binary. *Hexadecimal* was coined in the early 1960s to replace *sexadecimal*. *See also* **octal.** *See* Table 2 at **binary.**

HFS *Abbreviation of* **Hierarchical File System.** A file system developed by Apple Computers and used with its Macintosh operating systems. HFS has features that allow it to support the unique file structure used by Macintosh operating systems, and so is typically not supported by other operating systems. Since 1998, most releases of Macintosh operating systems have included a version called *HFS+*.

hidden file A file that is not ordinarily shown when listing or viewing the contents of a directory. In Windows, for example, many files used by the operating system are hidden files that cannot be seen unless a setting is changed. In Linux and Unix, any file whose name begins with a dot (.) is a hidden file.

hierarchical Organized into general groups that divide into more specific subgroups. Folders on Apple Macintosh computers and directories on computers running a Windows operating system are organized hierarchically, so that at the top level there is a small number of folders or root directories and at the bottom level there is a large number of files. *See also* **directory, folder, tree structure.**

Hierarchical File System   *See* **HFS.**

High-bandwidth Digital Content Protection   *See* **HDCP.**

High Color or **HiColor**   A format for encoding color with a bit depth of 15 or 16 bits per pixel and a color depth of 32,768 (2^{15}) or 65,536 (2^{16}) distinct colors.

high-definition   *Abbreviated* **high-def.** **1.** Relating to the reproduction of sound or images with exceptional clarity and precision. **2.** Relating to HDTV.

High-Definition Multimedia Interface connector   *See* **HDMI connector.**

high-definition television   *See* **HDTV.**

high-density disk   A floppy disk with more memory than a double-density disk. A 3.5-inch high-density disk can store 1.44 MB of data. *See also* **density.**

High Efficiency Advanced Audio Coding   *Abbreviated* **HE-AAC.** *See* **aac-Plus.**

high-end   Having or relating to high frequencies, typically above 5,000 hertz. Used mostly of audio signals or devices such as speakers that process audio signals. *See also* **tweeter.**

high-level language   A programming language, such as Java or Perl, that uses primarily words and symbols like those in natural language and allows programmers to avoid the details of how data is stored and processed by a CPU. Unlike assembly languages or machine languages, high-level languages are independent of the CPU architecture used to execute programs. Programs written in high-level languages must be processed by a compiler or interpreter in order to be executed. *Compare* **low-level language.**

highlight   To display text in a light color with a dark background or in some other manner different from normal text. Highlighting often indicates that the text is selected for some operation, such as deletion or copying.

High Performance Serial Bus   *Abbreviated* **HPSB.** *See* **IEEE 1394.**

high-resolution   *Abbreviated* **hi-res.** Relating to a display device or a printed or electronic image that has a high pixel density. High-resolution images are sharp and detailed. *Compare* **low-resolution.** *See also* **resolution.**

High-Speed Circuit-Switched Data   *See* **HSCSD.**

hints   **1.** Software instructions for improving the print and screen quality of fonts at low resolutions. Hints are especially useful when working with small point sizes. **2.** Small displays that appear when a user accesses a particular area of an application screen or window. Such displays typically contain a brief description indicating how that area is to be used.

hit **1.** An item, especially a webpage, that is identified or retrieved as a result of a search query. **2.** A record of a single instance of a webpage being loaded, used to track the number of actual visits to the page. *Also called* **page hit.**

home directory A directory assigned to a particular user that contains the user's configuration and preferences files and in which the user has permission to create, delete, and change files. Often, users do not have permission to create or change files outside their home directories. Home directories are used primarily with Linux and Unix operating systems.

Home key A key that shifts the contents of a window, such as a web browser, downward, so that the first or top part of text and images being viewed are displayed. In windows with a cursor, the Home key repositions the cursor to the beginning of the document or file being viewed. *Compare* **End key.**

homepage **1.** The main page of a website, usually containing general information about the owner of the site and information about using it. **2.** The first webpage that a web browser displays when the browser is opened.

home service area A geographic region within which a subscriber to some telephone service can make calls without incurring long-distance or roaming charges. The boundaries of a customer's home service area are usually defined in a service agreement. *Also called* **home coverage area.** *See also* **local calling area.**

home theater A system of sophisticated electronic equipment for the presentation of theater-quality images and sound in the home. A home theater usually includes a surround-sound audio system and a projector or television with a large screen.

home-theater-in-a-box *Abbreviated* **HTIB.** A home-theater audio system that is sold as a single package. An HTIB usually includes a set of surround-sound loudspeakers, a subwoofer, and an audio receiver with a built-in DVD/CD player.

host **1.** A computer connected to a TCP/IP network, such as the Internet. **2.** A computer containing data or programs that another computer can access over a network or by modem. For example, if a user logs on to a remote computer using a program such as Telnet, the remote computer is the host. *See also* **server.**

hostname **1.** The name used to identify a computer on a LAN. **2.** The domain name used to identify a computer or service on the Internet. The Internet hostname of a computer often includes its LAN hostname. *Also called* **fully qualified domain name.**

hot key *See* **keyboard shortcut.**

hotlink **1.** A connection between two files that allows one to be updated automatically every time you update the other. For example, an image stored on one website can be a hotlink on the webpage of another website. Every time the webpage is loaded, the stored version of the image is loaded. If the image file is changed, the webpage changes. Hotlinks are also used in office suites, where, for example, data from a spreadsheet might be used to create a graph in another document. When the data in the spreadsheet is updated, the graph changes automatically. *Also called* **link. 2.** *See* **hyperlink.**

hotspot **1.** The area surrounding a wireless access point in which computers with wireless cards and other devices with Wi-Fi transceivers can connect to a wireless LAN and thus get access to the Internet, often free of charge. **2.** An area of text or graphics that, when clicked, executes a command such as following a hyperlink or displaying a text box. Hotspots are found in webpages and in the GUIs of programs, and are usually indicated by a changes in the appearance of the cursor.

HPGL *Abbreviation of* **Hewlett-Packard Graphics Language.** A printer control language developed by Hewlett-Packard for plotting two-dimensional drawings by specifying the movement of a pen over paper. Many laser printers accept HPGL and can create output that simulates the movement of a pen to create an image on the paper.

HPSB *Abbreviation of* **High Performance Serial Bus.** *See* **IEEE 1394.**

.hqx An extension typically used for files in BinHex format.

HSB *Abbreviation of* **hue-saturation-brightness.** *See* **HSV.**

HSCSD *Abbreviation of* **High-Speed Circuit-Switched Data.** A circuit-switching protocol for transmitting and receiving digital data on GSM cellular networks. HSCSD allows users to communicate with the Internet and send and receive text and multimedia at transmission rates up to 57 Kbps. The EDGE standard enhances this protocol to allow transmission rates of up to 384 Kbps. *Compare* **CDPD, GPRS.**

HSV *Abbreviation of* **hue-saturation-value.** A color model that defines colors using varying levels of hue, saturation, and brightness. The HSV color model is commonly used in computer graphics. *Also called* **HSB.** *See also* **color model.**

HTIB   *Abbreviation of* **home-theater-in-a-box.**

HTML   *Abbreviation of* **hypertext markup language.**   A markup language used on the World Wide Web to design webpages. HTML provides a language for formatting text and setting up hyperlinks, among other functions. It was designed in SGML.

HTTP   *Abbreviation of* **hypertext transfer protocol.**   A client/server protocol used on the Internet to govern the transfer of data. HTTP is one of the standards that make the World Wide Web possible. It specifies how web browsers request webpages from servers, and how servers send webpages back in response. The lowercase prefix *http:* in URLs indicates that the web address that follows is to be interpreted using this protocol.

HTTPS   The use of SSL to encrypt HTTP transmissions. HTTPS is not an independent protocol, although the prefix *https:* is used for URLs that are accessed using a combination of SSL and HTTP. HTTPS stands for *HTTP, secure.*

hub   A device to which other devices are connected and through which they communicate. For example, in a star-topology network, the central device to which all the computers are connected is the hub.

hue   *See* **tint.**

hyperlink   In a hypertext document, a cross-reference that links to another related document or to another location within the same document. Hyperlinks are indicated on screen by a font or color change or by bold or underlined type, for example. *Also called* **hotlink, link.**

hypermedia   Information that is presented via computer-controlled displays so that readers can navigate easily and quickly between the distinct but integrative components or elements of text, graphics, video, and sound. Like hypertext, hypermedia employs hyperlinks between the various components.

hypertext   A format for presenting text that is heavily cross-referenced through hyperlinks. A document presented in hypertext may have links to other text documents or to graphic images, sound, or video as well. A book in hypertext format, for example, might allow the reader to use a mouse to click on words or sections that link to more detailed information about a subject.

hypertext markup language   *See* **HTML.**

hypertext transfer protocol   *See* **HTTP.**

Hz   *Abbreviation of* **hertz.**

I-beam pointer A mouse pointer having the shape of the letter *I*, indicating the place where a cursor or other marker will be placed on the screen to select or enter text.

IBM PC **1.** The first personal computer made by International Business Machines in 1981, using the Intel microprocessor 8088 and having 16 KB of RAM that was expandable to 64 KB. **2.** Any of the personal computers made by IBM, including the original IBM PC and later models. *See also* **PC-compatible.**

IBM PC-compatible *See* **PC-compatible.**

IC *Abbreviation of* **integrated circuit.**

ICMP *Abbreviation of* **Internet control message protocol.** A protocol defining error and information messages regarding Internet data transmission. One of the messages defined in ICMP is the *echo request,* which sends data to a remote computer and asks the remote computer to return the data. This message is used by the PING program, as well as other networking software, to determine if a remote computer is online and communicating.

icon A picture on a display screen that represents a specific file, directory, window, or program. Clicking on the icon opens the file, directory, or window, or starts the program.

ID3 A small attachment stored within an MP3 file, containing information relevant to the MP3, such as the album title, artist, track number, or genre.

IDE *Abbreviation of* **Integrated Drive Electronics.** A standard for the interface between the disk drives and the motherboard of a computer. The IDE standard locates the disk drive controller on the disk drive rather than on a separate expansion card. IDE disk drives are then connected by ribbon cables to sockets on the motherboard. The stages in the evolution of the standard are officially known as ATA 1-7 and Serial ATA (SATA) I-II. However, various versions are also labeled Fast ATA, Enhanced IDE (EIDE), Ultra ATA, or Ultra DMA (UDMA), and the protocols for drives other than hard drives often go by the name ATAPI. Before the Serial ATA protocols were introduced, all IDE interfaces used parallel data transfer. In the notation *ATA/133* or *DMA/133,* the *133* represents the maximum data transfer rate in Mbps. *Also called* **Advanced Technology Attachment.** *See also* **Serial ATA.** *See* Table C on page 358.

158

iDEN *Abbreviation of* **Integrated Digital Enhanced Network.** A digital mobile communications technology, used for voice, text messaging, data, and two-way radio services. iDEN is based on TDMA technology and is related to the GSM standard, but its inclusion of two-way radio capabilities is unique.

identifier A character or string of characters that identifies a file, record, variable, or other data. A filename, for example, is the identifier for a file.

IEC *Abbreviation of* **International Electrotechnical Commission.** A worldwide organization that maintains international standards for products and components in electronics and telecommunications. IEC and ISO work together closely through their Joint Technical Committee 1 (JTC1).

IEEE *Abbreviation of* **Institute of Electrical and Electronic Engineers.** An international professional organization of engineers, scientists, and students dedicated to the advancement and regulation of technology related to electricity. The IEEE has developed and set many standards used in the computer, telecommunications, and electronics industries.

IEEE 802 A set of standards developed by the IEEE involving the operation and management of local area networks. The standards labeled *802.11* deal with wireless LANs. Those labeled *802.3* deal with Ethernet. *See also* **Wi-Fi.** *See* Table D on page 360.

IEEE 1284 A parallel bus standard for connecting a peripheral device with a Centronic port, usually a printer, to a parallel port on a computer. IEEE 1284 cables have a 25-pin D-subminiature connector on the computer-end of the cable and a 36-pin D-subminiature connector on the device-end. *See* Table C on page 358.

IEEE 1394 A serial bus standard used for transferring data to and from digital devices at rates of up to 400 Mbps under the basic standard or up to 3200 Mbps under the IEEE 1394b standard. IEEE 1394 was originally developed by Apple Computer but is now also used in Windows-based applications to connect digital cameras and memory card readers to computers. FireWire is the Apple Computer trade name for this bus standard; iLink is the Sony trade name. FireWire 400 connectors, which transfer data at 100, 200, and 400 Mbps, have a four or six-pin plug depending on whether or not they are powered. FireWire 800 connectors, which conform to the IEEE 1394b standard, have an eight-pin plug. *Also called* **High Performance Serial Bus.** *See figure at* **connector.** *See* Table C on page 358.

illegal character A character that cannot be accepted by a computer in a particular command or statement, usually because it is reserved for another use. For example, in Microsoft Windows file names, the asterisk (*) is an illegal character.

iLink The Sony trade name for IEEE 1394.

IM *Abbreviation of* **instant messaging.**

iMac A compact desktop personal computer introduced by Apple Computer in 1998.

image map A graphic that is encoded with multiple HTML links so that clicking on various points on the image directs the web browser to those links. An example of an image map is a picture of a skeleton with embedded links associated with individual bones that, when clicked on, link to data specific to that bone.

image processing The use of a computer to analyze, manipulate, or modify images. Examples include changing the contrast of a picture, removing wrinkles from the photograph of a face, or adding color to a black and white image.

imagesetter A typesetting device that produces very high-resolution output by transferring an image to plates, graphics, or photosensitive paper directly from electronic text or graphic files. *Also called* **typesetter.**

IMAP *Abbreviation of* **Internet Message Access Protocol.** A protocol developed by Stanford University for retrieving and storing incoming email. With IMAP, email is stored on a mail server in a manner that allows easy access to it from multiple locations. IMAP allows users to set up multiple folders for sorting email on the server and provides support for multiple clients to connect to the same account. IMAP4, developed in the 1990s, is supported by most browsers and email programs. *See also* **POP.**

IMEI *Abbreviation of* **international mobile equipment identifier.** A unique number that identifies cell phones and other devices that use GSM technology. IMEIs are encoded in the chips of GSM devices and are designed to help prevent fraud. *Compare* **IMSI.** *See also* **MEID.**

impact printer A printer that prints by striking a pin or a character against an ink ribbon, which in turn hits the paper, leaving a mark. Dot-matrix printers are the most common impact printers; others, such as those that use a daisy-wheel as on some typewriters, are becoming increasingly uncommon as they are considerably slower and noisier.

impedance A measure of the total opposition to current flow in an alternating current circuit. Loudspeakers with an average impedance under four ohms require amplifiers capable of producing especially powerful signals.

import To acquire data or a file from some other program or computer system. The format of the data must be compatible with the program it is being imported into, or a conversion program will have to be used. Many programs are designed to be compatible with each other in order to allow importing and exporting. For example, a graphics file in PICT or JPEG format can be imported into most graphics software and desktop publishing programs. *See also* **export.**

IMSI *Abbreviation of* **international mobile subscriber identity.** A unique number used to identify a subscriber on a GSM network. IMSIs are encoded on removable SIM cards and are part of the data that is used to determine whether a user has the right to use a given network and to bill the user. The IMSI and other data on a SIM card is encrypted to help prevent the SIM card from being cloned. *Compare* **IMEI.**

inclusive OR *See* **OR.**

incremental backup A backup that copies only those files that have been added or changed since the last backup of any kind. When using incremental backups to restore files, both the last full backup and every incremental backup that has occurred since that last full backup must be available. *Compare* **differential backup.**

index *n.* A data structure used to search data more quickly. Indexes are used by search engines, database management systems, and other programs that need to look through large amounts of data quickly. They contain information about the location of basic data elements. For example, an index used by a web search engine records a list of webpages that contain various keywords.

v. To create an index for a data structure.

indexed sequential access method *See* **ISAM.**

Industry Standard Architecture *See* **ISA.**

.info A top-level domain operated by Afilias and intended to be used for informational websites. Any person or organization can register a domain name in the .info domain and there are no official rules for enforcing restrictions on the types of sites that have names in the domain.

information technology *Abbreviated* **IT.** The technology involved with the transmission and storage of information, especially the development, installation, implementation, and management of computer systems, networks, and applications within companies, universities, and other organizations.

infrared *Abbreviated* **IR.** **1.** Relating to wireless communication using infrared light waves. Infrared devices can exchange data by transmitting and receiving infrared light over short distances. Unlike other wireless communications technologies, infrared connections require an unobstructed path between the infrared ports on each device. *See also* **IrDA, remote. 2.** Relating to radiation slightly lower in frequency than visible light.

infrared adapter An external infrared port that connects to a device's USB or serial port and allows the device to make infrared connections to other devices. *Also called* **IrDA adapter.**

Infrared Data Association *See* **IrDA.**

Infrared Financial Messaging *See* **IrFM.**

infrared port A transceiver used for sending and receiving infrared waves, often found on PDAs, laptops, and smartphones. Two devices with infrared ports can exchange data at distances up to two meters (six feet). To make a connection between two infrared ports, there must be an unobstructed path between them. The infrared port is usually located in a small recess in the device's case and is usually covered with a dark red translucent plastic cover. *Also called* **infrared transceiver, IrDA port.** *See also* **infrared adapter.**

initialization file A file used by an application to establish the parameters that it uses upon startup. For example, a word-processing application might save parameters such as page margins, default fonts, or printer preferences in an initialization file, so that the next time the application is run, that file can be read and those parameters restored. Initialization files on many Windows operating systems have the *.ini* extension. *See also* **rc file.**

initialize **1.** To prepare a device, such as a printer, for use by resetting its parameters to the default values. *See also* **format. 2.** To prepare a disk for use by dividing it into sectors in which data can be stored and readily accessed. Information cannot be stored on the disk until it is initialized. All previous information existing on the disk is erased during the initialization process. *See also* **format.**

inkjet printer A printer consisting of a grid of ink nozzles that fire tiny streams of ink onto paper. Many inkjet printers are capable of producing high-quality pictures. *See also* **piezoelectric inkjet printer, printer, thermal inkjet printer.**

inline graphic **1.** A graphics file that is embedded in the same layer as the text of document, such as a word processing document. An inline graphic acts like a text item, so when the text is altered or moved, the graphic moves with it. *Compare* **floating graphic. 2.** A graphics file that is embedded within the text of a webpage or other HTML document, rather than being linked from another page. The graphic is displayed automatically when the document is opened. *See also* **hotlink.**

input   Information that is entered into a computer for processing, such as commands typed from a keyboard, a file read from a disk, or a bitmap created by scanning an image. *Compare* **output.**

input device   Hardware that transfers information into a computer. Keyboards, modems, mice, and scanners are examples of input devices. *See also* **output device.**

input/output   *See* I/O.

Ins   *Abbreviation of* **Insert key.**

insertion point   The point on a computer screen or window where newly typed characters will be inserted, or where deletions will be made, often indicated by a cursor appearing as a blinking vertical bar.

Insert key   *Abbreviated* **Ins.**   A computer key that allows the computer to toggle between insert mode and overwrite mode.

insert mode   In word processing, a mode for inserting new characters without typing over existing characters. *Compare* **overwrite mode.**

instant messaging   *Abbreviated* **IM.**   Any of various systems that allow two or more users connected to the Internet to exchange text messages quickly in the manner of a spoken conversation. A user typically types a short message, and the message is immediately visible to recipients in a sequential display that includes previous messages from all participants in a session. Most instant-messaging systems use a proprietary protocol in which users run client software that connects to a central server.

Institute of Electrical and Electronic Engineers   *See* **IEEE.**

instruction   A command, especially a single machine language command. *See also* **statement.**

instruction set   The set of machine language instructions that a microprocessor can recognize and execute. Different kinds of microprocessors use different instruction sets, so a piece of software that is compatible with computers using different microprocessors often requires very different executable code for each kind of computer. *See also* **RISC.**

integrated   Relating to hardware or software that combines two or more tasks. For example, a program that offers word processing, spreadsheets, communications, and database management in one program is integrated.

integrated circuit *Abbreviated* **IC.** **1.** An electronic circuit whose components, such as transistors and resistors, are etched or imprinted on a single slice of semiconductor material to produce a chip. Integrated circuits are often categorized by the number of electronic components they contain. **2.** *See* **chip.**

Integrated Digital Enhanced Network *See* **iDEN.**

Integrated Drive Electronics *See* **IDE.**

Integrated Services Digital Network *See* **ISDN.**

interactive Relating to a program or a kind of processing that accepts and responds to input from the user, such as data and commands. Word processing and spreadsheet applications as well as computer and video games are interactive programs.

interactive messaging The sending and receiving of text messages, especially short messages, to and from cell phones, pagers, and other handheld devices. Interactive messaging can use various protocols and systems, including SMS, email, and instant messaging.

interactive program guide *See* **electronic program guide.**

interface **1.** The graphics, commands, prompts, or other signals that enable a computer to communicate with any other entity, such as a printer, another computer, a network, or a user. For example, the ports and connector are parts of the interface between a computer and a printer. An interface that lets a user communicate with the computer is a user interface. *See also* **GUI. 2.** *See* **port** (sense 1).

interlacing A video format for CRT displays in which the successive images that constitute the video use in alternation only the odd or even lines of a given vertical resolution. Interlacing is used to transmit and display higher resolutions than would otherwise be possible due to bandwidth and other hardware limitations. If a CRT's electron guns do not draw images rapidly enough, the phosphor image fades before the next image is displayed, causing the video to flicker. Interlacing reduces the amount of time it takes for the electron guns to refresh the screen without reducing the apparent resolution. Interlaced video is typically displayed at 50 or 60 fields per second, which is twice the rate of progressive video, and is either recorded with an interlacing camera, or created from progressive video by dividing each frame into two fields. All NTSC video, a standard for analog television and VHS, is interlaced. Displays other than CRTs, such as LCDs or plasma displays, must convert interlaced signals into progressive signals through a process called deinterlacing. *Compare* **progressive scan.**

interLATA   *See* **long distance.**

interleaving   1. The arrangement of data on noncontiguous sectors of a disk to decrease access time. The platters of a disk spin very rapidly, meaning that once a sector has been fully read, the beginning of the next sector may already have spun under the read/write head. But sectors must be read in their entirety, so if data is stored contiguously so that each chunk of data is physically right next to the data it should follow, the head might miss part of the sector, and would have to wait a full rotation to read it when it comes around again. However, if the next chunk of the data is stored not on the adjacent sector but two or more sectors away, the read/write head will have enough time to be prepared to read the data without requiring a full rotation of the disk. **2.** A technique of storing information in RAM in which the RAM is divided into two or more sections, used to decrease access time. Generally, when the memory on a RAM chip is accessed, the memory cannot be accessed again without a brief pause for the chip to reset itself. To avoid this delay, interleaving allows the CPU to access alternate sections of RAM. While the memory just read is preparing to be read again, the CPU accesses the next piece of data from a different section. Interleaved memory is especially useful for increasing the effective speed of dynamic RAM (DRAM), which has relatively slow access time.

internal cache   *See* **level 1 cache.**

internal command   In DOS, a command that is defined in the core operating system program, rather than in an external utility program that comes with the operating system. *See also* **external command.**

internal font   *See* **resident font.**

internal modem   A modem that plugs into an expansion slot inside the computer instead of sitting outside the computer in a separate box. Internal modems usually use a standard telephone cable to connect to a telephone jack. *Also called* **onboard modem.**

International Electrotechnical Commission   *See* **IEC.**

international mobile equipment identifier   *See* **IMEI.**

international mobile subscriber identity   *See* **IMSI.**

International Organization for Standardization   *See* **ISO.**

International Telecommunication Union   *See* **ITU.**

internet   A network of computers, printers, disk drives, or other devices, connected in a network topology that allows the devices to communicate. *Compare* **Internet.**

Internet   A matrix of networks that interconnects millions of computers, including personal computers, workstations, mainframes, supercomputers, and handheld computers. The networks that make up the Internet use a standard set of communications protocols, thus allowing any computer equipped with basic software and hardware tools to communicate with others over the Internet. The Internet is used for email, file transfer, remote login, and as the basis for the entire World Wide Web. *Compare* **internet.**

Internet control message protocol   *See* **ICMP.**

Internet Explorer   A web browser developed by Microsoft Corporation and first released in 1995. Internet Explorer has been incorporated into Microsoft's Windows operating systems since 1997. It is available for Windows and Macintosh operating systems; however, the final Macintosh version was released in 2003.

Internet Message Access Protocol   *See* **IMAP.**

Internet Protocol   *See* **IP.**

Internet protocol television   *See* **IPTV.**

Internet Relay Chat   *See* **IRC.**

Internet Service Provider   *See* **ISP.**

interoperable   Relating to computer systems that are able to work together without being specially configured to do so. Interoperable devices and applications are able to exchange information, usually because of standard file formats and communication protocols.

interpolation   The process of calculating values of the intermediate sample points introduced in a digital signal, such as a pixelated image or a digital audio signal, that has been upsampled. Interpolation generally works by mathematical analysis of sample points that neighbor the newly introduced sample point, and then calculating an appropriate value that fits the overall shape of the signal.

interpreted language   A programming language whose programs are executed by an interpreter. Most scripting languages are interpreted languages. Programs written in some interpreted languages, such as Java, are compiled into an intermediate language before being interpreted.

interpreter   A program that executes other programs. Usually, interpreters are designed to be able to execute any program written in one specific language. In contrast to compilers, an interpreter does not output another version of a program. *Compare* **compiler.** *See also* **virtual machine.**

interprocess communication *Abbreviated* **IPC.** The ability for two applications running on a computer or two networked computers to share data. OLE is a form of interprocess communication.

intraLATA Relating to calls made within a telephone user's LATA (local access and transport area). IntraLATA calls are handled by the carrier that provides a user's basic telephone service. While they are not technically long-distance calls, some intraLATA calls incur extra charges. Such calls are usually referred to as *local toll* calls.

intranet A private network that provides services similar to those found on the Internet, composed of servers that communicate only with other servers on that network. An example of an intranet is a company's internal network.

I/O *Abbreviation of* **input/output.** Designating a program or device, such as a mouse or printer, that is used to input or output data rather than to process it. A modem, for example, is an I/O device, since it inputs and outputs data but does not process it (although it changes the form by which the data is encoded and transmitted).

IP *Abbreviation of* **Internet Protocol.** A packet-switching network protocol that allows computers on the Internet to communicate with each other. IP specifies the way packets of data are addressed and routed across the Internet to other computers. IP is a best-effort protocol, which means that it does not guarantee that all packets will make it to their destination. It is used in conjunction with TCP, which checks for lost or damaged packets. *See also* **IP address, TCP.**

IP address *Abbreviation of* **Internet protocol address.** The unique numerical sequence that serves as an identifier for a computer connected to the Internet. For most of the history of the Internet, an IP address has been a 32-bit number, written as a series of four decimal numbers between 0 and 255, separated by periods, as in 192.135.174.1. The latest version of IP uses a 128-bit address, typically written as eight groups of four hexadecimal digits separated by colons, as in 2005:0db9:85a3:08d3:1319:8a2e:0370:2334. *Compare* **MAC address.** *See also* **domain name.**

IPC *Abbreviation of* **interprocess communication.**

iPod A class of portable digital audio players developed by Apple Computer. Like other digital audio players, iPods can be used with both Macs and PCs and support a variety of audio formats, including MP3, AAC, WAV, and AIFF.

IP spoofing A technique of gaining unauthorized access to a computer or network, in which a message is sent to the target indicating that the party trying to gain access is from a trusted host computer or network;

this is done by modifying the message so that the message includes not the IP address of the sender's host, but the IP address of the trusted host. Some firewalls are able to detect the tampering required to modify the message in this way, thereby preventing unauthorized access.

IPTV   *Abbreviation of* **Internet protocol television.**   Digital television distributed over an IP-based network. IPTV requires a broadband Internet connection.

IPv4   *Abbreviation of* **Internet protocol version 4.**   The version of IP that has been used for most of the history of the Internet. The addressing scheme in IPv4 allows for about four billion unique computer addresses. Because of the rapid proliferation of the Internet, this was judged to be an insufficient number of addresses, and IPv6 was developed to replace IPv4. *See also* **IP address.**

IPv6   *Abbreviation of* **Internet protocol version 6.**   The latest version of IP, whose addressing scheme allows for about 3×10^{38} unique computer addresses. It was developed to replace IPv4, which allows fewer addresses. *See also* **IP address.**

IR   *Abbreviation of* **infrared.**

IRC   *Abbreviation of* **Internet Relay Chat.**   A protocol that allows users to hold real-time online conversations on one of several networks of servers worldwide. Using IRC, users can communicate with each other in ASCII text as part of a group discussion on any of a number of specified topics. *See also* **instant messaging.**

IR code   A specification of the infrared signals sent by a remote control to the device it controls, such as a television or DVD player. The required signals vary according to the signal's function, such as stop or play, and according to the make and model of the device being controlled. For this reason, replacement remote controls are often preprogrammed with multiple sets of IR codes in order to be compatible with a variety of makes and models. Some remote controls that are capable of receiving as well as sending infrared signals can learn IR codes from other remote controls. This feature is commonly found in universal remote controls.

IrDA   *Abbreviation of* **Infrared Data Association.**   **1.** A set of protocols for wireless communication using infrared light waves. The IrDA protocols allow two devices with infrared ports, such as handhelds, laptops, desktop computers, or peripherals, to exchange data at rates of up to 16 Mbps over distances of up to two meters (six feet). Infrared is commonly used with handhelds, often to synchronize such devices with a desktop computer or to exchange data with other handhelds. *See also* **beam, infrared, IrFM.** *See* Table D on page 360. **2.** The industry association responsible for maintaining the IrDA protocols and related standards for infrared wireless communication.

IrDA port   *See* **infrared port.**

IrFM   *Abbreviation of* **Infrared Financial Messaging.**   A mobile payment protocol designed by IrDA to allow users to pay for goods and services by sending infrared messages from their handheld devices. *Also called* **Point and Pay.**

ISA   *Abbreviation of* **Industry Standard Architecture.**   A bus architecture used in IBM PC and PC-compatible computers. The ISA bus was originally created for the IBM PC/XT and had an 8-bit data path. A later version created for the IBM PC/AT, known as the AT bus, has a 16-bit data path but is downward compatible with the older version. ISA is pronounced EYE-suh. *See* Table C on page 358.

ISAM   *Abbreviation of* **indexed sequential access method.**   An efficient method for managing the storage and retrieval of data on a hard disk. ISAM stores data in the order in which it is entered as well as in an index, allowing both sequential and random access to the data. The application using the disk may then retrieve the information in whichever manner is most efficient.

ISDN   *Abbreviation of* **Integrated Services Digital Network.**   A telecommunications standard for transmitting digital data over analog telephone lines. In order to transmit digital data over an older, analog telephone circuit, a computer modem must convert the digital signal into an analog one, while another modem must undo the translation at the receiving end. Since ISDN circuitry transmits all data digitally, the conversion to and from analog is avoided, thereby greatly increasing the bandwidth of the telephone lines for digital communication.

To transmit voice data on ISDN circuits, the analog sound signal picked up by the microphone is digitized; this digital signal is then transmitted across the circuit. At the receiving end it is reconverted into an anolog signal for the earpiece or speaker so that it can be heard.

In North America, an ISDN circuit is divided into B (or bearer) channels (2 for copper phone wires, 23 for fiber-optic lines), which carry voice and data, and a single D (or delta) channel, which carries control information. The B channels, running at 64 kilobits per second each, can be combined to yield a throughput of 128 kilobits per second for standard phone lines. *See also* **circuit switching, packet switching.**

ISO   A worldwide organization, the International Organization for Standardization, that maintains standards in many businesses and technologies, including computing and communications. While the term *ISO* uses the initial letters of the English name of the organization, it is not a typical abbreviation; it actually derives from the Greek word *īsos*, meaning equal, and is used as the short form of the name in every language.

ISO 8859   An ISO standard for encoding characters in digital files. ISO 8859 consists of 15 separate character encodings, each specifying how a particular group of 256 characters should be represented as eight-bit bytes.

The standard covers some of the most common scripts. For example, ISO Latin-1, also known as ISO 8859-1, encodes characters in the Latin alphabet. Because the standard uses eight-bit sequences, it is restricted to encodings containing at most 256 characters and does not cover common Asian languages.

ISO 10646   An ISO standard for encoding characters in digital files. ISO 10646 defines the universal character set, assigning code numbers and names to the characters of almost all known scripts. It uses the same set of characters and code numbers defined in the Unicode standard. The standard also includes two different ways of encoding character code numbers as sequences of bits in digital files: UCS-2 and UCS-4. These schemes are largely equivalent to UTF-16 and UTF-32, respectively.

ISO/IEC JTC1   *See* **JTC1.**

ISO Latin-1   An ISO standard character encoding covering the characters found in most Western European languages. ISO Latin-1 is HTML's and HTTP's default character set. It is an extended ASCII character set, in that the first 127 encodings are the same as ASCII without most of the control characters. ISO Latin-1 is more formally referred to as *ISO 8859-1,* because it is defined in the ISO 8859 standard, but the less formal term is very common. *See* Table 5 at **extended ASCII.**

ISP   *Abbreviation of* **Internet Service Provider.**   An organization that provides other organizations or individuals with access to the Internet. Larger ISPs often provide access by means of modem, fiber-optic cable, or other means to link computers to a central server that provides Internet access.

IT   *Abbreviation of* **information technology.**

italic   A font style in which characters slant to the right. *This sentence is printed in italic type.*

Itanium   A microprocessor developed jointly by Intel and Hewlett-Packard that has 64-bit registers and advanced features for processing instructions in parallel. Versions of Windows and Linux are available for computers with Itanium processors. *See also* **x86-64.**

ITU   *Abbreviation of* **International Telecommunication Union.**   A United Nations agency that sets standards for the telecommunications industry.

iTunes A media player developed by Apple Computers for downloading, playing, and organizing digital audio and video files. iTunes was originally developed for use on Apple Macintosh computers, but it is now supported on Windows platforms as well.

jack A socket, especially the socket of a registered jack or jack connector. Jack connectors were originally used on telephone switchboards, and the name *jack* was carried over from these original connectors to the connectors, called registered jacks, used to plug in modern telephones.

jack connector A connector consisting of a jack and a long single-pin plug that is used to carry an audio signal. The pin of a jack plug is divided into sections that transmit different signals, typically right and left audio. The plug comes in 1/4-, 1/8-, and, more rarely, 3/32-inch diameters. Jack connectors are probably most familiar as headphone connectors, but they are also used as general audio input and output connectors on computers and handheld devices.

    Jack connectors are sometimes referred to as phono connectors, though some restrict the sense of *phono connector* to *RCA connector. Also called* **TRS connector.** *See figure at* **connector.** *See* Table A on page 356.

jaggies In computer graphics, jagged artifacts that appear where there should be smooth curves or diagonals. *See also* **aliasing, artifact, pixelization.** *See figure at* **antialiasing.**

jar *Abbreviation of* **Java archive.** A zip format archive containing a computer program written in Java. Because Java programs often consist of multiple files, the files that make up a program are usually assembled into a jar file for distribution. When a program contained in a jar file is executed, the java interpreter extracts the necessary files from the archive. Jar files typically have the file extension *.jar.*

Java An object-oriented programming language initially developed by Sun Microsystems. Because of its extensive security features and because programs written in it run on many different operating systems, Java is popular for Internet applications. *Compare* **JavaScript.** *See also* **applet, JSP.**

Java archive *See* **jar.**

JavaScript A scripting language originally developed by Netscape Communications for embedding scripts in webpages. JavaScript runs in a web

171

browser and adds features like buttons and other interactive elements to webpages. It complies with the ECMAScript standard and is now maintained by the Mozilla Foundation. *Compare* **Java, JScript.**

JavaServer pages *See* **JSP.**

Java Virtual Machine *Abbreviated* **JVM.** An interpreter for the Java programming language that executes Java bytecode. Programs written in Java are compiled into bytecode, and the bytecode can be executed on any system that has a Java Virtual Machine. Java Virtual Machines are available for most modern operating systems and machines.

Jaz A disk drive developed by Iomega that is capable of transferring data at a rate of 330 MBps to a removable 1 GB disk. The Jaz drive is based on standard hard disk technology and can be installed either internally or externally using either a SCSI or parallel port. Jaz drives are no longer in common use due to the development of affordable and compact hardware for burning CDs and DVDs, which have higher storage capacity.

jitter A slight, rapid variation or distortion in a digital video or audio signal, usually caused by poor synchronization of the signal's digital pulses.

job A specified action or group of actions that the computer carries out as a single unit. For example, when a computer prints a document, the process is considered a print job. Often, a single program or application is responsible for carrying out multiple jobs.

Joint Photographic Experts Group *See* **JPEG.**

Joint Technical Committee 1 *See* **JTC1.**

joystick A handheld, button-activated input device consisting of an upright lever attached with a pivot to a plastic base. The motion of the lever is used to control some aspect of the computer software; for example, by moving a pointer on the screen in the same direction as the joystick lever, or by controlling the motion of some object being depicted on the screen, such as the flight of an airplane. Joysticks are popular control devices, especially for computer games and CAD/CAM systems.

JPEG **1.** *Abbreviation of* **Joint Photographic Experts Group.** A subcommittee of the ISO and the IEC that establishes standards for the digital compression of photographic images. **2.** The standard algorithm for image compression developed by this committee. JPEG compresses color or gray-scale digital images using lossy compression. It is not well-suited for line art or black-and-white images, due to the appearance of compression artifacts, but it is well-suited for photographic images. JPEG has become the standard format for encoding images on the Internet, and files of this type are usually identified by the *.jpg* extension after their filenames.

JScript   A scripting language that was developed by Microsoft Corporation to embed scripts in webpages and is compliant with the ECMAScript standard. JScript is similar to JavaScript, but the two are not fully compatible. *Compare* **JavaScript.**

JSP   *Abbreviation of* **JavaServer pages.**   A scripting language used to generate webpages. When a user requests a webpage that uses JSP, the script is interpreted and creates HTML to return to the user. *See also* **dynamic HTML, server-side script.**

JTC1   *Abbreviation of* **Joint Technical Committee 1.**   A joint committee of the ISO and the IEC that maintains standards in information technology. The JTC1 also has subcommittees, such as the Joint Photographic Experts Group (JPEG) and the Moving Pictures Experts Group (MPEG). *Also called* **ISO/IEC JTC1.**

jumper   A plug or wire designed to fit over pins in a circuit board, creating an electrical connection between them. Jumpers are used on some printed circuit boards, especially in disk drives and computer motherboards, as a kind of switch to enable or disable different parts of the circuit, allowing a variety of hardware configurations to be set up that may be changed if needed.

justification   The adjustment of spacing within a document so that lines end evenly at a straight margin. Newspaper articles and other typeset copy, for example, are usually justified both left and right, so that both the left and right margins of each column are even. Copy that is typed using a typewriter, on the other hand, is usually justified only at the left, so that the left margin is even but the right margin is ragged. Word processing and desktop publishing software generally allow the user to lay out text with or without justification. *Also called* **alignment.**

JVM   *Abbreviation of* **Java Virtual Machine.**

K   1. *Abbreviation of* **kilobyte.** 2. *Abbreviation of* **kelvin.**

Kb   *Abbreviation of* **kilobit.**

KB   *Abbreviation of* **kilobyte.**

K band   A band of microwave frequencies ranging from 10.7 to 18.4 gigahertz, used for satellite television broadcasting.

kbps or **kbit/s** *Abbreviations of* **kilobits per second.**

KBps or **KB/s** *Abbreviations of* **kilobytes per second.**

KDE *Abbreviation of* **K Desktop Environment.** A free, open-source desktop environment available for the Linux and Unix operating systems. KDE was the first complete desktop environment for Linux and Unix.

kelvin *Abbreviated* **K.** A unit of the Kelvin temperature scale, in which zero occurs at absolute zero. Water freezes at 273.15 K and boils at 373.15 K. Color temperature is measured in kelvins.

Kermit **1.** A file transfer protocol developed by Columbia University. While Kermit has largely been supplanted by FTP and SCP for file transfer over the Internet, the Kermit program can be used on such a wide variety of devices that the protocol remains in use. **2.** A program that uses the Kermit protocol to transfer files between two computers or other devices.

kernel The core module of an operating system that interacts directly with the hardware. The kernel typically processes tasks unseen by the user. These tasks usually include allocation of resources such as memory, CPU time, and synchronization of I/O peripherals.

kerning The adjustment of space between pairs of characters, usually in display type, so that the overall spacing of the letters appears even. Kerning makes certain combinations of letters, such as *WA, VA, TA, YA,* and *MW,* fit more neatly together on the page. Some page layout programs have an automatic kerning feature. Manual kerning can be performed with most page layout programs and some word processing programs.

without kerning   with kerning

kerning

key *n.* **1.** A button on a keyboard that is pressed to enter data or a command. **2.** A number used in cryptography, particularly in ciphers, in the encryption or decryption of information. The size of the key is usually measured in bits, with larger key sizes generally providing higher security. In Internet communication, keys are usually generated by the computers that are communicating and are not seen by the users. When a user is asked explicitly to type a password in order to encrypt or decrypt information, the password is typically not the key itself, but enables the use of the key. *See also* **private-key cryptography, public-key cryptography, one-time pad.**

v. To enter data into a computer by pressing buttons on the keyboard.

keyboard **1.** A device containing a set of keys and serving as the principal input device for most computers. Computer keyboards include a set of alphanumeric keys, usually in the standard layout of conventional type-writers, called the *QWERTY* keyboard layout. Many also have a numeric keypad to one side. All keyboards include a number of keys that perform functions other than typing characters, including the Control, Alt, function, and arrow keys. *See also* **Dvorak keyboard, Fitaly keyboard. 2.** *See* **keyboard layout.**

keyboard buffer A memory buffer for storing keystrokes until the CPU can act on them, allowing users to continue typing even if a program is not ready to accept input.

keyboard layout A specification of what characters are produced when specific keys and key combinations are pressed on a keyboard. Operating systems usually allow several different keyboard layouts, which makes it possible to type characters from different alphabets. More than one keyboard layout can be used for a given alphabet. For example, QWERTY and Dvorak are two different layouts for the Roman alphabet.

keyboard shortcut A combination of keystrokes that issue a command. For example, CTRL + C is a common keyboard shortcut used to copy text in word processing programs. Using keyboard shortcuts is often quicker than issuing commands by selecting from menus or toolbars. *Also called* **hot key, shortcut key.**

keyboard template A plastic or paper card that fits over or around the keys on a keyboard, especially the function keys, with printed information indicating each key's use in a particular program. *See also* **keyboard layout.**

key drive *See* **flash drive.**

key exchange The process by which two users or programs communicate over a public channel to establish a secret private key to be used to encrypt subsequent messages on the channel. Common security protocols such as SSL use a public-key cryptographic algorithm such as RSA to perform key exchange. *See also* **session key.**

keylogger Computer software or hardware that records a user's keystrokes and in some cases also periodic screen shots of a user's activity. This data is saved as a file or transferred through a network such as the Internet to a remote host. Keyloggers are used to monitor patterns of user behavior and for all manners of spying or stealing information, such as obtaining a user's passwords or credit card numbers. Keyloggers are installed without the user's knowledge, as by a worm or a Trojan horse. *Also called* **keystroke logger.**

keypad   An input device consisting of a set of keys usually arranged in a grid, as on a cell phone, calculator, or part of a standard computer keyboard. Keypads typically consist of numeric keys, but many can also be used to enter text characters or perform other functions. *See also* **numeric keypad.**

keystone   Distortion of an image that results from projecting the image from an angle that is not perpendicular to the projection screen. Some projectors can correct for keystone distortion by digitally adjusting the image or by moving the lens. *See also* **lens shift.**

keystroke   The striking of a key in order to enter a single character or command on a keyboard. Sometimes two or more keys are required for a single keystroke, as when entering an uppercase letter that requires holding down the shift key while striking another key.

keystroke logger   *See* **keylogger.**

keyword   **1.** A word used in a query to a search engine. Users enter keywords they think are likely to occur in documents they are interested in. **2.** A word or phrase included as metadata with a document, especially a webpage, in order to help identify the important concepts in the document so it can be retrieved by a search engine.

KHz or **kHz**   *Abbreviations of* **kilohertz.**

kill   **1.** To stop or end a process. **2.** To erase or delete a file permanently.

killer app   An application whose popularity forces out the competition or causes the competition to conform to it, as well as inducing consumers to purchase additional hardware in order to run the application.

killfile   A file containing lists of character strings, usually the names of authors or titles of threads, associated with Usenet news articles or emails that a user does not want to read. Many newsreaders and email clients can process a killfile when they start up, deleting posts or email that matches items in the killfile. Many also allow users to create killfiles by selecting messages. *See also* **filter.**

kilo-   *Abbreviated* **K.** **1.** A prefix indicating 1,000 (10^3), as in *kilohertz*. This is also the sense in which *kilo-* is generally used in terms of data transmission rates, where a bit is a signal pulse and is counted in the decimal system, which is based on multiples of 10. This decimal is sometimes abbreviated *kilo-* with a lowercase *k* to avoid confusion with the binary *kilo-*, which is abbreviated with an uppercase *K*. **2.** A prefix indicating 1,024 (2^{10}), as in *kilobyte*. This is the sense in which *kilo-* is generally used in terms of data storage capacity, which, due to the binary nature of bits, is based on powers of 2. This binary is sometimes abbreviated *kilo-* with an uppercase *K* to avoid confusion with the decimal *kilo-*, which is abbreviated with a lowercase *k*.

kilobit *Abbreviated* **Kb.** One thousand bits, used as a unit for expressing the rate of data transmission per unit of time (usually one second). In highly technical contexts involving data storage capacity, it can refer to 1,024 (2^{10}) bits.

kilobyte *Abbreviated* **K** or **KB.** **1.** A unit of measurement of computer memory or data storage capacity, equal to 1,024 (2^{10}) bytes. **2.** One thousand (1,000) bytes. While international standards indicate that the term *kilobyte* should be used to refer to units of 1,000 bytes, the term is almost always used to refer to units of 1,024 bytes.

kilohertz *Abbreviated* **KHz** or **kHz.** A unit of frequency equal to 1,000 hertz.

kludge A workable but poorly designed, often makeshift piece of hardware or software. Kludges are patched together from mismatched elements or elements designed for other uses.

L1 cache *Abbreviation of* **level 1 cache.**

L2 cache *Abbreviation of* **level 2 cache.**

label **1.** *See* **volume label. 2.** A heading placed in a cell of a spreadsheet to serve as a descriptive name for a row or column. **3.** A small piece of paper or other material, usually with an adhesive backing, that can be written on and attached to something for identification. Many word processors have a special option for creating sheets of labels.

LAN *Abbreviation of* **local area network.** A network that links together computers and peripherals within a limited area, such as a building or group of buildings. Each computer or device in a LAN is known as a node. The computers in a LAN have independent CPUs (central processing units), but they are able to exchange data and files with each other and to share such resources as laser printers.

The three principal LAN organizing structures, called topologies, are the bus, ring, and star structures. In a bus topology, all computers and other devices are connected to a central cable. In a ring topology, the computers are joined in a loop, so that a message from one passes through each node until it reaches its proper destination. In a star topology, all nodes are connected to one central computer, known as the hub.

Additionally, LANs are organized as either peer-to-peer networks, in which all computers are similarly equipped and communicate directly with one another, or client/server networks, in which one computer, the server, provides data and controls communication between other nodes.

Every LAN has a protocol that governs the exchange of data between nodes, and a network operating system (NOS), software that allows communication between devices to take place. *See also* **Ethernet, token-ring network.** *See* Table D on page 360.

land   **1.** The flat, light-reflecting layer on the playing surface of an optical disk. Data is encoded on the land in a series of microscopic pits etched by laser in a spiral-shaped track. **2.** A flat area between the pits on the playing surface of an optical disk. The pattern of intervals between lands and pits is detected by the disk player's read laser and converted into binary data to play the disk's content. *Compare* **pit.**

landline   A traditional telephone line in which a telephone is connected to the public network by cables. *See also* **landline, satellite phone.**

landscape   Relating to a mode in which a page or display screen is oriented so that it is wider than it is tall. *Compare* **portrait.**

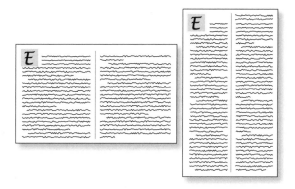

landscape (left) and portrait orientations

language   *See* **programming language.**

laptop   A portable computer small enough to fit on one's lap that provides most of the same functions and uses the same operating system as a desktop computer. In contrast to laptops, PDAs and other handhelds typically use special-purpose operating systems. Laptops usually have flat-panel displays that fold down and cover the keyboard. *Also called* **notebook.**

laser printer   A printer that uses one or more beams of light to produce an image on a rotating drum before transferring the image to paper. Laser printers are built around a rotating cylinder, called a print drum, that has an electrostatically charged surface. By shining a light—either a laser or a grid of LEDs or LCDs—on the drum, the printer creates a pattern of electrical charges corresponding to the image. As the drum rotates, these polarized charges attract particles of tinted powder, called toner. The drum then applies the toner to a piece of paper, and a heat lamp fuses the toner to the paper. Laser printers that print in color are typically more expensive than those that print only in black and white. *See also* **LCD printer, LED printer, printer.**

LaserWriter   A line of laser printers developed by Apple Computers and used with Macintosh computers. No longer manufactured, LaserWriters were one of the first laser printers available to consumers.

LATA   *Abbreviation of* **local access and transport area.**   A geographic region within which telephone calls are carried by a local carrier and are therefore not subject to long-distance charges. *See also* **intraLATA, local toll.**

latency   **1.** In a network, the amount of time that elapses in the transmission of a packet from its source to its destination. **2.** In disk drives, the amount of time that elapses in the rotation of the proper disk sector to a position under the read/write head. **3.** In SDRAM, the number of system bus cycles that elapse between a request to access a memory address and the reading of or writing to that address. The lower an SDRAM chip's latency, the faster data can be retrieved from it. *See also* **CAS latency.**

LaTeX   A page description language that is a component of the TeX word processing system. LaTeX was designed to have intuitive commands that allow the user to concentrate on content in contrast to appearance when typesetting. It has commands that make it easy to typeset special symbols and formulas, so it is widely used to produce scientific and mathematical papers. LaTeX documents can be transformed into PDF or PostScript documents for printing and viewing.

launch   To start a program. Most programs on personal computers can be launched by clicking on icons on the display screen of GUI interfaces. CD-ROM software usually launches automatically when the disk is inserted into the drive.

LAWN   *Abbreviation of* **local area wireless network.**   *See* **wireless LAN.**

layout   **1.** In desktop publishing and word processing, the art or process of arranging text and graphics on a page. Layout covers the overall design of a page, including elements such as page and type size, typeface, and the placement of graphics, titles, and page numbers. *See also* **page layout program, WYSIWYG. 2.** In database management systems, the arrangement of fields, leaders, and other elements when information is displayed in a report.

LCD *Abbreviation of* **liquid-crystal display.** A common display used in monitors, televisions, projectors, laptop computers, and handhelds, and also in devices such as calculators and digital watches.

An LCD is made of liquid crystals sandwiched between two layers of glass filters. Liquid crystals are rod-shaped molecules that flow like a liquid but have a crystalline order in their arrangement. Electric currents can be used to control the alignment of the molecules and therefore their transmission of light through the filters. Cells of liquid crystals are arranged in an array to form pixels, each cell acting as a tiny electronically controlled shutter.

Most large LCD panels, such as televisions and monitors, use thin film transistor technology, in which each pixel is controlled by a separate transistor. LCD projectors and rear-projection televisions use three small LCD panels. The panels produce three separate images, one green, one red, and one blue, which are combined into the single image that is projected on the screen.

LCD printer *Abbreviated* **liquid-crystal display printer.** A laser printer that uses a small LCD panel to produce an image on a rotating drum that transfers the image to paper. *Compare* **LED printer.** *See also* **laser printer.**

LCoS or **LCOS** **1.** *Abbreviations of* **liquid crystal on silicon.** A display used in projectors and rear-projection televisions. An LCoS display is made of liquid crystals arranged on three silicon chips that control the reflection of light from a mirror below. The chips produce three separate images, one green, one red, and one blue, which are combined into the single image that is projected on the screen. **2.** A projector or rear-projection television that uses such a display.

lead-in A circular data region in the inner part of an optical disk, 1.2 to 2 millimeters wide, inside the area where the main contents of the disk are stored. The lead-in contains information needed by the disk player to locate and read the main contents of the disk.

leading The vertical spacing between lines of text, measured in points. The measure includes the size of the font, so that 8-point type with 2-point spacing between lines is a leading of 10 points. Double-spaced 8-point type commonly has 18-point leading. *Leading* is pronounced with a short *e,* rhyming with *sledding. Also called* **line spacing.**

leading zero   In the display of numbers, a zero that is added as a place-holder to make a number fill up a field with a required amount of characters. For example, in 003.14159, the initial two zeroes are leading zeroes.

lead-out   A circular data region on an optical disk, 1.2 to 2 millimeters wide, surrounding the area where the main contents of the disk are stored. The lead-out serves as an instruction to the disk drive that no more data follows.

leased line   A telecommunications line that is leased from a telecommunications company for private use between two points, such as a T1 line connecting an organization's network to an ISP. *See also* **dedicated circuit.**

least significant bit   In the binary representation of a number, the bit representing the smallest exponent of 2. Binary numbers are usually written with their least significant bit at the right.

least significant digit   The rightmost digit in the written representation of a number. The least significant digit represents a multiple of the smallest exponent of the base used to represent the number; for example, in ordinary base 10 notation, the least significant digit of the number 5,783 is 3, which represents 3×10^0, that is, 3×1, which equals 3. (The other digits represent multiples of higher powers of 10; the 7, for example, represents 7×10^2, that is, 7×100, which equals 700.

LED   *Abbreviation of* **light-emitting diode.**

LED printer   *Abbreviation of* **light-emitting diode printer.**   A printer that uses a small LED panel to produce an image on a rotating drum that transfers the image to paper. *Compare* **LCD printer.** *See also* **laser printer.**

Left-arrow key   A key used to move the cursor to the left or back one character, or to scroll the contents of a window to the right so that the portions of its contents hidden on the left come into view. *Compare* **Right-arrow key.**

legacy   Relating to old or obsolete software, hardware, or data formats. Legacy software is often difficult to maintain because it may no longer be supported by its maker, and there may be few programmers who know how to work with it. Legacy data is difficult to work with because there may be few applications that can read and manipulate it.

lens shift   An adjustment on a projector that changes the position of the projected image and corrects for keystone distortion by moving the lens.

letterbox   A format for displaying widescreen images on a screen with narrower proportions. The letterbox format preserves the widescreen image by shrinking it until the full width can be seen, resulting in blank space above and below the image. *Compare* **pan-and-scan.** *See also* **anamorphic DVD.**

letter-quality   *Abbreviated* **LQ.**   Of or producing printed characters with a clarity greater than or equal to those produced by a conventional typewriter. Most modern printers produce letter-quality type.

level 1 cache   *Abbreviated* **L1 cache.**   In systems with multiple caches, the smallest and therefore fastest cache, which is checked first when data is needed by the CPU. The level 1 cache is usually an internal cache. *Also called* **internal cache, primary cache.**

level 2 cache   *Abbreviated* **L2 cache.**   The second level of cache memory in a microprocessor, which is larger and slower than the primary cache but smaller and faster than main memory. Very large level 2 caches can be so slow that they don't increase processing speeds significantly. The level 2 cache is often an external cache. *Also called* **secondary cache.** *See also* **level 1 cache.**

LF   *Abbreviation of* **linefeed.**

LFE channel   *Abbreviation of* **low-frequency effects channel.**   A surround-sound channel that only carries low-frequency audio signals of between 10 and 120 hertz. In surround-sound notation, the LFE channel is represented as *.1* after the number of full-range channels (20—20,000 hertz). For example, a six-channel surround-sound system with five full-range channels and one LFE channel is said to have *5.1* channels. The LFE channel is often directed to a subwoofer. *See also* **surround sound.**

library   **1.** A collection of standard routines, usually stored in executable form, that are used in programs. Some libraries, such as DLLs and shared libraries, contain routines whose instructions are not actually included in the programs that use them. In order to run a program that uses routines from such a library, the library must be installed. **2.** A collection of information, as in data files.

license   A legal agreement between the developer and the user of software that specifies the conditions for distributing, storing, and using that software. *See also* **clickwrap license, shrinkwrap license.**

light-emitting diode   *Abbreviated* **LED.**   An electronic semiconductor device that emits light when an electric current passes through it. LEDs are used for indicator lights, as on the front of a disk drive, and OLEDs, a type of LED, are used in displays. *See also* **OLED.**

light-emitting diode printer   *See* **LED printer.**

light pen or **light stylus**   A light-sensitive input device shaped like a pen, used to select objects on a CRT display screen.

Li-ion battery   *Abbreviation of* **lithium-ion battery.**

line   **1.** A wire, optical cable, or other channel, or a system of such channels, providing power or connecting communications systems. **2.** A string of characters in a horizontal row in a text file. Lines typically end with a standard control character indicating the end of the line. Empty lines with no characters (other than an end-of-line character) are still considered lines.

line art   An illustration consisting solely of solid black lines and white space, without shading.

line break   A command or tag in a word processing program, a page description language such as PDF, or a markup language such as HTML, indicating that a line should be ended and the cursor or printer should be moved to the beginning of the next line. Each program or language has its own line break commands and tags. *See also* **end of line, hard return, soft return.**

line editor   A simple program for editing text in which you can only edit or write one line at a time. Most line editors are obsolete.

linefeed   *Abbreviated* **LF.**   A control character that is often part of the indication of the end of a line in a text file. Linefeed is coded with a bit sequence corresponding to the number 10 in ASCII and in most other character encodings. It was originally designed to signal that the cursor on a text display should be moved to the next line or that the paper in a printer should be advanced one line. *Also called* **newline.** *See also* **carriage return, end of line, hard return.**

line noise   Unwanted electronic signals on a phone line that interfere with data transfers. Static is an example of line noise.

line printer   A high-speed impact printer, primarily used in business and industrial applications, that prints an entire line of type as a unit. The line printer differs from the dot-matrix printer, which prints each character individually, and the laser printer, which prints each page as a unit. Line printers usually serve more than one user and tend to be fast (up to 3,000 lines per minute) and loud.

line spacing   *See* **leading.**

link   **1.** *See* **hyperlink. 2.** On Linux or Unix operating systems, a hard link or a symbolic link. **3.** A connection between computers, devices, or programs, over which data is transmitted. **4.** *See* **hotlink.**

linked object A part of a document in the form of a link to another document or file. Since the information comprised by the linked object is not directly stored in the document, it may be altered or updated without altering the document itself. For a document containing linked objects to be fully visible or interpretable, the linked object files must be present and the links well-formed. *Compare* **embedded object.**

link rot The process or condition in which links on a website become irrelevant or cease to function, as when the locations they point to are webpages that have been modified, relocated, or no longer exist.

Linux A Unix-compatible operating system developed by Linus Torvalds and Gnu. Like Unix, Linux allows multiple users to work on the same computer at the same time. Unlike Unix or Windows, the core elements of the operating system are open-source and free of charge, as is much of the software that runs on it.

A complete Linux system consists of a number of different replaceable modules, such as a desktop environment and window manager, as well as other tools and accessories. Different organizations and companies distribute the core operating system with their own mix of open-source and proprietary modules, and users can modify the system on their own to create very different environments. Linux is usually installed on x86 computers, but it can run on many hardware platforms. *See also* **distribution, time-sharing.**

liquid-crystal display *See* **LCD.**

liquid-crystal display printer *See* **LCD printer.**

liquid crystal on silicon *See* **LCoS.**

Lisp *Abbreviation of* **list processing** or **list processor.** A programming language that is widely used in artificial intelligence. Invented in 1958 by John McCarthy at MIT and originally designed as a mathematical notation to use in the scientific study of computing and computer programs, Lisp was one of the first high-level programming languages.

list processor *See* **Lisp.**

listserv **1.** Popular software for list servers, owned by L-Soft International. Listserv is available for Linux, Unix, and Windows operating systems. **2.** *See* **mailing list.**

list server A program that manages email distribution and subscriptions for mailing lists. Users interact with a mailing list by sending email to a list server. Each list server can manage several mailing lists. *See also* **listserv.**

literal   A letter or symbol used in a computer, especially in a programming or markup language, acting in its everyday capacity as a symbol, rather than being a token for a feature, function, or entity associated with it. For example, * can be a symbol that refers to an arbitrary character, but as a literal, it is an asterisk.

lithium battery   A disposable battery that contains lithium. Lithium cells typically produce approximately three volts of electricity and have a larger energy storage capacity than alkaline cells of the same size.

lithium-ion battery   *Abbreviated* **Li-ion battery.**   A rechargeable battery that uses lithium ions. Li-ion cells typically produce around 3.6 volts of electricity and have a greater energy storage capacity than NiCad and NiMH cells of the same size.

lithium-ion polymer battery   *Abbreviated* **Li-ion polymer battery.**   A rechargeable battery similar to a lithium-ion battery but made of materials that permit the design of batteries with a greater variety of shapes and sizes and that make the battery less expensive to manufacture.

LMDS   *Abbreviation of* **local multipoint distribution system.**   A protocol for wireless communication that allows data transmission across distances as long as eight kilometers (five miles). LMDS uses microwave frequency transmissions and is designed to provide high-bandwidth wireless connections between a base station and several different transceivers at fixed locations.

load   **1.** To transfer a program or data from a storage device into a computer's memory. Before a program on a disk can be executed, it must be loaded into the computer's RAM (random-access memory). **2.** To import a large amount of data into a database. **3.** To mount an external storage device, such as a tape, floppy disk, or CD, into its drive.

loader   A computer program that transfers data from a mass storage device, usually a hard disk, into working memory.

local access and transport area   *See* **LATA.**

local area network   *See* **LAN.**

local area wireless network   *Abbreviated* **LAWN.**   *See* **wireless LAN.**

local call   An intraLATA call.

local calling area   A geographical region within which a telephone customer can make calls without incurring long-distance or local toll charges. For cell phone customers, the local calling area is often the same as the home service area. *Compare* **LATA.**

local echo   *See* **half duplex.**

185

local multipoint distribution system *See* **LMDS.**

local toll   Relating to intraLATA calls that incur an extra charge because they are placed to numbers outside a user's local calling area. *See also* **LATA.**

lock   **1.** In networking and other multi-user systems, to make a file or other unit of data inaccessible. The operating system locks a file or database record after one user has begun to work on it so that subsequent users cannot work on it at the same time. Write-locking only prevents the file or record from being altered, but read-locking prevents it from being viewed. **2.** To write-protect a floppy disk.

log file   A file that lists the actions of programs or users on a computer system in the order that the actions occurred. Programs and operating systems can often be configured to write data to log files. *Also called* **log.**

logical   Relating to the way the user perceives the organization of an element such as a database or a file. To the user, a file may be a discrete unit, but it is likely that the file is stored in pieces scattered throughout a computer's memory or on a disk. The term *physical* is used when referring to the actual location and structure of an element.

logical operator   An operator representing a function whose result can only be one of the values TRUE or FALSE. Common logical operators are AND, OR, XOR, and NOT. They are widely used in programming, spreadsheets, and searching. They join expressions that are TRUE or FALSE to create composite expressions. For example, $x > 4$ AND $x < 6$ is TRUE if x has the value 5.

In searching and database querying, logical operators are often used to describe the desired data. For example, the query *cat OR dog* will return all documents that contain the word *cat* as well as all documents that contain the word *dog*.

Logical operators are also essential to the functioning of logic gates in computer chips. *Also called* **Boolean operator, logical connective.**

logic gate   A mechanical, optical, or electronic system that performs a logical operation on an input signal. Logic gates, principally implementing the operations NAND and NOR (which are easily implemented as electronic circuits on a micro scale), are a major component of microchips. Almost all of the processing done in a CPU, for example, is done by millions of such interconnected logic gates. Memory and graphics accelerators also employ logic gates. *See* Table E on page 361.

log in   *See* **log on.**

login or **login name**   *See* **username.**

log off *See* **log out.**

log on To enter the information required to begin a session on a computer or multi-user computer system such as a network or website. Logging on typically consists of giving a username and a password. *Also called* **log in.** *Compare* **log off.**

log out To end a session on a computer or multi-user computer system such as a network or website. Logging out signals the system that you have finished communicating with it. It is recommended that users always log out of online accounts when leaving a computer to which others have access, and that they close the browser window to prevent others from accessing personal information. *Also called* **log off.** *Compare* **log in.**

long distance Relating to calls made to a location outside a telephone user's LATA. Long-distance calls are handled by specially designated long-distance carriers. *Also called* **interLATA.** *See also* **intraLATA, local toll.**

look-and-feel The general appearance and functioning of the user interface of a software product. Programs with the same look-and-feel appear essentially the same onscreen, and the user who knows one such program can run the others without learning new commands and menus. The look-and-feel of software, as opposed to its internal structure, has been a consideration in several legal cases concerning software copyright violations.

lossless compression Data compression that can be achieved with no loss of information.

lossy compression Data compression that results in some loss of information. Lossy compression is commonly used for storing and transmitting audio and visual information when some loss of picture or sound quality is considered acceptable as a tradeoff for smaller file sizes or faster transmission. Lossy compression can sometimes give rise to noticeable artifacts, such as high-pitched metallic sounds that accompany audio signals, and can cause a shifting patchwork effect on video images.

loudness **1.** The perceived intensity of a sound. Loudness is affected by a sound's amplitude, frequency, bandwidth, and duration. For example, sounds consisting of two notes of two different frequencies are generally perceived as louder than each of the notes separately, even if the amplitudes of the sounds are the same. *Compare* **amplitude, volume. 2.** A control that determines both the overall and relative volumes of the low-frequency, midrange, and high-frequency parts of an audio signal. Since the human ear is less responsive to high and low frequencies at low volumes than it is to midrange frequencies, lowering the overall volume of a signal causes a perceived decrease in the volume of high and low frequencies. Using a loudness control decreases the midrange frequencies relative to the high and low frequencies, maintaining the perception of balance of frequencies at the lower volume. *Compare* **volume.**

loudspeaker   *See* **speaker.**

low-end   Having or relating to low frequencies, typically below 300 hertz. Used mostly of audio signals or devices such as speakers that process audio signals.

lowercase   Relating to or being a noncapitalized letter. *See also* **case-sensitive.**

low-frequency effects channel   *See* **LFE channel.**

low-level language   A computer language, such as an assembly language or machine language, in which each statement is an individual instruction to be carried out directly by the CPU that the language is designed for. A high-level language, on the other hand, often combines several CPU instructions in each statement and is designed to work with any CPU. *Compare* **high-level language.**

low-resolution   *Abbreviated* **low-res.**   Relating to a display device or a printed or electronic image that has a low pixel density. Low-resolution images lack sharpness and may appear grainy. *Compare* **high-resolution.** *See also* **resolution.**

LPT   On a computer running Windows, one of three possible parallel ports, designated by MS-DOS as LPT1, LPT2, or LPT3. The letters *LPT* originally stood for *line print terminal.*

LQ   *Abbreviation of* **letter-quality.**

luminance   **1.** *See* **brightness** (sense 1). **2.** The black-and-white component of a video signal. *Also called* **luma.**

lurk   To read but not participate in ongoing discussions on a newsgroup or mailing list or in a chatroom. Proper netiquette dictates that newcomers to a newsgroup lurk for a while to get an understanding of the people and issues to avoid sending unwanted, irrelevant, or redundant messages.

Lynx   A web browser that displays text but not graphics. It is typically used with Unix-compatible operating systems.

m *Abbreviation of* **milli-.**

M *Abbreviation of* **mega-.**

M3U A file format used to store playlists of MP3s or other audio files. An M3U is formatted as a text file containing a queue of audio files and the paths or hyperlinks leading to each file's location. When the M3U is loaded in a media player, the queued files are played in the order that they are listed in.

M4A *Abbreviation of* **MPEG-4 Audio.** A file format that uses the audio layer of MPEG-4 to store and transmit digital audio. The information in M4A files is more highly compressed than information in MP3 files, so they require less bandwidth while maintaining higher quality. The extension *.m4a* distinguishes audio-only M4A files from MP4 files, which may contain both audio and video content. *See also* **AAC.** *Compare* **MP4.**

M4P A copy-protected file format developed by Apple Computer for use with files purchased from iTunes. M4P integrates the AAC format with an encryption scheme that makes the files unplayable on unauthorized computers. Files of this type usually have the *.m4p* extension. *Also called* **protected AAC.**

Mac *Abbreviation of* **Macintosh.**

MAC address *Abbreviation for* **Media Access Control address.** The unique numerical sequence that serves as an identifier for a device within a network. A MAC address commonly appears as a six-byte value expressed in hexadecimal notation. *Also called* **hardware address, physical address.** *Compare* **IP address.**

machine address *See* **absolute address.**

machine code Code written in machine language, taking the form of binary instructions that are interpreted by a CPU. Executable files consist of machine code, which is usually generated by compiling source code written by programmers. *See also* **machine language, programming language, source code.**

machine language The language used and understood by the CPU of a computer. Each CPU architecture has its own machine language. Machine language is the lowest-level language, and programs in high-level languages must be either converted to machine language or executed by an interpreter in order to run.

machine-readable   Relating to information encoded in a form that can be read by a peripheral device and interpreted by a computer, such as data on a disk. Most machine-readable data is in digital form.

Macintosh   *Abbreviated* **Mac.**   A line of personal computers introduced in 1984 by Apple Computer. Macintosh computers were the first popular computers to have an operating system with a GUI (graphical user interface) that employed windows, icons, onscreen menus, and the generalized use of a mouse. Other GUIs, such as Microsoft Windows, developed for the IBM operating environment, and Gnome, developed for the Linux environment, have incorporated many of the visual tools that originated in the Macintosh line.

Since Apple has provided a series of proprietary operating systems for use on Macintosh computers, the terms *Macintosh* and *Mac* have been used to refer both to the operating system and to the computer itself. Recent versions of the operating system have also gone by the name OS. In 1999, Apple introduced OS X, a new operating system based on Unix, which differs substantially from previous versions.

MacOS   The name for any of the Macintosh operating systems designed by Apple Computers. *See also* **OS X.**

macro   A set of stored commands created by a user to automatically perform a task. Macros can be specific to an application, as a series of commands that a spreadsheet or word processor performs at the click of a button, or they can be general-purpose, as an operating system macro that types a set of characters when a given key combination is pressed.

macroblocking   A type of blocking that occurs in DVDs, HDTV, and other forms of MPEG video. In macroblocking, rectangular sections of the image freeze when images on the screen are in rapid motion.

macro virus   A virus that consists of a macro and is spread by being embedded in a word processing or spreadsheet document.

Macrovision   An electronic copy protection system for analog video content, developed by a company of the same name. Macrovision prevents the unauthorized copying of DVDs and VHS tapes by implanting an extra signal, which does not interefere with initial playback, but which causes VCRs or DVD players in record mode to scramble or otherwise distort the image.

magnetic disk   Any of various storage media in which data is stored on a flat, rotating disk covered with magnetic material. The surface of a magnetic disk is divided into small zones, each of which stores one bit of data. Magnetic disks are read by means of a head that detects differences in the magnetic alignment of each zone, and written by means of a head that changes the magnetic alignment of these zones. Some magnetic disk technologies use a single head that can both read and write. Hard disks and floppy disks are two examples of magnetic disks. *Compare* **optical disk.** *See also* **magneto-optical disk.**

magnetic-ink character recognition *Abbreviated* **MICR.** A technique for making printed characters machine-readable by printing them with ink containing a magnetic powder. MICR is primarily used in the banking industry for the codes printed along the bottom of checks. MICR readers are highly accurate and use a device similar to an audiotape recorder head to detect the pattern of magnetism on the document. MICR printers generally use a special font developed for the purpose.

magnetic media Mass storage devices that store information magnetically. Hard disks and tapes are magnetic media.

magnetic RAM *See* **MRAM.**

magnetic tape A thin strip of plastic coated with iron oxide or some other material on which data can be recorded magnetically. Magnetic tape has been used for recording audio and video since the 1950s and was a natural choice as a storage medium for the earliest electronic computers. However, retrieving a computer file from a magnetic tape is slow because in order to retrieve data from any point on a reel of tape, it is necessary to move the entire tape until the head is under that point. With the development of the much faster access capabilities of hard disks, magnetic tape was no longer competitive as a primary storage medium. Because of its relatively low cost and high reliability, however, it continues to be used for long-term storage and backup. Magnetic tape is still commonly used for digital audio and video recording. *See also* **DV.**

magneto-optical disk or **magneto-optical disc** A high-density erasable disk that encodes data by magnetically aligning crystals that have been heated in the focus of an intense laser. The alignment of the crystals is stable at room temperature, and the disk is read by using the polarization of a reflected laser beam to determine this alignment. The focus of the laser beam can be made very small, allowing a high density of data to be stored. The data is read by a beam of lesser intensity (typically using the same laser apparatus); the magnetic alignment of the crystals affects the pattern of reflection, which is detected by a light sensor in much the same way as in an optical disk drive.

magnetoresistive RAM *See* **MRAM.**

mail *See* **email.**

Mail An email client developed by Apple and distributed with its OS X operating systems. Mail is available only for OS X and has most of the features currently available on email clients, including the ability to block spam and to automatically sort mail into folders based on rules. It cannot read newsgroups or web feeds.

mail bomb   To send email in quantities that are so large or with file attachments that are so large that the recipient's mail system crashes. Mail bombing is one form of online harassment.

mailing list   A discussion group dedicated to a particular topic or social group and conducted over email, usually using a list server to automatically distribute email to all subscribers. There are usually several email addresses associated with a list. One address is used to send messages to all subscribers, and another is used to manage subscriptions. *Also called* **listserv.**

mail merge   A feature in many word processing programs that creates personalized form letters. The main document contains the text of the form letter, along with codes that indicate where personalized information (such as names and addresses) goes. This information is usually contained in a separate text or spreadsheet file whose fields correspond to the codes in the form letter.

mainframe   A large, powerful computer used primarily by organizations that must handle large amounts of data and process large numbers of business transactions. Mainframes are typically very reliable and have very high rates of input and output. They often run specialized operating systems and typically function as servers in large client/server networks, doing the work of many smaller servers. *Compare* **supercomputer.**

main memory   Memory that is used by a computer's CPU to store executing programs and their working data. Main memory is distinct from the registers contained in a CPU. Modern computers use RAM for main memory.

Majordomo   A freeware mailing list server for managing mailing lists on the Unix platform.

male connector   A connector that has one or many exposed pins or plugs. *Compare* **female connector.**

malware   Malicious computer software that interferes with normal computer functions or sends personal data about the user to unauthorized parties over the Internet. Viruses, worms, and spyware are examples of malware.

management information system   *See* **MIS.**

man-in-the-middle attack   *Abbreviated* **MITM attack.**   An attempt by a malicious third party to intercept messages sent between two programs or users in order to get access to private information, such as passwords or credit card numbers. To avoid man-in-the-middle attacks, security protocols must have some way of ensuring that messages are being sent to the intended party. One type of man-in-the-middle attack uses a website designed to mimic the website of a legitimate business. If a user unwittingly connects to the fraudulent site and sends private information, that information can be read by the malicious user, even if it was sent over a secure connection. Most security protocols prevent this type of man-in-the-middle attack by using digital certificates to verify the identity of websites.

man page *Abbreviation of* **manual page.** On Linux and Unix systems, a page of online documentation for a command or program, formatted in a standard way. A man page can be read at the command prompt by typing *man* followed by the name of the command or program. Most man pages are also available on the World Wide Web.

MAPI *Abbreviation of* **Messaging Application Program Interface.** An API developed by Microsoft Corporation that allows different programs to send and receive email and other messages by using a library of executable code that is part of the Windows operating system.

markup language A formal way of annotating a document or digital data in order to indicate its structure and the contents of its data elements. HTML and PDF are well-known markup languages for displaying text and multimedia. XML and SGML are metalanguages in which markup languages can be designed.

massively multiplayer online game *Abbreviated* **MMO** or **MMOG.** A game in which numerous participants interact in a virtual environment over the Internet. Some MMOGs have millions of participants.

massively multiplayer online role-playing game *Abbreviated* **MMORPG.** An online role-playing game with numerous participants.

mass storage **1.** The storage devices and techniques used to supplement the main memory of a computer, including disks, memory cards, and magnetic tape. Mass storage devices are usually nonvolatile memory and can accommodate larger amounts of data than main memory. Mass storage capacity is usually expressed in bytes. **2.** A set of protocols for how storage devices such as hard drives, CD drives, flash memory devices, digital cameras, and digital audio players use USB to communicate. When such devices are connected to a computer's USB port, a mass storage protocol is typically used to make the contents of the device available to the computer.

master boot record The first sector of a hard disk, containing information that identifies where each partition is located on the disk and that specifies which partition to use for booting the computer.

math coprocessor A coprocessor that performs mathematical operations, used to increase the speed of mathematical calculations. Current CPUs have built-in circuits for performing these operations, so math coprocessors are seldom used. *Also called* **numeric coprocessor.** *See also* **floating-point coprocessor, floating-point notation.**

MathML An XML markup language for describing mathematical formulas. MathML is a W3C standard that allows formulas to be displayed on webpages and in XML documents.

matrix A multidimensional array of elements of the same kind, especially a two-dimensional array, arranged in rows and columns. Dot-matrix printers produce characters and images as matrices of ink dots. Matrices are also common data structures in computer applications, useful for the manipulation of spreadsheet tables and in mathematical calculations.

Matroska A container format used for the storage and transmission of audio and video over the Internet. Matroska is similar to containers such as ASF and QuickTime, but differs primarily in that it is an open-source format that can be freely used without licensing restrictions. Matroska audio files usually have the *.mka* extension and Matroska video files have the *.mkv* extension. *See* Table 4 at **container format.**

maximize To make a window on a display screen as large as possible.

Mb *Abbreviation of* **megabit.**

MB *Abbreviation of* **megabyte.**

Mbps or **Mbit/s** *Abbreviations of* **megabits per second.**

MBps or **MB/s** *Abbreviations of* **megabytes per second.**

MCGA *Abbreviation of* **MultiColor Graphics Array.** A graphics card, now obsolete, that was included in low-end models of the IBM PS/2. It had more graphics capabilities than CGA but was not as powerful as EGA or VGA.

MD *Abbreviation of* **MiniDisc.**

MD5 *Abbreviation of* **message digest 5.** A hash function used to create message digests. Message digests created with MD5 are commonly used to check the integrity of downloaded files. *See also* **checksum.**

MDA *Abbreviation of* **monochrome display adapter.** A monochrome graphics card used with some of the earliest personal computers. The MDA can display text but not graphics.

MDI *Abbreviation of* **multiple document interface.** A GUI (graphical user interface) in which each document open in the application is part of a single parent window. In MDIs, individual documents have their own windows, but these document windows do not have icons on the taskbar and they must be located within the borders of the application window. *Compare* **SDI**. *See also* **TDI**.

mean time between failures   *See* **MTBF**.

Media Access Control address   *See* **MAC address**.

media center PC   A personal computer designed for use in a home-entertainment system. Some media center PCs can perform the functions of a DVD player, a digital audio and video reciever, and a PVR.

media player   A program for playing, downloading, and organizing audio and video files. Most media players can play files in a wide variety of formats, including formats for streaming data. They can also be used to create playlists and rip audio data from CDs. Some media players support digital rights management formats, which only allow files to be played by a purchaser, and some can convert files into different formats and burn CDs or DVDs.

medium   **1.** An object or device used primarily for the storage of information.
   2. Any of various technologies by which information is disseminated, especially as a form of mass communication, such as radio, television, the Internet, and newspapers.
   The plural form of both of these senses is media.

meg   A megabyte. Used informally.

mega-   *Abbreviated* **M**. **1.** A prefix indicating one million, as in *megahertz*. This is also the sense in which *mega-* is generally used in terms of data transmission rates, where a bit is a signal pulse and is counted in the decimal system, which is based on multiples of 10. **2.** A prefix indicating 1,048,576 (2^{20}), as in *megabyte*. This is the sense in which *mega-* is generally used in terms of data storage capacity, which, due to the binary nature of bits, is based on powers of 2.

megabit   *Abbreviated* **Mb**.   One million bits, used as a unit for expressing the rate of data transmission per unit of time (usually one second). In highly technical contexts involving data storage capacity, the word *megabit* can refer to 1,048,576 (2^{20}) bits.

megabyte   *Abbreviated* **MB**. **1.** A unit of measurement of computer memory or data storage capacity equal to 1,048,576 (2^{20}) bytes. One megabyte equals 1,024 kilobytes. **2.** One million bytes, especially when reporting the storage capacity of a hard drive or DVD.

megaflop or **megaflops**   *Abbreviated* **MFLOP** or **MFLOPS**.   A measure of computing speed, equal to one million floating-point operations per second. *See also* **FLOPS**.

megahertz *Abbreviated* **MHz.** A unit of frequency equal to one million hertz.

megapixel A unit of resolution equal to one million pixels. Digital cameras are typically classified by the number of megapixels that they use to capture a single image. Most digital cameras can take a picture with a resolution between three and six megapixels.

MEID *Abbreviation of* **mobile equipment identifier.** A unique number that identifies newer cell phones and wireless devices that do not use GSM technology. MEIDs are 56-bit numbers that are permanently encoded in the chips of non-GSM cell phones and other devices in order to prevent cloning. Phones manufactured before 2005 used 32-bit ESNs. GSM devices use IMEIs. *Compare* **IMSI.**

membrane keyboard A keyboard covered by a thin plastic, having pressure-sensitive areas in place of keys. Membrane keyboards are often used in factories, restaurants, and other environments that have a lot of dirt and dust that would damage regular keyboards.

memory **1.** *See* **RAM. 2.** The capacity of a computer, chip, or other storage device to preserve data and programs for retrieval. Memory is measured in bytes. **3.** Any of various systems for preserving data and programs for retrieval, including chips, disks, and tapes. Volatile memory stores information only until the power is turned off. Nonvolatile memory retains information even when the power is off.

memory card A removable storage device that fits into a small slot in a host device and stores data in NVRAM (non-volatile RAM), so data is retained when power is shut down or the card is removed from the device. Memory cards typically store data on flash memory chips, though other types of NVRAM are sometimes used. They come in a wide variety of formats, and are used as storage media for a wide variety of devices, including digital cameras, PDAs, cell phones, and digital audio players.

memory card reader A device used to transfer data between a computer and a memory card. Memory card readers typically connect to a computer through a USB or FireWire port or a PCMCIA slot.

memory controller A chip on a computer's motherboard that controls the transfer of data between main memory and the CPU. The kind of memory controller that a computer has determines the kind and amount of main memory that it can have. Dual-channel memory controllers allow data to be transferred from main memory directly to another location, such as video display circuitry.

memory effect A property of NiCad batteries in which the amount of recharging they receive begins to fix the maximum amount of charging they can receive in subsequent recharges. The effect is noticed only if there is one specific drainage level at which the battery is recharged whenever it drains to that level. Memory effect is not known to affect the behavior of batteries used in personal technology. *See also* **voltage depression.**

memory management unit   *See* **MMU.**

memory module   A small printed circuit board that has several RAM chips mounted on it and is designed to be attached to a motherboard to provide RAM for a computer.

Memory Stick   A family of memory cards developed by Sony. Memory Sticks use flash memory for storage, and come in a variety of physical formats. Their design is proprietary, and they are primarily used as storage media for handheld devices made by Sony.

menu   An onscreen list of available options or commands for a computer program or for the computer's operating system. Usually the options are highlighted by a bar that moves from one item to another as the user moves a mouse or presses an arrow key. A menu item is chosen by keying in its code or by pointing and clicking with a mouse. Choosing an item may cause a cascading menu to appear, or a dialog box containing options that further refine the original menu selection. *See also* **menu bar, pull-down menu, tear-off menu.**

menu bar   A horizontal bar that runs across the top of a screen or a window and holds the names of available menu options. When a user chooses an option from the menu bar, as by clicking on it with a mouse or by using a keystroke, another list of commands or options drops down below the bar. *See also* **menu.**

menu-driven   Relating to software that is operated by making selections from onscreen menus, rather than by typing commands. *Compare* **command-driven.**

message board   A webpage or web application for holding discussions, usually about a particular topic or for a particular group of users. Message boards allow users to post messages for other users to read and respond to. They sometimes include instant messaging and other features, and usually allow users to post pictures and other kinds of content. Many message boards are moderated, meaning that special users are designated to monitor and control how they are used. *Also called* **electronic bulletin board, online forum.** *See also* **bulletin board system.**

message box   *See* **alert box.**

message digest   A compact digital signature for a stream of binary data, such as a message, password, or computer code. Message digests are typically used to verify that data has not been altered during trans-mission. If the digest made by the receiver matches the digest made by the sender, the data was almost certainly not altered over the course of transmission. *See also* **checksum.**

message digest 5   *See* **MD5.**

Messaging Application Program Interface   *See* **MAPI.**

metadata   Descriptive information about data. Metadata is used on the World Wide Web to provide information about content, such as author-ship, copyright information, keywords, or how the content is encoded. Word processing programs usually maintain metadata about documents, for example who has edited the file and when it was created. Database management systems maintain a large amount of metadata about data-bases, such as how many records each table contains and how many unique entries there are for a given field.

metalanguage   A computer language that is used to define the structure of another language. *See also* **markup language.**

metatag   An HTML tag used to add metadata—descriptive information about contents such as title, author, and keywords—to a webpage. The information in a metatag does not appear when the webpage is displayed in a web browser, but search engines often index the information.

MFLOPS or **MFLOP**   *Abbreviations of* **megaflop.**

MHz   *Abbreviation of* **megahertz.**

MICR   *Abbreviation of* **magnetic-ink character recognition.**

micro-   **1.** A prefix indicating something very small. **2.** A prefix indicating one millionth (10^{-6}), as in *microsecond.*

microchip   *See* **chip.**

Microcom Networking Protocol   *Abbreviated* **MNP.**   One of a group of communications protocols developed by Microcom, Inc., and used for transferring data with modems. Commonly used MNP protocols include data compression and error correction.

microcomputer   *See* **personal computer.**

microdisplay   **1.** A tiny display found inside projectors and on handheld devices and digital cameras. Microdisplays use a variety of display tech-nologies including LCoS, DLP, and LCD. **2.** A projector that projects an image onto a screen from a microdisplay.

Microdrive   A CompactFlash memory card that stores data on a very small hard drive. Microdrives were developed by IBM, and the name is now a trademark of Hitachi.

microkernel   An operating system kernel that contains only the minimum software necessary for managing the CPU and RAM. In operating systems that use a microkernel, tasks traditionally handled by the kernel, such as file system management and networking, are handled by separate programs, thus making it easier to modify the operating system for use on different devices. The Symbian OS uses a microkernel.

microphone   A device that converts sound waves into electrical signals. These signals are usually fed into an amplifier to provide sufficient energy for transmission, recording, or conversion to a digital signal. *See also* **digital microphone.**

microprocessor   An integrated circuit that contains the CPU (central processing unit) of a computer. When referring to personal computers, the terms *microprocessor* and *central processing unit* are often used synonymously.

Two major features that distinguish microprocessors are clock speed and register size (often called *register width*). The clock speed of a microprocessor determines the smallest amount of time that can elapse between individual steps in processing, thus contributing to how fast the computer can process data. For example, a one GHz processor operates at one billion cycles per second, meaning that there is only a nanosecond (one billionth of a second) between processing steps. The size of a microprocessor's registers also affects processing speed by determining the size of the numbers that it can process in a single step, as well as the size of the memory addresses it can work with. 32-bit microprocessors (i.e., microprocessors with a register size of 32-bits) are quite common, and 64-bit processors are becoming more common.

Multicore microprocessors, which contain more than one CPU and thus allow some parallel processing, are also becoming increasingly common. *See also* **processor speed.**

microSD   A memory card format developed by SanDisk and adopted by the Secure Digital Association. MicroSD is the smallest memory card format and is intended for use in handheld devices such as mobile phones and digital audio players. MicroSD cards can be used in devices that accept SD cards by using an adapter.

microsecond   *Abbreviated* **us, usec, μs,** or **μsec.**   A unit of time equal to one millionth (10^{-6}) of a second.

The letter *u* is used in some abbreviations (such as *us* and *usec*) to represent the Greek letter mu (μ). In this way, the *m* of the prefix *micro-* (abbreviated as *u*) is distinguished from the *m* of the prefix *milli-* (abbreviated as *m*). One also finds μs and μsec used when Greek characters are available.

microwave Electromagnetic radiation in the frequency range of 100 MHz to 30 GHz (lower than infrared but higher than other radio waves). Microwaves are used in satellite, WiMAX, and LMDS communications, as well as radar, cooking, and other applications.

Microsoft Internet Explorer *See* **Internet Explorer.**

Microsoft Outlook *See* **Outlook.**

Microsoft Windows *See* **Windows.**

middle area An area of unused physical space on a dual-layer OTP DVD that marks the transition between layer 0 and layer 1.

middleware Software that serves as an intermediary between systems software and an application, such as software that provides a single API through which an application can interact with several different database programs.

midrange Having or relating to frequencies between approximately 300 and 5,000 hertz. Used mostly of audio signals or devices that process audio signals.

midrange speaker A versatile speaker that produces low to high-pitched sounds, typically in the range of 300 to 5,000 hertz. *Also called* **mid-woofer.** *See also* **speaker.**

midtower A tower computer case that is larger than a minitower and smaller than a full-tower. A midtower is typically around 17 inches tall. *See also* **tower.**

midwoofer *See* **midrange speaker.**

MIDI *Abbreviation of* **Musical Instrument Digital Interface.** A protocol for the exchange of information between computers and musical devices such as synthesizers. Computers with a MIDI interface can control the playback of a compatible synthesizer, determining the pitch, tempo, volume, timbre, and other sound characteristics that the synthesizer produces. MIDI files thus do not necessarily contain encoded sound signals, but rather a set of playback instructions for the synthesizer. Some MIDI software also allows the display of MIDI files in the form of a musical score; some also allows the user to create MIDI files based on the way the synthesizer is played in real time, creating a MIDI file that can be played back and modified.

.mil A top-level domain operated by the US Defense Systems Agency and used by organizations in the US Department of Defense. The United States is the only country that has a separate top-level domain for its military.

milli- *Abbreviated* **m.** A prefix indicating one thousandth (10^{-3}), as in *millisecond.*

millisecond *Abbreviated* **ms** or **msec.** A unit of time equal to one thousandth (10^{-3}) of a second.

MIME *Abbreviation of* **Multipurpose Internet Mail Extensions.** A standard for the format of data transmitted between computers on the Internet. The MIME standard is used for transmissions sent with the SMTP protocol, which carry the contents of email, as well as transmissions sent with the HTTP protocol, which allow users to view webpages. MIME makes email attachments possible because it allows for multipart messages and provides standards for encoding data in formats other than ASCII text, as in image, audio, and word processor documents. *See also* **MIME type.**

MIME attachment *See* **attachment.**

MIME type One of the format codes specified in the MIME standard. These codes indicate the format of the data in each part of a message, such as an email message, so email viewers and web browsers know how to handle it. Text, HTML, and images are usually displayed, but many other file types, such as files from word processing or spreadsheet programs, need to be saved in a separate file in order to be viewed.

MIN *Abbreviation of* **mobile identification number.** A unique number used to identify a subscriber on a non-GSM cellular network. The MIN is used for billing and for determining if a user has the right to access a network. It is derived from the phone number assigned to the subscriber. Unlike ESNs, MEIDs, or IMEIs, which identify devices, the same MIN may be assigned to different devices at different times. Fraudulent users can clone a phone by illegally duplicating its MIN and ESN.

minicomputer A computer, usually fitting within a single cabinet, typically less powerful than a mainframe. Minicomputers can process input and output from many terminals simultaneously. Minicomputers are no longer in common use, due to the advent of powerful PCs and the ease with which they can communicate using network technology, such as the Internet or LANs.

Mini-DIN connector A small DIN connector used in S-Video and PS/2 connections. *See figure at* **connector.**

MiniDisc *Abbreviated* **MD.** A rewritable magneto-optical disk housed in a cassette and used especially for audio storage. The MiniDisc format was developed by Sony.

minidish A small satellite dish that receives signals from a direct broadcast satellite.

miniDV   A small form-factor videocassette used with the DV videotape format that is approximately 2.56 × 1.89 inches.

minijack   A jack connector that uses a 1/8-inch plug. Stereo minijacks are common for connecting audio devices, especially small headphones, into personal music players and laptop computers.

minimize   To hide a window so that it becomes a small moveable bar on the desktop or a button on the taskbar. A minimized window may be restored by clicking the associated button on the taskbar or, in the case of the small bar, by clicking the bar's restore button.

mini-PC   *See* **small form factor.**

miniSD   A memory card format developed by SanDisk and adopted by the Secure Digital Association. MiniSD is a smaller format than SD, but an adapter allows miniSD cards to be used in devices that accept SD cards.

minitower   A tower computer case that is smaller than a midtower. A minitower is typically around 14 inches tall. *See also* **tower.**

MIPS   *Abbreviation of* **million instructions per second.**   A measure of computing speed. MIPS refers to the number of instructions a computer's CPU (central processing unit) can carry out in one second. For example, a computer rated at 50 MIPS executes, on the average, 50 million instructions per second.

   MIPS is not the only variable to consider when judging a computer's speed. Other factors include the rate of data transfer between memory and the CPU and the speed of peripherals such as disk drives. *See also* **throughput.**

mirror site   A website that contains a duplicate of another website. Mirror sites are often at different locations in order to ensure the availability of data in case of a power failure and to give users located near the mirror site faster network access to the site.

MIS   *Abbreviation of* **management information system.**   The information system or systems used within an organization. Management information systems typically rely on large computer networks.

MITM attack   *Abbreviation of* **man-in-the-middle attack.**

.mka   The file extension for Matroska audio files.

.mkv   The file extension for Matroska video files.

MMC   *Abbreviation of* **MultiMediaCard.**   Any of various memory card formats standardized by a consortium of electronics manufacturers known as the MultiMediaCard Association. The original MMC format was designed by Siemens and SanDisk, and cards in this format can be used in devices with SD slots. Cards using MMC formats use flash memory for data storage, are manufactured by various companies, and are used as storage media for a range of products, including digital cameras, cell phones, PDAs, and computers. *See also* **RS-MMC.**

MMDS *Abbreviation of* **multichannel multipoint distribution service.** A subscription television and broadband Internet service that uses microwaves to carry signals between a local distribution antenna and a small antenna at the subscriber's location. *Also called* **wireless cable.**

MMO or **MMOG** *Abbreviations of* **massively multiplayer online game.**

MMORPG *Abbreviation of* **massively multiplayer online role-playing game.**

MMS *Abbreviation of* **Multimedia Messaging Service.** A standard for transmitting messages containing text, pictures, or audio on cell phone networks. MMS allows users who can record audio or take pictures with their phones, or can download audio and picture files to their phones, to send digital copies of these files to other users. MMS messages can consist of data in multiple formats, and there is no restriction on their size.

MMU *Abbreviation of* **memory management unit.** A device or circuit that handles memory requests for a computer's CPU (central processing unit). Among other functions, MMUs make virtual memory possible by translating virtual addresses to physical addresses and vice versa. An MMU can be part of the CPU, or it can be a separate chip.

MMX A technology introduced by Intel that enhances the x86 microprocessor architecture in order to handle multimedia and communications more efficiently. CPUs with MMX understand an extended set of instructions, designed to speed image processing, motion video, speech synthesis, telephony, and 3D graphics.

MNP *Abbreviation of* **Microcom Networking Protocol.**

mobile equipment identifier *See* **MEID.**

mobile identification number *See* **MIN.**

mobile payment The use of a cell phone or handheld to pay for goods and services. There are a variety of mobile payment systems, including systems in which users send specially-designed SMS messages or infrared messages. *Also called* **wireless payment.** *See also* **IrFM.**

mobile phone A portable telephone that can function over a wide area. The term is applied to both cell phones and satellite phones, although it is most often used as a synonym for *cell phone. Compare* **cordless phone.**

mode An operating state for a program or device, especially one that can be selected by the user. For example, when typing on a keyboard, users can usually choose between the insert mode, which adds text without deleting, and the overwrite mode, which replaces existing text with whatever is typed.

modem *Abbreviation of* **modulator/demodulator.** A device that transmits and receives data using a modulated carrier wave. Modems encode and transmit data by *modulation*—making a series of changes to a carrier signal. They decode and receive data by *demodulation*—detecting changes made by another modem to the carrier signal. Telephone modems, which transmit data over telephone lines, and cable modems, which transmit data over the coaxial cables used for cable television, are the most common ways to connect home computers to a network. Modems are also used for transmission on other cables, for example fiber-optic cables, as well as over the air, as with the transmission of microwave signals. Data transmission with modems is governed by communications protocols that specify how data is encoded in the carrier signal. *See also* **UART.**

moderate To oversee a forum for discussion, such as a newsgroup, mailing list, or chatroom, to ensure that the rules of that forum are followed, for example, by blocking people who are harassing others from entering a chatroom or by preventing spam from being posted to a newsgroup. Moderated newsgroups and mailing lists often require that messages be reviewed by a moderator before they can be viewed by other participants.

modifier key A key that is pressed in combination with another key to execute an alternate function. The Control key, Shift key, and Alt key are all modifier keys.

modular Relating to hardware or software systems made from distinct modules that operate independently and can be easily replaced with modules that have similar functions. In a modular system, each independent function is performed by an independent module.

modular arithmetic A form of arithmetic in which numbers that have the same remainder with respect to a set number called the *modulus* are considered equivalent. For example, with a modulus of 5, the number 7 is equivalent to the number 2, since 2 is the remainder of 7 divided by 5; this may be expressed as 2 = 7 mod 5. Modular arithmetic is used in many cryptographic algorithms that work with very high numbers.

modulation The process of changing a property of an electromagnetic wave or signal, such as its amplitude, frequency, or phase, in order to encode and transmit data. For example, digital data can be transferred from one computer to another by modulating a carrier signal on a telephone line. Each bit in the data is represented by a designated change in the carrier wave. In order to recreate the data on the receiving computer, the carrier signal is demodulated. *Compare* **demodulation.**

modulator/demodulator   *See* **modem.**

module   A self-contained hardware or software component that performs an independent function.

moiré effect   The perceived flickering or distortion of printed or displayed high-contrast images. The effect can be diminished or eliminated by altering the image's size or resolution.

monitor   A device that accepts video signals from a computer and displays information on a screen. A typical monitor has a screen that measures anywhere from 15 to 23 inches diagonally, with 17-inch and 19-inch models being the most common. Traditionally, monitors have had CRT displays, but now flat-panel LCDs are the most common. *Also called* **head, video display terminal.** *See also* **display, multihead.**

mono   Recording or reproducing sound using a single audio channel. *Also called* **monophonic.** *Compare* **stereo.**

monochrome   Relating to or being a display screen capable of displaying only one color on a dark or light background.

monochrome display adapter   *See* **MDA.**

monophonic   **1.** *See* **mono. 2.** Recording or reproducing audio in which only one tone is sounded at a time. *See also* **ringtone.**

monospace font   A font in which each character is given the same pitch, or width. *See also* **fixed space, proportional font.**

MOO   A MUD having an object-oriented language allowing the players to create objects, especially personalized characters and situations. The first of these went online in the early 1990s. MOOs were among the first virtual communities created on the Internet.

Moore's Law   The prediction that the number of transistors in an affordable chip will double every 18 months. In 1965, Gordon Moore, one of the founders of Intel Corporation, observed that the number of transistors that could be affordably put into an integrated circuit had been doubling every year. Moore later predicted that the number of transistors would double every two years, and claims never to have specified a period of 18 months. Nevertheless, the prediction has largely held true; chip components have become ever-smaller, resulting in increased computing power on affordable computers.

morphing   In video editing, the transformation of one image into another using an algorithm to create frames that depict the intermediate stages.

Mosaic   A web browser developed by the National Center for Supercomputing Applications. One of the first browsers available, Mosaic eventually became the basis for Microsoft Internet Explorer.

mosquito   A type of artifact that occurs in MPEG-compressed video. Mosquitoes appear as blurry dots or incorrectly colored pixels around the sharp edges of objects, and create a shimmering effect around objects in motion. *Also called* **Gibbs effect.**

most significant bit   In the binary representation of a number, the bit representing the largest exponent of 2. Binary numbers are usually written with their most significant bit at the left.

most significant digit   The leftmost digit in the written representation of a number. *See also* **least significant digit.**

motherboard   The main printed circuit board in a personal computer. It contains the CPU, main system memory, controllers for disk drives and other devices, serial and parallel ports, and sometimes expansion slots. *Also called* **system board.** *Compare* **daughter board.** *See also* **expansion card.**

motion capture   A technique that plots and records the movements of physical entities such as people and other material objects. The information about the way the entities move can then be used to simulate movement in computer graphics, as when creating realistic movement in animation, video games, and other computer-generated imagery.

mount   **1.** To make a file system available for use. In order for users to access files on a disk or other device, the file system on the device must be mounted. Usually, mounting is performed automatically by the operating system, though Linux and Unix operating systems sometimes require users to issue a command in order to mount a device. **2.** A program used for mounting a device on Linux and Unix systems.

mouse   An input device that is slid across a flat surface with the hand to control a pointer on a display. The mouse's movement is detected with a rubber ball or an optical sensor mounted on the underside. Buttons located on the top or side of the mouse execute various operations within programs or operating systems. Some mice also have scroll wheels to facilitate scrolling through documents. Most mice (or *mouses,* as they are sometimes called in the plural) connect to the computer through USB, serial, or PS/2 connectors, though wireless mice span part of the distance with an infrared connection.

mousepad   A flat piece of material, such as specially coated foam rubber, designed to provide an optimum surface on which to use a mouse.

mouse wheel   *See* **scroll wheel.**

.mov   A file extension typically used for QuickTime files.

Moving Picture Experts Group   *See* **MPEG.**

Mozilla **1.** A project for the development of a freely distributed, open-source web browser and email software. The Mozilla project began when Netscape Corporation released the source code for Netscape Communicator as an open-source application in 1998. Mozilla currently maintains the Firefox web browser and Thunderbird email viewer, as well as the Mozilla suite and other tools. It is sponsored by the Mozilla Foundation. **2.** A free, open-source suite of web applications, maintained by the Mozilla project. The suite includes a web browser, email and news client, and HTML editor.

MP3 *Abbreviation of* **MPEG-1 Audio Layer 3.** An MPEG standard used for storage of digital audio files and for transmitting music over the Internet. MP3 files can achieve a compression rate of up to 12 : 1 and can be stored in portable players and digital audio servers. Files of this type are usually identified by the *.mp3* extension after their filenames.

MP3 player *See* **digital audio player.**

mp3PRO An enhanced MP3 format used for the storage and transmission of high-quality digital audio. The mp3PRO format combines MP3 with spectral band replication to compress the data twice as efficiently as standard MP3; thus mp3PRO files require much less bandwidth to transmit and can be efficiently streamed through lower-speed connections. Files of this type use the *.mp3* extension and are backward compatible with standard MP3 players.

MP4 *Abbreviation of* **MPEG-4 Part 14.** An MPEG standard used as a container format to store digital audio and video content in files or to stream it over the Internet. MP4s use the AAC codec, which gives them better sound quality than MP3s. Files of this type are usually identified by the *.mp4* extension after their filenames.

MPEG **1.** *Abbreviation of* **Moving Picture Experts Group.** A subcommittee of the ISO and the IEC that establishes standards for the digital compression of moving images and associated audio content. **2.** Any of various algorithms for video and audio compression developed by this committee. MPEG uses lossy compression and achieves a high compression rate by storing only the changes from one frame to another instead of storing each entire frame. The MPEG standard continues to evolve and encompasses several phases for various forms of media. For example, MPEG-1 is the standard used for MP3s and VCDs, and MPEG-2 is used for broadcast video. **3.** A file format for files compressed using such an algorithm. MPEG files usually have filenames ending with the extension *.mpg*.

MPEG-1 Audio Layer 3 *See* **MP3.**

MPEG-2   A set of MPEG standards typically used in compressing digital audio and video signals for broadcast over high-bandwidth networks and for storage on DVD. MPEG-2 files have a low bit rate, which allows them to compress additional picture detail and multichannel sound, but they must be decoded in order to be displayed on standard televisions and monitors.

MPEG-4   A set of MPEG standards for the compression of digital audio and video data. MPEG-4 is currently composed of 21 individual standards, known as *parts*.

MPEG-4 AAC   *Abbreviation of* **MPEG-4 Advanced Audio Coding.**   *See* **AAC.**

MPEG-4 Audio   *See* **M4A.**

MPEG-4 AVC   *Abbreviation of* **MPEG-4 Advanced Video Coding.** *See* **H.264.**

MPEG-4 Part 10   *See* **H.264.**

MPEG-4 Part 14   *See* **MP4.**

MRAM   *Abbreviation of* **magnetic RAM** *or* **magnetoresistive RAM.** Nonvolatile memory that uses magnetic fields to store data. MRAM is similar to flash memory in that it retains data when it is not connected to a power source; however, unlike flash, it does not degrade over time and is as fast as SRAM. MRAM can serve as a replacement for both flash memory and SRAM, but it is more expensive to produce.

ms *or* **msec**   *Abbreviations of* **millisecond.**

MS-DOS   A version of DOS developed by Microsoft and used with its Windows operating system.

MS-Windows   *See* **Windows.**

MTBF   *Abbreviation of* **mean time between failures.**   A measure of the reliability of electronic and mechanical devices. The MTBF for a component reports its average working life, measured in hours, before its first failure requiring service.

MTS   *Abbreviation of* **multichannel television sound.**   A standard for encoding three audio or data channels in addition to the main audio channel in NTSC television signals. MTS channels are used to carry surround sound, broadcast information, and alternate soundtracks. *See also* **SAP.**

MUD   *Abbreviation of* **Multi-User Dungeon.**   A text-based cyberspace environment in which multiple users can interact and participate in virtual reality role-playing games.

multichannel audio   An audio stream that is split into more than two discrete channels. *See also* **mono, stereo, surround sound.**

multichannel multipoint distribution service *See* **MMDS.**

multichannel television sound *See* **MTS.**

MultiColor Graphics Array *See* **MCGA.**

multicore Relating to chips that contain more than one CPU or GPU. Multicore chips allow multiprocessing without the need for multiple chips. Multicore processing requires specially designed operating system and application software. *See also* **dual-core.**

multidimensional database A database system that can arrange data in forms other than tables of rows and columns, often used with OLAP software and data warehouses to view complex relationships in large bodies of data.

multidisplay Relating to a computer or graphics card that can simultaneously display images on multiple monitors. *Also called* **multihead, multimonitor.**

multihead *See* **multidisplay.**

multimedia Combining the use of several media, usually including sound and video.

MultiMediaCard *See* **MMC.**

Multimedia Messaging Service *See* **MMS.**

multimonitor *See* **multidisplay.**

multiplayer Relating to a game in which multiple players interact in a virtual environment. Multiplayer games are often played over the Internet.

multiple document interface *See* **MDI.**

multiplex To combine two or more message channels on a single transmission medium without interference, as when multiple radio transmissions are made on a shared frequency band. TDMA and CDMA cellular technologies function by multiplexing radio signals, as do Wi-Fi networks.

multiplexer or **multiplexor** *Abbreviated* **mux.** A hardware device that allows data signals from several sources to be transmitted over a common line.

multiprocessing The use of two or more CPUs on a single computer system to increase the speed at which tasks can be performed. Multiprocessing may involve different CPUs executing different programs, and is also useful when a single program consisting of distinct tasks, called *threads,* is processed on different CPUs at the same time. *Compare* **multitasking.** *See also* **coprocessor, multithreading, parallel processing.**

Multipurpose Internet Mail Extensions *See* **MIME.**

Multiread   The ability of an optical disk drive to read from a variety of CD media, including CD-ROM, CD-R, and CD-RW.

multisession   The capability of a compact disk to have data written on it incrementally in multiple recording sessions. Multisession CDs have an extended header format because lead-in and lead-out data must be written during each new session. *Compare* **single session.**

multisession drive   A drive capable of reading multisession CDs. A multisession drive can recognize the extended header format that is used when data is appended to a CD. Multisession drives are commonly used in conjunction with Photo CD technology and in some audio CD burners.

multitasking   The processing of several programs at once on a single CPU. With multitasking, each program residing in RAM takes turns using the CPU to execute the operations specified by that program. Although the CPU can perform operations for only one program at a time, the operating system controlling the execution switches from one program to another so quickly that it appears to the user as if the programs are all running simultaneously. *Compare* **multiprocessing, multithreading, time-sharing.** *See also* **process.**

multithreading   The processing of a program as a set of separate tasks, called *threads*. When a program is designed to run using multiple threads, each thread is treated by the operating system as a separate process. When one thread stops, as to wait for data, the operating system switches to another thread and thus does not lose time waiting. Multithreading is particularly effective for programs that require a large amount of user input. It is also useful in combination with multiprocessing. Multithreading is available on most modern operating systems. *Compare* **multitasking.**

multi-user   Relating to a computer system or application intended to be used by more than one person at a time. For example, database management systems are generally multi-user applications. Linux and Unix are multi-user operating systems that use time-sharing to allow different users to log in and run programs at the same time.

Multi-User Dungeon   *See* **MUD.**

Musical Instrument Digital Interface   *See* **MIDI.**

mux   *Abbreviation of* **multiplexer.**

MySQL   An open-source database management system owned and distributed by MySQL AB. MySQL is available for many operating systems and is commonly used with PHP to manage data for web servers.

n *Abbreviation of* **nano-.**

name server A computer server that translates domain names (which are easy for people to read) into IP addresses (which are easy for machines to read). A name server is part of the DNS. It stores information about the IP addresses in its own domain, and uses the DNS protocol to communicate with the name servers of other domains. Name servers can also translate IP addresses into domain names. *Also called* **DNS server.**

NAND A logical operator that returns the value TRUE as its output if either or both of its inputs (or *operands*) are FALSE, and that returns FALSE if both inputs are TRUE. It is equivalent to the logical operator AND followed by the operator NOT. NAND gates are especially easy to implement electronically, and a high proportion of the logic gates of microprocessors are NAND gates (together with NOR gates). *See* Table E on page 361.

nano- *Abbreviated* **n.** A prefix indicating one billionth (10^{-9}), as in *nanoseconds.*

nanosecond *Abbreviated* **ns** or **nsec.** A unit of time equal to one billionth (10^{-9}) of a second.

nanotechnology or **nanotech** A unit of time equal to one billionth (10^{-9}) of a second.

National Television System Committee *See* **NTSC.**

native application A program that is in the form of an executable file in the machine language of the computer's CPU. Native applications contrast both with programs in an interpreted language such as Java and programs in a machine language that is not understood by the computer's CPU and thus require some form of emulation in order to run.

native resolution The number of pixels or scan lines that a display uses to make an image. Most televisions and monitors can accept signals with a variety of resolutions, but in order to display them, all signals must be converted, or scaled, to the display's native resolution. Scaling requires a complex algorithm and sometimes diminishes picture quality.

navigation Any of various ways of changing what part of a database, network, document, or other kind of information is currently being accessed or viewed. Using a mouse or arrow key to scroll up and down a document is one example of navigation, as is using hyperlinks to jump from one webpage (or part of a webpage) on the Internet to another. Good navigation tools, such as well-placed hyperlinks, allow the user to gain access to the desired information quickly and easily.

near-letter quality *Abbreviated* **NLQ.** Of or producing printed characters that are nearly as clear as those produced by a conventional typewriter, but are of a lower resolution than letter-quality characters.

nest To embed a structure or set of data within another. For example, a nested table is a table within another table.

net **1.** *Abbreviation of* **network. 2.** *often* **Net** The Internet. The word *Net* is usually capitalized when referring to the Internet, as opposed simply to computer networks of any type, also known as internets (also spelled in lowercase). Thus one would speak of *the most frequently visited sites on the Net,* but *tools for net navigation,* since the latter might include tools that are designed for use on networks other than the Internet. **3.** A network of computers, printers, disk drives, or other devices, connected in a network topology that allows the devices to communicate; an internet. In this meaning the word *internet* is not capitalized.

.net A top-level domain operated by Verisign and originally intended for organizations providing network services, such as Internet service providers. Currently, any organization or individual can register a domain name in the .net domain.

NetBEUI *Abbreviation of* **NetBIOS Extended User Interface.** A protocol originally developed by IBM for transmitting data on networks that use NetBIOS. NetBEUI is used on some LANs that connect computers running Windows operating systems, but has been largely supplanted by TCP/IP.

NetBIOS *Abbreviation of* **Network BIOS.** An API developed by IBM that allows programs to exchange data across a network. NetBIOS is used on many LANs with Microsoft and IBM computers. *See also* **interprocess communication.**

NetBIOS Extended User Interface *See* **NetBEUI.**

netiquette A set of unofficial rules for good behavior and politeness that have been developed by users of Usenet, the Internet, email, chatrooms, and other modes of online communication. For example, it is considered good netiquette to refrain from posting messages intended for a single recipient on public newsgroups.

Netscape Browser A web browser distributed by AOL. Netscape Browser is a proprietary application based on the open-source Firefox browser. It is only available for the Windows operating system. *Also called* **Netscape.**

Netscape Communicator   A set of web-based applications, including the Netscape Navigator web browser, available from the Netscape Corporation between 1997 and 2002. *Also called* **Netscape.**

Netscape Navigator   A web browser first released by Netscape Corporation in 1994 and now owned by AOL. Before Microsoft's Internet Explorer became the market leader, Navigator was the most popular browser for a time. In 1998, it became an open-source application, part of the Mozilla project. In 2005, the name was officially changed to *Netscape Browser*. *Also called* **Netscape.**

NetWare   A network operating system designed by Novell Corporation for client/server networks. NetWare can be used with various communications protocols to operate LANs (local area networks) consisting of computers running almost any operating system.

network   A system of computers, and often peripherals such as printers, linked together. The smallest networks are local area networks (LANs), in which as few as 2 or as many as 500 computers are connected by cables within a small geographic area, often within the same building. Larger networks, called wide area networks (WANs), use telephone lines or radio waves to link computers that can be thousands of miles apart.

The geometric arrangement of the computers is called the topology of the network. Common topologies include the star, bus, and ring. LANs can also be connected to a backbone to build a larger LAN or WAN. Computers on a network communicate via a protocol, which standardizes rules and signals for interacting. AppleTalk, a protocol suitable for small networks, is built into all Apple Macintosh computers and laser printers. Popular protocols for LANs include Ethernet, and, specifically for PC-compatible computers, the IBM token-ring network. *See also* **client/ server network, extranet, intranet, peer-to-peer network.**

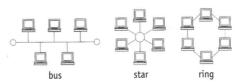

bus   star   ring

network

network adapter   *See* **network interface card.**

network administrator   A person who is responsible for maintaining, repairing, and sometimes creating a computer network. In smaller organizations, system administrators typically handle these tasks. *See also* **system administrator.**

Network BIOS   *See* **NetBIOS.**

network card   *See* **network interface card.**

Network File System   *See* **NFS.**

network interface card   *Abbreviated* **NIC.**   Any of various devices that allow a computer to be connected to a network through its external bus. Network interface cards contain both hardware to make a connection, such as jacks or antennas, and circuitry that allows the computer to use network protocol. They are usually made for a single type of network. The most common kinds are Ethernet cards and wireless cards. *Also called* **network adapter, network card.**

network number   A sequence of bits that serves as a prefix that is shared by the IP addresses of computers on the same subnet. For example, expressed using decimal numbers, 123.123.123 is the network number of a subnet that would include the IP addresses 123.123.123.1 and 123.123.123.2. Network numbers are often given with an *x* indicating the portion of the IP address that varies between computers on the subnet, for example, 123.123.123.x.

network operating system   *Abbreviated* **NOS.**   An operating system that provides the features necessary to operate a LAN, especially those that pro- vide sophisticated tools for administering a network. Opinions differ about which operating systems count as network operating systems, though Linux and Unix operating systems, as well as Windows NT, were designed for networking and are commonly considered network operating systems.

network server   *See* **server.**

network topology   The specific arrangement, or topology, of computers connected to a network, especially a LAN. Common network topologies include star, ring, and bus networks. *See figure at* **network.**

neural network   A computing system modeled after a biological network of neurons, in which interconnected processing elements, or nodes, play the role of neurons (nerve cells). Each node has a number of inputs, corre- sponding to the impulses a neuron may receive, either from an external source or from other neurons. The inputs determine each element's output, which corresponds to the nerve impulse that travels to the next neuron. The overall behavior of a neural network is controlled by the connectedness of the nodes, and by the effective influence or *strength* of each connection to a node on that node's output. Techniques exist for automatically adjust- ing the strength of the connections, based on how well the network per- forms and what mistakes it makes, allowing a sort of automatic learning.

Neural networks can be implemented either in software or in hardware, and have proven useful for some processing tasks, especially certain kinds of pattern recognition in audio and image processing. *See also* **artificial intelligence.**

newbie   A novice, especially someone new to some computer or Internet-related activity, such as someone who has just started using an online service, is learning how to use a particular kind of software, or has just begun participating in a newsgroup.

newline   *See* **linefeed.**

news aggregator   **1.** *See* **newsreader** (sense 1). **2.** *See* **aggregator.**

news client   *See* **newsreader** (sense 1).

newsgroup   A discussion forum on Usenet where users can post or read text messages as well as data in binary formats. Messages are stored on a news server and organized by newsgroup name, so they can be viewed with a newsreader or on a webpage. Newsgroup names consist of a string of words separated by periods, indicating the topic of discussion, as in rec.pets.cats.

newsreader   **1.** An application or website that allows users to read Usenet newsgroups. Many email clients, such as Microsoft Outlook and Mozilla Outlook, are also newsreaders. Trn is a popular newsreader for Linux and Unix. Many newsreaders can also collect and display web feeds. *Also called* **news aggregator, news client. 2.** *See* **aggregator.**

news server   A server that stores Usenet newsgroup messages so users can download and read them.

NFS   *Abbreviation of* **Network File System.**   A protocol developed by Sun Microsystems that allows a user to access files available on other computers and file servers as if they were on the same computer. NFS represents files on local devices together with files elsewhere on the network in a single hierarchical directory. It is commonly used with Linux and Unix operating systems, though it can also be used with MacOS and Windows.

nibble or **nybble**   A unit of data equal to four bits, or half of a byte.

NIC   *Abbreviation of* **network interface card.**

NiCad battery or **NiCd battery**   *Abbreviations of* **nickel-cadmium battery.** An inexpensive rechargeable battery with cells made of nickel and cadmium. In many applications, NiCad batteries have been replaced by longer lasting NiMH and lithium-ion batteries. NiCad cells typically produce around 1.2 volts of electricity.

NiMH battery   *Abbreviation of* **nickel-metal-hydride battery.**   A rechargeable battery similar to a NiCad battery but using nickel metal hydride rather than cadmium. NiMH cells avoid the problems of the use and disposal of cadmium, which is toxic, and have a larger storage capacity than

NiCad cells of the same size. Both NiMH and NiCad cells typically produce around 1.2 volts of electricity.

nit   *See* **candela per square meter.**

NLQ   *Abbreviation of* **near-letter quality.**

NNTP   *Abbreviation of* **network news transfer protocol.**   The protocol for transferring newsgroup messages across the Internet. NNTP is used for reading and posting Usenet articles, as well as transferring articles between news servers.

node   **1.** A workstation, server, printer, or other device that is connected to a network and is able to process data. **2.** An element of an XML or SGML document that does not contain another element. **3.** In a tree or graph structure as used in directory or network management and programming, a point where two or more lines or branches of the tree meet.

noise   A random signal on a communications channel that interferes with the desired signal or data. Noise can either be generated by the circuitry of the communications device itself or come from one of a variety of external sources, including radio and TV signals, lightning, power transmission lines, or interference with other signals.

noise-canceling headphone   A headphone that reduces ambient noise. Noise-canceling headphones detect external sound signals with microphones and create an inverted version of those signals, sending the inverted signals to the speaker elements in the headphones. The inverted signals largely cancel out the incoming external signals.

noise floor   The level of noise in the transmission of a signal such that parts of the transmitted signal below that level cannot be recovered.

nonimpact printer   A printer that does not physically strike the paper in order to transfer ink or wax to the page, such as a laser printer, an inkjet printer, or a thermal printer. Nonimpact printers are considerably quieter than impact printers, but they cannot be used for printing multipart forms. *See also* **printer.**

noninterlaced   Relating to video in which every line of resolution is used in every frame. *See also* **interlacing.**

nonvolatile memory   Memory whose contents are not lost when power is shut off. Disks, ROM, and flash memory are all examples of nonvolatile memory.

nonvolatile random access memory   *See* **NVRAM.**

NOR   A logical operator that returns the value TRUE as its output if and only if both of its inputs (or *operands*) are FALSE; if either input is TRUE, it returns FALSE. It is equivalent to the logical operator OR followed by the operator NOT. NOR gates are especially easy to implement electronically, and a high proportion of the logic gates of microprocessors are NOR gates (together with NAND gates). *See* Table E on page 361.

normalization   A method of determining the average volume level of the audio files in a playlist and automatically increasing or decreasing the levels of each individual file so that all are reproduced at roughly the same volume.

NOS   *Abbreviation of* **network operating system.**

NOT   A logical operator with just one input (or *operand*), returning the value TRUE as its output if its input is FALSE, and returning FALSE if its input is TRUE. *See* Table E on page 361.

notebook   *See* **laptop.**

notepad   A simple text editor that is distributed with the Microsoft Windows operating system.

ns or **nsec**   *Abbreviations of* **nanosecond.**

NTFS   *Abbreviation of* **NT file system.**   A file system developed by Microsoft and used in most versions of its Windows operating systems since 2000. NTFS replaced FAT as the default Windows file system because of its increased efficiency in using disk space, its improved security features, and its improved ability to recover lost files. Newer versions of Windows allow users to choose between FAT and NTFS. Other operating systems typically do not support NTFS.

NTSC   *Abbreviation of* **National Television System Committee** or **National Television Standards Committee.**   An analog television standard, used in the United States, that specifies how color is encoded in television radio signals. NTSC is used in conjunction with a transmission standard that has a vertical resolution of 525 lines per frame, an interlaced picture displayed at a rate of 59.94 fields per second, a channel bandwidth of 6 megahertz, and a 4 : 3 aspect ratio. *Compare* **PAL.** *See* Table B on page 357.

NuBus   A computer bus developed by Apple and used in older Macintosh computers. NuBus has a 32-bit bus width.

null character   A control character in the ASCII and Unicode character sets that functions as a placeholder and does not normally represent any information of its own. The null character stands in contrast to other control characters, which typically represent some nonalphanumeric character or an instruction. The null character is used to fill out data fields that require a certain number of characters, to terminate character strings, and to separate blocks of data. In the ASCII character set, the null character is symbolized by NUL and represented by the character code 0.

217

null-modem cable A cable that allows two computers to be connected together through their serial ports without using a modem. Two computers connected with a null-modem cable can communicate using protocols such as PPP or SLIP.

number cruncher A program or computer designed to perform complex, lengthy mathematical calculations. *See also* **supercomputer.**

numeric coprocessor *See* **math coprocessor.**

numeric keypad A keypad consisting of number keys, especially as part of a standard computer keyboard. The numeric keypad on a computer keyboard is usually to the right of the typing area and consists of the numbers 0–9, a decimal point, mathematical operators, and an Enter key. In numeric mode, the keys represent numbers. In cursor control mode, they function as arrow keys and function keys. The Num Lock key is pressed to toggle between modes.

   The numeric keypads on telephones and related devices are arranged in numeric order from right to left in rows starting with the lowest numbers on the top row. Those on calculators and computer keyboards have the lowest numbers on the bottom row.

Num Lock key A key that toggles the numeric keypad between numeric mode and cursor control mode.

Nuon An interface used to expand the capabilities of DVD players. A Nuon attachment enables a conventional DVD player to perform enhanced functions such as accessing interactive DVD-ROM content and playing CDs and video games.

NVRAM *Abbreviation of* **nonvolatile random access memory.** RAM whose contents are retained when the computer or device is shut off or power is disconnected. Some NVRAM is simply DRAM or SRAM with a dedicated battery to provide a constant power supply, but other forms of NVRAM, such as flash memory, can retain data without a power source.

nybble *See* **nibble.**

object **1.** In object-oriented programming, a discrete item that consists of data and the procedures necessary to operate on that data. **2.** A discrete item that can be selected and maneuvered, such as an onscreen graphic.

object code   Machine code or assembly language that is produced by a compiler from source code. Source code consists of the instructions written by the programmer in a high-level programming language such as C or VisualBasic. The object code is most often in the form of machine language that can be directly executed by a computer. It may, however, be in assembly language, an intermediate code that is then translated into machine language by an assembler.

object linking and embedding   *See* **OLE.**

object-oriented   Describing and handling data as a set of objects rather than as a collection of elements, bits, or points. Each object in an object-oriented system may contain data, but each object also contains procedures and functions for manipulating data.

object-oriented graphics   *See* **vector graphics.**

object-oriented interface   A user interface in which actions are performed by manipulating symbols on the screen that represent types of data as real objects, such as folders. Most common operating systems, such as Windows, Macintosh, and Linux, have an object-oriented interface.

object-oriented programming   *Abbreviated* **OOP.**   Computer programming that focuses on data instead of procedures. In conventional programming, the programmer lists the procedures to be performed on the data in order to accomplish a task. In object-oriented programming, a programmer designs a representation of the data that includes the operations that can be performed on it, as well as its relationships to other data. Java is an example of an OOP language.

Object-oriented programming is often used for graphical user interfaces, since an object can be represented onscreen by an icon, and the user can copy, reposition, or otherwise manipulate the object by dragging or clicking on its icon with a mouse.

oblique   A simulated italic type style created by slanting the roman characters of a font. Oblique letters lack the cursive appearance of italic letters.

OCR   *Abbreviation of* **optical character recognition.**

octal   Relating to the base 8 numeral system. In contrast with the commonly used decimal system, in which each place in a number represents a successive power of 10, each place in an octal number represents a power of 8. Thus the decimal number 1,165 is written in octal notation as 2215, which stands for $(2 \times 8^3) + (2 \times 8^2) + (1 \times 8) + (5 \times 1)$, or $1,024 + 128 + 8 + 5$. Octal notation is sometimes used in computer programming because it converts easily into the binary notation used by computers. *See also* **hexadecimal.** *See* Table 2 at **binary.**

octet   A set of eight bits, the usual size of a byte on a modern computer.

OCX   Former name of ActiveX control technology. ActiveX controls still retain the *.ocx* file extension.

ODBC   *Abbreviation of* **open database connectivity.**   A standard that allows different applications to communicate with different database servers. An ODBC driver translates standardized database requests from an application to a format that a particular database server understands.

odd footer   In word processing, a footer that appears on odd-numbered pages.

odd header   In word processing, a header that appears on odd-numbered pages.

OEM   *Abbreviation of* **original equipment manufacturer.**   The company that actually manufactures a product, which is then modified or repackaged and sold to the consumer by a different company.

office automation   The use of computers, computer networks, and related equipment to perform the tasks necessary to managing or operating an office efficiently.

office suite   A group of programs that perform typical office functions such as word processing, spreadsheets, presentations, scheduling, and email. Microsoft Office is a popular office suite, as is IBM's Lotus Smart-Suite and the free, open-source OpenOffice.

offline   Not connected to a computer or computer network.

offset   A value that specifies the distance of a byte, either in computer memory or in a digital file, from a reference point. For example, if a byte A is byte number 100, then A + 7, where 7 is the offset, specifies byte number 107.

Ogg Vorbis   A file format used for storing digital audio data and for transmitting music over the Internet with a higher sound quality and a lower bit rate than MP3. Unlike MP3, Ogg Vorbis is an open-source format and therefore can be freely used without licensing restrictions. Files of this type are usually identified by the *.ogg* extension.

ohm   A unit of impedance used to measure the total opposition to current flow through a circuit or component in a circuit. Loudspeakers with an average impedance under four ohms require amplifiers capable of producing a large amount of electrical power. The unit *ohm* is represented by the symbol O.

OLAP   *Abbreviation of* **online analytical processing.**   Software that works with a database management system and allows users to analyze large amounts of complex data quickly and interactively.

OLE *Abbreviation of* **Object Linking and Embedding.** A Microsoft standard for how different software modules interact. One application of this standard involves linking documents and establishing how updates to the data of one document affect the data in other documents. For example, a graph may be placed in a spreadsheet, which might be displayed on a webpage. The standard also provides ways for independent software modules to work together so that a single spell checker, for example, can provide spellchecking for different programs. *See also* **ActiveX.**

OLED *Abbreviation of* **organic LED.** A light-emitting diode that uses an organic compound to emit light. Screens made of OLEDs do not require backlighting like LCD displays, are energy-efficient, and may be made of flexible materials. OLED displays are used in some digital cameras and automotive display devices.

onboard Located on a circuit board.

onboard modem *See* **internal modem.**

on-demand Available for delivery to a customer immediately upon request, as by transmission over a network. On-demand software can be downloaded directly after purchasing it. *See* **video on demand.**

One-Finger Keyboard *See* **Fitaly Keyboard.**

100Base-T Any of various twisted-pair cables used for Fast Ethernet networks.

one-time pad A key used in private-key cryptography that is as long as the contents of the message being encrypted. The use of one-time pads is the only encryption method known to be unbreakable, but to guarantee its unbreakability, a one-time pad must be used with only one message. The generation of perfectly secure one-time pad systems is difficult to accomplish because it requires the generation of truly random numbers.

online Connected to or accessible by means of a computer or computer network.

online analytical processing *See* **OLAP.**

online forum *See* **message board.**

online help A website or software module that uses the Internet to provide information about how to use an application.

online service **1.** A commercial service that provides access to the Internet for a subscription fee. The access may be through telephone, cable, or wireless service. The provider often supplies email, ftp, conferencing, and other services. **2.** Access to large databases and other electronic information provided through a computer network. This access may or may not involve a fee, and may or may not include additional access to the Internet. For example, many libraries have their card catalogs set up as online services. Other examples include LexisNexis and the Dow Jones News/Retrieval service.

onscreen keyboard   *See* **soft keyboard.**

OOP   *Abbreviation of* **object-oriented programming.**

open   **1.** To make a file ready for reading or writing. *Compare* **close. 2.** To expand an icon into a window on a GUI (graphical user interface). *Compare* **close.**

open architecture   A computer hardware or software design whose specifications are publicly available, so that any third party is free to design and distribute components of the system or add-on products. *Compare* **closed architecture.** *See also* **proprietary.**

open database connectivity   *See* **ODBC.**

OpenDocument   A set of standard XML-based file formats for office suite documents, developed by the OASIS Group and based on formats used in the OpenOffice suite. The OpenDocument formats are open-source file formats suitable for spreadsheets, word processing documents, presentations, and related documents. These formats were designed as alternatives to the proprietary file formats used by Microsoft Office. OpenDocument format files can be displayed and created by programs in OpenOffice as well as other open-source programs. Typical file extensions used for OpenDocument format files begin with the letters *od.* For example, *.ods* is typically used for spreadsheets, and *.odt* is typically used for text files. OpenDocument is also known as *ODF,* which stands for *Open Document Format for Office Applications. See also* **Open XML Formats.**

Open Group   A computer industry consortium that maintains the Single Unix Standard and certifies Unix operating systems. The Open Group arose out of a merger between X/Open and the Open Software Foundation, organizations that had been developing competing Unix standards.

Open Software Foundation   *Abbreviated* **OSF.**   A computer industry consortium founded to create a standard for the Unix operating system and the X Window System. The Open Software Foundation merged with a competing consortium, X/Open, in 1996, to form the Open Group. The Open Group controls the Single Unix Specification.

open source   Relating to software that is available without restrictions regarding its installation and use, usually free of charge. Some open-source software is in the public domain, but more commonly, open-source software is covered by a license agreement such as the GPL, which allows users access to the source code so they can make changes to it and incorporate it into their own software. Open-source software is often written by unpaid volunteers who collaborate online. *Also called* **free software.** *Compare* **freeware, proprietary.** *See also* **copyleft.**

Open XML formats   A set of standard XML-based formats developed by Microsoft for office suite documents. The Open XML formats are open-source file formats suitable for spreadsheets, word processing documents, presentations, and related documents. They were developed to ensure compatibility with Microsoft Office. Because they are open-source for-mats, applications developed by companies other than Microsoft can dis-play and save documents in these formats. File extensions for Open XML formats are the same as those previously used for Microsoft Office docu-ments, with the addition of a trailing *x*. So, for example, the file exten-sion *.docx* is used for word processing documents designed to be read and saved by Microsoft Word. *See also* **OpenDocument.**

Opera   A web browser developed by Opera Software. Opera is proprietary, but a free version is available that displays advertisements while viewing webpages. Because of its proprietary technology for displaying webpages on a small screen, it is popular for use on handheld devices, such as PDAs and mobile phones.

operand   **1.** A number or variable on which a mathematical operation is performed. In the expression $8 + x$, 8 and x are the operands, and the operation is addition. **2.** In computing, the data on which a single instruction acts.

operating environment   The system software, key applications, and hard-ware configuration that are present on a computer. *See also* **environment.**

operating system   *Abbreviated* **OS.**   Software that controls the hardware of a specific computer system in order to allow users and application pro-grams to employ it easily. The operating system mediates between hard-ware and applications programs. It handles the details of sending instructions to the hardware and allocating system resources in case of conflicts, thus relieving applications developers of this burden and pro-viding a standard platform for new programs. Common operating systems for personal computers are Linux, Mac OS X and Windows XP.

operation   **1.** An action performed on one or more numbers or variables. Addition, subtraction, multiplication, and division are common arithmetic operations. *See also* **operand, operator. 2.** In computing, an action resulting from a single instruction.

operator   A symbol or character string that represents a function. In com-puting, the following symbols are used as common mathematical oper-ators: $+$ (addition), $-$ (subtraction), * (multiplication), / (division), and ^ (exponentiation). In programming, spreadsheets, and query languages, one encounters logical operators such as AND, OR, and NOT, and relational operators, such as > (greater than) and < (less than).

opposite track path *See* **OTP.**

optical Relating to or using visible light. While electronic communication often takes place by transmitting radio frequency energy, technologies such as fiber optics and some wireless data transmission systems use frequencies in the range of visible light. Data is read from optical disks using visible light.

optical character recognition *Abbreviated* **OCR.** The use of a device or software to identify and encode printed or handwritten characters on a page or in a digital image. OCR technology matches the patterns of light and dark in an image against patterns stored in memory to identify the letter of the alphabet, numerical character, or punctuation mark and encode it as a text character. Once a page or file has been processed, it can be stored as a text file instead of as a graphic.

optical disk A plastic-coated disk that digitally stores text, music, or other data as tiny pits etched into the surface that are to be read by a laser. Some optical disks are used for read-only data storage, others are erasable. CDs, DVDs, and MiniDiscs are well-known types of optical disks.

optical fiber A thin strand of glass or plastic, through which light can be transmitted over long distances. Optical fibers are used to create cables for transmitting data at high speed over long distances.

optical jukebox An automated device for storing, reading, and writing optical disks. A robotic arm moves the disks from the storage slots into the read/write drives for data retrieval or recording. *Also called* **optical library.**

optical mouse A mouse that senses motion by reflecting the light from a light-emitting diode (LED) off the surface it rests on and detecting changes in the reflected light. Optical mice are more precise than mechanical ones, and are less prone to breaking because they have no moving parts.

optical resolution The resolution at which a scanner or other video device can digitize images without being enhanced by software, measured in dots per inch.

optical scanner *See* **scanner.**

optical zoom On digital cameras, the use of a lens to magnify or zoom in on the subject being photographed. Optical zoom on a digital camera is the same as zoom on a traditional camera. *Compare* **digital zoom.**

optimization   The process of improving something based on the importance of some criteria. In computing, the processing speed and memory
requirements of a task are important criteria, so optimization often
involves reducing processing time and memory usage. An important cri-
terion for the success of a website is how many visitors it gets, so optimization involves making a site more likely to be returned in a web search.
See also **search engine optimization.**

Option key   A key on Apple Macintosh computer keyboards that when
pressed in combination with another key generates a number of special
characters or alternate commands.

OR   A logical operator that returns the value TRUE as its output if either or
both of its inputs (or *operands*) are TRUE. If both inputs are FALSE, it
returns FALSE. *Also called* **inclusive OR.** *See* Table E on page 361.

Oracle   A database management system developed by Oracle Corporation.
Oracle is one of the most widely used database systems, particularly for
large-scale commercial enterprises.

.org   A top-level domain operated by the Public Interest Registry and
intended to be used by organizations not covered by other top-level
domains, particularly non-profit organizations. Currently, any individual
or organization can register a domain name in the .org domain.

organic LED   *See* **OLED.**

orientation   The alignment of the text or graphics on a page or screen.
The two kinds of orientation are *portrait* and *landscape.*

original equipment manufacturer   *See* **OEM.**

OS   *Abbreviation of* **operating system.**

OS/2   An operating system for personal computers originally developed by
IBM and Microsoft Corporation to be the successor to DOS. Microsoft
eventually dropped its work on OS/2, and the system was for a time a
competitor of Windows. Now OS/2 is used on few computers. IBM stopped
selling it in December 2005, but planned to continue supporting it.

OSF   *Abbreviation of* **Open Software Foundation.**

OS X   Any of a set of Unix-based operating systems developed by Apple
Computer, Inc., for use on Apple Macintosh computers. OS X is compatible with older versions of the operating system, being able to run a simulation of System 9. Unlike earlier versions of MacOS, OS X features a
terminal window for command-line interface with the operating system.
Also called **System 10.**

OTA broadcasting   *Abbreviation of* **over-the-air broadcasting.**   *See* **terrestrial broadcasting.**

OTP *Abbreviation of* **opposite track path.** A form of dual-layer DVD in which layer 0 and layer 1 have opposite track directions. The DVD player reads layer 0 from the center to the outer edge of the disk, and then switches direction and reads layer 1 from the outer edge back to the center. OTP disks are designed for long programs that require continuous play, as they allow for seamless transition between layers. *Also called* **reverse spiral dual layer.** *Compare* **PTP.**

outline font A font in which the outlines of characters are defined by mathematical formulas. The printer then fills in the outlines at its maximum resolution. TrueType and PostScript are popular page description languages for defining outline fonts. Unlike bitmapped fonts, outline fonts are scalable; they can be adjusted in size without becoming distorted. Typically, an outline font is used for printing, and an associated bitmapped font is used for displaying text on the screen. *Also called* **printer font, scalable font, vector font.** *See also* **vector graphics.**

Outlook An email client developed by Microsoft. Outlook works with Microsoft's proprietary Microsoft Exchange email protocol as well as standard protocols such as POP and IMAP. A version of Outlook called Outlook Express, which can also read Usenet newsgroups, is included with the Microsoft Windows operating system.

output Information that a computer produces, such as the results of processing data input to the computer. Output can be printed, displayed on a screen, written to disk, sent from one application to another, or transferred via networks to other computers. *Compare* **input.**

output device Hardware that transfers data out of a computer. Printers, display screens, and speakers are examples of output devices. *See also* **input device.**

overclock To set the clock speed of a computer component, such as a CPU, memory module, or bus, to a higher speed than recommended by the manufacturer. Overclocking can improve a computer's performance to some degree. Problems associated with overclocking include overheating of the CPU or other components (which can permanently damage them), and the inability of the computer to synchronize with some peripherals. *See also* **clock speed.**

overflow error The condition that results when a unit of data is too large to be stored in the memory location allotted to it. Often, the extra data overwrites data the computer needs to continue processing. Overflow errors present a security risk because malicious users can often exploit them to overwrite data that should remain secure.

oversampling   The process of increasing the sampling rate of a digital signal by resampling it at a higher rate. Oversampling is often used for noise reduction and antialiasing in both audio and video applications. *See also* **upsampling.**

overscan   A portion of a video image, sometimes constituting as much as 10 to 20 percent of the original image, that exceeds the borders of the display screen and is unseen by the viewer. Overscan is deliberately included in analog television signals because CRT displays enlarge pictures to extend beyond the borders of the screen in order to obscure possible distortion and other imperfections at the edges of the image. *See also* **underscan.**

overstrike mode   **1.** *See* **overwrite mode. 2.** In word processing, a mode allowing the user to type two characters in the same position so as to create or simulate another character that may not be available, such as o and / for the character ∅. **3.** In the TeX page description language, a mode that produces horizontal bars on each letter, making the text look as if it has been crossed out.

over-the-air broadcasting   *Abbreviated* **OTA broadcasting.**   *See* **terrestrial broadcasting.**

overwrite   To write new data to a location where other data is already stored, thus destroying the old data.

overwrite mode   In word processing, a mode for typing over an existing character and replacing it with a new character. *Also called* **overstrike mode, typeover mode.** *Compare* **insert mode.**

owner   The user with privileged access to a file on a shared file system, typically the creator of the file. In some operating systems, only the owner of a file can modify its permissions.

P2P   *Abbreviation of* **peer-to-peer.**   *See* **peer-to-peer network.**

pack   *v. See* **compress.**
   n. A group of MPEG packets in a DVD-Video program stream. Each pack is 2048 bytes, or the size of one DVD sector.

packaged software   Software that is not designed for a specific client but is written for general use and distributed commercially through dealers and other channels. *Also called* **shrink-wrapped software.**

packed file   A file that has undergone data compression so as to take up less memory.

packet   A short block of data that is transmitted in a packet-switching network. *Also called* **datagram.**

Packet Internet Groper   *See* **PING.**

packet sniffer   A program that intercepts data transmitted over the Internet and translates it back into human-readable text. Network administrators use packet sniffers to help locate and relieve network congestion. The existence of packet sniffers means that unencrypted Internet transmissions are insecure. Packet sniffers are also used for illicit purposes such as obtaining passwords or credit card numbers. *Also called* **sniffer.**

packet switching   A technique for transmitting data between nodes in a network in which the data is divided into packets; each packet is independently provided with a path between the origin and the destination. This strategy is commonly used in local area networks (LANs) and wide area networks (WANs) such as the Internet. Packet switching capitalizes on the increase in efficiency that is obtained when there are many paths available and there is a large volume of traffic over these paths, since the least crowded path for a packet to follow might change over time, and the fastest route can be used for each packet. The original order of the packets must, however, be restored at the destination node. *See also* **circuit switching.**

page   *n.* Any fixed quantity of memory as used by an application, such as the amount of memory used by a graphics display program to display one screen's worth of a large image, or units of memory manipulated as in a system for virtual memory.

   v. In virtual memory systems, to swap pages of data between RAM and an auxiliary memory device, such as a hard disk. Data is paged into memory from swap space or paged out of memory to swap space.

page break   In word processing, a separation between pages of text. Most word processing programs create a page break automatically when the amount of text surpasses one printable page.

page description language   *Abbreviated* **PDL.**   A language for controlling the layout and contents of printed pages by stipulating fonts, margins, line paths and thicknesses, and other page characteristics. A page description language allows descriptions of characters and graphics that are scalable; that is, they can be displayed or printed at various sizes.

Originally developed for use in laser printers, page description languages are now commonly used for displaying text and graphics on computer screens. Popular page description languages include PostScript, PCL, and PDF.

Page Down key   *Abbreviated* **PgDn.**   A key that shifts the contents of a window, such as a web browser, upward, displacing its current content and revealing the next full window of text and images beneath. In windows with a cursor, the key repositions the cursor down one full screen or full window of lines in the document or file being viewed. *Compare* **Page Up key.** *See also* **End key, Home key.**

page fault   An attempt to read from or write to a memory address that is not in main memory. When this happens, the system must get the data from a swap file. *See also* **paging, virtual memory.**

page file   *See* **swap file.**

page hit   *See* **hit** (sense 2).

page layout program   An application that allows the user to arrange text and graphics from various files together on a page. Page layout programs generally support a variety of fonts, allow the structuring of text into columns or other arrangements, and provide automatic pagination and many other features. Some basic image processing is usually available as well, for resizing, cropping, or other adjustments. The page design being created is displayed as a graphics image onscreen. Two popular page layout programs are PageMaker from Aldus Corporation and QuarkXPress, developed by Quark, Inc. Page layout programs are widely used in desktop publishing and in the creation of formal documents such as reports or contracts. *See also* **desktop publishing.**

page preview   *See* **preview.**

page printer   A printer, such as a laser printer, that processes all the data for one page at the same time. Page printers require comparatively larger amounts of memory than other printers because the data for each page must be placed in memory before it is printed.

pager   A wireless communications device that receives and displays text messages sent through a terminal on the public telephone network. Messages received by the terminal are broadcast by transmitters. The pager that the message is intended for is identified by a code that precedes the message.

The earliest pagers merely beeped when a user called a dedicated phone number, alerting the user to call a central office for a message. Pager technology gradually developed so that pagers could first display the phone number of a caller, and later display messages transcribed by an operator. Now, protocols have been developed that allow the routing of email and SMS messages to pagers. Two-way pagers also allow users to send messages from pagers. *Also called* **beeper.** *See also* **cap code.**

pages per minute *Abbreviated* **ppm.** A measure of the speed of printers. A printer's ppm rating is usually based on how fast it can print a page that has text in a single typeface and no graphics or other special elements. Therefore, this rating is not a reliable measure for pages containing multiple typefaces or graphics. *Compare* **graphics pages per minute.**

Page Up key *Abbreviated* **PgUp.** A key that shifts the contents of a window, such as a web browser, downward, displacing its current content and revealing the previous full window of text and images above. In windows with a cursor, the key repositions the cursor up one full screen or full window of lines in the document or file being viewed. *Compare* **Page Down key.** *See also* **End key, Home key.**

pagination **1.** The numbering of the pages of a document at the top or bottom of each page. **2.** The dividing of a document into pages, as in word processing. Most programs do this automatically.

paging The use of pages for managing the main memory of a computer. In systems that use paging, memory is divided into pages of a specified size, and the operating system uses a data structure called a *page table* to keep track of how each page is being used. Most modern operating systems use paging, which requires that the computer have an MMU to manage the page table.

paint program A graphics application that allows the user to create images using virtual tools such as a paintbrush or a can of spray paint to color in shapes and tones. Unlike draw programs, images in paint programs are stored as bitmaps, and therefore tend to become distorted when they are resized. *See also* **draw program.**

PAL *Abbreviation of* **phase alternation line.** An analog television standard that is used in many parts of the world outside of North America and that specifies how color is encoded. PAL is used in conjunction with transmission standards that have a vertical resolution of 625 lines per frame, an interlaced picture displayed at a rate of 50 fields per second, and a 4 : 3 aspect ratio. *Compare* **NTSC.** *See* Table B on page 357.

palette **1.** The set of discrete colors that can be represented by an individual pixel. The size of the palette used by a device, file, or application is limited by the color depth of the pixels. The palette's colors are defined as a combination of values in a color model. **2.** In a graphics program, a group of colors or graphics tools.

Palm OS An operating system for PDAs and cell phones that have ARM processors. Palm OS was originally developed by US Robotics and is now licensed and developed by PalmSource. It is used on wireless handheld devices produced by a number of different manufacturers. PalmSource announced in 2004 that some versions of Palm OS will be based on a Linux operating system.

palmtop A computer that is small enough to fit in the hand. *See also* **PDA, subnotebook.**

PAN *Abbreviation of* **personal area network.** A small network consisting of connections between two or more devices, such as computers, handhelds, and printers, that are located close to one another. Most PANs use short-range wireless data transmission techniques, such as Bluetooth or IrDA.

pan-and-scan A technique for adjusting a widescreen image to fit the narrower aspect ratio of a conventional television screen by cropping off the sides of the image. *Compare* **letterbox.**

panel *See* **flat-panel display.**

Pantone Matching System *Abbreviated* **PMS.** A standard system developed by Pantone, Inc., for identifying approximately 500 ink colors, each assigned a specific number.

paper feed The mechanism that feeds paper through a printer. *See also* **friction feed, tractor feed.**

parallel **1.** Relating to or used in the simultaneous transmission of digital data over separate channels within a single communications connection. *Compare* **serial. 2.** Relating to or carrying out the simultaneous performance of separate tasks. *See also* **parallel processing.**

parallel bus A bus that transmits electrical signals over several wires simultaneously. The data transfer rate of a parallel bus is partially determined by its width, which is the number of wires that signals can be sent down, and thus the number of bits that can be sent at one time. The bus that connects the CPU to main memory is typically a parallel bus. *Compare* **serial bus.**

parallel port A port used for parallel data transmission, typically a 25-pin D-subminiature connector on a computer. A parallel port is used for communication with printers and other peripheral devices. The IEEE 1284 standard specifies both the hardware and communications protocols used with parallel ports. *See also* **serial port.** *See figure at* **connector.** *See* Table C on page 358.

parallel processing The simultaneous use of multiple computers or multiple CPUs or GPUs to complete a single computing task more quickly.

Parallel processing involves various methods for dividing up a computing task, distributing its parts to different computers or processors, and assembling the results. *See also* **cluster, distributed processing, multiprocessing.**

parallel track path   *See* **PTP.**

parameter   **1.** One of a group of adjustable factors that distinguish an environment or determine how a system will work. For example, when a user uses software to determine which colors will represent what items on a display screen, or sets margin and page length options in a document, the user is setting parameters. Parameter settings are often saved between sessions on a computer or with software. **2.** A specification that the user adds or changes in giving the computer a command. For example, if the user gives the DOS command COPY, the user must specify what should be copied and where the copy should go. For example, in the command COPY A:\DFILE.RUR, the filename "DFILE.RUR" is a parameter that tells the computer what to copy. **3.** In programming, a value that is passed to a function or routine so that it can be operated on to produce a result. *See also* **argument.**

parameter RAM   *See* **PRAM.**

parent directory   A directory in which a subdirectory is located. For example, a directory called Bird Photos, containing photographs of birds, might be kept within a directory called Photographs. Photographs would then be the parent directory of Bird Photos. Each directory has only one parent directory, unless it is a *root directory,* in which case it has no parent.

parity   **1.** The evenness or oddness of the number of 1's in a set of bits. The parity of a set of bits is often stored as a parity bit and is used to check the integrity of data or to recover data. **2.** Making use of a parity bit in storage or transmission. For example, a RAM chip with the designation *parity* stores a parity bit along with each memory address; a *nonparity* chip does not.

parity bit   A bit that indicates the parity of a given bit sequence so that the bit sequence can be checked for errors. If the parity of the bit sequence does not match the stored parity bit, it means that an odd number of bits (usually 1) has been changed.

park   To lock the heads of a hard disk drive on a part of the disk that contains no data in order to avoid a head crash. Current disk drives contain mechanisms that park the heads whenever the drive is turned off. Some disk drives designed for portable use also contain mechanisms that park the heads whenever there is a sudden change in motion.

parse To process a computer file by breaking the data into its component parts, such as commands, individual database records, or tags. For example, for a web browser to display a webpage, it must parse the HTML file and then process each individual element in the file. Parsing is accomplished by special-purpose software modules.

partition A section of a disk that has its own file system and functions as an independent disk. An entire disk may consist of only one partition, or it may have several.

passive Exhibiting no gain or contributing no energy to a signal, especially an electrical signal. *Compare* **active.**

pass phrase *See* **password.**

password A sequence of characters required by an application to grant a user access to some resource, such as the use of a computer, an email account, a network, or a cipher key for encrypting or decrypting messages. Many attempts to gain unauthorized access to computer resources often involve simply trying large numbers of common passwords, and various combinations of words that are likely to serve as passwords, so passwords should be chosen that are fairly long and do not consist entirely of recognizable words and phrases. *Also called* **pass phrase.**

paste To place copied text or graphics into a document or file. *See also* **copy, cut.**

patch A piece of code added to software in order to fix a bug without replacing the entire program, especially as a temporary correction between two releases.

path **1.** *See* **pathname. 2.** The ordered list of directories that a command line interpreter looks in to find the executable files necessary to execute each command. If the correct executable is not in the path, the command line interpreter cannot execute the command. The path is stored in a variable as part of the environment.

pathname A text string that identifies a file or directory, consisting of the name of the file or directory preceded by a list of directories above it in the hierarchy, ordered from highest to lowest. For example, if a file named *foo.txt* was in a directory called *bar,* which was itself located in a directory called *houghton,* then *houghton\bar\foo.txt* would be a pathname for the file. On Windows operating systems, directories in the pathname are separated from each other with a backslash. On Linux and Unix operating systems, a forward slash is used. *Also called* **path.** *See also* **absolute pathname, relative pathname.**

pattern recognition   The identification of patterns by a computer in order to classify or identify images, sounds, or sections of text. Examples of pattern recognition include speech recognition, handwriting recognition, the automatic recognition of human faces, and text classification.

Pause key   A key that, when pressed, interrupts a command, a program, or the onscreen display of data. Keyboards for PC-compatible computers have a Pause key that stops the display of data when you are scrolling through several screens. Many games have Pause keys so that you can interrupt the game and return to it later.

pay-per-view   *Abbreviated* **PPV.** A television service in which the customer pays a one-time fee to view a single television show, movie, special event, or period of programming, especially a scheduled broadcast.

pay TV   Television content that is provided for a fee.

PC   **1.** *Abbreviation of* **personal computer. 2.** A computer that is PC-compatible.

PCB   *Abbreviation of* **printed circuit board.**

PC Card   A standard developed by PCMCIA for the physical design of a variety of small, external cards used primarily with laptop computers. PC Cards have a variety of applications: modems, network adaptors, memory cards, and television tuners are all available as PC Cards. The standard specifies three card thicknesses: 3.3 mm (Type I), 5 mm (Type II), and 10.5 mm (Type III), with Type II being the most common. CardBus PC Cards have a length of 86 mm and a width of 54 mm. A 68-pin edge connector is located on the shorter side and data is transferred at a rate of 132 MBps along a 32-bit data path. The ExpressCard version, by contrast, specifies two sizes, 75 × 34 mm and 75 × 54 mm, both of which have a 16-pin edge connector. ExpressCards use high-speed PCI Express or USB 2.0 buses. *See* Table C on page 358.

PC-compatible   Designed to be compatible with the operation of Windows operating systems. The term originally referred to specific hardware configurations that commonly ran DOS operating systems; in fact, the term *IBM PC-compatible* is still often used, since such hardware was first developed by IBM for IBM personal computers. PC-compatible computers typically use x86 microprocessors. A wide variety of manufacturers (no longer including IBM) produce PC-compatible computers and peripherals, and the majority of personal computers on the market today are PC-compatible. PC-compatible computers are most commonly used with Windows operating systems, but other operating systems such as Unix or Linux are sometimes used as well. The terms *PC-compatible* and sometimes simply *PC* are sometimes used (inaccurately) to refer specifically to computers running Windows operating systems.

.pcd   A file extension typically used for data stored on Photo CDs.

PC-DOS   A version of DOS created and sold by IBM and originally used on its IBM PC computer.

PCI   *Abbreviation of* **Peripheral Component Interconnect.** A common computer bus standard. Most versions of PCI use parallel data transfer. Of these, some have bus widths of 32 bits and others 64 bits. Data transfer rates range from 133 MBps in the earliest versions to 533 MBps in the latest 64-bit version. The serial version of PCI is known as PCI Express. *See also* **bus.** *See* Table C on page 358.

PCI Express   A computer bus standard that is based on the PCI standard but uses serial data transfer to attain faster transfer rates. PCI Express expansion slots are sometimes used instead of Accelerated Graphics Ports. *See* Table C on page 358.

PCL   *Abbreviation of* **Printer Command Language** or **Printer Control Language.** A page description language developed by Hewlett-Packard that describes text and graphics in a way that allows for printing at any resolution. Printer drivers often convert documents to PCL before they are sent to a printer. A printer designed to understand PCL is sometimes called an *HP-compatible* printer.

PCM   *Abbreviation of* **pulse code modulation.** A method of encoding and sending analog signals in digital form in which the magnitude of the analog signal is measured and represented as digital information sent at rapid uniform intervals. PCM is used in modern modem protocols and in most conventional compact disks. *See also* **analog-to-digital converter.**

PCMCIA   *Abbreviation of* **Personal Computer Memory Card International Association.** The association that developed the PC Card.

PCS   *Abbreviation of* **personal communications service.** A system for mobile digital communications, including voice, text messaging, and data services, that transmits over the 1900 MHz frequency band. Restricted to the Americas, PCS systems use CDMA, GSM, or iDEN technologies.

PDA   *Abbreviation of* **personal digital assistant.** A lightweight handheld used primarily for the management of personal information, and often capable of running word processing and spreadsheet programs. Most PDAs can be synchronized with personal computers and some also have wireless interfaces that allow them to connect to the Internet. The most basic PDAs are pen computers but more sophisticated models incorporate keyboards or voice recognition as input devices. *See also* **palmtop, pen computer.**

PDF *Abbreviation of* **Portable Document Format.** A page description language used to describe text and graphics so they can be displayed or printed at any resolution by any operating system. PDF is a common format for exchanging documents containing text and graphics on the Internet. Files in PDF format often have the extension *.pdf* in their filename.

PDL *Abbreviation of* **page description language.**

PDP *Abbreviation of* **plasma display panel.** *See* **plasma display.**

peer-to-peer network A network of personal computers in which every computer acts as both a client and server, thus allowing every computer to exchange files and email directly with every other computer on the network. Computers in a peer-to-peer network can tap into each other's resources, although access can be restricted to files that a computer's user chooses to make public. Peer-to-peer networks are cheaper than client/server networks but are less efficient when large amounts of data need to be exchanged. *Compare* **client/server network.** *See also* **file sharing network.**

pel *Abbreviation of* **picture element.** *See* **pixel.**

pen computer A handheld that uses a touch screen and a stylus or light pen.

pen register A device that records routing or addressing information about electronic communication, such as one that records the phone numbers dialed from a phone line, or network addresses to which transmissions are routed. Pen registers are used to monitor communications, but they do not record the contents of messages. *See also* **trap and trace device.**

Pentium A microprocessor designed by Intel for personal computers and workstations and introduced in 1993. Pentium is so named because it represents the fifth generation of microprocessors from Intel, succeeding the popular 80486 series. Pentium performs calculations many times faster than the 486 microprocessor and is fast enough to support such CPU-intensive applications as speech recognition and high-bandwidth video.

peripheral A device, such as a printer, scanner, keyboard, monitor, or disk drive, perceived as distinct from and external to a computer's CPU, motherboard, power supply unit, and main memory. Peripherals are attached to a computer using a bus or connector.

Peripheral Component Interconnect *See* **PCI.**

Perl A scripting language developed by Larry Wall, designed for text processing. Perl is widely used for text and XML processing, system administration, and web server applications. A large number of programs written in Perl are freely available on the web. The name *Perl* stands for *Practical Extraction and Report Language.*

permalink   *Abbreviation of* **permanent link.**   A hyperlink to a location on a website, especially a regularly updated website, that has specific information that is not updated. For example, most blogs that are updated frequently allow permalinks to articles or other information that remains unchanged.

permanent link   *See* **permalink.**

permission   *often* **permissions**   The ability to access a file or directory in order to view, change, or execute it. Most operating systems have some system for managing permissions that keeps track of which users are allowed to access a resource as well as what each user is allowed to do with the resource. For example, a user with *read permission* on a file can usually only view its contents. To change the file, a user must usually have *write permission* on it.

personal area network   *See* **PAN.**

personal communications service   *See* **PCS.**

personal computer   *Abbreviated* **PC.**   A general-purpose computer, such as a desktop or laptop, that is designed to be used by one person. *Also called* **microcomputer.** *See also* **desktop computer, laptop.**

personal digital assistant   *See* **PDA.**

personal identification number   *See* **PIN.**

personal information manager   *See* **PIM.**

personal unblocking key   *See* **PUK.**

personal video recorder   *Abbreviated* **PVR.**   *See* **DVR.**

petabyte   *Abbreviated* **PB.**   A unit of measurement of computer memory or data storage capacity equal to 1,125,899,906,842,624 (2^{50} bytes). One petabyte equals 1,024 terabytes. Informally, the term is sometimes used to refer to one quadrillion (10^{12}) bytes.

PGA   *Abbreviation of* **pin grid array.**

PgDn   *Abbreviation of* **Page Down key.**

PGP   *Abbreviation of* **Pretty Good Privacy.**   A public key encryption algorithm created by Philip Zimmerman. This algorithm, which is in the public domain, is a common method of encrypting email and other information transmitted over the Internet. *See also* **public-key cryptography.**

PgUp   *Abbreviation of* **Page Up key.**

phase alternation line   *See* **PAL.**

phish   To request confidential information over the Internet under false pretenses in order to obtain credit card numbers, bank account numbers, and other personal data. Phishers often pose as well-known financial institutions through emails and fraudulent websites.

phono connector **1.** *See* **RCA connector. 2.** *See* **jack connector.**

phosphor A substance used in displays, such as plasma displays and CRTs, that emits light when exposed to radiation such as an electron beam or electrical current.

Photo CD A proprietary system developed by Eastman Kodak to read and write image data to CDs. Data on Photo CD disks is stored in files with the *.pcd* extension.

PHP *Abbreviation of* **PHP: hypertext preprocessor.** An interpreted programming language used mainly for server-side scripting and for creating web-based applications. PHP is commonly used on websites that require access to data stored in databases. Originally designed by Rasmus Lerdorf and called Personal Home Page Tools, PHP is an open source programming language.

phreak *v.* To manipulate telephone systems for amusement or for illegal purposes, for example to allow one to make free calls or charge them to others' accounts. One early form of phreaking involved replicating the tones used by the switching systems, effectively allowing the user to make free long-distance phone calls.

n. A person who engages in phreaking. *Also called* **phreaker.**

physical Relating to or being hardware. A physical hard disk, for example, is a piece of hardware that you can see and feel. It may be partitioned into a number of logical drives that function as if they were physically separate, so that there might exist several logical drives that appear to the user to exist as separate drives, but only one physical drive on which data is actually stored. *See also* **virtual.**

physical address **1.** A number identifying the actual storage location of data in a computer's physical memory. Programs that use virtual memory must translate virtual addresses into physical addresses in order to access data and transfer it to RAM. *Compare* **virtual address. 2.** *See* **MAC address.**

physical memory Memory stored on the circuitry of RAM chips. *See also* **virtual memory.**

pica In typesetting, word processing, and desktop publishing, a unit of measurement equal to twelve points or approximately 1/6 of an inch.

pico- *Abbreviated* **p.** A prefix indicating one trillionth (10^{-12}).

piconet A network of up to eight devices connected using Bluetooth protocols. Piconets always consist of a single central device that communicates with one or more peripheral devices. *See also* **PAN.**

picosecond   *Abbreviated* **ps** or **psec.**   A unit of time equal to one trillionth (10^{-12}) of a second.

PICT   A graphics file format that supports both object-oriented and bit-mapped graphics, as well as text. PICT was developed by Apple Computer and was commonly used by almost all Macintosh graphics programs to store and exchange graphics documents. Since the advent of OS X, PICT has been largely replaced by PDF. Files in the PICT format usually have filenames ending in a *.pict* extension.

picture   *See* **contrast** (sense 2).

picture-in-picture   *Abbreviated* **PIP.**   An option on a television to view other television channels or video signals in a small frame within the main image. *Compare* **split screen.**

piezoelectric inkjet printer   An inkjet printer that ejects ink from its grid of ink nozzles using tiny vibrating piezoelectric crystals that are attached to each nozzle. When the crystal moves in one direction, it forces ink onto the page; when it moves in the other direction, it draws more ink into the nozzle. *Compare* **thermal inkjet printer.** *See also* **inkjet printer.**

piezoelectric speaker   A speaker that produces sound by vibrating a piezoelectric film. Piezoelectric speakers are often used to produce high-pitched sounds, as in the alarm of a stopwatch and in the tweeters of speakers.

PIF   *Abbreviation of* **program information file.**   A file that contains the instructions that allow a non-Windows application to run in Microsoft Windows. PIFs usually have filenames ending with a *.pif* extension.

PIM   *Abbreviation of* **personal information manager.**   An application for keeping track of personal information, such as appointments, addresses, telephone numbers, and notes. PIMs are commonly used on PDAs.

pin   Any small prong designed to be inserted into a hole or gap, such as the tooth of a gear or electrical connectors on a chip that slide into sockets.

PIN   *Abbreviation of* **personal identification number.**   A numeric password, often short and used especially to authenticate users of bankcards, voice mail systems, cell phones, and other devices that have numeric keypads. *See also* **PUK.**

pincushion distortion   Distortion of an image in which horizontal and vertical lines that should appear straight instead curve inward toward the center of the image. Pincushion distortion often arises from imperfections in an optical system, such as a lens. *See also* **barrel distortion.**

pine A Unix program for reading and composing email, developed by the University of Washington as a replacement for early email and newsreading software called *elm*. Pine stands for *pine is not elm* or *Program for Internet News and Email*.

pin feed *See* **tractor feed.**

ping To send a message to a computer or person to find out whether or not they are present or able to communicate, as by a person sending an email or text message, or by a program automatically transmitting an echo request of the type sent by the PING program. *See also* **ICMP.**

PING A program that sends a message to another computer and waits for an acknowledgment in response. PING is normally used to check if another computer on the network is reachable. The type of message PING sends is part of the ICMP protocol, and is known as a *ping request* even if it is not sent by a PING program.

pin grid array *Abbreviated* **PGA.** The mounting of pins on a chip so that they protrude from the bottom rather than from the sides. This arrangement is often used for chips with a large number of pins.

PIN-to-PIN Relating to the transmission of messages from one Blackberry device directly to another by addressing the message to the receiving device's PIN, rather than routing it through an email server.

pin unblocking key *See* **PUK.**

PIP *Abbreviation of* **picture-in-picture.**

pipe **1.** A temporary connection in memory that acts a conduit in passing data, in which the output of one process is the input to another process. **2.** The symbol | on a keyboard, usually the shift character of the backslash (\). **3.** A Unix and DOS command that instructs the operating system to cause the output of one command to be the input to another command. For example, the command DIR lists the current directory's contents. The command MORE places breaks in long streams of data so that the data is displayed screen by screen instead of scrolling by all at once. Thus, DIR | MORE takes the output of DIR, the directory's contents, and makes that the input for the MORE command, so that the contents of the directory will appear one screen at a time.

pipelining In microprocessors, the processing of an instruction before the completion of the processing of previous instructions.

piracy The unauthorized copying and distribution of copyrighted digital media such as software, music, movies, and videogames. Some manufacturers attempt to combat piracy by installing copy protection in the media, which acts as a deterrent but is not foolproof against those with enough skill to circumvent it. *See also* **software piracy.**

pit   One of the series of microscopic holes etched by laser in a spiral track along the land surface of an optical disk. The pattern of intervals between lands and pits is detected by the disk player's read laser and converted into the binary data that encodes the disk's content. *Compare* **land.**

pitch   **1.** In word processing, the number of printed characters per inch. In proportional pitch fonts, pitch is an average. *Ten pitch,* for example, would mean an average of ten characters per inch in proportional pitch, or precisely ten characters per inch in fixed pitch or fixed space. **2.** *See* **dot pitch.**

pixel   *Abbreviation of* **picture element.**   **1.** The smallest unit in the digital representation of an image, representing the color or intensity of light in one small region of the image. *See also* **bit map, color depth, resolution. 2.** One of the tiny elements of a display that emit, reflect, or transmit light to produce an image. The pixels on some displays are composed of red, green, and blue subpixels. *See also* **native resolution.** *See* Table B on page 357. **3.** An individual light sensor in a digital camera, detecting the color and intensity of light at a particular point on the image.

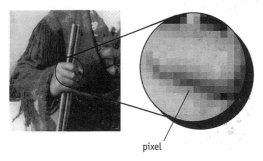

pixel

pixel

pixelization   **1.** The rendering of an image using pixels. **2.** An artifact of the rendering of an image, as on a screen or with a printer, in which individual pixels are too easily discerned, resulting in a dotted or jagged appearance of the image. *See also* **jaggies.**

pixel pitch   *See* **dot pitch.**

pixels per inch   *Abbreviated* **PPI.**   A measure of the pixel density of a display or digital camera. PPI is the number of pixels in a linear inch, usually measured along the horizontal axis. *Pixels per inch* may also be referred to as *dots per inch,* though some object to this usage. *See also* **resolution.**

PKUNZIP   A program for Windows operating systems that extracts files from zip format archives.

PKZIP   A program for Windows operating systems that creates compressed archives in the zip format and extracts files from zip archives.

plain old telephone service   *See* **POTS.**

plaintext   The original, unencrypted form of text or other information. *Also called* **cleartext.** *Compare* **ciphertext.** *See also* **decrypt, encrypt.**

plasma display   **1.** A display used in flat-panel televisions, consisting of an array of tiny, gas-filled cells that are coated with phosphor and sandwiched between two sheets of glass. Electrodes running to each cell change the gas, a mixture of xenon and neon, into a plasma state, releasing ultraviolet energy that illuminates the phosphor coating, making the cell glow. Each pixel of a plasma display has a red, green, and blue cell. Plasma displays generally have wide viewing angles and provide a bright picture even in brightly lit rooms. **2.** A television that uses such a display.

platform   The combination of hardware, software, and operating systems that determines which categories of programs are able to run on a computer or similar device. For instance, a Java platform consists mostly of certain software configurations that allow Java programs to run; various computer games require platforms using highly specific hardware and software.

platter   One of the round plates within a hard disk. Platters are coated with a magnetic film typically containing iron particles. Data is encoded by the alignment of these particles in a magnetic field. Each platter has two read/write heads, one on each side. *See figure at* **hard disk.**

playlist   A list of audio files arranged in the order they are to be played or saved. Playlists can be configured to play files in a programmed sequence or in random order.

PlayStation 2   *Abbreviated* **PS2.** A video game console developed by Sony. The PlayStation 2 belongs to the same generation of products as the Nintendo GameCube and the Microsoft Xbox.

PlayStation 3   *Abbreviated* **PS3.** A video game console developed by Sony. The PlayStation 3 belongs to the same generation of products as the Nintendo Revolution and the Microsoft Xbox 360.

PLC   *Abbreviation of* **power line communications.**

plotter   An output device that draws mechanically by moving a pen across the paper or other medium being drawn on. The computer sends instructions to the plotter indicating the points to which the pen should be moved and indicating whether the pen should be in contact with the paper or lifted away from it as it moves. In some plotters, the paper moves along one axis while the pen moves along the other.

plug A part of a connector, especially an electrical connector, which is inserted into a socket.

plug and play An architecture for the hardware and software of a computer, and of the components that attach to it, that allows the computer to detect the important characteristics of an attached component and adjust its own settings so that it can use that component. For example, graphics accelerator cards are usually plug and play, meaning that a computer user can simply install the card in an extension slot and the computer can immediately begin using it, without the user having to reconfigure any of the computer's internal settings.

plug-compatible Having the ability to connect to a computer or device made by a different company. For example, a plug-compatible modem can be plugged into a computer without the cables having to be rewired.

plug-in An accessory program designed to be used in conjunction with an existing application program, often a web browser, to extend its capabilities or provide additional functions. Sometimes a plug-in provides a major improvement, such as new functions or bug fixes. *Also called* **add-in, add-on.**

PMS *Abbreviation of* **Pantone Matching System.**

PNG *Abbreviation of* **Portable Network Graphics.** A bitmapped graphics file format that uses lossless compression and allows up to 48-bit color depth. Though designed as a replacement for GIF files for use in webpages, PNG is not commonly used on the web. PNG format files usually have the *.png* file extension.

Pocket PC A handheld device that uses the Microsoft Windows CE operating system. Pocket PCs typically include wireless networking, many are also cell phones, and a wide range of software is available for them.

podcast To broadcast over the Internet by making a series of audio files available to be automatically downloaded and played by a digital audio player. Podcasting makes use of RSS to describe the content of audio files so software can both detect when new files from a given podcast are available as well as display summary information about the files.

point *v.* To move a pointer to an item that the user wants to select on a display screen.

 n. **1.** In typography, approximately 1/72 of an inch, used to measure character height and leading between lines of text. **2.** In graphics, a pixel.

point and click   To choose an option on a display screen by sliding a mouse that controls the cursor position (*pointing*) over a level surface and activating one of the mouse buttons (*clicking*) one or more times. It is the primary means of command execution when the GUI cursor is controlled by a mouse.

Point and Pay   *See* **IrFM.**

pointer   **1.** A cursor associated with a mouse, touchpad, directional pad, or similar input device. Pointers often appear in the shape of an arrow. Sometimes a change in the pointer is used to indicate that different functions are available to the user. **2.** In programming and database management systems, a variable that gives the memory address of a piece of data.

pointing device   An input device that controls a pointer. Common pointing devices are mice, touchpads, and trackballs.

point of presence   *See* **POP** (sense 2).

point-to-point protocol   *See* **PPP.**

polling   The ongoing requests that a computer makes sequentially to each device with which it is connected as a way of determining if any device has data that it needs to transmit.

polyphonic   Relating to a system of recording or reproducing audio in which two or more tones can be sounded simultaneously.

POP   **1.** *Abbreviation of* **Post Office Protocol.**   A protocol for storing and retrieving incoming email. Servers using POP store email and transmit it to users who connect with a client program. With POP, messages for each user are stored in a single folder and typically removed from the server when they are downloaded for viewing. Email can be organized into multiple folders only after it is downloaded from a POP server. **2.** *Abbreviation of* **point of presence.**   A physical location in a wide area network (WAN) from which dial-up access to the Internet can be obtained with a local telephone call. Most Internet service providers (ISPs) provide POPs in many of the cities and towns that they serve.

pop-up   A new window produced by a web browser in response to a command from the webpage being viewed. Sometimes simply viewing a webpage will cause pop-ups to appear; many commercial sites install such pop-ups to display advertising. Because pop-ups can be great annoyances when they are not wanted, web browsers now let users effectively turn off pop-ups by setting the browser to disallow them, although it is sometimes possible for webpages to circumvent this setting.

pop-up menu   A menu that appears on the screen in response to a user action and is separate from the primary application menus. It generally remains onscreen until the user selects a command from the menu. *See also* **pull-down menu.**

pop-up utility   A program that can be accessed from within any application, typically by pressing a designated key on the keyboard.

pop-up window   A window that appears on the screen when the user selects an option or presses a function key. The window may display options to choose from. Generally, the window will remain open until the user selects an option or it is explicitly closed by the user. Often, all other processing in that application is inhibited until the window closes.

port   *n.* **1.** A component of hardware or region of memory where data can pass into or out of a CPU, computer, or peripheral. In computers and peripherals, a port is generally a socket into which a connector can be plugged. In microprocessors, a port is a particular point in memory reserved for incoming and outgoing data. *Also called* **interface. 2.** A number used as an address to route data transmitted over a network to different applications on the same host computer. Communication protocols usually specify a port number to be used for transmissions. For example, port 80 is used for transmissions using the HTTP protocol. Requests to view a webpage are sent to port 80 on a web server computer, allowing the operating system to route the request to the web server application running on that computer.

   v. To modify software so that it may be run on a different machine or platform.

portable   **1.** Designating software that is capable of running on two or more kinds of computers or with two or more kinds of operating systems; machine-independent. **2.** Designating hardware that is capable of being carried around. The first computers considered portable weighed more than 25 pounds, although today most people would not consider anything heavier than a laptop truly portable.

Portable Document Format   *See* **PDF.**

Portable Network Graphics   *See* **PNG.**

portal   A website that serves as an entry point to other websites. *Also called* **doorway page, gateway page.**

portrait   Relating to a mode in which a page or display screen is oriented so that it is taller than it is wide. *Compare* **landscape.**

POSIX   *Abbreviation of* **Portable Operating System Interface (Unix).**   A set of standards that defines the way in which software applications and operating systems interact. Software that complies with the POSIX standard will run on any operating system that also complies with the standard. The standard is based on Unix, but most operating systems are compliant with it.

post *v.* To send a message to a public forum on a network, such as to a newsgroup, website, or bulletin board.

n. A message sent to a public forum on a network.

POST *Abbreviation of* **power-on self-test.** On a PC-compatible computer, a program executed by the BIOS that tests a computer's components when the power is turned on. If POST detects a problem, the BIOS will issue a beep or series of beeps and may display an error message on the screen. If the POST does not detect any problems, the computer begins to boot.

posterize To transform an image, especially a photograph, by reproducing it with a smaller number of colors, substituting the colors of the original palette with the nearest shade in the restricted palette. With posterization, gradations of color and brightness are replaced with patches or bands of solid color. In a photograph, this has the effect of impairing the illusion of depth.

Post Office Protocol *See* **POP** (sense 1).

PostScript A page description language that uses vector graphics, allowing for printing at any size or resolution. Developed by Adobe and originally used primarily with laser printers, PostScript is now widely used as a language in which to typeset scientific and technical papers so they can be displayed or printed using any operating system. PostScript files typically have the extension *.ps. Compare* **SVG.** *See also* **Encapsulated PostScript.**

POTS *Abbreviation of* **plain old telephone service.** Traditional analog telephone service provided on a landline.

power A measure of how much energy is used, emitted, or transferred over the course of time. In electrical and electronics applications, power is measured in watts and is equal to the amount of energy, measured in joules, that is used, emitted, or transferred in one second. For example, the amount of energy given off by a 60 watt light bulb in 5 seconds would be 60 × 5, or 300 joules.

The power used or provided by an electronic device or component is equal to the voltage across the device (measured in volts) multiplied by the amount of current running through it (measured in amperes). For example, an amplifier that provides an output of 100 volts and a current flow of 2 amperes provides 200 watts of power.

power down   To turn off a computer or other device. Powering down an electronic device often involves a series of steps that prepare the various components of the device to be disconnected from the power supply, although in many cases the device handles this process automatically when the user attempts to shut off the device. *See also* **shut down.**

power line communications   *Abbreviated* **PLC.**   The transmission of data though existing power lines rather than special-purpose cables in order to provide telecommunications services or to create a LAN using the electrical wiring in a home or other building. Technologies for power line communications add a high-frequency carrier wave to the energy already carried in power lines. *See also* **BPL.** *See* Table D on page 360 for an example.

power-on self test   *See* **POST.**

PowerPC   A RISC-based microprocessor jointly developed by IBM, Motorola, and Apple Computer. PowerPC chips were originally designed for personal computers and are used in many models sold by Apple. They are also popular for use in game consoles and embedded systems, such as those used in automobiles.

power strip   An electrical device for distributing electrical power to other devices. A power strip has a cable that plugs into an electrical socket, and two or more sockets of its own for other devices to plug into. Power strips often have a power indicator light and an on-off switch; some also have built-in circuit breakers or surge protectors for the protection of every device that plugs into them.

power supply unit   *Abbreviated* **PSU.**   The electrical device that converts the alternating current (AC) of standard outlets to the lower-voltage direct current (DC) that a computer requires. Most computer power supplies provide between 250 and 600 watts, and most desktop computers require a power supply of at least 250 watts. The higher the speed of the computer, and the more peripherals that are built into it, the more electrical power the computer needs.

power up   To turn a computer or other device on. Powering up a computer or other device is often not instantaneous; often a period of time is required for various components to reach full power and be ready to function.

PPI   *Abbreviation of* **pixels per inch.**

ppm   *Abbreviation of* **pages per minute.**

PPP   *Abbreviation of* **point-to-point protocol.**   A communications protocol that establishes a direct serial connection between two computers over any full-duplex path. PPP then emulates other protocols, such as TCP/IP, allowing network connections over the serial line. PPP includes built-in error detection, security, and line-monitoring functions, and is a common protocol for connecting personal computers to the Internet via a modem.

.ppt The file extension typically used for presentations created by Microsoft's PowerPoint presentation software, part of its Microsoft Office suite.

PPV *Abbreviation of* **pay-per-view.**

PRAM *Abbreviation of* **parameter RAM.** In Apple Macintosh computers, a RAM chip that is powered by a battery and stores information about the system configuration, including date and time. Other computers typically use a CMOS chip for the same purpose. Deleting the information stored in PRAM, which returns the computer settings to their defaults, is referred to as *zapping* PRAM, and is performed by holding down the Command, Option, p, and r keys during a boot. PRAM is pronounced PEE-ram.

preemptive multitasking Multitasking in which the operating system determines when to interrupt an active program in order to process instructions from another program. Preemptive multitasking requires a more complex operating system than cooperative multitasking, because the operating system must determine how to schedule each program. It leads to more efficient processing, because it prevents any one program from monopolizing the CPU (central processing unit). Preemptive multitasking is used by all Linux and Unix operating systems, Windows operating systems since Windows NT, and Macintosh operating systems since OS X. *Compare* **cooperative multitasking.**

preinstall To install software on a computer before it is sold.

prepaging A virtual memory technique in which all the data that a program is likely to need is swapped into working memory from the disk whenever the CPU begins processing instructions from that program. Prepaging is designed to be more efficient than demand paging because it attempts to reduce the number of times that data has to be accessed from the disk. *Compare* **demand paging.**

presence technology Any of various technologies developed for computer networks that allow users to know when others are connected to the network and to communicate with them. Instant messaging, both text-based and telephonic, is an example of presence technology.

presentation graphics A kind of graphics geared to business presentations of statistical information and featuring a wide variety of graphs and charts including pie charts, flow charts, and bar graphs.

Pretty Good Privacy *See* **PGP.**

preview A feature in many programs that allows the user to format a document for the printer and then view it on the display screen before printing. The user can check to see whether the appearance of the printed document will be satisfactory or if it will require further editing. *Also called* **page preview.** *See also* **greeking, thumbnail.**

primary cache   *See* **level 1 cache.**

primary storage   *See* **main memory.**

print   **1.** To send a document to the printer in order to obtain a hard copy; to route output to a printer rather than to a disk file. **2.** To convert a document into a file format designed for print or electronic publication.

print buffer   A memory location where information is temporarily stored before it is printed. Print buffers are usually RAM that is located in the printer. They are necessary because computers send data to printers faster than it can be printed. Printers with larger buffers can usually print large print jobs faster. *See also* **spooler.**

print drum   The electrostatically charged cylinder in a laser printer on which the image is formed before it is transferred to the paper.

printed circuit board   *Abbreviated* **PCB.**   A flat plastic or fiberglass board on which electrically conductive paths have been etched or laminated in order to provide connections between electrical components mounted on the board. The conductive paths may also be used to provide electrical connections to external devices; many boards are designed to fit into slots for this purpose. In computers, the board that contains the CPU is typically called the motherboard; others are often called cards or adapters. *See also* **expansion card.**

printed circuit board (left) and detail (right)

printer   A device for printing text and graphics, especially onto paper. Printers are typically classified by the technology they use to apply ink to a surface. Inkjet printers spray liquid ink through a nozzle. Dot-matrix printers hammer the ends of pins against an ink ribbon, stamping dots onto the page. Dye-sublimation printers, which are often used to reproduce photos, vaporize dye from a sheet of film, producing a soft-edged pixel. Laser printers create the image first on a rotating drum using an ink powder that is then transferred and melted to the page. The most common printers for home use are probably inkjet printers because they are relatively inexpensive (though the cost of replacement ink cartridges can be high) and are capable of printing high-quality text and graphics. *See also* **dot-matrix printer, dye-sublimation printer, inkjet printer, laser printer, thermal printer, thermal wax printer.**

Printer Command Language or **Printer Control Language** *See* **PCL.**

printer driver   A program that enables a computer to work and communicate with a particular brand and model of printer. *See also* **device driver.**

printer font   *See* **outline font.**

print head   The element of a printer, especially an inkjet printer, that applies the mark or image to the paper.

print job   A computer file that stores data which is scheduled to be printed. When a user gives a print command, the program often sends data to a spooler for processing. The spooler puts the data into a file on the disk until the printer can print it. *See also* **print queue.**

printout   The printed output of text or other data from a computer. *See also* **hard copy.**

print queue   A list that a spooler uses to determine the order in which files will be printed. The spooler usually sends files to the printer in the order that they are received, but most spoolers also provide some way to prioritize files, such that more important documents are printed before less important documents that may have been received first. *See also* **print job.**

Print Screen key   A key on many keyboards that copies the image currently on the screen to the clipboard so it can be pasted into a document. *See also* **screen shot.**

print server   **1.** A computer that connects a printer to a network and allows users of the network to share the printer. **2.** A program that manages printing services and controls a shared printer on a network. *See also* **client/server network.**

print spooler   *See* **spooler.**

private key   **1.** In public-key cryptography, the key used by the recipient of an encrypted message to decrypt the message. A message encrypted using the recipient's public key, which is made available to the sender, can only be decrypted using the recipient's private key. Private and public keys are always generated in pairs. A private key can also be used by a sender to verify his or her identity when sending a message by creating a digital signature for that message. *Also called* **secret key. 2.** In private-key cryptography, the key shared and kept secret by both the sender and receiver of a message. The private key is used both to encrypt and to decrypt the message. *Also called* **secret key.**

private-key cryptography   A technique for the encryption and decryption of messages that uses the same key, called the private key, to encrypt and decrypt. When the key is used for communication, both the sender and receiver must have access to it, and it must remain secret. Private-key cryptography is also used to store information securely, as in keeping private files on a computer in an encrypted form that only their owner may access.

The algorithms that encode messages in private-key cryptography, such as DES, tend to run more efficiently than those used for public-key cryptography; however, they require a secure way for the two parties to agree on the private key they will use. For these reasons, private-key cryptography is commonly used within public-key cryptography systems, such as PGP. Public-key cryptography is used to encrypt not the message itself, but rather a randomly generated private key, which is generally much shorter than the actual message and can be encrypted and decrypted more efficiently. Thus, the message encrypted with a private key is sent along with the encrypted private key, and the private key is decrypted with the public key and then used to decrypt the message quickly. *Also called* **private-key encryption, secret-key cryptography, symmetric-key cryptography.** *Compare* **public-key cryptography.**

process   *n.* A program running on a computer. Typically, many processes are running simultaneously on a computer. Each process takes up some space in RAM, and different processes take turns using the CPU. Some processes correspond to applications that the user has started, and others are daemons that are automatically started by the operating system. *See also* **background process, foreground process, multitasking.**

v. To perform an operation, such as sorting or calculating, on data.

processor   **1.** *See* **microprocessor. 2.** *See* **CPU.**

processor speed   The clock speed of a microprocessor. Because the processor speed determines the smallest amount of time that elapses between individual steps of processing, it is an important factor in determining how quickly a computer can execute instructions. However, many other factors are also important, including the size of the processor's registers, the speed and width of the system bus, the presence and speed of caches, and the architecture used by the microprocessor. In general, it is not possible to compare two microprocessors based on their processor speed unless they use the same architecture.

program *n.* **1.** A set of instructions that direct the activity of a computer or other processor. The act of writing a program is called *programming*. Programs are written in what are called *programming languages.* The most elemental programming language in a computer is machine language, in which each instruction takes the form of a binary number that is interpreted directly by the CPU. Most programming, however, is done in more abstract, or *high-level,* programming languages; programs in these languages are written with letters, numbers, and other characters, according to the rules of the programming language being used.

Programming instructions are often referred to as *code,* and the program as written by the programmer is called the *source code.* A program that is ready to run, especially having been translated into machine language by a compiler, is known as an *executable program* or *executable code.* Software consists of one or more executable programs.

2. An individual radio or television broadcast, especially a scheduled one.

v. To write a set of instructions directing the activity of a computer or other processor.

program area The largest data region on an optical disk, about 33 millimeters wide, located between the lead-in and lead-out regions. The program area stores the main contents of the disk. *Also called* **data area.** *See also* **lead-in, lead-out.**

program file A file that contains an executable program. *Compare* **data file.** *See also* **executable file.**

program information file *Abbreviated* **PIF.** *See* **PIF.**

programmable read-only memory *See* **PROM.**

programming language An artificial language used to program or control the activity of a computer. Programming languages are ways of spelling out commands to the computer, including the order and conditions by which the commands should be performed. The term *programming language* usually refers to high-level languages, such as C, C++, Java, or VisualBasic, which are abstract languages commonly used by programmers and employ a set of standard words, symbols, and rules for combining them to form complex programs. Lying below high-level languages are assembly languages, which more directly reflect the machine language understood by the computer's CPU. Programmers sometimes also program in assembly languages. Regardless of the language in which it is written, the program is ultimately executed as a series of machine language instructions, thus a program in a higher-level language must either be compiled or interpreted.

progressive scan   *n.* A video format in which all the lines of a given resolution are used in every frame. CRT televisions can display progressive or interlaced video. Displays other than CRTs, such as LCDs or plasma displays, must convert interlaced signals into progressive signals through a process called deinterlacing. *Compare* **interlacing.**

   adj. Capable of deinterlacing an interlaced signal and outputting or displaying progressive video. Many progressive-scan DVD players and televisions are not only capable of displaying progressive video but also of converting interlaced video into progressive video, using a built-in algorithm.

projection screen   A screen on which a projector displays an image. Projection screens can be hung from a stand or mounted on the wall or ceiling. Fixed screens are often preferred over flexible screens because unevenness of the screen can distort the image. Different kinds of surfaces are used to control the screen's reflectivity, or gain. A light-gray matte surface has a gain of around 0.8, and a surface made of glass beads has a gain of around 2.5. Low-gain screens have wider viewing angles than high-gain screens, but they can be difficult to see in a lighted room.

projection television   A television that uses a lens to project an image from an internal display onto a screen. Projection televisions use LCD, DLP, CRT, and LCoS display technologies. *See also* **projector, rear-projection television.**

projector   A television or monitor that uses a lens to project an image from an internal display onto a separate projection screen. Projectors use a variety of display technologies including LCD, DLP, CRT, and LCoS, which either reflect or transmit light from the projector's lamp. Most projector lamps are replaceable and have a life of 1,000 to 2,000 hours. *See also* **projection screen, rear-projection television.**

PROLOG   A high-level language widely used for programming in the field of artificial intelligence, especially expert systems. It was developed in the early 1970s by Alain Colmerauer and Philippe Roussel. PROLOG is design to work with logical relationships established between pieces of data, and PROLOG programs are constructed as a set of facts and a set of rules for deriving new facts. The name PROLOG comes from *programming in logic.*

PROM   *Abbreviation of* **programmable read-only memory.**   A type of nonvolatile memory chip that can be reprogrammed once after manufacturing.

Unlike ROM chips, PROM chips can be manufactured as blank memory. They were frequently used for video games, but have been largely superseded by erasable forms of memory such as EEPROM.

prompt A symbol or phrase that appears on a display screen or window to indicate that the computer is ready to receive input. Common prompts are a colon (:), a backslash (\), a greater-than sign (>), or a word followed by one of these characters. Some programs will wait indefinitely for input; others will resume execution after a time-out, a set interval of time that passes without user input.

propagated error An error in a piece of data that is passed on as input to some operation or calculation, causing another error in the output of that operation or calculation.

proportional font A font in which the characters have varying pitches, or widths. *See also* **fixed space, monospace font.**

proportional space An amount of space that varies according to the width of the different characters in a font. Proportional space contrasts with fixed space or fixed pitch, in which each character is given a space of the same width. Thus, in a proportional space font, narrow letters such as *i* and *l* are given a smaller width than wide letters such as *m* and *w*. *Also called* **proportional pitch.**

proprietary Privately owned, under the restriction of copyright, patent, or other laws. A proprietary product, program, or technology cannot be duplicated or used unless an explicit license is purchased from its owner. To legally use proprietary software, for example, one must either purchase it or obtain permission from the owner. *Compare* **freeware, open source, shareware.**

prosumer Relating to video and audio production equipment whose price, performance, and quality fall between that of consumer and professional grade products.

protected AAC *See* **M4P.**

protocol A standard procedure for sending, receiving, or storing data. *See also* **communications protocol.**

proxy A program or device that acts as an intermediary on a network, particularly one that stands between a computer and the Internet for security reasons. Client software sends requests, such as a request to view a webpage, to a proxy, which then sends the request on to the appropriate server. When data comes back in response to the request, the proxy passes it back to the computer that originated the request. Whenever data passes through the proxy, it can be checked to ensure that it is secure, or it can be translated in various ways. Some proxies are able to store webpages that have been requested by clients in order to provide them more quickly when they are requested again. Web browser software and network configuration software usually have settings that allow them to work with a proxy.

ps or **psec**   *Abbreviations of* **picosecond.**

PS2   *Abbreviation of* **PlayStation 2.**

PS/2 connector   A keyboard and mouse connector having a six-pin Mini-DIN plug and socket. *See figure at* **connector.** *See* Table A on page 356.

PS3   *Abbreviation of* **PlayStation 3.**

PSU   *Abbreviation of* **power supply unit.**

PTP   *Abbreviation of* **parallel track path.**   A form of dual-layer DVD in which layer 0 and layer 1 both have the same track direction. The DVD player reads both layers from the center to the outer edge of the disk. PTP discs are mostly used for separate programs (such as widescreen and pan and scan versions of the same movie) on a single disk. *Also called* **RSDL.** *Compare* **OTP.**

PTT   *Abbreviation of* **push-to-talk.**

public domain   The status of inventions and creative work such as software, images, songs, or written texts that are not protected under copyright, patent, or other laws. Work in the public domain is available without charge or restriction. *See also* **open source.**

public key   In public-key cryptography, a key created by someone who wants to receive encrypted messages, used by the sender of a message to encrypt it. The public key need not be kept secret: the recipient may make his or her public key available to anyone who might want to send a secure message. A second key, called the *private key,* is kept secret by the recipient, since a message encrypted using the public key can be decrypted only with the private key, and thus only by the intended recipient. Public and private keys are always generated in pairs. *Compare* **private key.**

public-key cryptography   Any of various cryptographic techniques that use two different keys, one public and one private, to encrypt and decrypt data. Public-key cryptography is crucial in situations in which a sender and a recipient wish to communicate securely but have no private channel of communication.

Public-key cryptography is different from traditional cryptography (known now as *private-key* or *secret-key cryptography*), in which the encryption and decryption keys are the same. In public-key cryptography, two keys are generated together in such a way that, using the appropriate algorithm, a message encrypted with the public key can be decrypted only by using the private key. Thus, someone who wishes to receive messages securely may make his or her public key freely available; a message encrypted with it can be decrypted only by the recipient, who keeps the private key securely out of public view. Thus, public-key cryptography may be used over nonsecure channels of communication and is regularly used in the transmission of private information (such as passwords and credit card numbers) on the Internet.

In practice, public-key cryptography, as in SSL or PGP, is combined with traditional private-key cryptography. Public-key cryptography algorithms are relatively slow compared with traditional, private-key algorithms, and this can be a disadvantage with long messages. To resolve this problem, much faster private-key cryptography algorithms are used to encrypt the message, and the key that was used is then itself encrypted using public-key cryptography and is transmitted along with the message. *See also* **ciphertext, cryptography, plaintext.**

publish/subscribe   Relating to technology for distributing information in which a sender creates messages labeled with particular topics, which are then sent to any users who subscribe to those topics. Publish/subscribe systems can be either push systems, in which messages on a topic are delivered without a specific request from the user, or pull systems, in which users must take an action in order to receive messages on a topic.

puck   An input device that resembles a mouse but has a clear plastic section that is marked with cross hairs. It is used on a digitizing tablet to make accurate traces of a hard copy of a graphical image into a form that can be used by the computer. Pucks are often used in architectural and engineering applications.

PUK   *Abbreviation of* **personal unblocking key** or **pin unblocking key.**   An eight-digit code used to activate a SIM card after it has been blocked because of three successive failed attempts to enter a PIN. Each SIM card comes with a PIN and a PUK.

pull   Relating to technology for distributing information in which a server sends out messages or data only when a user or client program makes a request. Most World Wide Web services, such as websites, use pull technology. *Compare* **push.**

pull-down menu   A pop-up window that appears directly beneath the item selected on a menu bar. *Also called* **drop-down menu.** *See also* **menu.**

pulse code modulation   *See* **PCM.**

punch card   A medium for feeding data into a computer, essentially a card punched with holes or notches to represent letters, numbers, or other information.

purity   *See* **saturation** (sense 1).

push   Relating to technology for distributing information in which a server sends out messages or data without being prompted by a client program or user. For example, push email service for PDAs ensures that any incoming email is sent to the device without the user entering a command to download it. Similarly, push news services send news reports to users' computers at regular intervals. *Compare* **pull.**

pushbutton   *See* **button** (sense 1).

push-pull   Relating to an arrangement of two electronic devices or signal paths that carry or process the same electrical signal in opposite phases. For example, in a push-pull amplifier, one half of the amplifier produces a rising signal in response to the input being amplified, and the other half produces a falling signal. The difference between these two halves then constitutes the final, amplified signal. Push-pull circuitry is used for various purposes, such as minimizing distortion or electrical interference, or increasing the efficiency of amplifiers.

push-to-talk   *Abbreviated* **PTT.**   A method of operation for two-way radios and similar devices, in which users connect directly to other users and communicate in half-duplex mode. Users of a push-to-talk device or service push a button to transmit and release it to hear the transmissions of others. Some cell phone networks provide push-to-talk service. *Also called* **walkie-talkie.**

PVR   *Abbreviation of* **personal video recorder.**   *See* **DVR.**

Python   An object-oriented, interpreted programming language developed by Guido Van Rossum. Python is commonly used for web server applications, as well as for many other programming tasks. It was designed to allow a wide range of programming styles and be easy for beginners to use.

QBE   *Abbreviation of* **query by example.**

QIC   *Abbreviation of* **quarter-inch cartridge.**   A tape cartridge in which the magnetic tape is 11/44 inch wide, used especially for backups. Such cartridges may be the same size as standard cassette tapes, or they may be miniature. The manufacturers of these tapes have established a set of standards for identifying and distinguishing their different sizes. QIC is pronounced like the word *quick*.

.qt   A file extension sometimes used for QuickTime files.

quantization   The process of converting a continuous analog signal, such as an audio wave form, into a discrete set of digital values that approximate the shape of the signal. Quantization is used in analog-to-digital conversion in audio and video.

quarter-inch cartridge   *See* **QIC.**

query   A request to a database or search engine for information. For example, for a database containing the wholesale prices of widgets from every company in the United States and the United Kingdom for every month from 1999 to 2009, a useful query might ask for a list of companies selling widgets in a certain price range in January 2000.

query by example   *Abbreviated* **QBE.**   **1.** A graphical system for constructing database queries in which the user can select database fields, specify the data required for each field, and graphically specify relations between database tables. Query-by-example systems are easier to use than SQL, so database management systems intended for consumers often provide a query-by-example interface. **2.** A feature of some search engines that allows users to refine searches by selecting documents or text that are similar to the information they are looking for.

query language   A language used to express queries intended for a database management system or search engine. Query languages allow users to specify properties of the data they are looking for, including the absence or presence of keywords or the contents of particular fields. *See also* **SQL.**

queue   *n.* A list of items in the order they will be processed, as documents to be printed or other commands to be performed by a computer.

   v. To place items in a queue. For example, when a user prints several documents at the same time, the print spooler queues the documents until they can be printed.

QuickTime   **1.** A multimedia file format and player developed by Apple Computer and used for the storage, transmission, and playback of digital video and audio on personal computers and over the Internet. The Quick-Time file format is a container format that can hold several tracks of video, audio, text, animation, and other media. Files of this type usually have *.mov* or *.qt* as their extension. **2.** A media player designed to play video and audio using the QuickTime standard, as well as other formats such as JPEG and MPEG. The QuickTime player is compatible with most computer platforms.

quit **1.** To end the use of a program with the appropriate command, such as *quit* or *exit*. **2.** To terminate. Used of computer processes, especially computer programs. Programs may be designed to quit on their own under certain circumstances; they may also quit unexpectedly due to software or hardware errors, often resulting in loss of data that was being used or manipulated by the program.

QWERTY keyboard **1.** A keyboard having the traditional arrangement of keys on a standard English keyboard or typewriter. The name comes from the letters of the first six keys on the left side at the top row of the keyboard. Several alternative keyboards have been designed to facilitate faster typing, of which the best known is the Dvorak keyboard. **2.** A keyboard layout that uses the QWERTY key arrangement.

QWERTY keyboard

.ra One of several filename extensions used for standard RealAudio files.

radio **1.** The distribution of video content to the public or subscribers over broadcast networks. Traditional radio broadcasters, such as AM and FM radio stations, distribute radio content using terrestrial broadcasting, while some subscription services use satellite networks. Radio content is also available over the Internet. *See also* **digital radio, satellite radio, terrestrial broadcasting. 2.** A device for playing such signals. **3.** Audio content distributed over a broadcast network. Radio available over the Internet is often no more than a series of songs arranged according to a particular theme or genre.

radio button A button on a window, dialog box, or other part of an application representing one of a group of mutually exclusive options. For example, a menu may have radio buttons for various fonts. Since only one font can be selected at a time, clicking on a particular radio button selects that font and rejects all the others.

Radio Corporation of America connector   *See* **RCA connector.**

radio frequency   Having or using a frequency in the same range as the frequency of radio waves, from roughly 30 kilohertz to 100 gigahertz. Electronic devices that send or receive radio transmissions have circuits that operate at radio frequency. Cell phones, Wi-Fi connections, and traditional radio broadcast technologies all use radio waves to carry signals of many different kinds and thus contain radio frequency electronics.

radio frequency cable   *See* **coaxial cable.**

radio frequency connector   *See* **RF connector.**

radio frequency fingerprinting   **1.** A technique for identifying cell phones by minor variations in the radio waves they transmit. Radio frequency fingerprinting is used to prevent the fraudulent use of cell phones. **2.** A technique for determining the location of a wireless communications device within a region served by a wireless network. By using information about how radio waves are affected by the objects and surfaces located in a region, radio frequency fingerprinting can locate a device within that region based on minor variations in the radio waves it transmits.

radio frequency identification   *See* **RFID.**

ragged   Not aligned evenly with a margin. *Ragged right* refers to text that is not aligned, or justified, along the right margin. *See also* **flush, justification.**

RAID   *Abbreviation of* **redundant array of independent disks** or **redundant array of inexpensive disks.**   A group of disk drives over which data is distributed. The disk drives are used together to achieve faster rates of storage and retrieval and greater security against data loss than is possible with a single disk drive.

.ram   *Abbreviation of* **RealAudio media.**   One of several filename extensions used for standard RealAudio files.

RAM   *Abbreviation of* **random-access memory.**   **1.** Computer memory into which data may be both read and written, consisting entirely of electronic components rather than moving parts. Random access entails that every location where data is stored can be accessed without having to scan through other locations; the speed with which information is stored or retrieved is therefore independent of where it is located in RAM. This makes RAM significantly faster than memory that requires sequential access, such as magnetic tape; thus, data that is being actively proc-essed, as well as the software that processes it, is generally loaded into RAM. In volatile RAM, often used as the main memory of computers, information is lost when power is lost. Flash memory and NVRAM, how-ever, are not volatile and preserve information without external power. *See also* **ROM. 2.** *See* **main memory.**

RAM cache *See* **cache** (sense 2).

RAM disk A part of RAM that is configured so as to be treated as a pe-ripheral disk by the operating system and to be used as a temporary stor-age device. RAM disks have many uses, especially in cases where a program needs to write information to a storage device very quickly but not permanently. The contents of RAM disks are lost when the computer is shut down unless they have been previously saved in another more per-manent memory device such as a hard disk. *Also called* **virtual disk.**

random access A method of storing and retrieving information in which any given data item can be accessed directly from its address in the same or nearly the same amount of time as any other data item. With random access, as in the case of RAM (in contrast with storage on magnetic tape), no irrelevant data needs to be scanned in order to locate the desired data. *Compare* **sequential access.**

random-access memory *See* **RAM.**

RAR 1. A proprietary format for archiving and compressing files. RAR format files are created by programs such as RAR and WinRAR. Creating an archive in RAR format usually results in a smaller file size than that produced by zip format, but creation of the archive takes more time. Files in RAR format typically have the extension *.rar.* **2.** A file archiving and compression program for Linux and MacOS operating systems. RAR can create compressed archives in RAR and zip formats, and can extract and decompress files in a range of formats.

raster A scanning pattern of parallel lines that forms the image on a CRT display. *See also* **cathode-ray tube.**

raster font *See* **bitmapped font.**

raster graphics *See* **bitmapped graphics.**

raster image processor *Abbreviated* **RIP.** A device that converts vector graphics into a bitmapped image, usually so that the image can be printed. This term includes both the hardware and the software that make up this device.

raster scanning A process for creating and refreshing an image on a CRT display. In raster scanning, the cathode-ray tube (CRT) sends electrons

261

across the top of the screen from the left edge to the right edge. The CRT then begins again from the left edge, but this time it directs the electron path to begin each line slightly below the line just covered. When the electron beams reach the bottom right corner, the process begins again.

RAW Any of a variety of file formats that directly encode the data produced in a digital camera, without converting it into a standard file format such as JPEG or TIFF. RAW files thus involve no digital processing of the data picked up by the sensor and digitized by the camera, giving the user full control over how the information is processed (for example, by use of graphics software on a computer). RAW files tend to be considerably larger than other files, so fewer photographs can be stored in a digital camera's memory than with other formats. RAW file formats differ depending on the make and brand of the camera. Files in such formats are often given filenames ending in .*raw*.

RAX *Abbreviation of* **RealAudio 10.** An enhanced RealAudio format used for the downloading and streaming of digital audio over the Internet. RAX transmits data over a wide range of bandwidths by using the standard RealAudio codec for files of low- and mid-range bit rates, and switching to AAC for higher bit rates. Files of this type usually have the .*rax* extension.

RCA connector *Abbreviation of* **Radio Corporation of America connector.** A connector comprising a jack and a single-pin plug that is used to carry a video or audio signal. RCA connectors are widely found on consumer audio and video equipment. Since they can only carry one signal at a time, separate cables are needed to transmit audio and video and to carry each signal to and from a device. RCA connectors often come in sets of three, each color-coded for a different signal. One common set contains a yellow composite-video cable, a white left-audio cable, and a red right-audio cable. Sets consisting of a red, blue, and green cable are typically used to transmit component video. *Also called* **phono connector.** *See figure at* **connector.** *See* Table A on page 356.

rc file An initialization file used on Linux and Unix systems. The letters *rn* stand for *runcom,* the name of a facility for running commands stored in a computer file in old Unix systems.

RDBMS *Abbreviation of* **relational database management system.**

RDF *Abbreviation of* **resource description framework.** A format for exchanging data on the Web, usually implemented in XML. RDF is used to create machine-readable descriptions of resources available on the Internet. RDF descriptions contain metadata, such as the author or creation date of a webpage, the topic of an article, or who is allowed to use a resource.

An important component of RDF is a framework that allows users to create and standardize new vocabularies to be used in describing objects. This framework makes it easier for new applications to make use of RDF descriptions. *See also* **metadata, RSS, semantic web.**

RDF site summary   *See* **RSS.**

read   To get data from a storage device such as a hard disk, DVD, or CD. When a computer reads a hard disk, it often copies the data it needs into RAM. Users sometimes have permission to read a file but not change or delete it. *Compare* **write.** *See also* **read-only.**

read laser   The laser in an optical disk player that detects the lands and pits on the surface of an optical disk by the respective amounts of light they reflect. The disk player converts this pattern into a binary pattern of 1's and 0's that constitutes the data stored on the disk. *Compare* **write laser.**

readme file   A text file in many programs that tells the user of any modifications in or requirements for the program. It is often the first file a user will be given the option to use after a program is installed. A readme file may, for example, explain how to install the program and warn about bugs recently discovered in the program and provide tips on how to deal with them.

read-only   Relating to information that is stored in such a way that it can be read but not changed or deleted. The content of a file marked as read-only, for example, cannot be altered unless the file is changed into a file that is not marked as read-only. The instructions and information contained in ROM (read-only memory) cannot be dynamically altered, and in many cases can never be altered. *See also* **permission, ROM, write-protect.**

read-only memory   *See* **ROM.**

read/write   Relating to a storage device that is capable of both having data written to it and having data read from it.

read/write head   A head of a disk or tape drive capable of both reading and recording data.

real address   *See* **absolute address.**

RealAudio   A client/server system developed by RealNetworks for streaming digital audio over the Internet. The RealAudio server compresses audio data and sends it to the RealAudio client, which decompresses the data and plays it on the client computer. RealAudio files usually have *.ra, .ram,* or *.rm* as their extension.

RealAudio 10   *See* **RAX.**

really simple syndication   *See* **RSS.**

RealPlayer A media player developed by RealNetworks. RealPlayer downloads, plays, and organizes audio and video files in a wide variety of formats, including RealAudio and other streaming formats. It is available for Windows, Macintosh, and Linux operating systems.

real-time clock *Abbreviated* **RTC.** A battery-powered clock that is part of a computer's circuitry and that keeps the time regardless of whether the computer is off or on.

real-time computing **1.** The processing of data by a computer as rapidly as the data is input or within some small upper limit of response time, typically milliseconds or microseconds. For example, an automatic pilot must respond to data on changing flight conditions or the position of other aircraft immediately. Accordingly, automatic aircraft guidance systems must use real-time computing. **2.** Animated computer graphics or multimedia applications in which real-life situations are simulated at the speed at which they would normally occur. For example, flight simulation programs used to train pilots use real-time computing.

RealVideo A client/server system developed by RealNetworks for streaming digital video over the Internet. The RealVideo server compresses video data and sends it to the RealVideo client, which decompresses the data and plays it on the client computer. RealVideo files usually have *.rv* or *.rm* as their extension.

rear-projection television *Abbreviated* **RPTV.** A television that uses a lens to project an image from a small internal display onto the rear of an attached screen. Rear-projection televisions typically have large screens and, depending on the type of display, can be as thin as a flat-panel television. Rear-projection televisions use a variety of display technologies including LCD, DLP, CRT, and LCoS. *Compare* **direct-view television.** *See also* **projector.**

reboot To boot a computer that has either not been turned off (as a warm boot) or has been turned off for a short time (as a cold boot).

receiver **1.** An audio device consisting of a tuner and an amplifier. Audio receivers are typically equipped with a variety of connectors and can accept signals from most home theater components. **2.** A device, such as a part of a radio, television, or telephone, that receives incoming signals and converts them to perceptible forms, such as sound or light, or to electrical signals for further processing.

record In a database or spreadsheet, a single set of related data organized into fields. *See also* **field, report.**

record locking A database feature that prevents a data record from being edited. This feature is useful when more than one person has access to a database, because if a record is locked while one person is editing it, a second person is prevented from editing that record until the first person has finished and the document is unlocked, preventing the possibility of conflicting or overwritten changes.

recoverable error   A computer error that does not cause a crash or the loss of data. A recoverable error can be dealt with by the user, the computer, or the software so as to continue working without serious or lasting consequences.

recycle bin   A system folder in Microsoft Windows where deleted files are held until the user either restores or expunges them. This folder is represented on the desktop by an icon of a recycling bin. *See also* **trash.**

Red Book   A standard for audio CDs, developed by Phillips and Sony and approved by the ISO. It is one of several CD standards now in use.

redirect   *v.* To direct a program to send output to a device that is not the program's default output device, or accept input from a device that is not the program's default input device. Often, output that would normally be sent to a text window is redirected to a file.

   n. A webpage that serves only to guide users to another webpage, typically used when a webpage at one URL has been moved to a different URL.

reduced instruction set computer   *See* **RISC.**

Reduced-Size MultiMediaCard   *See* **RS-MMC.**

redundant array of independent disks   *See* **RAID.**

redundant array of inexpensive disks   *See* **RAID.**

reformat   To erase existing address tables on a storage device and reinitialize it so that it can be reused. Reformatting a disk destroys or makes inaccessible any data that had been stored on it.

refresh   **1.** To renew the image on a CRT monitor or television screen by renewing the beam of electrons in the cathode ray tube that form the image on the screen. **2.** To renew the data in dynamic RAM by sending a new electric pulse to recharge the chips.

refresh rate   **1.** The number of times per second a CRT monitor or television refreshes an image. On 17-inch monitors, a flicker is often noticeable at refresh rates below 75 hertz; larger monitors require higher refresh rates to avoid perceptible flickering. **2.** The maximum number of frames or fields that a monitor or television can display per second.

regional management   A method of content protection that marks a DVD as playable only on players in specific geographical regions of the world. This allows the producers or owners of the content to control various aspects of its release, including date and price, on a region-by-region basis. *See* Table 6.

Table 6   Regional Management: DVD Geographical Regions

Region Code	Geographical Region
0	all
1	Bermuda, Canada, United States, and U.S. territories
2	Europe, Egypt, Greenland, Japan, Lesotho, the Middle East, South Africa, Swaziland
3	Hong Kong, Macao, Southeast Asia, South Korea, Taiwan
4	Australia, Central America, Mexico, New Zealand, South America
5	Africa (excluding South Africa and Swaziland), Eastern Europe, Mongolia, North Korea, Russia, South Asia
6	Mainland China
7	reserved for unspecified future use
8	international venues such as aircraft and cruise ships

register   A temporary storage area in a microprocessor. Registers typically hold bits of data, addresses for data that are currently being processed, or instructions for the CPU.

registered jack connector   *Abbreviated* **RJ connector.**   A jack-and-plug connector commonly used with twisted-pair cables such as telephone and Ethernet cords. Registered jack plugs are normally made of clear plastic and attach to the jack with a small clip. Most telephone jacks consist of a six-position registered jack that accepts a two, four, or six-pin plug (common types include RJ-11, RJ-14, RJ-12, and RJ-25). Ethernet cords usually have a larger eight-pin plug and connect to an eight-position jack (RJ-45). *See figure at* **connector.**

registry   A database maintained by all versions of Microsoft Windows that contains configuration information. It is used to hold information about hardware and software in the system, such as the amount of memory installed, modem or ethernet settings, desktop preferences, and so on. *See also* **environment variable.**

relational database   A database that is organized as a set of related tables. Each table consists of a list of records, and each record consists of data organized into fields. For example, a table storing information about addresses may have one record for each person's address. Each record might have one field for the person's name, another field for the street address, and another for the Zip Code. Tables are related to one another on the basis of common fields, so when searching, data from a field in one table is matched with data from an equivalent field in a second table, resulting in a third table that combines the data from both tables.

relational database management system *Abbreviated* **RDMBS.** A program that allows the user to create and manipulate relational databases.

relational operator An operator, such as =, $>$, or $<$, that is used to compare two or more values. *See also* **arithmetic operator, logical operator.**

relative pathname A pathname that identifies the location of a file or directory with respect to the current directory. A relative pathname consists of the name of the file or directory, preceded by a list of any directories above it, but below the current directory, ordered from highest to lowest. For example, if a file named *foo.txt* was located in a directory called *bar,* which was itself located in the current directory, a relative pathname of the file would be *bar/foo.txt. Compare* **absolute pathname.**

remote *n.* A device used for remote control, as of a television or DVD player. Remotes often use infrared light to send signals to the device being controlled.

    adj. Relating to a device that is controlled, operated, or used from a distance, as by modem or over cables, or with wireless technology.

remote access Access to a network or host computer through a modem instead of by a direct connection to a local access network (LAN).

remote procedure call *Abbreviated* **RPC.** A request made by one computer on a network for another computer to execute a program for it.

remote terminal A terminal that is at a different location than its host computer and is not directly linked by cables or similar hardware. Personal computers are commonly used as remote terminals in SSH and Telnet applications.

removable cartridge *See* **removable hard disk** (sense 1).

removable disk A disk that can be inserted into a disk drive to be read from or written to, and removed when not in use. Removable disks come in various forms, including floppy disks, optical disks, and removable hard disks.

removable hard disk **1.** A disk built into a plastic or metal cartridge that can be removed from the disk drive. Removable hard disks allow efficient storage of multiple disks, and make it possible to transfer hard disks between drives. *Also called* **removable cartridge. 2.** A hard disk drive that can be housed in a computer chassis but is designed to be easily removed. Removable hard disks are often used as backup drives, since they can be removed and stored.

render To create a graphical image for the display of something whose properties are described as an object in graphics software. For example, the shape of an airplane can be described as a mathematical object which, together with information about its position and orientation, can be rendered as a depiction of the airplane on a computer screen. Graphics cards often include hardware designed to perform high-speed rendering.

repaginate In word processing, to scan a document that has been altered, updating the page breaks to reflect the current content of the document. Most word processors can repaginate automatically or upon request.

repeater A device used to amplify digital or analog signals in order to strengthen them for retransmission, as on a computer network or in telephone or radio transmission.

repetitive strain injury *Abbreviated* **RSI.** Any of various injuries to tendons, nerves, and other soft tissues that are caused by the repeated performance of a limited number of physical movements. A common form of repetitive strain injury among computer users is carpal tunnel syndrome.

replication Creating and maintaining a copy of a database, usually on a different computer in a network, in such a way that the copy is regularly updated to reflect any changes made in the original. In two-way replication, changes to the copy may also result in changes to the original.

report Information that has been output from a database in response to a query and organized and presented according to particular specifications.

report generator A program that creates reports from a database in response to a query about its contents. Most database management systems come with a report generator. The report generator generally allows the user to specify the form of the report, which may be a table, graph, or chart, for example. *Also called* **report writer.**

report writer *See* **report generator.**

resampling The sampling of a digital signal that is itself the result of digital sampling. Resampling is typically done at a higher or lower sampling rate than the original sample. *See also* **downsampling, upsampling.**

reset button   A button, key, or sequence of keystrokes pressed to bring an application or device back to a default state or to restart the application or device.

resident font   A font stored in a printer's memory, typically a hard disk or ROM (read-only memory). All laser printers come with one or more resident fonts, but additional fonts can usually be added to a printer's repertoire by downloading soft fonts. *Also called* **built-in font, internal font.**

resize   To shrink or enlarge an object. Resizing a window means enlarging or reducing it on the screen. For example, in word processing, text can be resized to fit a new page size. When a vector graphics object is resized, its mathematical description is recalculated, yielding an enlargement or reduction that is not distorted.

resolution   **1.** The level of clarity or fineness of detail that can be distinguished in an image. The resolution of digital images is usually measured as the number of pixels on the horizontal axis by the number of pixels on the vertical axis. For example, widescreen HDTV has a resolution of either 1280×720 or 1920×1080. The resolution of images captured by digital cameras is often measured as the total number of pixels, usually expressed in megapixels (millions of pixels). A digital camera capable of taking a three-megapixel image allows the printing of a photograph up to 8×10 inches without noticeable loss in image quality; higher resolutions allow correspondingly larger and sharper images. For scanned and printed images, resolution is generally measured as dots per inch (dpi) or samples per inch (spi). A high-quality inkjet printer can produce a color image that has 4800 dpi on the horizontal axis and 1200 dpi along the vertical, and a good scanner is capable of capturing an image of 3200 spi $\times$ 6400 spi. *See also* **dots per inch. 2.** The maximum resolution that can be captured or reproduced by a display, camera, scanner, or printer. *See also* **native resolution, pixels per inch.** *See* Table B on page 357.

resource description framework   *See* **RDF.**

response time   For LCD displays, the minimum time it takes a pixel to turn from black to white and back to black. Response time is measured in milliseconds. An LCD with a high response time may not be able to display video without artifacts such as ghosting. Manufacturers use a variety of methods to calculate response time, making it difficult to compare actual figures for different models.

restart   To boot a computer that has not been turned off. When a computer is restarted, all data is erased from RAM, and the operating system is reloaded.

restore   **1.** To retrieve a file from a storage device on which a backup copy of the file has been made. Software used to perform a backup can usually automate this process as well. **2.** In graphical user interfaces, to bring back a window to its previous size after it has been minimized or maximized.

retrieve   To access information or a file, as from a database or storage device.

Return key   **1.** *See* **Enter key. 2.** In word processing, the key used to enter a hard return, or a carriage return and linefeed.

reverse spiral dual layer   *Abbreviated* **RSDL.**   *See* **OTP.**

Revolution   A video game console developed by Nintendo. The Revolution belongs to the same generation of products as the Sony PlayStation 3 and the Microsoft Xbox 360.

revolutions per minute   *Abbreviated* **rpm.**   A measure of the speed of a rotating object. The speed of the spindle that rotates the magnetic platters in a hard drive is often measured in revolutions per minute. Standard hard drive speeds include 5,400 rpm, 7,200 rpm, and 10,000 rpm.

RF cable   *Abbreviation of* **radio frequency cable.**   *See* **coaxial cable.**

RF connector   *Abbreviation of* **radio frequency connector.**   A class of single-pin connectors that are typically used in conjunction with coaxial cables for high-frequency transmissions. Various models of RF connectors incorporate mechanisms such as threads, bayonets, and braces to lock them in place. *Also called* **coax plug.** *See figure at* **connector.** *See* Table A on page 356.

RFID   *Abbreviation of* **radio frequency identification.**   A method of identifying objects by affixing very small radio transmitters that contain a chip and antenna. When such a transmitter, known as a *tag,* comes near the device used to identify the object, known as a *reader,* the tag receives a radio signal emitted by the reader and responds with a unique code. RFID technology is used in a wide range of tracking and identification systems, including systems that identify and track various kinds of manufactured goods and systems that collect electronic tolls.

RGB   *Abbreviation of* **red-green-blue.**   **1.** A color model that uses varying values of red, green, and blue to define a color. The colors are added together, on a computer display for example, with a brightness generally proportional to the value for each color, and the blend of the three colors yields a final visible color. For example, maximal values of red, green, and blue yield a bright white, while high values of red and green mixed together with low values of blue yield yellow. **2.** A video signal in which the red, green, and blue components of the signal are transmitted over separate cables.

ribbon cable   A flat, broad cable, containing from 8 to 100 parallel conducting wires. Ribbon cables are often used in connections between disk drives and the motherboard of a computer. *Also called* **flat cable.**

rich site summary   *See* **RSS.**

rich text format   *Abbreviated* **RTF.**   A standard developed by Microsoft Corporation for specifying simple text formatting. This standard allows documents to be run on many different platforms. RTF supports basic formatting information, such as the choice of font size or typeface, but not more complex formatting such as column width and footnotes.

Right-arrow key   A key used to move the cursor to the right or forward one character, or to scroll the contents of a window to the left so that the portions of its contents hidden on the right come into view. *Compare* **Left-arrow key.**

right justify   To align the right side of each line of text with the right margin, so that the right edge of the text is even. *See also* **justification.**

ringback tone   A tone or audio recording that callers hear on the line when the phone they are calling is ringing. Some cell phone networks allow customers to choose custom ringback tones.

ring network   A network in which all computers and devices (network nodes) are configured like points on a circle, with each device connected by cable to two others. Data is passed in one direction along the ring from one computer or device to the next. When the data reaches its destination, the computer or device to which it is addressed copies it before sending it to the next node in the network. When the data returns to the sender, the sender takes it out of circulation. Many local area networks (LANs) are configured as ring networks. *See also* **bus network, network topology, star network**. *See figure at* **network.**

ringtone   A digital sound file that a cell phone plays to indicate an incoming call. Most cell phones allow users to choose between several different ringtones stored on the phone and to store new ringtones.

Monophonic ringtones are simple audio files that consist of a single tone being played at a time. Polyphonic ringtones are more complex and can consist of any audio recording.

rip   To copy data, especially music or video data, from a CD or DVD and store it on another CD or DVD or on a hard disk. *See also* **digital audio extraction.**

RIP   *Abbreviation of* **raster image processor.**

RISC *Abbreviation of* **reduced instruction set computer.** A simple microprocessor design that reduces the complexity of the instructions that the CPU recognizes and carries out. RISC architecture is intended to increase processing speed by simplifying the tasks required of the CPU. Few personal computers have CPUs with RISC architecture, though the ARM chips found in many PDAs and cell phones do use this design. *See also* **CISC.**

.rm One of several filename extensions used for standard RealAudio and RealVideo files.

roam To use a cell phone network outside of a home service area as defined by a service plan. While most cell phone service providers own networks that cover a wide geographic area, they often charge an extra fee for using networks outside of the home service area.

robot **1.** A mechanical device capable of performing a variety of often complex tasks on command or by being programmed in advance. Many factories use robots to do repetitive mechanical work. *Also called* **bot. 2.** *See* **bot** (sense 1). **3.** *See* **spider.**

robotics The science or study of the technology associated with the design, fabrication, theory, and application of robots.

role-playing game *Abbreviated* **RPG.** A game in which players assume the roles of characters and act out adventures, usually in fantasy or science fiction environments. Computer role-playing games typically provide a three-dimensional virtual world in which characters interact, as well as keeping track of the changing characteristics and possessions of characters.

ROM *Abbreviation of* **read-only memory.** Memory that stores data in such a way that it cannot be modified. ROM typically refers to chips installed in computers and related devices, although other types of data storage, such as CD-ROMs, are also a kind of ROM, because once data is written on them it cannot be altered. The data in computer-internal ROM chips is generally written onto the chips when they are manufactured. ROM of all kinds is typically nonvolatile, though on some ROM chips the contents may be completely erased and new contents added under certain conditions. ROM is especially useful for devices that must always perform the same specific routines, such as the initial processes involved in starting up a computer. On personal computers, for example, the BIOS and sometimes parts of the operating system are stored in ROM. *See also* **EPROM, PROM, RAM.**

root The superuser account on many Linux and Unix systems.

root directory The uppermost directory in a hierarchy of directories or folders.

rootkit   A set of software tools used to gain unauthorized access to a computer system on a network and to control its operation. Rootkit tools are often used maliciously to alter or destroy files on the system, to attack other computers on the network, or as spyware. *See also* **Trojan horse.**

router   A device in a network that handles message transfer between computers. A router receives information and forwards it based on what the router determines to be the most efficient route at the time of transfer. *See also* **bridge, gateway.**

routine   A set of instructions designed to perform a specific task within a program.

row   A horizontal arrangement of data. On a display screen in character mode, a row is a horizontal line that is one character wide and extends from the left side of the screen to the right. In a spreadsheet, a row is a set of horizontally aligned cells.

RPG   *Abbreviation of* **role-playing game.**

rpm   *Abbreviation of* **revolutions per minute.**

RPTV   *Abbreviation of* **rear-projection television.**

RS-232   A standard for serial data transmission developed by the Telecommunications Industry Association and the Electronics Industries Alliance. The serial port found on older computers is one of the connectors specified in the RS-232 standard. *See* Table C on page 358 (serial port).

RSA   *Abbreviation of* **Rivest, Shamir, and Adleman.**   An algorithm used in public-key cryptography and secure digital signatures. RSA is the most commonly used algorithm for encryption and authentication on the Internet, being used with protocols such as PGP and SSH. RSA was described by Ron Rivest, Adi Shamir, and Len Adleman in 1977. However it was determined in 1997 that RSA had been independently discovered by Clifford Cocks in 1973 and kept secret by a British intelligence agency. RSA is now in the public domain.

RSDL   *Abbreviation of* **reverse spiral dual layer.**   *See* **OTP.**

RSI   *Abbreviation of* **repetitive strain injury.**

RS-MMC   *Abbreviation of* **Reduced-Size MultiMediaCard.**   A smaller version of the MMC memory card format. With an adapter, RS-MMC cards can be used in slots for MMC and SD cards.

RSS   *Abbreviation of* **RDF site summary** or **really simple syndication** or **rich site summary.**   An XML language for representing headlines and summary information about web content. RSS is used for distributing news briefs, as well as alerting people about new content available on websites. *See also* **web feed, web syndication.**

RSS reader *See* **aggregator.**

RTC *Abbreviation of* **real-time clock.**

RTF *Abbreviation of* **rich text format.**

run **1.** To process or execute a program. **2.** To be processed or executed. Used of a program. **3.** To be in operation. Used of a device such as a printer.

runtime The period of time during which a program is being executed. *Compare* **compile time.**

runtime error An error that occurs while a program is being executed, as opposed to while it is being compiled.

.rv A filename extension used for RealVideo files.

SACD *Abbreviation of* **Super Audio Compact Disk.**

Safari A web browser developed by Apple Computer and distributed with its Mac OS X operating system. Safari is only available for Macintosh computers.

safe mode A mode of operation in Windows 2000 that results in a clean boot. During startup, users can choose to start in safe mode, which prevents software such as device drivers and services from being loaded.

sample **1.** A number used to digitally represent the value of some variable quantity, such as the amplitude of a sound wave or the brightness of a color at different parts of an image. *See also* **sampling. 2.** A small audio file of prerecorded sound, typically used in the creation of larger audio files or in audio performances.

samples per inch *Abbreviated* **spi.** A measure of the resolution of a scanner; the more samples per inch, the higher the resolution. A scanner with a resolution of 2400 spi can capture 2400 samples of an image per linear inch, or 5.8 million (2400 × 2400) samples per square inch. *See also* **resolution.**

sampling The process of creating a digital representation of a signal or of data, especially audio or video data. For example, in sampling a sound, the amplitude of the sound wave is sampled many times per second, and each measurement is recorded as a number represented digitally; the sequence of these numbers constitutes a digital sample of the sound. Sampled sounds can be digitally manipulated, mixed with other sampled sounds, and so on, before being played back.

In sampling digital video, each component of the color model is sampled. For instance, the DV format uses the YCbCr color model and thus records one measurement for luminance (Y) and two measurements for chrominance (Cb and Cr). *See also* **analog-to-digital converter, digital-to-analog converter, sample.**

sampling rate The number of samples used to represent a signal, especially an audio or video signal, when converted to digital form, expressed as the frequency of samples captured per unit time, distance, or area. The greater this frequency, the more accurately the original signal can be represented digitally, making possible high-quality sound or video reproduction. High sampling rates generate more data per unit time than low rates, and thus require more memory and processing power. Sampling rates for digital video often vary for each component of the color model. For example, the luminance component of the DV format has a sampling rate of 13.5 MHz but the two chrominance components are sampled at 3.375 MHz, resulting in a ratio between sampling rates of 4 : 1 : 1. *See also* **analog-to-digital converter, digital-to-analog converter.**

sans serif A category of type in which the characters lack serifs. Common fonts with such characters include Helvetica, Geneva, and Arial. *See also* **serif.**

SAP *Abbreviation of* **secondary audio program.** A channel of an MTS television signal used to transmit audio or data. The SAP channel often carries the main soundtrack in another language.

SAR *Abbreviation of* **specific absorption rate.**

SAS *Abbreviation of* **Serial Attached SCSI.** A version of the SCSI standard for hardware interfaces. SAS is the only version of SCSI that uses serial data transmission. SAS is compatible with SATA devices. *See also* **SCSI.** *See* Table C on page 358.

SATA *Abbreviation of* **Serial ATA.**

SATA II *Abbreviation of* **Serial ATA II.**

satellite A device put into planetary orbit to aid telecommunications, as by reflecting or relaying a radio signal.

satellite dish A dish antenna that receives and transmits signals relayed by satellite.

satellite phone   A mobile phone that functions by transmitting radio-waves to orbiting satellites. A satellite receiving a message sends it to a gateway, which routes it to a landline. *See also* **cell phone, landline.**

satellite radio   A subscription service in which digital radio content is transmitted by satellite to the receivers of subscribers. Satellite radio services offer a variety of radio programs, which can be selected using the radio receiver. *See also* **digital radio.**

satellite speaker   One of the loudspeakers, other than the subwoofer, that is positioned around the listener in a surround-sound setup.

satellite television   Television received by satellite dish. *See also* **DBS, TVRO.**

saturation   **1.** The vividness of a color, measured as a degree of difference from a gray of the same lightness or brightness. *Also called* **purity. 2.** The state of a ferromagnetic substance in which an increase in applied magnetic field strength does not produce an increase in magnetization.

save   To copy a file or files from a buffer to a disk or other long-term storage device. Most software for manipulating data, such as a word processor, requires some portion of that data to be in RAM, which requires power to store the data; saving data frequently is therefore advisable in case of accidental power outage, or a crash of the computer that requires restarting it. Saving backup copies of important data on more than one medium is also highly advisable. *See also* **autosave.**

SBR   *See* **spectral band replication.**

scalable   Relating to a computer file, particularly a multimedia file, that can be displayed, printed, or played at different sizes or on different systems without a loss of quality.

scalable font   *See* **outline font.**

scalable vector graphics   *See* **SVG.**

scaling   **1.** The process of adjusting the size of an image or font without changing its proportions. **2.** The process of changing the resolution of an image to match the native resolution of the display. Scaling requires a complex algorithm and almost always entails some loss in picture quality. **3.** The process of adjusting the scale of an image, such as a graph or design, so as to change the perspective from which the image is viewed. Many graphics programs, for example, allow scaling of the y-axis on bar graphs to highlight certain features.

scan   **1.** To move a finely focused beam of light or electrons in a systematic pattern over a surface in order to reproduce and subsequently transmit an image, as when using a scanner; most photocopying machines also use this technique. **2.** To search systematically through stored data for a specific data item. **3.** To draw one of the horizontal lines that constitute an image on a CRT display by shooting a beam of electrons at the phosphor screen, using magnets or electric fields to bend the beam and guide it from one side to the other. *See also* **interlacing.**

scanner A device that converts printed text and images into digital information that can be stored as a computer file and processed by graphics software. Scanners work by sensing the light and dark areas on a page and digitizing the lightness values, converting them into numerical values that are recorded in electronic form as a bitmapped graphic.

Scanners are often used to insert graphics or text copied from other sources into a document. Because all images are stored in bitmap form, however, text copied by a scanner cannot be edited in a word processing program unless the image is processed by an optical character recognition program. *Also called* **optical scanner.**

scanning velocity The speed at which the spiral track of an optical disk passes under the disk player's laser pickup head.

scheduler **1.** In an operating system, a program that allocates the use of such resources as the CPU (central processing unit) or a printer so that several tasks can be handled at the same time without interfering with each other. **2.** A program that helps people schedule meetings or other events. A scheduler compares the relevant calendars, sends out invitations, and distributes follow-up reminders. **3.** A program that schedules tasks to run automatically on a computer. Users create entries specifying how and when programs are to run.

schema **1.** A formal definition of the structure of a given type of XML document. The schema lists the constraints on the structure of the document and the kind of data that each of its components may contain. Several different markup languages can be used for creating schemas, the most common being XML Schema. **2.** The structure of a database, including what data is represented in each field of each table and how different tables are related to each other.

scientific notation A way of representing a number, especially a very large or a very small number, by showing it as the product of a power of 10 and a number between 1 and 10. For example, the number 23,456,000,000,000,000 would be written in scientific notation as 2.3456×10^{16} or as 2.3456E16, with "E" standing for "10 to the exponential power of." Similarly, 0.0000007 would be written as 7×10^{-7} or as 7E-7. *Also called* **exponential notation.** *See also* **floating-point notation.** *See* Table 7.

Table 7   Examples of Scientific Notation

Scientific Notation	Decimal Expansion
1.2345E4	12,345.0
1.0E–5	0.00001
–6.789E3	–6,789.0
–9.0E–2	–0.09

SCP   *Abbreviation of* **secure copy.**   **1.** A file transfer protocol that encrypts files being transferred over the Internet. SCP uses the SSH protocol to perform authentication and encryption. **2.** A program common on Linux and Unix operating systems that uses the SCP protocol to transfer files between computers on the Internet. The SCP program performs both as a client requesting files from other computers and as a server sending files to other computers.

screen   **1.** The surface on which an image is displayed. Screen size is measured diagonally across the screen from corner to corner. Most screen measurements only include the area within the frame or bezel; however, the measurements for CRT screens also include the part of the screen that is covered by the frame, so the display surface is smaller than the dimensions would indicate. Monitor screens typically measure 15 to 23 inches, while television screens range from handheld size to over 70 inches. Common aspect ratios (screen proportions of width to height) are 4 : 3 and 16 : 10 for monitors, and 4 : 3 and 16 : 9 for televisions, with widescreen formats becoming increasingly popular. *See also* **projection screen. 2.** A still image displayed on a screen.

screen capture   *See* **screen shot.**

screendoor effect   Pixelization resulting from spaces between the pixels on a display. The screendoor effect is a problem in displays with a high dot pitch.

screen dump   *See* **screen shot.**

screen flicker   The blinking of a video image. Screen flicker can result from a monitor with a low refresh rate or a video signal with a low frame rate. It is also an artifact of deinterlacing.

screen font   *See* **bitmapped font.**

screen name   A nickname used in online chatrooms and on instantmessaging services. *Also called* **handle.**

screen saver   A utility program that detects when the computer has been idle for a certain amount of time and then replaces the screen image with an empty screen or an image that moves continuously. Screen savers were originally designed to protect CRT monitors from damage called ghosting or burn-in, which was caused by displaying a still image for an extended period of time. Technological innovations in screen design have made screen savers mostly ornamental.

screen shot   The act or process of sending a copy of whatever is on the display screen to the clipboard or to a file so it can be saved or printed. On Linux and Windows operating systems, the Print Screen key can usually be used to take a screen shot. On Mac OS X, the key combination Command + Shift + 3 is used.

script   A program written in a scripting language. Scripts are typically shorter and less complex than other kinds of programs, and are often used to launch other programs. Batch files are a common kind of script.

scripting language   An interpreted language, especially one that is typically used for simpler tasks such as combining different programs or accessing data from a database so it can be displayed on a webpage. Scripting languages sometimes lack features found in more powerful languages. JavaScript and Perl are two commonly used scripting languages. *See also* **macro.**

script kiddie   A person who uses existing scripts, code, or other tools illicitly to gain entry to a computer system or network, without understanding the way the tools function or the way the system or network is designed.

scroll   To shift the whole of the virtual area partially displayed by a window so that a part of the area that was hidden is brought into view. The presence of a horizontal or vertical scroll bar will usually indicate whether or not the entire area is contained within the window. A hidden area can be scrolled into view using the scroll bar or an input device. *See also* **scroll wheel.**

scroll bar   A narrow bar that appears on the side of or beneath a window when the contents of a window are part of a larger virtual area. Scroll bars usually have a box that slides along the bar and indicates the extent of the virtual area not included in the window and the position of the window within this area. Parts of a virtual area may be shifted into or out of the window with the cursor using buttons on either end of the scroll bar or by dragging the scroll box. *See figure at* **frame.**

scroll box   A box within a window's scroll bar that indicates the extent of the virtual area not included in the window and the position of the window within this area. The length of the scroll box indicates how much of the virtual area is not contained in the window. The box's position relative to the ends of the bar indicates the position of the contents of the window relative to the boundaries of the virtual area. *See figure at* **frame.**

Scroll Lock key   A toggle key that is sometimes used to change the effect of the arrow keys in a way determined by the application. In some applications, for example, when the Scroll Lock key is activated, the arrow keys scroll the document rather than move the cursor. In Linux command line interpreters, activating the Scroll Lock key pauses text output to the screen. Most keyboards have a light that goes on when the Scroll Lock key is active.

scroll wheel   A small wheel typically located between the right and left buttons of a computer mouse, used especially for scrolling up and down through a document such as a webpage, text file, or graphic image, through a menu, or through any other information that does not fit entirely on a single window. *Also called* **mouse wheel.**

SCSI   *Abbreviation of* **small computer systems interface.**   A computer bus standard that allows multiple devices, especially disk drives and scanners, to be linked in a daisy chain to a single port. There are many versions of the SCSI (pronounced SKUZ-ee) standard; most represent increases in the speed that data is carried. Early versions, including SCSI-1 and SCSI-2, transferred data at 8 Mbps. Subsequent versions, such as Wide SCSI, Fast Wide SCSI, and Ultra SCSI, increased the speed to 20 Mbps. Wide Ultra SCSI and Ultra2 SCSI increased the speed to 40 Mbps, and Wide Ultra2 SCSI doubled it to 80 Mbps. Ultra3 SCSI and Ultra4 SCSI, which are sometimes written Ultra-160 and Ultra-320, transfer at 160 Mbps and 320 Mbps, respectively. Serial Attached SCSI (SAS), the only version to transfer data serially, has a data transfer rate of 300 Mbps. Most versions that are designated *Wide* use a 68-pin cable as opposed to the 50-pin cable introduced in the SCSI-2 version—though Ultra3 SCSI and Ultra4 SCSI, which do not carry the designation, also use 68-pin cables. *See* Table C on page 358.

SD   *Abbreviation of* **Secure Digital.**   A memory card format based on the earlier MMC format and developed by a consortium of electronics manufacturers called the Secure Digital Association. SD is one of the most popular memory card formats for digital cameras, and SD cards are used as a storage medium for cameras and other handheld devices manufactured by a range of different companies. *See also* **microSD, miniSD, SDIO card.**

SDI **1.** *Abbreviation of* **single document interface.** A GUI (graphical user interface) in which each document open in the application gets its own window and its own icon on the taskbar. *Compare* **MDI.** *See also* **TDI. 2.** *Abbreviation of* **Serial Digital Interface.** A standard for the serial transmission of digital video over coaxial cables. SDI is widely used in television broadcasting.

SDIO card *Abbreviation of* **SD Input/Output Card.** An external device that fits into the slot for an SD memory card and allows users to add functions like wireless connectivity, scanning, and digital photography to devices that have such a slot, for example, cell phones, PDAs, and digital cameras.

SDK *Abbreviation of* **software development kit.** A set of software tools for programmers. Some SDKs provide the tools programmers need to create applications in a given programming language. Other SDKs allow programmers to modify an existing application or access it from within other applications.

SDR *Abbreviation of* **single data rate.** Relating to SDRAM that transfers data once during each bus cycle, in contrast to DDR SDRAM, which transfers data twice during each cycle. *See also* **DDR.**

SDRAM *Abbreviation of* **synchronous DRAM.** DRAM whose processing is synchronized with the bus that the CPU uses to communicate with main memory, thus reducing the amount of time the CPU spends waiting for data. SDRAM is much quicker than earlier forms of DRAM. SDRAM chips are rated in hertz (Hz) for the clock speeds at which they operate, and sometimes rated in nanoseconds (ns) for the amount of time between clock cycles.

SDRAM chips are generally categorized according to standards set forth by JEDEC, using a numerical system and the prefix *PC. PC100,* for example, is the name for a standard SDRAM module that runs at 100 MHz. *PC3200* is the name for a standard DDR SDRAM module that runs at 400 MHz.

SDTV *Abbreviation of* **standard-definition television.** A class of television display formats that have 576 or fewer visible lines per frame and typically have an aspect ratio (the ratio between the width and height of an image) of 4 : 3. Common SDTV formats include 480p30, 480i60, and 576i50. The first number refers to the vertical resolution in visible lines per frame, the letter to *progressive* scanning or *interlacing,* and the second number to the fields or frames per second. *See* Table B on page 357.

seamless playback The ability of a DVD player to switch between streams of a program (especially separate audio tracks) without a noticeable break in playback.

281

search   To look for strings of characters in a document, or to look for documents or files on the World Wide Web, in a database, or in some other collection.

search and replace   A feature of most word processor and text editor programs allowing users to automatically change a string of characters to a different string of characters throughout a document. For example, a user might want to replace *don't* with *do not* in a letter. The search and replace feature usually comes with an option to review and confirm each instance of a replacement.

search bot   *See* **spider.**

search engine   A program that allows the user to search for data on the Internet by entering keywords in a search field.

search engine optimization   The process of making a website appear prominently or frequently in the results of web searches. Search engine optimization is a strategy used by site owners to increase revenue by increasing the number of visitors to their site. It often involves changes to the website itself, especially adding common search terms. Sometimes other tactics are used, including the creation of links to the site from other sites.

SECAM   *Abbreviation of* **système électronique couleur avec mémoire.**   An analog television standard, used in many parts of the world excluding North America, that specifies how color is encoded. SECAM is used in conjunction with transmission standards that have a vertical resolution of 625 lines per frame, an interlaced picture displayed at a rate of 50 fields per second, and a 4 : 3 aspect ratio. PAL has replaced SECAM in many countries.

secondary audio program   *See* **SAP.**

secondary cache   *See* **level 2 cache.**

second extended file system   *See* **ext2.**

second-generation   *See* **2G.**

secret key   *See* **private key.**

secret-key cryptography   *See* **private-key cryptography.**

sector   **1.** An area on a disk that contains the smallest addressable unit of information. When a disk is formatted, the operating system divides it into sectors and tracks. A sector is the theoretically minimal region of the disk upon which data can be read or written at one time, although in some formatting schemes, larger units called clusters are the minimal units. Tracks are concentric circles around the disk; sectors are segments within each circle. The operating system and disk drive keep track of where information is stored on the disk by noting the range of track and sector numbers, i.e., the addresses, of the information. Some hard disk drives use zoned-bit recording, in which tracks on the outside have more sectors than tracks on the inside. *Also called* **track sector.** *See also* **bad sector. 2.** *See* **disk sector.**

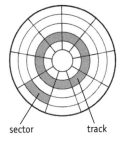 

sector   track   zoned-bit recording

sector and track

secure copy *See* **SCP.**

Secure Digital *See* **SD.**

Secure Hash Algorithm 1 *See* **SHA-1.**

secure MIME *See* **S/MIME.**

secure shell *See* **SSH.**

Secure Sockets Layer *See* **SSL.**

security The prevention of unauthorized use of a program or device. On networks or any other system where more than one user can access programs and data, security usually involves the use of passwords to identify authorized users, and encryption, which renders data unintelligible to unauthorized users. More recently, companies with access to the Internet have been installing firewalls to prevent unauthorized users from accessing their local area networks. Viruses and other forms of malware can also damage, alter, or steal data; software such as antivirus programs are thus also important to security. *See also* **password.**

seek time The amount of time required for a disk drive's read/write head to move to a track on a disk. Seek time is expressed in milliseconds, or thousandths of a second. It is one of the components of access time, the total amount of time that elapses before the read/write head locates a piece of data and is ready to transfer it from the disk. *See also* **disk drive, head.**

select 1. To choose a portion of a document, spreadsheet, or database by highlighting it, as by changing the background color, so that an operation can be performed specifically on that portion. *See also* **block. 2.** To choose a command or action on a display screen by moving the mouse or other pointing device until the pointer touches a specific object and then clicking on that object.

semantic web   A project led by the W3C to make it easier for computers to find and work with the information available on the web. The project is based on RDF and XML, and primarily involves finding ways of coding metadata so that information can be exchanged more easily between different applications in different domains. *See also* **metadata.**

semiconductor   **1.** A crystalline substance, such as silicon or germanium, having electrical conductivity that is greater than an insulator (such as rubber) but less than a good conductor (copper, for example). By adding impurities called dopants to semiconductors, manufacturers can precisely control their electrical properties in order to create transistors, diodes, and other basic components of electronic devices such as computer chips. **2.** An integrated circuit or another device that is made up of semiconductor material.

sequential access   A method of storing and retrieving information in which data items are accessed by searching, from some given starting point, along a sequence of physical locations until the desired data items are located. Storage devices such as magnetic tape require sequential access of data. *Compare* **random access.**

serial   **1.** Relating to the transmission of digital data over a single channel, usually one bit at a time. *Compare* **parallel.** *See also* **serial bus, serial port. 2.** Performing actions, such as computer instructions, one at a time. *Compare* **parallel.**

Serial ATA   *Abbreviated* **SATA.**   A standard for the interface between the disk drives and the motherboard of a computer. SATA is based on the IDE standard but uses serial data transmission to transfer data over less bulky cables. In the notation *SATA/150,* the *150* represents the maximum data transfer rate in MBps. *See also* **IDE, Serial ATA II.** *See* Table C on page 358.

Serial ATA II   *Abbreviated* **SATA II.**   A version of the SATA standard for the interface between the disk drives and the motherboard of a computer. SATA II has a maximum data transfer rate of 300 MBps. *See also* **IDE.**

Serial Attached SCSI   *See* **SAS.**

serial bus   A bus that uses one or a few wires to transmit electrical signals, typically transmitting one bit at a time. USB is an example of a serial bus. Because of increased speeds, serial buses are becoming more and more popular for communication between the motherboard and external devices. *Compare* **parallel bus.**

Serial Infrared   *See* **SIR.**

Serial Line Internet Protocol   *See* **SLIP.**

serial port   A port used for parallel data transmission, typically a nine-pin D-subminiature connector on a computer. A serial port is used for communication with keyboards, mice, modems, and other peripheral devices. The RS-232 standard specifies both the hardware and communications protocols used with serial ports. *See also* **parallel port.** *See figure at* **connector.** *See* Table C on page 358.

serif   A fine line finishing off the main strokes of a letter. Typefaces without these fine lines are called sans serif.

server   **1.** A computer that provides services such as file storage or printing to other computers on a network. *See also* **client/server network, file server. 2.** A program that provides services to other programs, known as *clients*. Servers often provide services to clients running on different computers on the network. Web servers and mail servers are examples of server programs.

server-side script   A script that runs on a web server and is used to generate webpages or information that is used on webpages. Server-side scripts can create HTML based on frequently changing data that is often stored in a database on the server. For example, server-side scripts are often used to change and display information that is specific to a user or a session, such as online user profiles and shopping carts used in Internet commerce. VBScript, JSP, PHP, Perl, and Python are the languages mostly commonly used for server-side scripts. *Compare* **client-side script.** *See also* **ASP, CGI.**

service   **1.** The provision of a resource such as a computer or telephone network to the public. ISPs, for example, offer Internet service to customers, and cellular carriers offer cell phone service. **2.** A specific system that constitutes such a resource. For example, ISPs typically maintain an email service for use by their customers. **3.** A program that runs as a daemon on a Windows operating system. Services are automatically started when the computer starts up, and do not require user input. An example of a service is a program that handles network connections for a computer.

service provider   *See* **ISP.**

session   The period of time when a user or program is logged in or connected to a website, computer, or online service.

session key   A key used for encryption and decryption of private messages or information transmitted over a public channel. Session keys are usually established automatically by the applications controlling the communication, such as a user's web browser and the software controlling a commercial website, or two nodes communicating in a local area network. This process is called key agreement. The session key is established at the start of communication along the channel before any private information is transmitted.

set-top box   *Abbreviated* **STB.**   A device connected to a television or computer that converts or decodes television signals received via cable or antenna. Most subscription television services require subscribers to purchase or rent a set-top box. Some set-top boxes can also transmit signals or function as personal video recorders.

7z   An open-source format used for archiving and compressing files. 7z allows the use of several different compression algorithms, and supports encryption of compressed archives. The file extension *.7z* is usually used for archives in the 7z format.

7zip   An open-source archiving and compression program using the 7z compression format. 7zip is available for Windows operating systems.

SFF   *Abbreviation of* **small form factor.**

SFTP   *Abbreviation of* **SSH file transfer protocol.**   **1.** A file transfer protocol that encrypts files being transferred over the Internet. Unlike SCP, the SFTP protocol also allows users to delete, rename, and move files on a remote computer. It uses the SSH protocol for authentication and encryption. **2.** A program common on Linux and Unix platforms that uses the SFTP protocol to transfer files between computers on the Internet. SFTP is a client program that requires different server software to be installed on the computer to which it connects.

SGML   *Abbreviation of* **Standard Generalized Markup Language.**   An international standard metalanguage for creating markup languages. HTML is an example of a markup language that was designed using SGML. SGML-based languages structure text and other data by embedding textual tags. The tags provide extra information about the form or content of the data, for example, text formatting. The advantage of such a tag system is that it is independent of the software or hardware used. *Compare* **XML.**

SHA-1   *Abbreviation of* **Standard Hash Algorithm 1.**   A hash function used with Internet security protocols such as SSL, SSH, and TLS.

shadowing   A technique for speeding up processing in which certain data stored in slower ROM (read-only memory) is copied to RAM (random-access memory) at startup for faster access. The upper memory area of main memory is typically used for shadowing.

shadow mask   A perforated metal plate on the inside of a CRT screen that prevents stray electrons beamed at the phosphors of one color (red, green, or blue) from striking either of the others, thereby keeping the colors clear and distinct. *Compare* **aperture grill.**

shared library   A library file on Linux and Unix operating systems that contains executable routines used by various programs. A program that uses routines from a shared library cannot run unless the shared library is installed. Shared libraries normally have *.so* as their filename extension. *See also* **DLL.**

shareware   Programs that are made available under a license that allows them to be used free of charge for a trial period and freely distributed to other users. Users who continue to use a shareware program after the trial period are supposed to pay a fee. Some shareware ceases to function after the trial period, and some has functions that are not available until the fee is paid. *See also* **freeware, public domain.**

sharpness   A display setting that adds artificial edges and highlights to objects within the image. The minimum sharpness setting displays the image without any alterations. *Also called* **detail.**

sheet-fed scanner   An optical scanner into which documents can be fed. In a sheet-fed scanner, the document is rolled past the scan head. A flatbed scanner, on the other hand, moves the scan head past a stationary page, in much the same way as a photocopier. A sheet-fed scanner is suited for scanning unbound documents or single pages, while a flatbed scanner can handle bound books. *See also* **handheld scanner.**

sheet feeder   A mechanism that holds a stack of paper and feeds it one sheet at a time. Sheet feeders are standard with laser printers and most kinds of fax machines. *Also called* **cut-sheet feeder.**

shell   A program that interprets commands for an operating system kernel. Some shells provide a text window containing a command prompt; commands are typed at the prompt, and results are displayed in the text window. Other shells provide a GUI (graphical user interface) that allows users to interact with the operating system by pointing and clicking on icons or choosing menu options.

shell script   A text file that contains a set of commands to an operating system shell. Shell scripts are often used to execute commonly used sequences of commands, but some shells allow scripts to contain complex calculations. On Windows systems, shell scripts are called *batch files.*

shielded twisted pair   *See* **STP.**

shift clicking   The act of holding down the Shift key and clicking the mouse button at the same time. Shift clicking can have different effects depending on the application being used, but on Apple Macintosh computers and in Microsoft Windows, it allows the user to simultaneously select multiple items from a screen.

Shift key   A key on a computer keyboard that, when pressed and held down, changes letters from lowercase to uppercase. In many applications, the Shift key changes the meaning of a function key when the two keys are pushed at the same time. The Shift key can also change the function of the mouse button.

shortcut   In Microsoft Windows, a file that points to another file. Shortcut icons are often used on the desktop as a convenient way to open files located in less accessible parts of the directory. Deleting a shortcut does not delete the main file.

shortcut key   *See* **keyboard shortcut.**

Short Message Service   *See* **SMS.**

shrinkwrap license   A software license for which the user indicates acceptance of the term of use by opening the shrinkwrap that encloses the product when it is purchased. *See also* **clickwrap license.**

shrinkwrapped software   *See* **packaged software.**

S-HTTP   An extension of HTTP, originally developed by Enterprise Integration Technologies and the National Center for Supercomputer Applications, for transmitting data securely over the World Wide Web using encryption and authentication. S-HTTP is commonly used for business and other secure transactions. *See also* **SSL.**

shut down   To exit applications and the operating system properly in preparation for turning off the computer. If a computer is switched off while applications are running, data may be lost or damaged, and the configuration of the operating system may be incorrect the next time the computer is started up; the process of shutting down the computer (most of which is automatically handled by the computer itself) obviates these dangers. *See also* **power down.**

sigfile   A file that contains the text of a signature automatically appended to email messages. Sigfiles may also include code that determines the content of the signature dynamically, as by changing the content periodically or varying it according to the recipient's email address.

signal-to-noise ratio   *Abbreviated* **SNR.**   The ratio of the magnitude of desired data in a signal to the magnitude of the extraneous noise that accompanies it, often measured in decibels. Digitally processed audio and video recordings generally have higher signal-to-noise ratios than analog recordings, resulting in less hiss and a sharper image during playback than analog recordings.

signature   **1.** Text or pictures, such as names, contact information, personal photographs, slogans, or even animated images, that are automatically appended to an email message before it is sent. On some email systems, the signature is kept in a file called the *sigfile,* which may also contain code that determines the content of the signature. **2.** *See* **digital signature.**

Silicon Valley   A region of California south of San Francisco known for its high-technology design and manufacturing industries. Once encompassing the communities immediately southeast of San Francisco, in which many companies that design and engineer silicon-based computer chips were located, the term *Silicon Valley* now describes the entire region, which contains companies in a wide range of high-technology industries.

silver-oxide battery   A disposable battery containing silver oxide. Because of the high cost of silver, silver-oxide batteries generally come only in button-cell sizes. Silver-oxide cells typically produce around 1.6 volts of electricity and have a larger energy storage capacity than alkaline cells of the same size.

SIM   *Abbreviation of* **Subscriber Identity Module.**   A small circuit board that stores data necessary for identifying subscribers on a mobile digital communications network. SIM cards are inserted into devices such as mobile phones and PDAs and allow the devices to be used on a network. They are primarily used on GSM networks but can be used on other networks. They also contain memory for a personal directory of numbers and other details specific to each user. *See also* **smart card.**

SIMM   *Abbreviation of* **single inline memory module.**   A memory module used to provide RAM for personal computers, having either 30 or 72 pins and providing up to 256 MB of memory. SIMMs must be installed in pairs. They have largely been superseded by DIMMs. *See figure at* **chip.**

Simple Mail Transfer Protocol   *See* **SMTP.**

simple object access protocol   *See* **SOAP.**

simplex   Any mode or channel of communication that proceeds in only one direction, from sender to receiver. Television and radio broadcasting are examples of simplex transmission. *Compare* **duplex, half duplex.**

simplex printing   A printing process in which the printer only prints on one side of a piece of paper. Many printers have modes for simplex and duplex printing. *Compare* **duplex printing.**

simulcast   *v.* To broadcast simultaneously at two or more locations or on two or more distribution channels. Television and radio programs are often simulcast on the studio's website or on separate television channels or radio stations. Sporting events are commonly simulcast at multiple off-track betting locations.

n. A broadcast so transmitted.

single data rate   *See* **SDR.**

single-density disk   A floppy disk with far less storage capacity than a double-density or high-density disk. Single-density disks are now obsolete.

single document interface   *See* **SDI.**

single inline memory module   *See* **SIMM.**

single inline package   *See* **SIP.**

single-lens reflex   *Abbreviated* **SLR.**   A camera fitted with a mirror that reflects the image from the lens into the viewfinder and, when the shutter is released, retracts to permit the image to reach the film or image sensors. Many digital SLRs can accommodate traditional camera lenses.

single session   The capability of a compact disk to allow data to be written to it only once and in a single chunk. *Compare* **multisession.**

single-sided disk   A disk, such as a CD or floppy disk, that stores data on one side only.

Single Unix Specification   The standard for Unix operating systems, controlled by the Open Group. Operating systems are only certified to be Unix after they complete extensive testing to ensure that they conform to the standard. The Single Unix Specification emerged in 1994 after several years of competing standards. *See also* **Open Software Foundation, X/Open.**

SIP   *Abbreviation of* **single inline package.**   An electronic component housing used for chips, having a single line of connecting pins sticking out from one side. *Compare* **DIP.** *See figure at* **chip.**

SIR   *Abbreviation of* **Serial Infrared.**   An IrDA protocol for infrared data transmission at rates of between 9.6 and 115.2 kbps, the same data transmission rates as a standard serial port.

site   *See* **website.**

skin   A software module that controls the appearance of a program's GUI (graphical user interface), sometimes simply changing the colors and shapes of various elements and sometimes completely rearranging the interface. Skins can be purchased or downloaded free from the Word Wide Web and are most commonly used with instant messengers and media players. *See also* **theme.**

slave   A machine or component that is controlled by another machine or component. For example, when two hard drives share a single link to the motherboard, one drive is given priority in using the link while the other must wait until the link is free. In such configurations, the latter drive is the slave.

sleep mode   A power-saving mode of operation for a device such as a computer or cell phone in which some of the device's functions are shut off. Many devices enter sleep mode automatically after the device has been idle for a specified period of time. Unlike devices in standby mode, devices in sleep mode may not be ready for immediate use. Sleep mode usually involves shutting down displays, which consume a large amount of energy.

slider phone   A cell phone consisting of two sections that are positioned one underneath the other in a way that allows them to be slid apart. The keypad is typically located on the lower section, so it can be hidden underneath the section that houses the display.

slimline computer   A thin, rectangular desktop computer that is usually no bigger than a laptop and that uses small-form-factor components. *See also* **small form factor.**

SLIP   *Abbreviation of* **Serial Line Internet Protocol.**   A communications protocol allowing TCP/IP communication over a serial connection, such as a dial-up Internet connection. SLIP has largely been replaced by PPP.

SLR   *Abbreviation of* **single-lens reflex.**

slot   *See* **expansion slot.**

small computer systems interface   *See* **SCSI.**

small form factor   *Abbreviated* **SFF.**   *n.* A compact desktop computer with components that are smaller than those used in traditional desktops. A typical SFF is 8 inches wide, 12 inches deep, and 6 inches high, but there are also models that are much smaller. *Also called* **mini-PC.** *See also* **slimline computer.**

   adj. Having smaller dimensions than is typical.

Small Office/Home Office   *See* **SoHo.**

small outline DIMM   *See* **SODIMM.**

Smalltalk   An object-oriented programming language designed by Xerox researchers in the 1970s. Smalltalk was one of the first object-oriented programming languages and introduced several ideas that have been incorporated into popular programming languages such as Java.

smart   Relating to or being a highly automated device, especially one that contains computer components such as a microprocessor. For example, a *smart terminal* is a terminal that has its own microprocessor. *Compare* **dumb.**

smart card   A small plastic card containing a computer chip. Many smart cards contain memory chips to store data, but most also contain microprocessors that can process data. Smart cards are part of systems that enable cardholders to purchase goods and services, enter restricted areas, connect to cell phone networks, or perform other operations that require the storage and processing of identifying information. SIM cards are a popular type of smart card.

SmartMedia   A memory card format developed by Toshiba. SmartMedia cards are available in 5- and 3.3-volt versions and have storage capacities up to 128 MB.

smartphone   A cell phone that includes features of a PDA, such as software that runs email, calendar, word processing, and web browsing functions.

smart quote   A quotation mark oriented toward an adjacent character (' ' " or ") and automatically chosen by a computer program when a user types the simple straight quotation mark (' or ") on the keyboard. Because most keyboard layouts do not have character-oriented quotation marks, many word processors provide the option of formatting text with smart quotes, thereby saving a user from having to enter them as special characters.

smart terminal   A terminal in a multiuser system that has a processor and therefore has processing capabilities independent of the host computer. *Compare* **dumb terminal.** *See also* **diskless workstation.**

SMIL   *Abbreviation for* **synchronized media integration language.**   An XML markup language for integrating different media, such as audio, video, and text, into a single synchronized multimedia presentation.

smiley   Characters typed next to each other that together resemble a smiling face, such as :-) or :). Smileys are emoticons that are very popular in email and text messaging.

S/MIME   *Abbreviation of* **secure MIME.**   An extension of the MIME protocol for the transmission of encrypted email over the Internet. S/MIME capabilities are built into most email clients.

smoothing   A technique for eliminating jaggies, the jagged distortions that appear on curves. Smoothing usually involves reducing the size or alignment of the dots that make up a curved line. *See also* **antialiasing.**

SMR   *Abbreviation of*   **specialized mobile radio.**   A system for wireless communications in which a network of mobile two-way radios and base stations transmit and receive analog signals over a wide geographic area through the use of repeaters. SMR systems are used by public organizations such as police and fire departments, as well as taxi dispatch systems and similar private organizations. The two-way radios used in SMR systems are like walkie-talkies in that users must alternate transmissions but SMR systems cover a wider area and allow transmissions to be routed to the public telephone network. *See also* **ESMR, half duplex.**

SMS   **1.** *Abbreviation of* **Short Message Service.**   The standard for sending text messages on mobile communications networks. Part of the GSM recommendation, SMS allows for messages of up to 160 characters. **2.** *See* **text message.**

SMTP   *Abbreviation of* **Simple Mail Transfer Protocol.**   A protocol that governs the sending of email over the Internet. In order to send an email, an email client must contact a server that can use SMTP.

smurf   To disable a network maliciously by flooding it with replies to ping requests. Attackers send out ping requests to large numbers of computers using the forged return address of the network being attacked. The responses are all sent to the network, flooding it with too much traffic and sometimes causing it to crash. Smurfing is one kind of a denial-of-service attack.

snail mail   Mail delivered by a postal system, as distinct from email.

sniffer   *See* **packet sniffer.**

snow   White specks on a television screen resulting from weak reception.

SNR   *Abbreviation of* **signal-to-noise ratio.**

SOAP   *Abbreviation of* **simple object access protocol.**   An XML language for communication between software applications. SOAP provides a standardized way for web service applications to exchange information such as the data necessary to make purchases on the web.

socket   **1.** The combination of an IP address, the name of a communications protocol, and a port number, used to route data transmitted over the Internet to a program running on a host. The IP address identifies the host on which the program is running, and the port number is used to route the data to the program. **2.** An electrical component consisting of one or more holes into which the prongs of a plug are inserted to make a connection, as between a connector and an electrical device.

SODIMM   *Abbreviation of* **small outline DIMM.**   A memory module similar to a DIMM, but smaller and having either 72 or 144 pins. Because SODIMMs are roughly half the size of DIMMs, they are often used in portable computers.

soft copy   An electronic version of a printed document or image, such as a scanned version of the document or a PDF or PostScript file. *Compare* **hard copy.**

soft hyphen   A command, tag, or character in a word processing program or a markup language such as HTML, indicating where a word can be broken to end a line. Soft hyphens do not display if the word does not occur at the end of a line, and are often automatically inserted by word processing programs. Character encodings such as ISO Latin-1 and Unicode contain soft hyphen characters.

soft key   A key on the keypad, especially of a cell phone, that performs a range of different functions. Often, a soft key is located below the device's display and the function that it will perform in a given situation is shown near the key on the display.

soft keyboard   A keyboard displayed on a touch screen, allowing a user to type text by touching the screen with a finger or stylus. *Also called* **onscreen keyboard, software keyboard.**

soft line break   *See* **soft return.**

soft link   *See* **symbolic link.**

soft return   An instruction in a word processing program that ends a line and begins a new one in the same paragraph. Unlike hard returns, which are typically inserted by a user to indicate a new paragraph, soft returns are typically indicated by a program's word wrap feature and can be moved automatically when the document changes. Soft returns can be inserted by users, usually by typing Shift + return. *Also called* **soft line break.** *See also* **hard return, line break.**

software   Information in the form of programs and data that serves as instructions to a computer or similar device, determining how data is to be processed, stored, retrieved, manipulated, entered, or displayed. Software may also control the operation of hardware devices such as displays, storage devices, and modems.

Computer software is usually divided into two categories: system software and applications software. System software controls the basic workings of the computer, determining how memory should be managed and providing basic tools for other software to function on the machine. It includes operating systems, utilities, and file management tools. Applications software handles the multitude of tasks that users want their computers to perform. Examples are word processing programs, database management systems, spreadsheets, Internet browsers, and games. Applications software is unable to run without the operating system and utilities.

Two additional categories that contain elements of system and applications software are network software, which enables computers to communicate, and programming languages, which give programmers the tools to write software of their own.

Software is generally understood as an abstract set of instructions rather than any particular piece of hardware that contains the binary data encoding the instructions. For example, a word processing program is considered software, but the disk on which the information describing the program is recorded is hardware. *Compare* **hardware.** *See also* **firmware.**

software development kit *See* **SDK.**

software keyboard *See* **soft keyboard.**

software piracy The unauthorized copying, distribution, or use of copyrighted software. Software piracy occurs in various forms, including the unlicensed installation of a single copy of a program on multiple computers, illegal downloading from the Internet, and unauthorized resale of software by a third party.

Some software companies have responded to piracy with incentives for purchasing licensed software, such as documentation, free upgrades, and support, as well as disincentives in the form of lawsuits against those who deal in large-scale piracy. Still other software developers make shareware as an alternative to standard copyright ownership. *See also* **copy protection, dongle.**

SoHo or **SOHO** *Abbreviations of* **Small Office/Home Office.** Relating to computer and computer-related products that are more sophisticated and expensive than what the average consumer would need, while being less expensive (and less functional) than the equipment used in larger offices.

Sony/Phillips Digital Interface *See* **S/PDIF connector.**

sort An operation that takes a set of data and arranges it in alphabetical or numerical order. Sorting is a common procedure in word processing, database, and spreadsheet programs. *See also* **ASCII sort, dictionary sort.**

sound card A computer expansion card that processes and converts audio signals. Sound cards typically have a variety of audio connectors such as those for sending signals to speakers and for receiving signals from a microphone, and contain A/D and D/A converters. On some motherboards, the sound card is integrated into the system. *Also called* **audio card.**

soundtrack The audio portion of a film or video recording.

source code Code in high-level language, such as C++, as written by a programmer. In order to run a program, its source code must first be converted into machine code by a compiler or executed by an interpreter. *See also* **high-level language, machine code, object code, programming language.**

space bar   A bar at the bottom of the keyboard. In word processing, pressing the space bar down introduces a blank space to the right of the preceding character. In other software, pressing the space bar can serve a variety of purposes, such as selecting a field or executing some function.

spam   Unsolicited email, often of a commercial nature, sent indiscriminately to multiple mailing lists, individuals, or newsgroups. Most email providers have filters that identify spam and separate it from other email.

S/PDIF connector   *Abbreviation of* **Sony/Phillips Digital Interface.** A connector used primarily for transferring digital audio to and from CD and DVD players. Consumer S/PDIF connectors typically consist either of a coaxial cable with an RCA plug and socket or an optical fiber cable with a TOSLINK plug and socket. *See also* **AES/EBU.** *See* Table A on page 356.

speaker   **1.** A device that converts electric signals to audible sound. Most speakers consist of a driver that vibrates a flexible cone or dome by means of an electromagnet. The size of the cone or dome determines the pitch of the sounds that the speaker can produce. Speakers designed to produce the lowest range of sounds, called *subwoofers* or *woofers,* have large cones, while those made for high-pitched sounds, called *tweeters,* have small cones or domes. Tweeters and woofers are often used in combination to reproduce a single audio channel. In such a setup, a device called a *crossover* divides the signal into the appropriate frequency ranges. *Also called* **loudspeaker.** *See also* **electrostatic speaker, midrange speaker. 2.** A set of such devices, sometimes assembled into a single structure, that work together to reproduce a single sound signal. Speaker units are often classified as two-way, three-way, and so on, depending on how many individual speakers they contain. *Also called* **loudspeaker.**

special character   A character that has a special meaning in a given context. For example, the left angle bracket (<) is a special character in HTML, where it is used to introduce a tag. Control characters are special characters in almost all circumstances. Escape sequences often must be used in order to include a special character as a literal character in a document.

specialized mobile radio   *See* **SMR.**

specific absorption rate   A measure of the rate at which the human body absorbs radio frequency energy from a cell phone, usually reported in watts per kilogram (W/kg). By law, the maximum specific absorption rate for cell phones sold in the United States is 1.6 W/kg.

spectral band replication *Abbreviated* **SBR.** An audio coding technology that is used to enhance the capabilities of audio codecs such as MP3 and AAC. Spectral band replication predicts and reconstructs some of the high-frequency information that is lost when the signals are compressed using lossy compression. It therefore allows audio signals to be transmitted quickly in compressed form (i.e., at a higher bandwidth), but with less noticeable decrease in signal quality. *See also* **aacPlus, mp3PRO.**

spectrum A set of frequencies, especially of electromagnetic radiation such as light and radio waves, within some continuous range.

speech recognition The interpretation of human speech by software or by a device. Speech recognition technology allows computers to identify spoken words so that computers can respond to commands or translate speech into text. *Also called* **automatic speech recognition, voice recognition.** *See also* **handwriting recognition.**

speech synthesis The production of speech sounds by a computer or other machine, as distinct from playing back recorded speech. Speech synthesis can be performed by software or by special-purpose hardware systems. *See also* **text-to-speech.**

speed dial A feature available on many telephones that allows a user to make a call by pressing fewer buttons. Speed dial systems allow the user to store full telephone numbers in memory and typically associate them with single digits or pairs of digits; to use speed dial to make a call to a stored number, a user dials the digits associated with that number and presses another button.

spell checker A program that searches a document for misspelled words by comparing each word in the document to a dictionary file of correctly spelled words. Many spell checkers can lead a user through the document, stopping at each word it cannot find in its dictionary; some spell checkers then offer a list of possible substitute words with which the user can replace the unrecognized word. Most spell checkers on personal computers allow the creation of custom dictionaries, where users can enter words or abbreviations they frequently use but which are not part of the basic dictionary used by the spell checker.

spi *Abbreviation of* **samples per inch.**

spider A program that automatically retrieves webpages and follows the links on them to retrieve more webpages. Spiders are used by search engines to retrieve publicly accessible webpages for indexing, and can also be used to check for links to webpages that no longer exist. *Also called* **bot, crawler, robot, search bot, webcrawler.**

split screen A display option that divides the screen into sections, each of which can display a different video signal or television channel. *Compare* **picture-in-picture.**

spoofing **1.** email spoofing **2.** The assumption of the identity of another user in order to gain access to a system. Logging in to a database using another user's password is an example of spoofing. **3.** The emulation of the identity of another device. For example, devices such as routers and bridges can be programmed to spoof remote nodes in a wide area network.

spool *See* **queue.**

spooler A program that temporarily stores data on disk until a printer is able to process it. Spoolers are used because even with large print buffers, printers cannot process data as fast as computers can send it. Programs send documents to the spooler, which maintains a queue of documents to be printed. The spooler communicates with the printer, sending data whenever the printer has free space in its buffer. Spoolers are part of most modern operating systems. *Also called* **print spooler.** *See also* **background printing, print buffer.**

spreadsheet A table of values arranged in columns and rows in an onscreen display. The intersections of columns and rows are called *cells.* The columns are alphabetized and the rows are numbered, so each cell can be identified by its column letter and row number. B9, for instance, is the cell in column B and row 9.

   The role of each cell on the spreadsheet can be defined through a numerical relation with other cells, often called a *formula.* For example, one cell, labeled "total," could be defined to hold the value of the sum of all the values in the cells above it; a cell named "sales tax" could be defined as 7% of the value of the cell "total." Changing the values of the undefined cells will then automatically result in changes for the cells defined by formulas, allowing the user to update the data, or experiment with different possible values without having to do any manual recalculation.

   Spreadsheet applications allow the user to perform accounting, bookkeeping, and related calculations easily. Specialized spreadsheets are particularly popular for calculating taxes.

   2. A document created in a spreadsheet application.

spread spectrum A set of techniques for radio transmission in which a signal is transmitted over more frequencies than are required by the signal itself. The use of greater bandwidth reduces the possibility of interference and noise, and it allows for the private transmission of messages over a shared frequency band. CDMA cellular networks and Wi-Fi networks are examples of spread spectrum technology.

spyware   **1.** Software that secretly gathers information about a person or organization. On the Internet, where spyware is sometimes called a spybot or tracking software, spyware gathers information about the user, keeping track of such things as which websites have been visited, and relays this information to advertisers or other interested parties. Spyware is often inadvertently installed on computers when users visit certain websites, install certain software, or open specially coded email messages that automatically download it. Some programs that perform a legitimate task also secretly function as spyware. *See also* **malware. 2.** Any malicious software designed to take partial or full control of a computer's operation without the knowledge of its user. *See also* **malware, Trojan horse.**

SQL   A standard language for managing a relational database. SQL commands allow users to create, modify, and query databases. SQL can be issued at a command line or embedded in a program. The name of the language was originally *Structured English Query Language.* Because the abbreviation *SEQUEL* was already trademarked, the name was changed to *SQL,* which is pronounced SEE-kwel.

SRAM   *Abbreviation of* **static RAM.**   A type of RAM chip that can store information as long as it is attached to a power supply. Unlike dynamic RAM, static RAM does not need to be refreshed. Substantially faster than dynamic RAM, static RAM chips are also more expensive and so are primarily used for a computer's cache.

SRS   A trademark for any of a variety of audio technologies developed by SRS Labs. SRS WOW enhances 3D audio signals for playback on small speakers, and SRS TruSurround enhances six-channel audio signals for playback on two speakers.

SSH   *Abbreviation of* **secure shell.**   **1.** A protocol that provides a secure, encrypted connection between two computers on a network, often used to allow users to log in and execute commands on a remote computer. Because the SSH protocol includes methods for authenticating users and encrypting communication between two computers, it is the preferred method for logging in to a remote computer on the Internet. In combination with other protocols, it allows secure file transfer between computers on a network, as well as several other types of communication. **2.** A client program that uses the SSH protocol to allow users to log in and execute commands on a remote computer. SSH is available on most Linux and Unix operating systems.

SSH file transfer protocol   *See* **SFTP.**

SSL   *Abbreviation of* **Secure Sockets Layer.**   An encryption protocol developed by Netscape for transmitting data securely over the Internet. SSL uses public-key encryption to exchange keys, and private-key encryption to send data. SSL operates on the network level, allowing for the encryption of data transmitted by other protocols, such as TCP or HTTP. *See also* **HTTPS, S-HTTP.**

SSL certificate *See* **digital certificate.**

stack overflow An overflow error that occurs when a unit of data is too large to be stored on the stack that it is written to. *Also called* **stack overrun.**

standard A procedure or structure that is agreed upon for a specific type of communication. There are standard physical structures that enable a device such as a printer to plug into a variety of different computers, and there are standard communications methods, called protocols, that make the data in one computer usable by other computers and devices.

Some standards are set by an official organization, such as ANSI (American National Standards Institute), which establishes standards for programming languages. Other standards evolve naturally as hardware and software developers attempt to create products that will be compatible with the more popular computers and devices. Some commonly used standards include the Unicode standards for digital representations of written characters in different alphabets, and TCP/IP, a communications protocol for transmitting digital data.

standard-definition television *See* **SDTV.**

Standard Generalized Markup Language *See* **SGML.**

Standard Hash Algorithm 1 *See* **SHA-1.**

standby A mode of operation for a device such as a computer or cell phone that is not being used but is on and ready for immediate use. In order to conserve energy, displays may be dimmed and other functions may be shut down when the device is on standby. *Compare* **sleep mode.**

star network A network in which all computers and devices (the network nodes) are connected to one central computer, known as the hub. All communication between nodes is routed by the hub. Many local area networks (LANs) are configured as star networks. *See also* **bus network, network topology, ring network.** *See figure at* **network.**

start bit In some asynchronous communication protocols, the bit that signals the beginning of a unit of data. The start bit indicates to the receiver that a transmission is starting. *See also* **stop bit.**

startup *See* **boot.**

startup disk A disk that contains the operating system files that a computer needs to start working. The startup disk is usually a hard disk, although in some situations, for example when reinstalling a computer's operating system, an optical disk or other external medium may be used. *Also called* **boot disk, system disk.**

statement   An instruction or set of instructions in a programming language, especially a high-level language.

static   Random noise, such as crackling in a receiver or specks on a television screen, that is produced by atmospheric disturbance of the signal.

static RAM   *See* **SRAM.**

STB   *Abbreviation of* **set-top box.**

steganography   The concealment of data, especially by embedding it in some other form of data. For example, binary data representing a secret message can be hidden in a graphics image by distributing it within the representations of color values. *Compare* **cryptography.**

stereo   *adj.* Recording, transmitting, or playing back audio that uses two or more separate channels to give a more natural distribution of sound. *Also called* **stereophonic.** *Compare* **mono.**

    n. An audio receiver and related devices for playing back recorded sound.

stop bit   In some asynchronous communication protocols, the bit that signals the end of a unit of data. The stop bit indicates to the receiver that a complete unit has been transmitted. *See also* **start bit.**

storage   Devices that hold data for processing or retrieval. There are two types of storage: primary storage consists of a computer's working memory; secondary storage, or mass storage, refers to the places, such as hard disks, where large amounts of information can be permanently stored.

storage device   Any of various devices used to record and store computer data. Storage devices include hard disks, floppy disks, optical disks, tapes, and memory cards.

store   To copy data onto a storage device, for example onto a disk or into RAM.

STP   *Abbreviation of* **shielded twisted pair.**   A cable consisting of two copper wires twisted around each other and sheathed in insulated metallic tubing that functions as a ground. STP cables are often used in Ethernet networks and some professional digital audio equipment.

streaming   A technique for transmitting audio and video content over the Internet that allows the content to be played in real time while the transmission is still in progress. The data is played in a continuous stream of small packets, as opposed to being downloaded as a single large file.

string   A set of consecutive characters treated by a computer as a single unit. Computers often perform operations on text by grouping characters together into strings; this is especially common in word processing, in which consecutive letters, spaces, and other characters are manipulated as strings. *Also called* **character string.**

stripe   To distribute data over several disks in a RAID. Striping is accomplished by storing different pieces of a file on different disks. It reduces the likelihood of data loss and allows faster access to the data because pieces can be retrieved in parallel. *See also* **RAID.**

stripe pitch   A measure of the distance between the pixels of a CRT display with an aperture grill; the lower the stripe pitch, the denser the pixels. Stripe pitch is measured horizontally between like-colored stripes of phosphor subpixels.

stuck pixel   An LCD pixel that has stopped responding to signals from the transistor, especially a pixel that cannot be turned off. *Compare* **dead pixel.**

style sheet   A file of instructions for the visual format of a webpage, usually written in the cascading style sheets language. A style sheet is stored separately from the content of the webpage, making it easier to make global changes in the way a group of webpages look and allowing the creator of a webpage to have more influence on how the page is displayed in different browsers.

stylus   A pen-shaped instrument used for pressing and drawing on a touch screen. Handhelds with touch screens typically come with a stylus.

subdirectory   A directory that is contained within another directory, located lower in the directory structure or directory tree. The directory containing a subdirectory is called the parent directory. *See also* **subfolder.**

subfolder   A folder that can be opened from within another folder. *See also* **directory.**

submenu   *See* **cascading menu.**

subnet or **subnetwork**   A network that is part of a larger network. On an IP network, the IP addresses of machines on a subnet all have the same network number.

subnotebook   A portable computer that is smaller and lighter than typical laptops.

subpixel   One of the red, green, or blue components of a pixel. Most flat-panel and direct-view displays render color using subpixels.

Subscriber Identity Module   *See* **SIM.**

subtitle   A transcription or translation of speech used in film or video, or on stage, that is displayed in synchronization with the speech.

subtractive color   Color that is produced by absorbing and reflecting light, as ink on a sheet of paper, rather than by emitting light, as pixels on a display. Subtractive colors are usually a mix of cyan, magenta, and yellow. *Compare* **additive color.** *See also* **color model.**

subwoofer   A large speaker that produces low-pitched sounds, typically in the range of 20 to 120 hertz. Subwoofers are usually enclosed in a wooden box to increase their resonance. Since the human ear cannot determine the location of low-pitched sounds, subwoofers can be positioned anywhere that is most suitable to the acoustics of the room. Some subwoofers, often described as *powered* or *active* subwoofers, come with their own amplifiers. *See also* **speaker.**

suite   A group of software products with related functions that are packaged and sold together. Each component of a suite typically has certain things in common with the others, including a consistent look-and-feel, a common installation, and shared software modules. Office suites such as Microsoft Office are one common type of suite.

Super Audio Compact Disk   *Abbreviated* **Super Audio CD** or **SACD.**   A CD format developed jointly by Sony and Philips. Super Audio CDs offer high-resolution or multichannel sound when played in dedicated SACD players. Many SACDs are now hybrid discs, containing an additional CD layer that allows them to be played in standard CD players, but without the advantages of SACD sound. SACDs use DSD coding rather than the PCM used in standard compact disks.

supercomputer   A fast, powerful computer designed to execute computation-intensive programs as quickly as possible. Supercomputers generally execute fewer programs at one time than ordinary mainframes and are used in scientific research to perform the enormous number of calculations required in modeling complex phenomena such as weather patterns or nuclear explosions. They often use parallel processing to achieve their computation speed and require specialized software.

SuperDrive   **1.** An optical drive developed by Apple that can read and write both CDs and DVDs. SuperDrives support all major CD and DVD formats, and are now standard on Macintosh computers. **2.** A 3.5-inch floppy disk drive that can read all Apple Macintosh formats (400 KB, 800 KB, and 1.4 MB) and can read and format 720-KB and 1.4-MB DOS disks. SuperDrives were formerly the standard floppy drive on Macintosh computers.

superscalar architecture   A CPU (central processing unit) architecture that allows for the execution of more than one instruction during each cycle of the system clock by including multiple ALUs (arithmetic-logic units) as well as one or more FPUs (floating-point units) on the micro-processor. The presence of multiple units for performing particular kinds of operations allows CPUs with superscalar architecture to process instructions in parallel. *See also* **control unit.**

superuser A special user account with unlimited access to files and other resources on an operating system. The superuser account can create other accounts and modify the configuration of the operating system. Access to this account is normally restricted to system administrators, and the superuser account is used solely to perform administrative tasks. On Linux and Unix systems, this account typically has the username *root, superuser,* or *avatar.* Windows systems have a superuser account with the username *Administrator.*

Super VGA   *See* **SVGA.**

support To have the ability to work in a certain way, to interact with a certain device or program, or to perform a certain task. For example, older televisions do not support HDTV.

supra-aural headphone A headphone that lays flat against the outer part of the ear. *See also* **headphone.**

surf To browse through information presented on the World Wide Web by casually following links from site to site, in contrast to the focused activity of trying to find specific information.

surge protector A device that protects electronic devices, especially computers, from damaging increases in voltage caused by lightning and other sources. Surge protectors work by diverting excess voltage. *Also called* **surge suppressor.**

surround sound A system of recording and playing back audio that uses multiple separate channels to give a more natural distribution of sound. Audio can either be recorded in surround sound or converted into sur-round sound by a receiver. Movie soundtracks are often recorded in sur-round sound so that audio effects can be made to appear to come from different positions around the listener.

Surround-sound formats typically have between two and six channels that each support a full range of frequencies (20–20,000 hertz) and one smaller channel, called the LFE channel, that carries only very low-fre-quency signals (10–120 hertz). Each format usually assumes a specific arrangement of speakers with respect to the listener, with each full-range channel assigned to a particular speaker position. For example, a 5.1-channel surround-sound system has left, center, and right front-channels, and left and right rear-channels, plus an LFE channel. (The notation 5.1

means that there are five main channels and one LFE channel.) The LFE channel can be directed to a subwoofer or combined with the other channels. Some surround-sound receivers create the illusion of multiple audio sources from a single speaker unit.

SVG *Abbreviation of* **scalable vector graphics.** A nonproprietary XML markup language for describing two-dimensional graphics, used to transmit graphics on the Internet. SVG allows graphics to be represented in XML format in such a way that they can be displayed with equal resolution at any size, and allows for animation. It is usually viewed with a web browser plug-in. *Compare* **Flash, PostScript.** *See also* **vector graphics.**

SVGA *Abbreviation of* **Super Video Graphics Array.** A display standard for PC-compatible computers that offers higher resolution than VGA (Video Graphics Array). SVGA video adapters and monitors are able to display images of up to 1,280 by 1,024 pixels and over 16 million different colors. *Also called* **extended VGA.** *See* Table B on page 357.

S-VHS *Abbreviation of* **Super VHS.** A videotape format that is based on the VHS format but has a horizontal resolution of 400 lines.

S-Video An analog video signal in which the luminance and chrominance components are transmitted along two separate channels contained within a single cable, resulting in a sharper onscreen picture than composite video. S-Video cables have a Mini-DIN connector with four or seven pins. *See figure at* **connector.** *See* Table A on page 356.

swap **1.** In a system using virtual memory, to copy a segment or page that is not currently in use from RAM to the hard disk, replacing it with a needed segment or page. **2.** In a multitasking system, to move all the data associated with a given program to swap space on the hard disk in order to make room in main memory for another program. *See also* **swap file.**

swap file A file used as swap space by a virtual memory system. *Also called* **page file.**

swap space A section of a disk or other mass storage device that an operating system uses to hold data that is needed by running programs, but that does not fit in main memory. Many operating systems use files for swap space, but Linux and Unix systems typically use partitions. *See also* **virtual memory.**

.swf An extension commonly used for Flash files.

switch A point in an electric circuit or network at which a power source or signal may be turned on or off, or its path through the circuit or network changed. Switches control the delivery of power to different parts of an electrical system and are used as the basis of logic gates that switch each other on and off in order to perform the operations carried out in microprocessors and other computer devices.

Symbian OS An operating system designed primarily for handhelds and used especially on smartphones. Symbian OS is licensed by Symbian, Ltd. Although it is not open-source software, it has a published, standard interface, and so open-source software is available for devices that run it.

symbolic link In Linux and Unix operating systems, an alternative name for a file or directory, which allows the file or directory to show up in multiple directories. Unlike hard links, which are stored as references to the actual location of the file on the disk, symbolic links are stored as references to a filename. If the file is renamed or moved to a different directory, a symbolic link will no longer function. *Also called* **soft link, symlink.** *Compare* **hard link.**

symlink *n. See* **symbolic link.**

v. In Linux and Unix operating systems, to create a symbolic link to a file.

symmetric-key cryptography *See* **private-key cryptography.**

sync or **synch** To synchronize.

synchronize **1.** To transfer data between two devices in order to ensure that the same data is stored on both. Usually, a desktop computer or other server and a handheld device are synchronized, so that the same files are available to calendar, scheduling, email, and related applications. **2.** To align a video with its soundtrack so that the sound coincides with the appropriate image.

synchronized multimedia integration language *See* **SMIL.**

synchronous Relating to an electronic communication system in which the flow of data is synchronized by an electronic clock. The internal bus of a computer transfers data between various internal components using a synchronous communication system. *Compare* **asynchronous.**

synchronous DRAM *See* **SDRAM.**

syndicate **1.** To include the contents of a website on another webpage or in a newsreader by using a web feed. New content that is added to the original website, commonly news articles and blog entries, is automatically available on the syndicating webpage or in the newsreader. **2.** To create a web feed for a website, allowing users to include content from the website in other websites or to view the content in a newsreader. *See also* **aggregate.**

sysadmin A system administrator.

sysop A system operator.

system   A combination of components that work together to perform a specific set of tasks. A computer system, for example, is made up of all of the hardware and software that allow a computer to accept input, to process and store it, and to produce output. The operating system of a computer is often referred to simply as its system.

system administrator   A person who manages and maintains computer systems and software, as for a business, institution, or organization. *See also* **network administrator.**

System 10   *See* **OS X.**

system board   *See* **motherboard.**

system bus   **1.** The communication pathway between the CPU, main memory, and core components of a computer. **2.** The communication pathway between the CPU, expansion slots (excluding memory slots), and other peripheral components that rely on technologies such as PCI, PCI Express, USB, and IEEE 1394.

system clock   An electronic timer circuit that sends out electrical pulses at regular intervals. The rate of the pulses is measured in megahertz. Most processes executed by a computer are synchronized according to these pulses. *See also* **clock cycle, clock speed. 2.** A clock maintained by a computer and used for various purposes, including logging the times at which various events happen and scheduling tasks to run automatically. Operating systems usually display the system clock and provide a way to set it.

system disk   *See* **startup disk.**

système électronique couleur avec mémoire   *See* **SECAM.**

system operator   A person who manages a computer system.

systems analysis   The design of computer systems to solve particular problems or accomplish particular tasks, including analysis of the cost, feasibility, and schedule of a project.

systems analyst   A person who performs systems analyses, designing, recommending, and sometimes overseeing the implementation of computer systems for specific settings and requirements.

system software   Software that is concerned with the actual operation of the computer as opposed to the work that is done with it. System software primarily includes the operating system and related utility programs, as well as configuration files, compilers, linkers, and other files and programs that cannot be considered applications software. *Compare* **applications software.** *See also* **software.**

T   *Abbreviation of* **tera-.**

T1   A North American standard for digital transmission over cables at a transmission rate of 1.544 Mbps. T1 lines are commonly used for dedicated circuits.

T2   A North American standard for digital transmission over cables at a transmission rate of 6.312 Mbps. T2 lines are commonly used for dedicated circuits.

T3   A North American standard for data transmission using fiber-optic cables or microwaves at a transmission rate of 44.736 Mbps. T3 lines are commonly used for dedicated circuits.

T4   A North American standard for data transmission using fiber-optic cables or microwaves at a transmission rate of 275.176 Mbps. T4 lines are primarily used by telecommunications carriers for network backbones.

TA   *Abbreviation of* **terminal adapter.**

tab   **1.** A blank character often indicating that the cursor or print head should move to the next tab stop, leaving blank space in between. In applications that do not use tab stops, a tab usually indicates that several blank spaces should be inserted; the number inserted depends on configuration settings. *See also* **TSV. 2.** A small graphical element in a GUI (graphical user interface) that allows users to select a window for viewing. Tabs are usually located at the top or bottom of the window in which documents are viewed. *See also* **TDI.**

tabbed browsing   The use of a TDI, especially to open multiple webpages in a web browser.

tabbed document interface   *See* **TDI.**

tab-delimited   Relating to data tables stored as text by representing each row as a line in the file and separating columns of data with tabs. *See also* **TSV.**

Tab key   A key that moves the cursor a preset distance, as to the next cell in a spreadsheet or to another part of a dialog box, or that inserts a tab.

table   An arrangement of information using rows and columns. Spreadsheets and databases use tables as their basic data structures. Word processing programs make it easy to include tables in documents, and HTML allows tables to be displayed in webpages.

tablet *See* **digitizing tablet.**

tablet PC A notebook computer or PDA that has a surface on which a user can draw or write with a stylus. A tablet PC can store what is written or drawn as a bitmap file, or it can use handwriting recognition to translate printed words, numbers, and punctuation into ASCII characters in order to enter commands or data. *See also* **digitizing tablet.**

tab-separated values *See* **TSV.**

tab stop In word processing, a position in a line of text where the cursor will stop when the Tab key is pressed. Tab stops are useful for indenting the first line of a paragraph, and also make it easier to type text in columns without filling lines with spaces. Most word processors set default tab stops every half inch. Usually tab stops can be set to align text flush left or flush right with the stop, or centered on it.

tag A character or string that is attached to an item of data, such as a string of text or a database field, and encodes information about that item. In HTML, tags are used to indicate how text should be formatted. For example, placing text between the tag $< I >$ and the tag $< /I >$ indicates that the text should be italicized.

Tagged Image File Format *Abbreviated* **TIFF.** A bitmap graphics file format that uses no compression or lossless compression. Because TIFF format does not allow lossy compression, TIFF files are often large but store higher-quality images.

talk time The length of time that a particular model of cell phone can transmit without its battery being recharged. When a cell phone is transmitting, it uses much more energy than when it is on standby.

tape **1.** A magnetic tape. **2.** A videotape. **3.** An audiotape. **4.** A DAT.

tape bias A high-frequency signal that is added to an audio signal to improve the degree to which it can be recorded on magnetic tape. The tape bias, typically having a frequency of 10–150 kHz, has sufficient energy to free the electric particles on the tape, allowing them to align themselves magnetically with the lower-frequency (and lower-energy) audio signal. Using the wrong bias frequency when recording can significantly decrease recording quality.

tape deck A recorder and player for magnetic tape, especially audiocassette, having no built-in amplifiers or speakers, used as a component in an audio system.

tape drive A device that holds magnetic tape, mounted on reels or in cartridges, and includes a transport mechanism that moves the tape across read/write heads that read data from it and write new data to it. Tape drives are still in wide use for recording and storing audio and video, though the speed and storage capacity of hard disks has led to the replacement of tape drives with hard drives in more recent technology. Tape drives are also used as backup or archival storage devices for computer data.

tar **1.** A file format used for archives, especially on Linux and Unix systems. The tar format preserves information about archived files and directories, such as their permissions and directory structures. Windows programs like WinZip can read tar archives.

The word *tar* takes its name from the phrase *tape archive,* since magnetic tape was once the most common storage medium for archived files.

2. A program on the Linux and Unix operating systems that employs the tar file format to create archive files and to retrieve files out of a tar archive.

task   A set of computer program instructions that is in memory and either ready for execution or being executed. *See also* **process.**

taskbar   A row of buttons or graphical controls on a computer screen that represent open programs. The user can switch back and forth between programs by clicking on the appropriate button.

TB   *Abbreviation of* **terabyte.**

TCP   *Abbreviation of* **Transmission** or **Transfer Control Protocol.**   A network protocol that specifies the way two computers on the Internet are connected and the way data is exchanged between them. TCP specifies how data transmitted from one computer to another is broken into packets. It is generally used with IP, which is responsible for routing packets to their destination. TCP also has procedures for making sure that the packets arrive undamaged and are assembled in the correct order. *See also* **IP, TCP/IP.**

TCP/IP   *Abbreviation of* **Transmission** or **Transfer Control Protocol/Internet Protocol.**   The combination of the two protocols TCP and IP, used to route and transfer data on the Internet. While TCP/IP specifies how data is transmitted between computers on a network, protocols like HTTP and SMTP specify how different applications use the network to perform tasks like viewing webpages and sending email.

tcsh   *Abbreviation of* **Tenex C shell.**   A popular shell that interprets commands for Linux and Unix operating systems and that is the default command line shell for the MacOS. Tcsh is an extension of the C shell.

TDD   *Abbreviation of* **telecommunications device for the deaf.**   A teletypewriter designed to allow people who are hearing-impaired or speech-impaired to use telephone lines for communication. TDDs transmit data over a serial connection on a standard telephone line. They typically have a standard QWERTY keyboard for typing messages and an LCD or LED display for displaying received messages. TDDs are often used with a tele-communications relay service, allowing the user to communicate with people who do not have TDDs.

TDI   *Abbreviation of* **tabbed document interface.**   A GUI (graphical user interface) commonly used with web browsers, in which only one open document is visible and active at any time. In a TDI, users make a document active and visible by clicking on a tab associated with it. Applications can often be configured to use a TDI. *See also* **MDI, SDI.**

TDMA   *Abbreviation of* **Time Division Multiple Access.**   A method of transmission for digital mobile communications, such as voice and text messaging, in which multiple transmissions occur on the same frequency channel. Interference is avoided by giving users unique time slots. *Compare* **CDMA.** *See also* **multiplex.**

tear-off menu   A pop-up menu that can be moved around the screen. A tear-off menu remains on the screen after one of its options has been selected.

technical support   *Abbreviated* **tech support.**   Assistance with the installation or use of a product or service. Most vendors offer telephone and online technical support, and some hardware vendors also offer onsite support.

telecommunications   The transmission and reception of information over the air or through cables. Telecommunications includes television, telephone, the Internet, and other media.

telecommunications device for the deaf   *See* **TDD.**

telecommunications relay service, MOVE   *Abbreviated* **TRS.**   A service that allows hearing- and speech-impaired people to place voice calls via a TDD, computer, or similar device. To place a call with a telecommunications relay service, a user makes a connection to an operator, who then places a call to a third party. The user types messages to the operator, who reads them to the third party. The third party speaks to the operator, who types the messages and sends them to the user. Telecommunications relay services were developed for use with TDDs, but are increasingly using the Internet for messages sent between the user and the operator. *See also* **video relay service.**

telecommuting   The practice of working at home or some other location outside of a traditional business office by means of a computer that is connected to the Internet or a company network.

telematics   **1.** The integration of wireless communication, tracking technology such as GPS, and computers. Telematics is used for a variety of purposes, including car navigation systems, the monitoring of transportation involved in shipping to increase efficiency, and other technologies that involve electronic communication with or among vehicles. *See also* **DSRC.** **2.** The use of computers in telecommunications, or the study of that use.

telephone A communications device that allows users to transmit and receive audio signals over long distances using a worldwide public circuit-switching network. Traditional telephones are connected to the largely digital network over dedicated telephone cables, often using analog technology. Cell phones, satellite phones, and VoIP phones use the same network, but connect to it using different technologies. *See also* **circuit switching.**

teletypewriter *Abbreviated* **TTY.** A device that transmits and receives typed messages over a telephone or other connection. Teletypewriters were formerly a common way to transmit text quickly over long distances. The Internet and other telecommunications technologies have made them largely obsolete, except as TDDs allowing people who are deaf or hearing-impaired to communicate over telephone lines.

television *Abbreviated* **TV.** **1.** The distribution of video content to the public or subscribers over broadcast networks. Television broadcasters, such as NBC, CBS, and ABC, use terrestrial broadcasting, while subscription-based providers use cable or satellite broadcasting. Television content is also distributed over the Internet. *See also* **cable, digital television, satellite television, terrestrial broadcasting. 2.** An electronic apparatus for displaying and playing such signals. The difference between televisions and monitors is rapidly disappearing: some displays are designed to perform both functions and some computers have television tuners. Televisions are usually larger than monitors and can receive television signals (such as over-the-air NTSC or ATSC signals) and are designed to display television formats (such as HDTV). Television sets can have an integrated screen, such as a flat-panel, direct-view, or rear-projection television, or can have a separate screen such as a projector. Television display technologies include CRT, LCD, DLP, LCoS, and plasma. *Also called* **television set. 3.** High-resolution video content, such as television shows or movies, that is distributed by special providers to the public or to subscribers. While most television providers still have scheduled programming, many make movies and television shows available for viewing at any time. Television shows can also be recorded, as on a DVR or a DVD.

television receive-only *See* **TVRO.**

TELNET **1.** A protocol that allows a computer connected to a network to act as a terminal for another computer on the network, allowing a user to log in and execute commands on a remote computer. Because TELNET does not provide encryption or authentication, it is insecure and has largely been supplanted by SSH. **2.** A client program that uses the TELNET protocol to allow users to log in and execute commands on remote computers. TELNET is available on most operating systems. *See also* **SSH.**

template **1.** A file or form that serves as the standard layout for a document, which the user may add to or modify as needed. **2.** A sheet of paper or plastic that fits over all or part of a keyboard and contains labels describing the functions of each key within a particular program.

Tenex C shell *See* **tcsh.**

tera- *Abbreviated* **T.** **1.** A prefix indicating one trillion (10^{12}), as in *terahertz.* **2.** A prefix indicating 1,099,511,627,776 (2^{40}), as in *terabyte.* This is the sense in which *tera-* is generally used in terms of data storage capacity, which, due to the binary nature of bits, is based on powers of two.

terabyte *Abbreviated* **TB.** A unit of measurement of computer memory or data storage capacity equal to 1,099,511,627,776 (2^{40}) bytes. One terabyte equals 1,024 gigabytes. Informally, the term is sometimes used to refer to one trillion (10^{12}) bytes.

terminal **1.** A device with a keyboard and a video display, through which data or information can enter or leave a computer. Personal computers running terminal emulators are commonly used as terminals for interacting with remote computers. Dumb terminals, which lack any data processing and storage capabilities of their own, are sometimes used to interact with mainframes. *Also called* **video terminal.** *See also* **diskless workstation, thin client. 2.** *See* **terminal window. 3.** An electrical component, such as a pin, a socket, or a metal screw, to which a wire or plug may be attached in order to establish an electrical connection and allow current flow.

terminal adapter *Abbreviated* **TA.** An adapter that enables a computer to connect to an ISDN communications line. The signals that are passed to and from a terminal adapter are purely digital, unlike those sent by a modem, which converts the computer's output to analog. Many terminal adapters provide a separate analog jack so that analog (voice) data can be sent through the same line, allowing users to talk on the phone and simultaneously access the Internet using a single line.

terminal emulator A program that simulates the behavior of a terminal, providing a way to interact with a computer. Terminal emulators display terminal windows, where commands can be typed and where the results of commands are displayed. Terminal emulators are often used to interact with remote computers, but on Macintosh and Linux systems, they are commonly used to interact with the local computer.

terminal window   A text window into which users type commands and in which the results of commands are displayed. Terminal windows are displayed by terminal emulators. They are often used to interact with remote computers, but on some operating systems, such as Macintosh OS X and Linux, they are commonly used to interact with the local computer. *Also called* **console, terminal.**

terrestrial broadcasting   The public distribution of radio and television programming using ground-based antennas. Terrestrial broadcasts can be received using a standard tuner and antenna. In the United States, terrestrial television is distributed using the NTSC and ATSC standards. Terrestrial radio is broadcast using the FM, AM, Digital Radio Mondiale, and HD Radio standards. *Also called* **over-the-air broadcasting.** *See also* **digital terrestrial television.**

TeX   A page description language and word processing system developed by Donald Knuth. Unlike most other word processing systems, TeX is not WYSIWYG; it involves creating a text file that contains special formatting commands. The file is displayed and printed by programs other than the one used to create it. TeX gives the user very precise control over the typesetting of a document. *See also* **LaTeX.**

text   *n.* **1.** Data in the form of words and sentences, as distinct from material such as graphics, tabular material, charts, and graphs. **2.** Data consisting of only standard ASCII characters, without formatting or any other codes.

   adj. Relating to information in the form of text. *Compare* **audiovisual.**

text-based   Relating to applications that represent, display, and allow manipulation of information using text input and output. Examples of text-based software include many interactive computer games such as role-playing games, as well as command-line interfaces. *Compare* **graphics-based.**

text box   A window or full screen in which a user interacts with a computer by typing text, as when using a command line interface at a terminal window. *See also* **terminal window.**

TextEdit   A simple text editor that is distributed with the Macintosh OS X operating system.

text editor   A program used to create and edit text files. Text editors typically do not have the text formatting capabilities that word processors have, although some have features that make it easier to create and edit files in languages that allow advanced text formatting, such as HTML and LaTeX. Advanced text editors include a range of features, such as allowing the user to search and replace text, defining keyboard macros, creating backup files, and saving files in a range of character encodings.

text file   A file that contains only characters defined in a standard character encoding and does not contain formatting codes or tags. Although text files are stored as sets of binary numbers, they are usually contrasted with binary files, such as image files or executable files, which contain non-character data. They can also be contrasted with files written in a markup language such as HTML, XML, or SGML; such files contain only characters defined in standard character encodings, but the characters are used to represent tags. Text files often have the *.txt* extension. *Compare* **binary file.**

text flow   The way text, for example, in a word processing document or a webpage, continues in different columns, text boxes, or pages. Most word processors and editors automatically manage text flow, moving text between locations when it is added or deleted. *See also* **text wrap.**

text message   *n.* An alphanumeric message sent to or from a mobile phone, computer, PDA, or two-way pager. *Also called* **SMS.**
   v. To send a text message.

text-to-speech   The automatic production of speech sounds from computer text. Text-to-speech is a form of speech synthesis in which the speech synthesis software or hardware is given computer text and generates a spoken version of the text.

text wrap   A feature in word processing software that automatically shortens, lengthens, or interrupts lines of text so that they fit around an inserted graphic. *Also called* **wraparound text.**

TFT display   *Abbreviation of* **thin film transistor display.**

theme   A software module that determines the appearance of a desktop environment or program. Operating systems usually allow users to choose between themes, and new themes can often be purchased or downloaded free from the World Wide Web. Themes are similar to skins, but usually involve controlling relatively minor aspects of an environment or program's appearance, such as icons and color schemes. *See also* **skin.**

thermal inkjet printer   An inkjet printer that ejects ink from its grid of ink nozzles using heating elements that are embedded in each nozzle. The heat creates an ink-bubble that forces the ink onto the page and, upon bursting, draws more ink into the nozzle. *Compare* **piezoelectric inkjet printer.** *See also* **inkjet printer.**

thermal printer   A printer that works by pushing heated pins against specially treated paper. The thermal paper reacts to the heat by becoming dark where the hot pins have come in contact with it; hence no ink is required for a thermal printer. Thermal printers are used in calculators, fax machines, and other devices for which it is convenient not to use ink. *See also* **printer.**

thermal wax printer   A printer that works by applying heated pins to a ribbon covered with strips of colored wax. The wax melts onto the paper and hardens, forming the image. Thermal wax printers are commonly used in industrial label printing. *See also* **printer.**

thin client   A client computer or program that relies on a server for most of its processing and storage needs. A thin client computer may be a diskless workstation. A thin client program may be one that mainly displays the results of processing by a server program.

thin film transistor display   *Abbreviated* **TFT display.**   A display using a refinement of LCD technology in which each liquid-crystal cell, or pixel, is controlled by three separate transistors, one each for red, blue, and green. Most LCD televisions and monitors have TFT displays.

third extended file system   *See* **ext3.**

third-generation   *See* **3G.**

thread   **1.** A portion of a program designed to be processed separately from the rest. For example, to ensure that a program responds quickly to user commands, a programmer might design it to have one thread that handles interactions with the user and one thread that makes calculations. The CPU can quickly switch to processing the interaction thread when user input is detected. When multiprocessing is available, different threads can be processed by different CPUs. *See also* **multithreading. 2.** A series of email, newsgroup, or bulletin board messages on a certain topic. Newsreaders and email clients usually allow users to group messages by thread.

3 : 2 pulldown   **1.** A process for converting video with a frame rate of 24 frames per second (fps), the standard for movies shot on film, to a rate of 30 fps, the predominant television standard in North America. To increase 24 fps video by six frames per second, one frame needs to be added every four frames. Because this process requires combining fields from different frames of the original video, it usually reduces the quality of the picture.

3 : 2 pulldown creates the required extra frame by taking an interlaced version of the video and duplicating two fields for every four frames. Using alternating horizontal lines of resolution, each frame of the 24 fps video is divided into two fields (a frame with half the lines of resolution), resulting in two sets of fields, one composed of the even lines of the original frames and one composed of the odd. Every fourth field of both sets is duplicated in such a way that none of the duplicated fields coincide

between the two sets and that successive frames of the original video appear alternately in two fields and three fields. Thus, if the fields in a one-second section of each set were labeled A—X according to the original frame from which they were extracted (there are 24 fields per second before duplication), one set would began A, B, B, C, D, E, F, F, G, H, and the other A, B, C, D, D, E, F, G, H, H. After the duplication, the odd and even sets of fields are merged to produce a video with 30 full-resolution frames per second. *See also* **frame rate.**

2. A feature on some television and DVD players that reverses the process of 3 : 2 pulldown.

3D 1. Relating to the modeling of three-dimensional objects, especially in order to produce realistic depictions of them in computer graphics. **2.** Relating to the reproduction of sound by surround-sound speakers according to the apparent position of the sound in an interactive virtual environment, as in computer gaming.

3G *Abbreviation of* **third-generation.** In mobile phone technology, the proposed third generation of voice and data transmission networks, allowing for the faster transmission of digital data and thus providing high-quality multimedia on mobile devices. The UMTS standard in Europe, and the cdma2000 standard in the US are considered 3G standards.

3GP A container format based on MP4 and used for storing and transmitting multimedia content on 3G mobile phones. Files of this type usually have the *.3gp* extension. *See* Table 4 at **container format.**

three-letter acronym *See* **TLA.**

three-way calling A telephone service that allows a user to initiate a conference call by adding a third participant to a call in progress.

throughput The data transfer rate, usually measured in characters or bytes per second, at which data passes through a communications channel or processing device. *See also* **bandwidth.**

thumb drive *See* **flash drive.**

thumbnail A small, low-resolution image showing the contents of a computer file, especially a graphics file. Thumbnails are often used for previewing full-size images. *See also* **greeking, preview.**

thumbstick *See* **analog stick.**

TIFF *Abbreviation of* **Tagged Image File Format.**

tile To arrange the active windows on a display screen so that they are all completely visible. Tiled windows do not overlap. Applications often have a single command or menu option for tiling windows. *Compare* **cascade.**

time code A digital signal associated with other digital signals to mark those signals along a time line. For example, a time code is generally encoded onto videotape during recording to identify each frame of elapsed tape by hour, minute, second, and frame number. Time code serves as an index that makes it easier to locate exact frames during editing and sound synchronization and to make sure that the signals are played back at the appropriate speed and in the right order.

timed backup *See* **autosave.**

Time Division Multiple Access *See* **TDMA.**

time-out The automatic cancellation of a process if the expected input is not received after a specified time. For example, when an online session times-out, the user is automatically logged off.

time-sharing The scheduling process by which an operating system allows different users of the same computer to share the CPU. Time-sharing is the most common way to create an operating system that allows multiple simultaneous users. It is used in Linux and Unix operating systems. *Compare* **multitasking.**

time-shift To record a scheduled broadcast on a DVR or VCR and watch it at another time.

tint A display setting that adjusts the color balance. At one end of the setting skin tones appear green, and at the other end they appear magenta; skin tones are often used to adjust tint. *Also called* **hue.**

tip-ring-sleeve connector *Abbreviated* **TRS connector.** *See* **jack connector.**

title bar A line at the top of a window that shows the name of the program or file in that window.

TLA *Abbreviation of* **three-letter acronym.** An acronym or initialism that consists of three letters, such as PDA, RAM, or VIN. The highly technological field of computer science lends itself to cumbersome phrases that are frequently reduced to acronyms or initialisms. Because the bulk of these consist of three letters, the term *TLA* was introduced as a jocular comment on this phenomenon. *See also* **ETLA.**

TLD *Abbreviation of* **top-level domain.**

TNC connector A threaded version of the BNC connector, used for terminating thin coaxial cables carrying microwave frequency transmissions, such as with Wi-Fi equipment.

toggle To switch from one to the other of two possible states. For example, the Insert key usually toggles between insert mode and overwrite mode.

token   **1.** A small data file passed from one computer to another in a network, especially a token-ring network, that authorizes them to communicate. **2.** A small hardware device that contains cryptographic information such as a password.

token-ring network   A type of local area network in which permission to transmit over the network is contained in a special file called a token. The basic topology of the network is the same as that of a ring network, and allows the token to be circulated continuously from one station to the next. When a station wishes to transmit, it seizes the token, marks it as busy, inserts its message together with the intended address, and sends the package back into the loop. All other stations on the network must pass the busy token along to its destination and are prohibited from transmitting any new data themselves. After the message is delivered, the token returns to the originating station, where it is once again marked as free and returned to circulation.

toner   A fine, electrically charged, powdered pigment that is fused to paper to form an image in laser printers and photocopying machines.

toolbar   A row of icons or words across the top of a window that serve as buttons to activate commands or functions.

top-level domain   *Abbreviated* **TLD.**   One of the set of the broadest domains in the hierarchy of Internet addresses. In a domain name, the name of the top-level domain appears at the very end. Each top-level domain is controlled by an organization, called a *registrar,* that charges individuals and organizations a fee to register and use names within that domain. Registrars can establish guidelines for the types or locations of individuals that can register names within a given top-level domain. For example, the *.edu* domain is operated by Educause; only accredited post-secondary institutions are allowed to register names within it. Each country has a top-level domain, such as *.de* for Germany and *.mx* for Mexico.

 Because the registrars for many domains, including many country domains as well as domains like *.com,* place no restrictions on registration, the top-level domain generally does not provide good information about the nature or location of a website.

topology   The geometric arrangement in which devices are connected to each other, such as computers in a LAN. *See also* **network topology.**

TOSLINK   A digital audio connector developed by Toshiba consisting of an optical fiber cable and a plug and socket. TOSLINK connectors are typically used in conjunction with the S/PDIF standard to transmit digital audio to and from a CD or DVD player. *See figure at* **connector.** *See* Table A on page 356.

touchpad   An input device consisting of a soft pad or flat metallic plate that is sensitive to finger pressure and movement, used especially on laptop computers as an alternative to a mouse or trackball.

touch screen   An input technology consisting of a pressure-sensitive transparent panel mounted over a display. Every point on the panel corresponds to the position on the screen directly underneath it, and touching the panel, as with the fingertip or a stylus, not only issues a command but also designates a position. Thus, touch screens do not require an onscreen pointer like other input devices. Touch screens are commonly found on PDAs and other handhelds. *Also called* **touch-sensitive display.**

tower   A rectangular computer case that is designed to stand upright, often on the floor, with components, such as the power supply and storage devices, stacked on top of each other. *Compare* **desktop.** *See also* **full-tower, midtower, minitower.**

TPI   *Abbreviation of* **tracks per inch.**   A measure of the storage density of magnetic disks. TPI represents the number of concentric tracks per inch on the radius of the disk. While 3.5-inch floppy disks have 135 TPI, hard disks have tens of thousands. *Also called* **track density.** *See also* **areal density.**

track   **1.** One of the series of concentric rings that form the separate data storage areas on a floppy, optical, or hard disk. Tracks are created in the process of formatting a disk, and data is read from or written to the tracks as they pass in a fixed path under the read or write head. *See also* **cylinder.** *See figure at* **sector. 2.** A file or set of files that constitutes one channel of audio or video data.

trackball   An input device consisting of a ball that is rotated with the fingers or palm to control a pointer on a display. Unlike a mouse, the ball is mounted on top of a stationary housing, which typically contains one or more buttons.

track density   *See* **TPI.**

track sector   *See* **sector** (sense 1).

tracks per inch   *See* **TPI.**

tractor feed   A mechanism for advancing continuous-form paper through a printer by means of two pin-studded rotating belts. The pins catch matching perforations along the edges of the paper. Many early printers had tractor feeds, but they are much less common now. *Also called* **pin feed.** *Compare* **friction feed.** *See also* **paper feed.**

transaction processing   Processing that controls how data is entered into a database or updated in a storage location, generally used with database applications. Transaction processing is used to ensure database integrity even in the event of catastrophic failure such as a drive crash or power failure.

transceiver   A device that can both transmit and receive radio signals, either by antenna or through a wire. Cell phones, for example, contain transceivers that transmit and receive radio signals by antenna. Most network interface cards contain transceivers that transmit and receive radio signals through Ethernet cable.

transducer   A substance or device, such as a piezoelectric crystal, microphone, or photoelectric cell, that converts input energy of one form into output energy of another. Transducers are commonly used to transform sound vibrations into electrical signals.

Transfer Control Protocol/Internet Protocol   *See* **TCP/IP.**

transfer rate   *See* **data transfer rate.**

transformer   An electrical device that converts an electrical signal from one voltage to another. Transformers are commonly used to convert the voltage of household electrical outlets (around 120 volts in the US) to the lower voltage levels used in electronic and other devices. Transformers are capable of converting the voltage of alternating currents; they cannot be used to convert the voltage of a steady source of direct current, such as a battery.

transistor   An electronic component made of semiconductors, typically having three electrical contacts. The strength of an electrical signal at one of these contacts controls the voltage across, or current flow thorough, the other two contacts, in the manner of a faucet regulating the pressure or flow of a liquid. Transistors are used to amplify electrical signals such as audio signals and are also used as switches in the design of logic gates and memory circuits found on chips.

Transmission Control Protocol or **Transfer Control Protocol**   *See* **TCP.**

trap and trace device   A device that records information identifying the origin of incoming electronic messages, such as a device that records the phone numbers from which incoming calls originate or one that records the network addresses from which incoming messages are transmitted. Trap and trace devices are used to monitor communications, but do not record the contents of messages. *See also* **pen register.**

trash   A folder in Macintosh operating systems where deleted files are held until the user either restores or expunges them. This folder is represented on the desktop by an icon of a trash can. *See also* **recycle bin.**

tree structure   A hierarchical structure for classifying and organizing data in which every item is arranged in a unique position beneath a unique root. Such a structure may be represented graphically in the manner of an inverted tree, with a *root node* at the top branching out into other nodes, often called *subnodes,* which the root node contains, or *dominates.* A subnode may in turn branch off into its own subnodes. Nodes that do not branch and contain no subnodes are called *terminal nodes.* A node may also be referred to as the *child* or *daughter* of the node containing it, which in turn may be called its *parent.* No node in a tree structure may have more than one parent node.

Tree structures are often used in computing as a way of organizing directories and the files they contain. The root node typically represents a storage device, such as a disk, while the directories and files the disk contains are subnodes. Files and applications are terminal nodes, while directories are nodes that may themselves have subnodes—files, further directories, or both. *See also* **filename, folder, pathname.**

tri-band phone A cellular phone that transmits at three different frequency bands. Most tri-band phones use 900 MHz, 1800 MHz, and 1900 MHz. The 900-MHz and 1800-MHz bands are both used outside the Americas. The 800-MHz band sometimes replaces the 900-MHz or 1800-MHz band on tri-band phones sold in the US.

trn A newsreader for reading Usenet newsgroups on Unix or Linux platforms. Trn was one of the first newsreaders to allows users to read posts in the order that they appear in a thread.

Trojan horse A computer program in which malicious code is hidden within an apparently benign application such as a utility or a game. A Trojan horse differs from a virus in that the damaging code is unable to replicate itself and spread to other programs. *See also* **spyware, worm.**

TRS *Abbreviation of* **telecommunications relay service.**

TRS connector *Abbreviation of* **tip-ring-sleeve connector.** *See* **jack connector.**

TRUE One of two values used in logic gates, equivalent to the binary value one. *Compare* **FALSE.** *See* Table E on page 361.

True Color A format for encoding color with a bit depth of 24 bits per pixel and a color depth of around 16.7 million (2^{24}) distinct colors.

truetone A polyphonic ring tone that is an accurate reproduction of a piece of music rather than a simplified version with fewer tones.

TrueType A standard format developed by Apple Computer for creating outline fonts. TrueType fonts are commonly used on Macintosh and Windows operating systems.

TSV *Abbreviation of* **tab-separated values.** A file format for storing tables in which each line of the file represents a row of a table and columns of data are separated by tabs. TSV files contain only character data. They often have the file extension *.tsv. See also* **tab-delimited.**

TTY **1.** *Abbreviation of* **teletypewriter. 2.** In a Linux or Unix operating system, a serial connection, typically one connecting a terminal to the computer.

tuner A device that receives television or radio signals, especially an electronic circuit or device used to select signals at a specific radio frequency for amplification and conversion to sound or images. A tuner can be located inside a television, radio, set-top box, or computer, or it can be a separate component. A digital or HDTV tuner is required to receive digital terrestrial television. *See also* **set-top box.**

turnkey Relating to computer systems or applications assembled and delivered to customers ready to use. A turnkey system includes all necessary hardware or software and requires very little, if any, work to configure.

tutorial A program that instructs the user of a system or software package by simulating the capabilities of the system or software or by guiding the user through actual use of the software. Most large commercial applications provide tutorials that usually consist of a series of short, graduated lessons demonstrating how to use the features of the program.

TV *Abbreviation of* **television.**

TVRO *Abbreviation of* **television receive-only.** Satellite television or radio transmission in which a standard satellite receiver and a large moveable satellite dish, usually six to ten feet in diameter, are used to receive or intercept signals from different satellites. While TVRO users have access to many free channels and unedited feeds, some channels are encrypted and require the user to purchase an access code to unscramble the signal. *Compare* **DBS.**

tween To create the successive steps that occur as one shape is transformed into another when creating an animation in a graphics program.

tweeter A small speaker that produces high-pitched sounds, typically in the range of 5,000 to 20,000 hertz. Tweeters can be located on a separate speaker cabinet or combined with mid-range speakers or woofers. *See also* **speaker.**

twisted-pair cable A cable consisting of two strands of thin, insulated copper wire twisted around each other in a regular spiral pattern. One wire carries the signal, and the other wire is grounded. Twisted-pair cables are often used for data transmission in telephone communications and in networking. They typically use a registered jack connector. *See* Table C on page 358.

2D **1.** Relating to the coding or rendering of images in two dimensions. **2.** Relating to the reproduction of sound without regard to the user's position in an interactive virtual environment, as in computer gaming. 2D sound is not dependent upon the user's position in a virtual space. 2D audio may be surround sound, but the way it is played back is not affected by the actions of the user.

2G *Abbreviation of* **second-generation.** In mobile phone technology, the second generation of voice and data transmission networks. These networks use digital protocols such as GSM, CDMA, TDMA, or iDEN as replacements for first-generation analog protocols. *Compare* **3G.**

two-way radio A device that can both transmit and receive audio signals using radio waves. Walkie-talkies are one kind of two-way radio.

.txt An extension commonly used for text files.

type To enter text by pressing keys on a keyboard or touching a screen.

typeface The design of a set of printed letters. The typeface specifies the exact shape of each letter and character. Some traditional typefaces are Courier, Helvetica, Times Roman, and Times New Roman. Typefaces that have the same shapes but differ in obliqueness (e.g., italic) and weight (bold, semibold, lightface, etc.) are grouped into font families. The two broad categories of typefaces are serif and sans serif. Most word processing and desktop publishing programs feature a large inventory of typefaces, and when used in conjunction with a good printer, output can match that of professionally printed documents. Additionally, with the appropriate software, users can create new typefaces or modify existing ones.

typeover mode *See* **overwrite mode.**

typesetter *See* **imagesetter.**

UART *Abbreviation of* **universal asynchronous receiver-transmitter.** A computer component, typically a microchip, that controls certain kinds of serial communication, such as between the computer and other devices connected to it. Data in a computer is generally handled in chunks that are transmitted in parallel each on a separate circuit path; the UART converts data sent as one serial signal to and from a parallel form. Some internal modems also have UARTs. The maximum speed of data transmission to and from any personal computer is delimited by the speed of its UART; thus a very fast modem cannot operate at full speed if that speed exceeds the capacity of the UART to process the information. UART is pronounced YOU-art.

UCS *Abbreviation of* **universal character set.**

UCS-2 *See* **UTF-16.**

UCS-4 *See* **UTF-32.**

UDMA *Abbreviation of* **Ultra DMA.**

UDP *Abbreviation of* **user datagram protocol.** A network protocol that specifies a way to break data into packets so it can be sent over the Internet to another computer. UDP is generally used with IP, which is responsible for routing packets to their destination. UDP is similar to TCP, but does not provide any way to ensure that all packets arrive and are assembled in the correct order. Because it is faster than TCP, UDP is used for applications in which the speed of data transmission is important, such as VoIP and online games.

UHF *Abbreviation for* **ultra high frequency.**

Ultra ATA *See* **Ultra DMA.**

Ultra DMA *Abbreviated* **UDMA.** Any of various versions of the IDE standard that allow data to be transferred between the main memory and the disk drive without involving the CPU. *Also called* **DMA, Ultra ATA.** *See also* **IDE.**

Ultra Extended Graphics Array *See* **UXGA.**

ultra high frequency *Abbreviated* **UHF.** A band of radio frequencies from 300 to 3,000 megahertz. UHF includes television channels 14 through 83.

UMTS *Abbreviation of* **Universal Mobile Telecommunications System.** A W-CDMA standard for digital mobile communication, which allows for data transmission speeds of up to 2 Mbps. Considered a 3G standard, UMTS is an incompatible competitor with cdma2000 and is licensed by the European Telecommunications Standards Institute. *See also* **W-CDMA.**

unbalanced cable A cable that transmits signals using two separate conductors. One conductor carries the signal and the other serves as the ground. Unbalanced cables are used in consumer audio and video equipment but are avoided in professional settings in which long cables must be used, as they are susceptible to interference from external signals. *Compare* **balanced cable.**

uncompress *v.* To restore a compressed file to its original state. *Also called* **decompress, unpack.**

n. A program available on Linux and Unix operating systems that restores files that have been compressed by means of the compress program.

undelete To restore information such as text or graphics to a document, or a file to a directory, after it has been deleted. When files are deleted from a file system, the file's data stays on the disk until the disk space is used by another file. Utility programs can often undelete such files. *See also* **recycle bin, undo.**

underclock To set the clock speed of a computer component, such as a CPU or memory module, to a lower speed than that set at the factory. CPUs are often underclocked in order to reduce power consumption and heat production. Many laptops come with features that automatically underclock the CPU when the processing load is light or when operating on battery power. *See also* **clock speed.**

underflow error An error that arises when a computed quantity is a smaller number than the floating point unit is capable of representing. Underflow errors typically occur when dividing a very small number by a very large number.

underscan The process of displaying a video image at a slightly smaller size than the display screen. Many displays and DVD players have an underscan feature, which allows the viewer to recover overscan, a portion of the image not normally seen.

underscore **1.** A straight line that is placed under other characters in text, usually for emphasis. This sentence is written with an underscore under it. **2.** The character (_); it is often used to create text strings containing multiple words, as in *average_length*.

undo A command in many programs that allows the user to reverse the action of the last command executed and return to a previous state.

Unicode A standard for digitally encoding text characters so that they can be stored and transmitted by computers. The Unicode standard assigns almost all known characters, including the letters of most written languages, a code number and a name. It provides three separate standards, UTF-8, UTF-16, and UTF-32, for encoding character code numbers as sequences of bits in digital files. *See also* **character encoding.** *See* Table 8.

Unicode transformation format *See* **UTF.**

Table 8   Selected Unicode Characters

Character	Unicode Number	Description
s	0073	Latin letter
c	0441	Cyrillic letter
š	0161	Latin letter with caron
洒	6D12	Chinese character
س	0633	Arabic letter
ש	05E9	Hebrew letter
さ	3055	Hiragana letter
ϡ	03E1	Greek letter sampi (archaic Greek; used in mathematics)
σ	03C3	Greek lowercase sigma
Σ	03A3	Greek uppercase sigma
∑	2211	mathematical symbol for summation
♄	2644	symbol for Saturn
€	20AC	symbol for euro currency
⌦	2326	symbol for erase to the right
☺	263A	smiley face

Uniform Resource Identifier   *See* **URI.**

Uniform Resource Locator   *See* **URL.**

Uniform Resource Name   *See* **URN.**

uninstall   To remove the software associated with a program completely from a computer. Much software consists of a set of separate programs that can be hard to track down, since they are placed in a variety of parts of the computer's file structure; thus software is best uninstalled using a utility program called an *uninstaller,* which finds and removes all the component programs.

uninterruptible power supply   *See* **UPS.**

universal character set   *Abbreviated* **UCS.**   The set of characters defined in ISO 10646 and used in the Unicode standard for encoding characters in digital files. It contains the characters used in printing most written languages.

Universal Mobile Telecommunications System   *See* **UMTS.**

327

universal remote control   A programmable remote control that can operate multiple devices, such as a television, DVD player, and audio receiver.

Universal Resource Locator   *See* **URL.**

Universal Serial Bus   *See* **USB.**

Unix or **UNIX**   A proprietary operating system that allows multiple simultaneous users. Unix was originally invented in 1969 at AT&T Bell Labs.
When it was later implemented in the C programming language, it
became the first operating system that could be easily adapted for use on
any computer. There are several varieties (often called *flavors*) of Unix,
among them versions developed at the University of California at Berkeley from 1979 on, and AT&T's own later version, System V. The name *Unix*
is now a trademark of the Open Group, which developed the Single Unix
Specification. The open-source Linux operating systems were based on
Unix but are not certified as conforming to the Single Unix Specification.
  Unix has long been favored in technical, scientific, and educational
circles for its flexibility, power, security, and networking capabilities. In
recent years, improvements in graphical user interfaces have made Unix
much easier to use. *See also* **POSIX.**

Unix to Unix copy   *See* **UUCP.**

unpack   *See* **uncompress.**

unzip   **1.** To retrieve files from a zip-format archive by using a program
such as WinZip, PKZIP, or unzip. **2.** A program commonly used on Linux
and Unix systems to retrieve files from zip archives. *See also* **zip.**

up   Functioning or in operation, especially after being set up for the first
time or after a period of not functioning. Used especially of computers,
servers, networks, or connections. *Compare* **down.**

Up-arrow key   A key used to move the cursor up one line of text, or to
scroll down the contents of a window so that the lower portions of its
contents come into view. *Compare* **Down-arrow key.**

upconversion   The process of increasing the apparent resolution of an
image by inserting additional visual data extrapolated from the existing
pixels. Upconversion is applied in such tasks as upgrading SDTV signals
for broadcast on HDTV televisions. *See also* **interpolation, upsampling.**

upgrade   To replace a software or hardware product with a more recently
released version or one that provides better performance.

upload   To transfer a copy of a file from a local computer or other device
to a central computer or host. For example, files can be uploaded from a
computer to a website or a network file server, or from a handheld device
to a desktop computer. *See also* **download.**

uppercase   Relating to or being a capital letter. *See also* **case-sensitive.**

upper memory area   In PC-compatible computers, the 384 kilobytes of memory addresses between conventional memory and extended memory. Upper memory addresses are used for BIOS data and video memory. BIOS data and video memory are not physically stored in main memory. Nevertheless, the addresses in the upper memory area are reserved for these purposes and often can't be used for anything else.

UPS   *Abbreviation of* **uninterruptible power supply.**   A power supply containing a rechargeable battery source that will maintain a constant supply of power to a computer or other electronic system in case electrical power fluctuates or fails. A UPS can prevent accidental shutdown or data loss.

upsampling   The process of increasing the sampling rate of a digital signal by inserting zero-valued samples in between the signal's original samples. Upsampling is applied in such tasks as magnifying pixelated digital images, since more pixels are being used to display the same image. Interpolation of the values of the zero-valued signals is generally required to remove unwanted spectral images, or in the case of audio signals, to prevent distortion. *Compare* **downsampling.**

upward compatible   Relating to technology that is compatible with later versions that have been modified or improved. For example, software that runs on PC-compatibles based on the Intel 80486 microprocessor will also run on later models based on the Pentium series; this software is thus upward compatible. Software developers strive for upward compatibility because it enables users to upgrade their computer systems without the expense of replacing software and data. New systems can become technologically advanced, however, to the point that the upward compatibility of older versions must be sacrificed. *Also called* **forward compatible.** *See also* **backward compatible, compatible.**

URI   *Abbreviation of* **Uniform Resource Identifier.**   An identifier for some resource available on the Internet, such as a webpage, digital document, or application. URLs and URNs are the two types of URIs.

URL   *Abbreviation of* **Uniform Resource Locator** or **Universal Resource Locator.**   An identifier of a resource available on the Internet, such as a webpage. URLs are made up of an address on the Internet with a prefix indicating the protocol that should be used to access that location. For example, *http://www.whitehouse.gov* is a URL for a resource located at the domain name *www.whitehouse.gov*. The prefix *http* indicates that the resource can be accessed with the HTTP protocol, meaning it is a webpage. URLs can be used for many other protocols, such as FTP or Telnet.

URN *Abbreviation of* **Uniform Resource Name.** An identifier for resources available on the Internet. URNs are designed to refer to a digital resource, such as an online journal, in a way that is independent of its location. One important type of URN is based on the International Standard Serial Number, which identifies periodicals. The locations of resources identified with URNs must be maintained in a central registry, which can then be used to locate the resource. Such registries are not yet widely available, so URNs are not widely used.

.us A top-level domain operated by the US Department of Commerce, which registers domain names for US city and state governments, citizens, businesses and other organizations. Until 2002, only city and state governments were allowed domain names in the *.us* top-level domain.

us or **usec** *Abbreviations of* **microsecond.** The letter *u* is used in some abbreviations (such as *us* and *usec*) to represent the Greek letter mu (μ). In this way, the *m* of the prefix *micro-* (abbreviated as *u*) is distinguished from the *m* of the prefix *milli-* (abbreviated as *m*). When Greek characters are available, the abbreviation may be styled as μs or μsec.

USB *Abbreviation of* **Universal Serial Bus.** A serial bus standard used for transferring data to and from digital devices. USB version 1.0 has a data transfer rate of up to 12 Mbps, but it can also support slower devices, such as mice and keyboards, which transfer data at 1.5 Mbps. The faster USB 2.0 standard has a maximum transfer rate of 480 Mbps, which is comparable to that of the IEEE 1394 standard. USB devices such as mice and flash drives are often powered by their USB connection. Computers typically have a rectangular Type A socket, while peripheral devices, if they have a detachable cord, have a square Type B socket. Thus, USB cords that are not permanently attached to a peripheral device usually end in two different types of plugs. *See figure at* **connector.** *See* Table C on page 358.

USB flash drive *See* **flash drive.**

USB key *See* **flash drive.**

Usenet A worldwide public network on the Internet that can be accessed with a newsreader. The material on Usenet consists of a large number of newsgroups on various topics. A user can follow a thread by reading a sequence of messages posted on a single topic, or respond to a message through a newsgroup or one-on-one through email.

user account A set of files that allow a user to log in and use a computer system. Each user account on a system has a unique username and contains a password, a set of configuration files, and a set of permissions. User accounts often include a home directory. They are usually associated with individual users, though sometimes more than one user has access to a given user account, and a user may have access to more than one user account.

user datagram protocol *See* **UDP.**

user-friendly Easy to use or learn to use.

user group or **users' group** A group of people who share a common interest in a particular topic that relates to computers or computer programming. Many have online discussion forums such as Usenet newsgroups or message boards where pertinent information is regularly discussed. Some have developed into large organizations which hold conventions or seminars.

user ID *See* **username.**

user interface An interface, such as a GUI or a terminal window on a computer screen, or pushbuttons and display lights on a printer, permitting communication or interaction between a computer or other device and a person using it.

username An alphanumeric string used to identify users of a computer system, network, or device, especially when logging on. Usernames often have associated passwords. *Also called* **account ID, account name, login, login name, user ID.** *See also* **PIN.**

UTF *Abbreviation of* **Unicode transformation format.** One of the standards used to translate Unicode character codes into bit sequences.

UTF-8 A standard for encoding characters in digital files, UTF-8 specifies a mapping from Unicode character code numbers to eight-bit bytes. It is a variable-length encoding scheme, meaning that some characters take up more than one byte.

UTF-16 A standard for encoding characters in digital files. UTF-16 specifies a mapping from Unicode character code numbers to sequences of 16 bits. It is a variable-length encoding scheme, meaning that some characters take up more than one 16-bit sequence. *Also called* **UCS-2.**

UTF-32 A standard for encoding characters in digital files. UTF-32 specifies a mapping from Unicode character code numbers to sequences of 32 bits. *Also called* **UCS-4.**

utility A program that performs a specific task related to the management of computer functions, resources, or files. Utility programs range from the simple to the sophisticated, and many programmers specialize in producing and distributing them as shareware. There are utilities that perform file and directory management, data compression, disk defragmentation and repair, system diagnostics, and system security, for example. Many operating systems incorporate such popular utility functions as undeleting, password protection, uninstalling, memory management, virus protection, and file compression.

.uu   An extension commonly used for uuencoded files.

UUCP   *Abbreviation of* **Unix to Unix copy.**   A protocol used on Linux and Unix operating systems for transmitting data over temporary phone line connections, allowing email and file transfer. While these functions are now usually provided by Internet protocols, UUCP is still in use for computers that do not have permanent Internet connections.

uudecode   *n.* A program for converting uuencoded data back to binary form. *Uudecode* is pronounced yoo-yoo-dee-KODE.

v. To convert ASCII text in uuencode format back into binary data. *See also* **uuencode.**

.uue   An extension commonly used for uuencoded files.

uuencode   *n.* A file format that encodes binary data as ASCII text, as for including graphics or other binary files in email or newsgroup messages. Uuencode, pronounced yoo-yoo-en-KODE, was designed to be used with UUCP. Uuencoded files often have *.uu* or *.uue* file extensions.

v. To encode binary data as ASCII text in this format. *See also* **base64, BinHex, uudecode, yEnc.**

UXGA   *Abbreviation of* **Ultra Extended Graphics Array.**   A standard of video resolution that supports a maximum of 1600 horizontal by 1200 vertical pixels. *See* Table B on page 357.

V   *Abbreviation of* **volt.**

vaporware   Software that has been announced or marketed but has not yet been delivered to a customer, especially software that seems unlikely ever to be produced.

variable bit rate or **variable bitrate**   *Abbreviated* **VBR.**   A method of encoding data, especially audio or video, so that the rate at which it is transmitted automatically adjusts itself according to the varying levels of the data. For example, in an audio file, areas of silence require a lower bit rate than areas of full sound. *Compare* **constant bit rate.**

VBR   *Abbreviation of* **variable bit rate.**

VBScript   A scripting language developed by Microsoft resembling Visual Basic and similar in function to JavaScript. VBScript can be used with Microsoft Internet Explorer and Microsoft web servers.

VCD   *Abbreviation of* **video compact disk.**   A format for storing video and audio content on compact disk. Because they use the older MPEG-1 compression format, VCDs have lower resolution than DVDs and can only store up to 74 minutes of VHS-quality video on a single disk. They are playable on most DVD players and computers that have set-top boxes.

V-Chip   A television filter used to censor television content. V-Chips interpret the FCC content ratings that are sent along with television broadcasts and can be set to block shows and movies with ratings that exceed a specified level.

VCR   *Abbreviation of* **videocassette recorder.**   A device for recording and playing back video images and sound on a videocassette. Most VCRs use the VHS format and are compatible with one of the major television standards (NTSC in North America). VCRs have three different recording speeds, designated SP, LP, and EP. When recording an NTSC signal on a standard videocassette, SP produces a two-hour recording, LP a four-hour recording, and EP a six-hour recording. Four-head VCRs have a separate head for recording and playing back in both SP and EP modes.

VDT   *Abbreviation of* **video display terminal.**   *See* **monitor.**

VDT radiation   The electromagnetic radiation emitted by video display terminals. Studies have shown that exposure to these emissions may have harmful effects on users' health, but other studies have reached contradictory conclusions.

vector   An array of only one dimension.

vector font   *See* **outline font.**

vector graphics   Graphics that use mathematical descriptions to represent images, allowing the images to be resized or otherwise modified without reducing their quality. The mathematical descriptions are ultimately converted into bitmapped representations for printing or display. For example, the shape of an airplane may be represented as a set of lines and surfaces at some position in space; movement of the airplane would then involve changing the mathematical representation of its position, and the airplane would appear to move as changing bitmapped representations of it appeared on a monitor. *Also called* **object-oriented graphics.** *Compare* **bitmapped graphics.** *See also* **graphics card.**

Veronica *Abbreviation of* **Very Easy Rodent-Oriented Netwide Index to Computerized Archives.** A search engine used to find files on gopher servers.

vertical justification In word processing, the automatic alignment of columns so that they end evenly at the bottom margin.

Very Fast Infrared *See* **VFIR.**

very high frequency *Abbreviated* **VHF.** A band of radio frequencies from 30 to 300 megahertz. VHF includes television channels 2 through 13.

VESA *Abbreviation of* **Video Electronics Standards Association.** An international professional organization of personal computer manufacturers, dedicated to the establishment and improvement of industry standards for graphics and multimedia in PC-compatible computers. Standards introduced by VESA include VGA and SVGA. VESA is pronounced VEE-suh.

VFIR *Abbreviation of* **Very Fast Infrared.** An IrDA protocol for infrared data transmission at rates of up to 16 Mbps.

VGA *Abbreviation of* **Video Graphics Array.** The graphics display system introduced by IBM in 1987 that was an industry standard for IBM PC and PC-compatible computers. VGA works with an analog monitor and offers a palette of 16 to 256 continuously variable colors. When displaying text, VGA has a resolution of 720 pixels across by 400 down. When displaying graphics and using 16 colors, VGA has a resolution of 640 pixels across by 480 down. VGA is compatible with all earlier IBM graphics display systems. Higher resolution interfaces have replaced VGA for desktop usage. However, VGA is still used as a minimum graphics standard for the configuration of new systems and in instances where integration problems prevent display at higher resolutions. *See* Table B on page 357.

VGA connector A video connector used to connect a VGA, SVGA, or XGA monitor to a computer. VGA connectors have a 15-pin D-subminiature (DE-15) plug and socket. *See* Table A on page 356.

VHF *Abbreviation of* **very high frequency.**

VHS *Abbreviation of* **Video Home System.** A common analog videotape format that stores up to 240 lines of horizontal resolution. VHS tapes have a 1/2-inch magnetic tape and a large 7 3/8 × 4 1/16 cassette. Video can be recorded on VHS tapes in any of the standard analog television formats including NTSC, PAL, and SECAM and played back on a compatible VCR. NTSC, which is the predominant standard in North America, allows approximately 480 lines of vertical resolution. *See also* **D-VHS, S-VHS.**

video **1.** A signal carrying images, including still images and moving pictures. **2.** A sequence of recorded images that are electronically displayed with sufficient rapidity as to create the illusion of motion and continuity. *See also* **frame. 3.** A video recording and its soundtrack.

video accelerator   *See* **graphics accelerator.**

video adapter   *See* **graphics card.**

video camera   A camera that captures moving images and converts them into electronic signals so that they can be saved on a storage device, such as a videotape or hard drive, or viewed on a monitor. *See also* **camcorder.**

video capture card   *See* **capture card.**

video card   *See* **graphics card.**

videocassette   A cassette containing blank or prerecorded videotape.

videocassette recorder   *See* **VCR.**

video compact disk   *See* **VCD.**

video display terminal   *Abbreviated* **VDT.**   *See* **monitor.**

video game   **1.** An electronic game played by manipulating images on a display. **2.** An electronic game, usually stored on a disk or cartridge, that is designed for play on a specific video game console or handheld device. *Also called* **console game.** *Compare* **computer game.**

video game console   A computer designed to play a specific format of video games using an external display. Video game consoles are operated with a controller. Most modern consoles can play CDs and DVDs in addition to video games.

Video Graphics Array   *See* **VGA.**

Video Home System   *See* **VHS.**

video memory   *See* **VRAM.**

video object   *See* **VOB.**

video on demand   *Abbreviated* **VOD** or **VoD.**   A subscription or pay-per-view television service in which television shows or movies are made available to customers for viewing at any time.

videophone   Any of various devices that transmit both audio and video data so users can see each other when speaking. Videophones can use ordinary phone lines as well as Internet connections.

video RAM   *See* **VRAM.**

video relay service   *Abbreviated* **VRS.**   A service that allows people who are hearing-impaired or speech-impaired to place calls and communicate via American Sign Language or some other visual mode of communication. Users of video relay services make a connection to an operator using a

335

videophone or a computer with a video camera. They sign messages to the operator, who relays them in spoken form to a third party. The operator also uses sign language to relay spoken messages from the third party to the user.

videotape   **1.** A relatively wide magnetic tape for recording and playing back or broadcasting visual images and associated sound. *Also called* **tape. 2.** *See* **videocassette.**

video terminal   *See* **terminal** (sense 1).

VIDEO_TS   A folder in the directory of a DVD where files in the DVD-Video format are stored.

viewable image size   *Abbreviated* **VIS.**   A measure of the size of a display screen that includes only the area of the screen that is not covered by the frame or bezel. Viewable image size is measured diagonally across the screen from corner to corner.

viewing angle   **1.** The maximum angle between positions from which a display screen can be viewed without unacceptable distortion. CRTs have very wide viewing angles, but other types of displays, such as LCDs, have narrower viewing angles.

Viewing angle is difficult to use as a standard of comparison among display screens because manufacturers usually demarcate unacceptable distortion in terms of contrast ratios; as long as the ratio is high enough, the level of distortion is considered acceptable, but the level considered acceptable often varies. For example, one manufacturer may advertise a viewing angle of 90 degrees at a contrast ratio of 100 : 1 for an LCD panel, while another may claim a viewing angle of 140 degrees at a contrast ratio of 10 : 1 for a very similar panel, thus making it difficult to determine which panel provides a better picture.

2. The angle from which a screen is viewed, measured against an imaginary line perpendicular to the screen.

3. The angle formed by imaginary lines from the corners of a display screen to a viewer at the vertex of the angle. This angle widens as the viewer approaches a point at the middle of the screen and narrows when the viewer moves back from the screen or toward the sides.

Viiv   One of several combinations of a chipset, a network card, and a CPU, sold by Intel for multimedia computing. Viiv is designed to allow users to view and hear DRM-protected content.

virtual   **1.** Capable of functioning or being used as, but not constituting, the physical object or entity represented. For example, virtual memory is memory that a microprocessor can use, but it doesn't correspond to actual chips in RAM. **2.** Existing in the form of, or by making use of, digital media. For example, groups of people who do not live near each other but who share a common interest or concern and keep in contact by means of the web can be said to be a virtual community. **3.** Relating to or existing in virtual reality.

virtual address A number identifying the location of data stored in a computer's virtual memory. The operating system must map the virtual address onto an address in a physical storage device (such as a hard disk drive) in order to access the necessary data and transfer it to RAM. *Compare* **physical address.**

virtual disk *See* **RAM disk.**

virtual machine **1.** An interpreter that executes programs written in bytecode. Because bytecode shares some features with machine languages, and CPUs execute machine language, virtual machines are thought of as emulating CPUs. **2.** A program that emulates a particular CPU architecture by executing the machine language designed for that CPU. Virtual machines allow programs compiled for one architecture, such as x86, to run on another, such as the Macintosh PowerPC architecture. They also allow more than one operating system to run on a single CPU.

virtual memory A way of organizing computer memory so that applications may act as if more RAM were available than is actually available on the physical memory on RAM chips. To create virtual memory, the operating system keeps track of which parts of a program or data are in active use and loads only those parts into RAM, swapping them for other parts only if necessary. This means that large programs or files do not need to be completely loaded into RAM in order to be used, allowing multiple programs to run or very large programs to be in use at the same time, just as if there were more RAM available.

Since creating virtual memory requires the operating system to read and write from the hard disk more often, it can reduce the performance of the computer. If too many programs are active at once, or if a program is structured in such a way that many different parts of it must be active one after another, the operating system may spend so much time swapping programs and data back and forth from RAM to disk that the programs run sluggishly.

Since the operating system copies program pieces into arbitrary places in memory and may even move them about to make room for others, the addresses in virtual memory that the program references do not correspond to actual bytes in physical RAM. These virtual addresses are converted into physical addresses by the operating system, usually with the help of special tables in the CPU. *See also* **demand paging, paging, prepaging, swap space.**

virtual private network   *Abbreviated* **VPN.**   An encrypted communication channel between two computers that are connected to a public network. Virtual private networks allow users to transmit private data securely over the Internet, and are often used to access an organization's intranet from a remote location. In order to establish a virtual private network, a computer running client software contacts a computer running host software and requests a connection.

virtual reality   *Abbreviated* **VR.**   A technology that simulates reality by using three-dimensional graphics and such input/output devices as gloves that transmit information about the position of the user's hands and fingers, goggles that use a small display screen for each eye to provide a stereoscopic view of the virtual world, and headphones. One use of virtual reality systems is in training; for example, pilots train with virtual reality systems that imitate flight conditions and respond to input as an actual airplane might.

Virtual Reality Modeling Language   *See* **VRML.**

virus   A program or series of commands that can replicate itself and spreads by inserting copies of itself into other files or programs which users later transfer to other computers. Viruses can be damaging, but the amount of damage varies; viruses may erase all the data on a disk or do nothing but reproduce themselves. They may be in a system for a long time before they cause any damage. There are many antivirus programs now available to identify and remove viruses. *Compare* **worm.** *See also* **Trojan horse.**

VIS   *Abbreviation of* **viewable image size.**

Visual Basic   A programming language developed by Microsoft Corporation. It is widely used for creating Windows applications, since it provides extensive tools for creating GUIs. It is often used as an interpreted language, but it can also be compiled to create executable programs. A major change to Visual Basic was made in 2002, and applications written with versions released since that time are not compatible with earlier versions.

vlog   *Abbreviation of* **video blog.**   A blog that makes primary use of video content, typically accompanied by text annotations for the video provided.

VOB   *Abbreviation of* **video object.**   A container format used in DVDs for storing MPEG-2 video and audio, subtitles, menu, and navigation data in stream form. Files of this type usually have the extension *.vob* or *.mpg*.

VOD or **VoD**   *Abbreviations of* **video on demand.**

voice-activated   Relating to systems, devices, or modes of operation in which speech can be used to control how a device functions. For example, voice-activated mode in audio recorders is a mode in which recording begins when an audio signal is detected, and a voice-activated television remote allows users to control a television set with voice commands. *See also* **speech recognition.**

voice mail   1. Any of various systems for answering telephone calls and recording and saving messages. Some computer voice mail systems can also route and record calls, relay messages, page users, or convert messages to text for transmission as an email or SMS. **2.** A recorded message left by a caller on a voice mail system or answering machine.

voice over IP   *Abbreviated* **VoIP.** A method for routing telephone calls over the Internet that involves digitizing audio data and splitting it into packets. It includes a means for connecting to the public telephone network; thus, a voice over IP call can be placed to or from devices connected to the Internet, such as computers or specially designed phones, as well as phones connected to the public telephone network, such as traditional phones or cell phones.

voice recognition   *See* **speech recognition.**

VoIP   *Abbreviation of* **voice over IP.**

volatile memory   Memory that loses its data when the power is turned off or disconnected. For example, the DRAM usually used for a computer's main memory is volatile memory, in contrast to a hard disk, which is non-volatile memory.

volt   *Abbreviated* **V.**   The International System unit of electric potential and electromotive force, equal to the difference of electric potential between two points on a conducting wire carrying a constant current of one ampere when the power dissipated between the points is one watt.

The notion of a volt is a relational one; voltage is always measured between two points, especially two points in a circuit. There can be a difference of many volts between two points, yet no current flow, as between the empty sockets of a two-prong electrical outlet that is not in use.

voltage depression   A reduction in the amount of time a rechargable battery can maintain its peak voltage. Normally, a fully charged battery drops in voltage very gradually until it is almost out of energy and needs to be recharged. With voltage depression, the amount of voltage supplied drops quickly after recharging. This drop in voltage can be a problem even if the battery still has plenty of energy available, since sensors that measure battery charge generally measure the voltage supplied by the battery and may automatically turn off the device being powered if they sense that the voltage of the battery is too low.

volume   **1.** The amplitude or loudness of a sound. *Compare* **amplitude,** **loudness. 2.** A control, as on a television, for adjusting sound amplitude or loudness. *Compare* **loudness. 3.** A predetermined amount of memory on a tape or disk. The volume usually comprises all the memory on the storage device, but sometimes a single disk is divided into two or more volumes, and sometimes one volume is distributed over two or more disks. **4.** A disk or tape used to store data.

volume label   The name assigned to a disk, tape, or other storage device. Operating systems usually allow users to choose volume labels. *Also called* **volume name.**

VPN   *Abbreviation of* **virtual private network.**

VR   *Abbreviation of* **virtual reality.**

VRAM   *Abbreviation of* **Video Random Access Memory.**   RAM used for visual data that is located on the graphics card. It is usually dual-ported RAM that features separate communication paths for the microprocessor and the video display circuitry. Pronounced VEE-ram, it is useful for video applications that require high-speed processing.

VRML   *Abbreviation of* **Virtual Reality Modeling Language.**   A standard XML markup language used to represent three-dimensional vector graphics. X3D is replacing VRML in most circumstances. VRML can be pronounced VUR-mull or by saying the letters individually. *See also* **X3D.**

VRS   *Abbreviation of* **video relay service.**

W   *Abbreviation of* **watt.**

W3C   *Abbreviation of* **World Wide Web Consortium.**   An international consortium that develops standards for Internet communication. The W3C maintains the HTML and XML standards, among others.

wait state   A clock cycle in which the CPU (central processing unit) waits for data from working memory. Since CPUs operate at clock speeds much higher than RAM chips, there are sometimes several wait states between when the CPU requests data from working memory and when the RAM chip can supply the data. Techniques such as using caches and pipelining are designed to reduce the number of wait states. A *zero wait state* computer would have a CPU and working memory that work together at maximum efficiency.

walkie-talkie   1. A portable, handheld two-way radio that uses half-duplex communication, so users have to alternate transmissions. Walkie-talkies are used with various systems for radio communication, including CB, FRS, GMRS, and SMR. **2.** *See* **push-to-talk.**

wallpaper   A picture or design in the background of a display screen. *See also* **desktop.**

WAN   *Abbreviation of* **wide area network.**

WAP   *Abbreviation of* **Wireless Application Protocol.**   A group of standards designed to allow web browsing and similar Internet-based services on wireless devices such as cell phones and PDAs. In addition to protocols for transmitting data on wireless networks, WAP defines the WML markup language. WAP is maintained by the Open Mobile Alliance.

warez   A slang term for proprietary programs, movies, games and other digital files that are illegally distributed after their copy protection has been overidden. Transmitting and using such pirated files is in violation of copyright laws. *See also* **piracy.**

warm boot   The process of restarting a computer that is currently in operation. *Compare* **cold boot.**

watermarking   *See* **digital watermarking.**

watt   *Abbreviated* **W.**   An International System unit of power equal to one joule per second. The amount of energy used by an electrical component is equal to the power it uses multiplied by the amount of time it uses that power. In general, the amount of power in a simple electrical component is equal to the current running through the component (measured in amperes) multiplied by the voltage difference between the input and output of the component (measured in volts).

WAV   *Abbreviation of* **Waveform Audio.**   A file format developed by Microsoft for storing and transmitting sound files. The WAV format is often used with codecs that encode CD-quality audio signals, but can be used with codecs that use lossy compression techniques and thus result in lower quality sound. Files of this type usually have the *.wav* extension.

wavelength   The distance traveled by a wave as it completes one full cycle. Since the speed of electromagnetic radiation is relatively constant, the wavelength of such radiation is directly related to its frequency, and either wavelength or frequency can be used to characterize the radiation. *Compare* **frequency.**

wavetable synthesis A technique for mimicking the sound of a musical instrument used by systems that utilize MIDI. Wavetable synthesis operates by retrieving from a memory bank a recorded digital sample of the sound of a musical instrument. *See also* **FM synthesis.**

W-CDMA A 3G digital mobile technology that uses CDMA techniques but allows for faster transmission rates by using a wider spectrum of frequencies. The W-CDMA standard is the basis for the UMTS and FOMA protocols and was developed by the European Telecommunications Standards Institute.

web or **Web** The World Wide Web.

web browser A program, such Mozilla Firefox or Microsoft Internet Explorer, that allows the user to access hyperlinks to different sites on the World Wide Web.

webcam A digital camera or video camera whose images are made available on a website, usually being updated once every interval of seconds or minutes, or at the request of the viewer. Some webcams provide new images continuously and use streaming video to transmit them. Home webcams are typically attached to or near a computer, but some may be mounted elsewhere, for example for outdoor views; some may also be rotated in different dimensions upon command. Websites often use Java applets to link the images to the desired webpage.

webcast A broadcast of an event or a recording of an event over the World Wide Web. Webcasts are usually scheduled and often live broadcasts, and are generally not interactive.

web conference A conference in which participants who are remote from each other use telephone and World Wide Web communication to converse and exchange information such as text, audio, and video files.

webcrawler *See* **spider.**

web feed An XML document that contains links to and descriptions of content available on the Internet, such as text, pictures, audio, or video. The document is frequently updated and provides a way for other users to access the content easily. Most web feeds use an RSS format.

webinar A kind of web conference in which remote participants interact with a teacher and with each other to conduct a seminar, exchanging text, audio, or video files over the Internet, usually while simultaneously conversing by telephone or using streaming audio or video. *See also* **webcast.**

weblog *See* **blog.**

webmail A system for reading and sending email at a website. Many free email services only allow users to access their email accounts via webmail. ISPs typically provide webmail access as well as access via client programs such as Mozilla Thunderbird or Microsoft Outlook.

webmaster   The person responsible for designing, developing, marketing, or maintaining a website.

webpage or **Web page**   A file on the World Wide Web that is accessible using a web browser. Most webpages consist of code written in HTML that serves as a set of instructions to the browser used to view it. This code defines the structure and content of the webpage, and may include text, images, and links to other webpages or files. *See also* **hyperlink.**

web server   **1.** A program or set of programs that responds to HTTP requests for webpages. Web servers retrieve HTML from their local file system and run server-side scripts, sending the results to the web browser that made the request. **2.** A computer that has such software installed on it.

web service   A software application that interacts with other applications on the Internet by using standardized XML protocols such as SOAP. Web services perform tasks, such as authorizing a charge on a credit card or searching a database, in response to queries by other applications on the web, rather to than direct human input.

website or **Web site**   A webpage or a set of interconnected webpages, usually including a homepage and generally located on the same server. Websites are typically prepared and maintained as a collection of information by a person, group, or organization.

web syndication   To make web content, such as text, pictures, audio, or video, available to other websites or users. Syndication often involves licensing content to other users, and it is often accomplished by using RSS web feeds.

white level   *See* **contrast** (sense 2).

whitespace   **1.** The space on a piece of paper where no characters or graphics appear when a document, record, or file is printed. **2.** *See* **blank character.**

wide area network   *Abbreviated* **WAN.** A network that spans a larger geographic area than can be covered by a LAN. The Internet is an example of a very large wide area network.

widescreen   Having a screen or image with an aspect ratio greater than 4 : 3 (1.33 : 1), which is the NTSC standard for analog television and a common monitor format. Widescreen televisions typically have screens with an aspect ratio of 16 : 9 (1.78 : 1) for displaying widescreen HDTV signals. Widescreen aspect ratios of 1.85 : 1 or 2.35 : 1 are common in cinematography. Common aspect ratios for widescreen monitors are 16 : 10 and

15 : 9. To display widescreen images on a 4 : 3 screen, the image must be reduced either by shrinking it, resulting in blank space above and below the image, or less commonly by cropping the sides. *See also* **anamorphic DVD.** *See* Table B on page 357.

widget Data and program instructions that constitute a functional part of a GUI (graphical user interface), such as a text box or a button. Window managers and operating systems provide standard widgets for programs to use.

Wi-Fi or **WiFi** *Abbreviations of* **Wireless Fidelity.** A commonly used set of protocols for data transmission on wireless LANs. Wi-Fi can refer to any of the protocols defined in the IEEE 802.11 standard. These protocols operate at 2.4 or 5 GHz and transmit simultaneously at a spectrum of frequencies. The most recent Wi-Fi protocol is 802.11n, which supports maximum data transfer rates of 100 Mbps and above. *See also* **spread spectrum, wireless LAN.** *See* Table D on page 360.

Wi-Fi adapter *See* **wireless card.**

Wi-Fi card *See* **wireless card.**

wiki A website that allows users to collaborate by editing its contents. The pages of a wiki are written in wikitext.

wikitext **1.** A simple markup language used for creating and editing the pages of a wiki. Wikitext allows basic text formatting and hyperlinking. **2.** Text that is written using wikitext markup language. The web server for a wiki stores wikitext in a database and converts it to HTML for display.

wild card A character that stands for one or more of a specified set of characters. Wild cards are used in many computer systems, such as search engines and word processors, that search for character sequences in text. An asterisk (*) often stands for any sequence of characters and a question mark (?) often stands for any single character. For example, *FIL?.DOC* would match *FILE.DOC, FILL.DOC, FILM.DOC,* and so on. **.DOC* would match all file names ending in the extension *.DOC*.

wild feed or **wildfeed** A satellite television transmission, not intended for a broadcast audience, that is intercepted by a TVRO satellite dish.

WiMAX *Abbreviation of* **worldwide interoperability for microwave access.** A protocol for wireless communication that allows data to be transmitted over distances as far as 50 kilometers (31 miles). WiMAX allows data rates of up to 70 Mbps and is designed to provide Internet connectivity for both fixed and mobile devices. *See* Table D on page 360.

Win32 An API by which programs can interact with versions of the Windows operating system that run on 32-bit architectures.

Win64 An API by which programs can interact with versions of the Windows operating system that run on 64-bit architectures.

Winamp A media player created by Nullsoft that downloads, plays, and organizes audio and video files in a wide variety of formats, including some used for streaming. Winamp is available for Windows operating systems in both free and for-purchase versions.

Winchester drive A hard disk. This term is largely obsolete, but was originated by IBM in the early 1970s when it was applied to their model 3340 hard drive, the first hard drive whose head and disk assembly were sealed in an airtight compartment. The 3340 had two spindles, each with a 30-MB capacity, so the hard disk was named after Winchester's 30-30 rifle. Subsequent hard disks all had sealed head and disk assemblies, and so were referred to as *Winchester drives.*

window A box on a display screen that displays information independently of the rest of the screen. Windows are used by many operating systems and applications to allow the user to work with multiple files or programs at once. Windows can overlap other windows within a desktop or application, and clicking on a partially obscured window brings that window to the front. Most windows can be resized and repositioned using the cursor, and many have buttons at the top to minimize, maximize, and close the window. The contents of a window are often only part of a larger virtual area, some of which is hidden. Hidden areas can be shifted into the window by scrolling.

windowing Relating to the creation and management of windows and other parts of a GUI by an operating system such as Mac OS X or Microsoft Windows, or by a window manager on a Linux or Unix system. Windowing systems create a consistent look-and-feel by providing basic GUI elements, such as windows, menus, and buttons, for programs to use.

window manager An application that controls the GUI (graphical user interface) for a Unix-compatible operating system by moving, resizing, opening, and closing windows for all applications. The window manager determines the appearance of windows, as well as what features they have, such as title bars and buttons. These functions are incorporated into operating systems like Windows and Macintosh OS X. *See also* **X Window System.**

Windows Any of a set of GUI-based operating systems, developed by Microsoft Corporation, in use in 90 percent of all computers sold today. Windows was originally designed to be a GUI for MS-DOS, though Windows ME (Millennium Edition) and subsequent editions have been full-fledged operating systems that include DOS.

PC-compatible computers have long been associated with Windows, since Windows has been designed to run on such machines (though other operating systems, such as Linux, can be run on PC-compatible machines as well). The family of Windows operating systems developed by Microsoft includes Microsoft Windows, Windows NT, Windows 95, Windows 98, Windows 2000, and Windows ME. Both Windows NT and Windows 95 and later versions, unlike Microsoft Windows, do not rely upon the presence of MS-DOS and are true operating systems. They also support the 32-bit API Win32, and take full advantage of the 32-bit processing offered by the Intel and AMD families of microprocessors.

The term *Windows* is now generally used to refer to any of the specific Windows operating systems currently in use.

Windows-1252   A character encoding designed by IBM and used in Windows. It encodes characters of the Latin alphabet as used in most Western European languages and largely overlaps with ISO Latin-1. It is an extended ASCII encoding, in that the first 128 encodings are the same as ASCII. *See* Table 5 at **extended ASCII.**

Windows CE   A version of the Windows operating system developed by Microsoft Corporation that is designed to run on handheld devices such as PDAs and cell phones.

Windows keyboard   A 104-key keyboard that is similar to an enhanced keyboard but has 3 additional keys that activate functions specific to Windows operating systems. The Windows keyboard and the enhanced keyboard are the most common keyboards on PC-compatible computers.

Windows Media Audio   *See* **WMA.**

Windows Media Player   A media player software for playing audio and video content on personal computers using the Microsoft Windows platform. Among the file formats supported by this software are MP3, WMA, WMV, and ASF.

Windows Media Video   *See* **WMV.**

Windows Metafile   *See* **WMF.**

Windows Vista   A version of the Windows operating system scheduled to be released by Microsoft in late 2006. Windows Vista was previously known as *Longhorn*. Though it is based on previous versions of Windows, Vista is to include major revisions to much of Windows core technology, as well as many new features.

WinRAR   A file archiving and compression program for Windows operating systems. WinRAR can create compressed archives in RAR and zip formats, and can extract and decompress files in a range of formats.

WinZip   A program for Windows operating systems that creates compressed archive files in the zip format and extracts files from zip archives.

wireless   Relating to or enabling communication that takes place by the transmission of electromagnetic waves through the atmosphere. Most techniques for wireless communication involve transmitting radio frequency waves. However, some techniques use infrared and optical frequencies. *See also* **wireline.**

wireless access point   A device that sends and receives signals from wireless devices such as portable computers or communications devices, allowing them to communicate with each other and thereby establish a wireless network. Typical wireless access points have a communication range of about 100 meters (328 feet); some may additionally provide a connection to another network such as an Ethernet or the Internet. *Also called* **base station.**

wireless adapter   **1.** *See* **wireless card. 2.** An adapter that allows a device that normally transmits information through a wire to transmit the information over the air. For example, wireless adapters can be used to transmit audio signals from a home stereo to speakers.

Wireless Application Protocol   *See* **WAP.**

wireless cable   *See* **MMDS.**

wireless card   A network interface card that allows a computer to be connected to a wireless network. Wireless cards contain an antenna for transmitting and receiving radio waves. *Also called* **Wi-Fi adapter, Wi-Fi card, wireless adapter, wireless interface card.**

wireless cloud   A wireless network encompassing a large region, such as an office building, campus, or city, especially one that provides access to the Internet. *Also called* **cloud.**

Wireless Fidelity   *See* **Wi-Fi.**

wireless interface card   *See* **wireless card.**

wireless LAN   *Abbreviation of* **wireless local area network.**   A LAN that uses high-frequency radio waves or infrared beams to link together computers and other devices. *Also called* **LAWN, local area wireless network.**

Wireless Markup Language   *See* **WML.**

wireless payment   *See* **mobile payment.**

wireline   Relating to or enabling communication that takes place by the transmission of radio frequency waves through wires. Cable television and traditional telephone service over landlines are examples of wireline technologies. *See also* **wireless.**

Wizard   An automated guide that assists users in accomplishing a task in an application or operating system. Wizards guide users through tasks that require multiple steps. For example, a Wizard in Microsoft Windows can help a user configure a new printer by following simple steps.

WMA   *Abbreviation of* **Windows Media Audio.**   A file format developed by Microsoft for digitally transmitting audio content over the Internet. Files of this type were designed for the Windows Media Player application but can be played by a variety of applications and digital audio players. They usually have the *.wma* extension.

WMF   *Abbreviation of* **Windows Metafile.**   A vector graphics file format developed by Microsoft and used primarily on their Windows operating systems. Like other vector graphics formats, WMF files retain smooth lines when viewed or printed at different sizes and resolutions. They typically have the file extension *.wmf. See also* **EMF.**

WML   *Abbreviation of* **Wireless Markup Language.**   An XML markup language designed for creating webpages and similar content that can be viewed on small displays such as those on cell phones. WML provides many of the features of HTML and is part of WAP.

WMV   *Abbreviation of* **Windows Media Video.**   A file format developed by Microsoft for digital video and audio content, commonly used on the Internet. Files of this type were designed for the Windows Media Player application, but can be played by a variety of applications and devices. They usually have the *.wmv* extension.

woofer   A large speaker designed to reproduce bass frequencies, typically in the range of 80 to 300 hertz. *See also* **speaker.**

word   A unit of information for a computer, measured in bits. The length of a word for a given computer is equal to the largest amount of data that it can handle in one operation. Words are usually made up of a set number of bytes. Because computers generally use 8-bit bytes, common word lengths for personal computers are 8, 16, 32, and 64 bits.

word processing   The use of a word processor to create, edit, and store documents.

word processor   A computer software application that allows the user to create, edit, and print out documents such as letters, papers, and manuscripts. With a word processor the tasks of deleting, inserting, and moving sections of text can be made through a few keystrokes rather than by laborious retyping, and the format of the document can be easily manipulated. Most word processors include a variety of features, such as spell checking and grammar checking, word wrap, the ability to set margins, spacing, fonts, and font sizes, page numbering and generation of page headings, and automatic footnote numbering. Text and graphics can typically be merged into single documents using word processors. *See also* **desktop publishing, text editor, WYSIWYG.**

word wrap A feature of word processing applications that automatically moves a word to the beginning of a new line if it goes beyond the margin of the document. If the user has chosen to have the program hyphenate the document automatically, the word wrap feature hyphenates the word and moves the second portion to a new line. When the margins or other layout parameters of the document are changed, word wrap automatically rearranges the text to fit the new specifications.

workgroup A group of individuals working together on a single project. Often, the computers of workgroup members are linked together in a local area network (LAN), allowing the members to easily share common data files, software, and hardware such as printers.

working directory *See* **current directory.**

workstation **1.** A personal computer designed and marketed for professional use, often in domains such as engineering and graphic design that require more computing power. Workstations are usually faster, more powerful, and more reliable than computers designed for home use, and they typically come equipped with software and operating systems that are also designed for professional use. **2.** One of the computers connected to a LAN, especially the LAN of a business or other organization.

worldwide interoperability for wireless access *See* **WiMAX.**

World Wide Web, web, or **Web** *Abbreviated* **WWW.** All of the files residing on Internet servers that are accessible to other users by using hyperlinks. The documents comprising these files are called webpages, which generally consist of text and/or other elements, such as graphics, audio, and video. Web browsers are used to view the content of webpages. To access a webpage, a browser typically sends a request (usually in the form of an HTTP message) to the server on which the page is kept, and the server responds by sending the webpage to the browser in the form of HTML. The web was first developed at the European Laboratory for Particle Physics (CERN), in Geneva, Switzerland.

World Wide Web Consortium *See* **W3C.**

worm A malicious computer program that can replicate itself and spreads by using communication protocols to send itself across a network. Worms often harm computer networks as well as the individual computers they infect. They may also be designed to take control of the computers they infect in order to perform denial-of-service attacks or make some other unauthorized use of computer resources. Worms are now more common than viruses, which only spread when a user transfers an infected file to another machine. *Compare* **virus.** *See also* **Trojan horse.**

WORM *Abbreviation of* **write once read many.** Relating to storage media that can be written to once but read many times. Once the data has been written, it cannot be changed. Optical disks such as CD-R and DVD-R are examples of WORM disks.

wraparound text *See* **text wrap.**

write To copy information from memory to a storage device such as a hard disk, CD, or DVD. Writing data can create new files or change old ones. *Compare* **read.** *See also* **write-protect.**

write laser The laser in an optical disk burner that writes encoded data onto a blank disk by etching a spiral pattern of pits into the disk's land surface. *Compare* **read laser.**

write-once Relating to a medium that allows data to be written to it only once. Data written to a write-once medium cannot be modified or deleted. For example, CD-R is a write-once medium as opposed to CD-RW, which can be written to more than once.

write once read many *See* **WORM.**

write-protect To modify a file or disk so that its data cannot be edited or erased. A file or disk modified in this way is read-only. Many operating systems enable users to write-protect individual files or directories. *See also* **lock, permission.**

WWW *Abbreviation of* **World Wide Web.**

WYSIWYG Relating to or being a computer system in which the screen displays text and graphics exactly as they will be printed. One advantage of a WYSIWYG system is that the layout of a document is much easier to set up. Pronounced WIS-ee-wig, this term stands for *what you see is what you get.*

X *See* **X Window System.**

X3D A standard XML markup language for representing three-dimensional vector graphics. X3D is used to create animated, three-dimensional scenes, called *worlds,* for use in engineering, medicine, education, and entertainment. X3D files typically have the extension *.x3d* and can be viewed by special-purpose programs. Additionally, plug-ins are available that allow some web browsers to view X3D files.

x86 A general microprocessor architecture designed by Intel. Computers with x86 microprocessors typically use the Windows or Linux operating systems. The name *x86* refers to the fact that the earliest microprocessors using this architecture had names that ended in *86*. x86 processors use a CISC design and models since the 80386, released in 1985, have had 32-bit registers. Intel's Pentium and Celeron and AMD's Athlon are popular x86 processors. *See also* **x86-64.**

x86-64 A microprocessor architecture based on x86, but using 64-bit registers. x86-64 was developed by Advance Micro Devices (AMD) and later renamed *AMD64*. A similar 64-bit architecture developed by Intel, the originators of the x86 architecture, is called *EM64T*. Windows and Linux operating systems are available for x86-64 processors. *See also* **Itanium.**

x-axis 1. The horizontal axis in a two-dimensional graph or coordinate system. 2. A horizontal axis in a three-dimensional graph or coordinate system. The x-axis is usually depicted as running from left to right.

Xbox A video game console developed by Microsoft. The Xbox belongs to the same generation of products as the Sony PlayStation 2 and the Nintendo GameCube.

Xbox 360 A video game console developed by Microsoft. The Xbox 360 belongs to the same generation of products as the Sony PlayStation 3 and the Nintendo Revolution.

xD-Picture Card A memory card format developed by Olympus and Fujifilm that stores data on flash memory chips. Memory cards using the xD-Picture format are manufactured by several different companies and are typically used as storage media for digital cameras manufactured by Olympus, Kodak, and Fujifilm. Adapters also make it possible to use xD-Picture Cards with devices designed for other memory card formats. The letters *xD* stand for *extreme digital.*

XDR *Abbreviation of* **extreme data rate.** Relating to DRAM employing an interface that allows data transfer rates of eight bits per bus cycle. XDR chips transfer data at much faster rates than DDR2 chips. The XDR interface was designed by Rambus.

XFree86 A free, open-source software package that implements the standard X Windows System for Linux and Unix.

XGA *Abbreviation of* **Extended Graphics Array.** A video standard developed by IBM that is fully compatible with VGA, but supports higher resolutions and more colors. *See* Table B on page 357.

XHTML *Abbreviation of* **extensible hypertext markup language.** An XML markup language designed to replace HTML. XHTML adds to the capabilities of HTML and is intended to make it easier to create content that can be displayed on different kinds of devices, including cell phones and PDAs as well as browsers.

XLR connector A locking, balanced audio connector often used in professional audio equipment. XLR connectors provide high sound quality with low noise when long cables are used. In appearance, they generally resemble DIN connectors and the most common type has three pins.

.xls The file extension typically used for files created with Microsoft's popular Excel spreadsheet program, part of its Microsoft Office suite.

XML *Abbreviation of* **extensible markup language.** An international standard metalanguage for creating markup languages. XML uses textual tags to structure digital information so it can be exchanged, displayed, and stored in a device- and system-independent way. It is a subset of SGML, and has become an important method of data exchange on the Internet. Most industry-standard markup languages are now designed in XML. Examples are RSS, SOAP, and SVG.

Xmodem A file transfer protocol designed to transfer files using a modem and a standard telephone line. Xmodem has largely been replaced by FTP, SCP, and SFTP, all of which transfer files more quickly over current modem connections. *See also* **Ymodem, Zmodem.**

XMS memory *Abbreviation of* **Extended Memory Specification memory.** *See* **extended memory.**

X/Open A computer industry consortium founded to create a standard for the Unix operating system and the X Window System. X/Open merged with a competing consortium, OSF, in 1996, to form the Open Group. The Open Group controls the Single Unix Specification.

XOR A logical operator that returns the value TRUE as its output if one of its inputs (or *operands*) is TRUE and the other FALSE, but returns the value FALSE if both are TRUE or both are FALSE. *Also called* **exclusive OR.** *See* Table E on page 361.

X protocol The protocol used on Unix and Linux operating systems for communicating data between applications and the X Window System software. The X protocol allows display data to be sent over the Internet, so a computer can display windows created by applications running on remote machines.

XSL *Abbreviation of* **extensible stylesheet language.** A markup language for specifying the visual format of XML documents. Unlike HTML, XML does not by itself specify how to format text and graphics for display. XSL provides ways to specify fonts, colors, spacing, and many other properties of XML documents, allowing them to be displayed by web browsers. *See also* **CSS.**

XviD An open-source video codec originally developed to compete with and eventually replace the DivX format. XviD encodes video files into MPEG-4-compliant data streams that can be embedded in various container formats. Because they most often use the AVI container, XviD files usually have the *.avi* extension. *See* Table 3 at **codec.**

X Window System A standard for software used by Linux and Unix operating systems to communicate with display-related devices, such as the monitor, the mouse, and the keyboard. The X Window System software converts commands from applications into a form that the devices understand and manages settings for the devices. It requires a window manager to control how windows are displayed. Because it uses a client/server protocol, it allows a computer to display windows from graphical applications that are running on different machines. *Also called* **X, X11, X Windows.** *See also* **XFree86, X protocol.**

Y *Symbol for* **luminance.**

y-axis **1.** The vertical axis in a two-dimensional graph or coordinate system. **2.** A horizontal axis in a three-dimensional graph or coordinate system. The y-axis is usually depicted as running toward and away from the viewer.

YCbCr A color model used by digital video formats consisting of a luminance component (Y) and two chrominance components (Cb and Cr). MPEG, DV, and JPEG formats rely on this model. *Compare* **YPbPr.**

yEnc A nonstandard format that encodes binary data as ASCII text, as for including graphics or other binary data in email or newsgroup messages. While there are no official standards for yEnc, it is widely used for posting binary files on newsgroups. Files in yEnc format often have the *.ync* file extension. *See also* **base64, BinHex, uuencode.**

Ymodem   An enhanced version of the Xmodem file transfer protocol that allows batch file transfers. Like Xmodem, Ymodem has largely been replaced by file transfer protocols that transfer data more quickly over current modem connections. *See also* **Zmodem.**

.ync   An extension commonly used for files with the yEnc format.

YPbPr   A color model used in analog video transmission consisting of a luminance component (Y) and two chrominance components. YPbPr component video connections consist of three separate cables, one for each component. YPbPr connectors are sometimes found on televisions and DVD players. *Compare* **YCbCr.** *See* Table A on page 356.

YUV   A color model used in PAL and NTSC television consisting of a luminance component (Y) and two chrominance components (U and V). The YPbPr and YCbCr color models are derivatives of YUV.

.Z   An extension used for files compressed with the compress program in the Unix operating system.

Zapruder   To analyze a movie or video frame by frame in order to discover details in the image that are not easily seen during normal playback. DVD players, DVRs, and computer software have made it easy to Zapruder video images such as television shows. The term is named after Abraham Zapruder, whose amateur film footage of the assasination of John F. Kennedy has undergone detailed frame-by-frame analysis.

z-axis   A vertical axis in a three-dimensional graph or coordinate system. The z-axis is usually depicted as running up and down, intersecting the plane on which the x-axis and the y-axis lie.

zero insertion force socket   *See* **ZIF socket.**

ZIF socket   *Abbreviation of* **zero insertion force socket.** A chip socket designed so that the chip can be inserted or pulled out easily, with very little resistance. The chip is made secure in the ZIF socket by moving a small lever that clamps the socket shut, locking the pins in.

zinc-air battery   A lightweight disposable battery that relies on the oxidation of zinc to produce electricity. Zinc-air cells typically produce approximately 1.4 volts of electricity and have a larger energy storage capacity than alkaline cells of the same size.

zinc-carbon battery   A disposable battery made of zinc and carbon. Zinc-carbon cells typically produce approximately 1.5 volts of electricity. While they are less expensive than alkaline cells, they typically do not last as long.

zip   *n.* **1.** A format used for archiving and compressing files. One zip file may contain several compressed files. Zip format archives are created by archiving programs such as WinZip, PKzip, and zip. They commonly have the file extension *.zip*. The format is also used by the jar program for storing Java programs and by the OpenOffice suite to store word processing and related documents. **2.** *usually* **Zip**   A floppy disk technology developed by Iomega Corporation that can store up to 750 megabytes of data on a single disk. Zip disks are similar in size to standard 3.5-inch floppy disks, but they store much more data, and the data can be accessed more quickly. **3.** A program commonly used on Linux and Unix systems to create archives having the zip format. *See also* **unzip.**

   v. To create a zip archive by using an archiving program such as WinZip, PKZip, or zip. *See also* **unzip.**

Zmodem   An enhanced version of the Xmodem file transfer protocol that allows faster data transfer rates and the ability to restart interrupted transfers. Like Xmodem, Zmodem has largely been replaced by file transfer protocols that transfer data more quickly over current modem connections. *See also* **Ymodem.**

zoned-bit recording   A technique for recording data on a disk, in which tracks on the outside of the disk have more sectors than the tracks on the inside. Zoned-bit recording is used on most hard disks. Earlier disks used an inefficient technique in which the longer outside tracks had the same number of sectors as inside tracks. By making better use of the outside tracks, zoned-bit recording allows more data to be stored on the same disk. *See figure at* **sector.**

zoom   On cameras, a feature that allows a range of increased magnification of the central part of the image being photographed. Traditional film cameras use optical zoom; some digital cameras also feature digital zoom. **2.** To make a window on a display screen larger by selecting the zoom box in one corner of the window. Clicking the zoom box once enlarges the window to fill the entire display screen. Clicking it again restores the window to its original size.

Appendix

TABLE A Common Audio-visual Interfaces and Connectors

	Plug/Socket	*Application*
HDMI		
A	19-pin	digital video and audio
B	29-pin	digital video and audio
DVI		
I	23-pin	analog and digital video
I-DL	29-pin	analog and digital video
D	19-pin	digital video
D-DL	25-pin	digital video
A	17-pin	analog video
component video (YPbPr or RGB)	RCA (3 cables)	analog video
S/PDIF	TOSLINK (used with optical fiber cable) or RCA (used with coaxial cable)	digital audio
S-Video	4-pin Mini-DIN	analog video
VGA connector	15-pin D-sub (DE-15)	analog video
jack connector (TRS)	1/4", 1/8", or 3/32" jack plug	analog audio (esp. headphones)
RF cable/coaxial cable	RF connector	cable TV
RCA connector	RCA	analog audio, digital audio, or analog video (composite or component signal)

TABLE B Common Display Resolutions

Resolution horizontal × vertical	Pixels	Aspect Ratio*	Standards
640 × 480	307,200	1.33 : 1 (4 : 3)	VGA, NTSC, SDTV, EDTV
720 × 576	414,720	1.25 : 1 (5 : 4)	PAL, SDTV, EDTV
800 × 600	480,000	1.33 : 1 (4 : 3)	SVGA
1024 × 768	786,432	1.33 : 1 (4 : 3)	XGA
1152 × 870	1,002,240	1.33 : 1 (4 : 3)	Apple Macintosh
1280 × 720	921,600	1.78 : 1 (16 : 9)	HDTV
1280 × 768	983,040	1.69 : 1	WXGA
1280 × 800	1,024,000	1.6 : 1 (16 : 10)	WXGA
1280 × 1024	1,310,720	1.25 : 1 (5 : 4)	SXGA
1366 × 768	1,049,088	1.78 : 1 (16 : 9)	WXGA
1400 × 1050	1,470,000	1.33 : 1 (4 : 3)	SXGA+
1440 × 900	1,296,000	1.6 : 1 (16 : 10)	WXGA+, WSXGA
1680 × 1050	1,764,000	1.6 : 1 (16 : 10)	WSXGA+
1600 × 1200	1,920,000	1.33 : 1 (4 : 3)	UXGA
1920 × 1080	2,073,600	1.78 : 1 (16 : 9)	HDTV
1920 × 1200	2,304,000	1.6 : 1 (16 : 10)	WUXGA
2048 × 1536	3,145,728	1.33 : 1 (4 : 3)	QXGA
2560 × 1600	4,096,000	1.6 : 1 (16 : 10)	WQXGA

*Films typically have an aspect ratio of 2.39 : 1, 1.85 : 1, 1.37 : 1, or 1.33 : 1.

TABLE C Common Data Interfaces and Computer Buses

	Plug / Socket	Application	Data Transfer Rate
PCI			
parallel versions	32- or 64-pin slot	internal expansion cards	133-533.3 MBps
PCI Express (serial)	1-, 2-, 4-, 8-, 12-, 16-, or 32-pin slot	internal expansion cards	2.5 Gbps (250 MBps) per lane (up to 32 lanes)
ISA	8- or 16-pin slot	internal expansion cards	32 MBps
PC Card			
CardBus (parallel)	68-pin slot	external laptop cards	132 MBps
ExpressCard (serial)	16-pin slot	external laptop cards	480 Mbps or 2.5 Gbps
IDE			
ATA (parallel)	40- or 80-pin	internal disk drives	4.2-133 MBps
SATA (serial)	7-pin	internal disk drives	1.5-3.0 Gbps (150-300 MBps)
SCSI			
parallel versions	50- or 68-pin	internal and external peripherals	5-320 MBps
SAS (serial)	7-pin	internal and external peripherals	3 Gbps (300 MBps)
IEEE 1394	FireWire (4-, 6-, or 9-pin) or iLink (4-pin)	external peripherals	100-800 Mbps

	Plug / Socket	Application	Data Transfer Rate
USB			
1.0	USB Type A and Type B	external peripherals	1.5-12 Mbps
2.0	USB Type A and Type B	external peripherals	480 Mbps
parallel port (IEEE 1284)	25-pin D-sub (DB-25) and 36-pin Centronics	printers	150 KBps-1.5 MBps
serial port (RS-232)	9-pin D-sub (DE-9)	mouse and keyboard	20 Kbps
PS/2	6-pin Mini-DIN	mouse and keyboard	~20 Kbps
Ethernet			
Ethernet	8-pin registered jack	networking	10 Mbps
Fast Ethernet	8-pin registered jack	networking	100 Mbps
Gigabit Ethernet	8-pin registered jack	networking	1 Gbps
telephone cord	2-, 4-, or 6-pin registered jack	networking	56 Kbps

TABLE D   Common Networking Standards

	Maximum Data Transfer Rate*	Frequency	Range
Wireless			
Wi-Fi (IEEE 802.11)			
802.11b	54 Mbps	2.4 GHz	100 ft
802.11a	54 Mbps	5.0 GHz	100 ft
802.11g	54 Mbps	2.4 GHz	100 ft
802.11n	>500 Mbps	2.4 GHz	>100 ft
WiMAX (IEEE 802.16)	70 Mbps	2.0-66 GHz	50 km
Bluetooth	720 Kbps	2.4 GHz	30 ft
IrDA	115 Kbps	infrared	3 ft
Wireline			
power line (HomePlug)	14 Mbps		
Ethernet (IEEE 802.3)			
Ethernet	10 Mbps		
Fast Ethernet	100 Mbps		
Gigabit Ethernet	1 Gbps		

*Actual data transfer rates are usually much lower and typically decline as distance increases.

TABLE E   Truth Tables for Logic Gates

Input		Output						
A	B	NOT A	NOT B	A AND B	A OR B	A NAND B	A NOR B	A XOR B
FALSE	FALSE	TRUE	TRUE	FALSE	FALSE	TRUE	TRUE	FALSE
FALSE	TRUE	TRUE	FALSE	FALSE	TRUE	TRUE	FALSE	TRUE
TRUE	FALSE	FALSE	TRUE	FALSE	TRUE	TRUE	FALSE	TRUE
TRUE	TRUE	FALSE	FALSE	TRUE	TRUE	FALSE	FALSE	FALSE

Input		Output						
A	B	NOT A	NOT B	A AND B	A OR B	A NAND B	A NOR B	A XOR B
0	0	1	1	0	0	1	1	0
0	1	1	0	0	1	1	0	1
1	0	0	1	0	1	1	0	1
1	1	0	0	1	1	0	0	0

These tables show the output of the standard logic gates NOT, AND, OR, NAND, NOR, and XOR, given the four possible combinations of values of inputs A and B. The NOT gate takes only one of either A or B as its input; the rest take both A and B as their inputs. The tables are logically equivalent; in the second table, the binary numbers 0 and 1 are in direct correspondence with the logical values FALSE and TRUE in the first table. In actual logic gates, these values are represented by low and high voltages respectively at the input and output of the logic gate's circuitry.